The Charitable Crescent

The Charitable Crescent

Politics of Aid in the Muslim World

Jonathan Benthall

and

Jérôme Bellion-Jourdan

I.B. TAURIS

LONDON · NEW YORK

Paperback edition published in 2009 by I.B. Tauris & Co Ltd
6 Salem Road, London W2 4BU
175 Fifth Avenue, New York NY 10010
www.ibtauris.com

In the United States of America and Canada
distributed by Palgrave Macmillan, a division of St Martin's Press
175 Fifth Avenue, New York NY 10010

First published in 2003 by I.B. Tauris & Co Ltd

ISBN 978 1 84511 899 0

A full CIP record for this book is available from the British Library
A full CIP record is available from the Library of Congress

Library of Congress Catalog Card Number: available

Printed and bound in India by Thomson Press India Ltd
from camera-ready copy edited and supplied by the authors

To the memory of
Yehudi Menuhin

Contents

	page
Acknowledgments	*ix*
Note on transliteration and translation	*x*
Preface to the paperback edition	*xi*
Preface	*xv*
Introduction	1
1. Financial worship	7
2. Waqf and Islamic finance: two resources for charity	29
3. Red Crescent politics	45
4. Helping the 'brothers': the medic, the militant and the fighter	69
5. NGOs in the contemporary Muslim World	85
6. Western versus Islamic aid? International Muslim charities and humanitarian aid in Sudan	111
7. The Balkan case: transnational Islamic networks in Bosnia-Herzegovina	128
Conclusion	153
Abbreviations	*157*
Glossary of Islamic and Arabic terms	*159*
Notes	*163*
Postscript	*174*
Bibliography	*175*
Index	*187*

Acknowledgments

Jonathan Benthall writes:
I am grateful to the Nuffield Foundation for a research grant; to the Royal Anthropological Institute for giving me six months' sabbatical leave in 1996 while employed as its Director; to the Department of Anthropology, University College London, for appointing me an Honorary Research Fellow; and to the French research centre CERMOC in Amman for hospitality. Numerous individuals and institutions have been generous with information, especially officials of the Red Cross and Red Crescent Movement. Among many people whom I thank for information, help and encouragement I would like to mention specially Sadruddin Aga Khan, Akbar Ahmed, Khaldoon Ahmed, Jon Anderson, Simon Barrington-Ward, Jean-Nicolas Bitter, Riccardo Bocco, Bernard Botiveau, Hastings Donnan, Mary Douglas, Dale Eickelman, Adele Harmer, Arthur Hertzberg, Hana Jaber, Mu'in Kassis, Ziba Mir-Hussaini, Joanna Macrae, Randa Mukhar, Riyad Mustafa, François Nordmann, Jamal Nusseibeh, Sari and Lucy Nusseibeh, Edward L. Queen, Hugh Roberts, John de Salis, Arlette Tadié, Alex de Waal, Pnina Werbner, William C. Young and Ameur Zemmali. More generally, I have learnt much from association with Save the Children Fund (1981 to 1998) and with the International NGO Training and Research Centre (INTRAC) since 1996.

Previous versions of some of my research material have been published in the *British Journal of Middle Eastern Studies* (24.4, November 1997), the *Journal of the Royal Anthropological Institute* (5.1, March 1999), *Interpreting Islam* (edited by Hastings Donnan, Sage Publications, 2002) and *Sacrifice in Religious Experience* (edited by Albert I. Baumgarten, Brill, 2002).

Jérôme Bellion-Jourdan writes:
I am grateful to various bodies for the logistical and financial support which allowed me to conduct research in various parts of the world, mainly to the Centre d'Etudes et de Recherches Internationales (CERI, Paris) where I was affiliated with research finance from the French Ministry of Research for three years; to St Antony's College (Oxford) where I spent a year in 1996-97; to the Direction des Affaires Stratégiques

of the French Defence Ministry; to the Centre d'Etudes et de Documentation Juridique, Economique et Sociale (CEDEJ, Cairo) and its branch in Khartoum; and to the Cultural Service of the French Embassy in Islamabad. Despite the difficulties of being an outsider in the field of charity, I benefited from the cooperation of many heads and employees of Muslim charities: among them, I would like to thank Kamal al-Sherif (head of International Islamic Council for Da`wa and Relief, Cairo), Abdallah Suleyman al-'Awad (Islamic Relief Agency, Khartoum), Hany El Banna (Islamic Relief Worldwide, Birmingham), Mahmood al-Hassan (Muslim Aid, London) and Abdul Samad Summers (ISRA-UK) as well as Ahmed Barakat (Islamic Call Committee, Peshawar). My thanks also go to individuals working in other NGOs and international organisations, including the ICRC and UN agencies. I am grateful to Jean Leca who supervised my D.Phil. research, to Mariam AbouZahab, Fariba Adelkha, Bertrand Badie, Xavier Bougarel, Jean-Paul Burdy, François Burgat, Gilles Kepel, Remy Leveau, James Piscatori, Olivier Roy, Johanna Simeant and Jacques Sommet for their encouragement and support in my research. I am last but not least grateful to my friends and relatives who have supported me in both the French and the English senses of the term throughout the period of this research.

On this topic, I have contributed to several publications, including *Genèses* (September 2002), *Esprit* (August-September 2001, p.173-185), *Le nouvel islam balkanique. Les musulmans acteurs du post-communisme. 1990-2000* (edited by Xavier Bougarel and Nathalie Clayer, Maisonneuve et Larose, 2001), and *Politique Africaine* (no. 66, June 1997).

Note on transliteration and translation

A highly simplified convention for transliterating Arabic words has been used throughout this book. Arabic nouns in the plural are generally treated as English nouns, e.g. *waqf*s rather than the correct Arabic plural *awqaf*.

Abdullah Yusuf Ali's translation of the Quran has mainly been used (Beltsville, MD: Amana Publications, 1989).

PREFACE TO THE
PAPERBACK EDITION

The Charitable Crescent was prepared for publication after the attacks of 11th September 2001 in New York and Washington, and was based on research we had each carried out since the mid-1990s. This new preface to the paperback edition is meant to summarize what has changed in the world of Islamic charity in the five years since publication in 2003.

In Iraq, the Preface we wrote in 2003 mentioned the United States administration's aim of delivering humanitarian aid to 'win the hearts and minds of the people and make them accept the occupying force', amid fears from the voluntary sector that 'factionalism and violence would persist in the new political vacuum'. We anticipated that the US government would set out to exercise tight control over interventions by external Islamic charities. The extent of aid provided in this devastated country since 2003 by Iranian foundations and by Gulf-based Sunni charities has not yet been clear.

External aid to Iraq has met with acute challenges. The international aid community was traumatized in late 2004, when a British employee in Iraq of CARE, the secular NGO, Margaret Hassan, who was married to an Iraqi and who had personally opposed the war in Iraq, was abducted and brutally murdered. In many cases the motive for such violence, including the murderous attack on the UN offices in August 2003, appears to have been more to sow indiscriminate chaos against agencies seen as promoting 'Western' interests than to single out any particular agency for its political affiliations. Médecins Sans Frontières withdrew at the end of 2004 because of the dangers to staff, though it returned to northern Iraq in 2007. Oxfam GB decided in 2004 to work only through Iraqi partner organizations, because of the exceptionally difficult and uncertain environment. But the UK-based Muslim Aid and Islamic Relief Worldwide have been consistently operational in Iraq, focussing on help for orphans and Internally Displaced Persons as well as other programmes.

More broadly, the trend towards professionalization continued. Particularly in Great Britain, Muslim charities continued to cooperate with the international aid system. Thus Islamic Relief Worldwide became a member of the Disasters Emergency Committee, the elite of aid agencies that join forces in national media appeals. Muslim Aid, the second largest UK Islamic aid agency, worked regularly with the secular Oxfam and formed a partnership with the US-based United Methodist Committee on Relief (UMCOR). In the USA too, Islamic Relief

Worldwide has been allowed to raise funds without impediment, and was even awarded the maximum rating of four stars by Charity Navigator for four years running. The example set by these Muslim charities in working towards practical integration deserves reflection on the part of those who are impatient with the otherworldliness of much 'inter-faith dialogue' and others who prefer to focus on what divides Islam from the 'West' rather than on unifying factors.

Médecins Sans Frontières experienced serious difficulties affecting its work in several Muslim countries, and has been exploring the potential of collaboration with Islamic charities. The reproach sometimes directed against Islamic charities that they concentrate their efforts on aid to Muslim beneficiaries is somewhat unfair, given the large proportion of Muslims among the suffering people of the world. Increasingly, Islamic charities have joined the consensus of the international aid system that, within any particular region where aid is supplied, there must be no discrimination on the basis of religion or ethnicity. This has not excluded a measure of competition between Islamic and Christian humanitarianism, especially in those countries of west Africa which have mixed religious populations.

In the USA, Islamic charities would probably – but for 9/11 – have evolved on similar lines to the UK, but on a larger scale. However, when *The Charitable Crescent* came out in early 2003, we noted that the US administration had taken steps before 9/11 against Islamic charities held to be associated with Palestinian opposition movements (p.106), and that these measures had been extended since 9/11 to target a wider range of Islamic charities (pp.2, 163). Our chapters on Afghanistan, Sudan and Bosnia offered some historical depth on the complex links between humanitarian aid, religious militancy and politics, and there is evidence that the privileges of some charities may have been abused in order to fund the 9/11 or other attacks. Since 9/11, the George W. Bush administration decided to black-list a number of major Islamic charities, in the USA and elsewhere, and to prosecute them and their organizers on serious criminal charges including the alleged support of terrorism (though the success rate in securing convictions was low to date). Civil litigation was also launched by individual plaintiffs against Islamic charities, and even against commercial banks that provided services for them, on the alleged grounds that charitable funds had been abused to finance suicide bombing. A complicating factor was that the US and Israeli authorities minimized the distinction between movements such as Hamas and Hizbullah, with essentially nationalist as well as religious goals, and international movements more or less tied to Al-Qaʾida that caused global disruption.

Not until 2004 did the mainstream non-Muslim voluntary sector in the USA begin to notice that the concerted campaign against Islamic charities, apparently without realistic rights of defence and appeal, constituted a wider threat to the freedom of charities to direct relief and development aid where they believe it will be of most practical benefit. One result of 9/11 that impacted particularly on charities was the expansion of 'compliance' procedures in international banks, setting obstacles in the path of financial transfers, especially to conflict zones. Many observers concluded that the effort to control the financing of extremism through the banking system was in fact counter-productive, driving money into informal channels where it was subject to no control at all. These and related issues were explored in *Understanding Islamic Charities* (ed. Alterman and von Hippel, CSIS Press, 2007), a set of articles some of which, in an editorial context of US foreign policy concerns, cast doubt on the wisdom of the Bush administration's policy.

Tensions between the British and the US approaches came to a head with the case of the British Islamic charity Interpal, set up to bring aid to Palestinians, which was designated by the US government as a terrorist entity on the grounds that it allegedly gave material support to Hamas. Interpal earned wide support from the British Muslim community and was cleared twice by the Charity Commission of any wrongdoing. As this preface went to press, the results of a third investigation by the Charity Commission had yet to be announced. Similar controversial cases relating to aid to Palestinians arose in half a dozen other European countries.

Two international efforts were launched in 2005, in response to the US government's measures and to other pressures such as those exerted by the Financial Action Task Force (FATF), which had been set up by the G-7 members, the European Commission and eight other countries. One of these efforts was the Humanitarian Forum, initiated by Islamic Relief Worldwide, with a broad objective of promoting interaction and understanding between different humanitarian organizations. The other was the Montreux Initiative, sponsored by the Swiss Federal Department of Foreign Affairs as a joint confidence-building exercise involving both Muslim and non-Muslim participants – with the aim of helping to remove unjustified obstacles from Islamic charities through a system of self-regulation and monitoring.

International Islamic charities based in the Gulf states have not escaped the political turbulence since 9/11, and some of the largest have had to scale down their activities. Rival versions of Islam, expressed in humanitarian programmes, have continued to compete in countries such as Pakistan. Some of the wealth generated by the petroleum boom has spun off into philanthropic foundations pursuing an Islamic agenda. Islamic banking and finance have continued to expand.

As regards research, two books on Islamic charities published by leading university presses in the genre of counter-terrorism adopted an approach completely different to that of *The Charitable Crescent*. This was not surprising, since we set out to 'supply a fresh perspective for considering the politics of global humanitarianism through the exercise of "decentring", or unsettling of prior assumptions' (p.5). A more serious criticism is that the evidential base of these books is weak.

More encouragingly, a number of research papers on Islamic charities appeared recently, grounded in field studies, and several dissertations and doctoral theses are in preparation. The *ISIM Review* (International Institute for the Study of Islam in the Modern World, Leiden) published several articles on the topic in its Autumn 2007 issue (no. 20). We anticipate that this will prove to be a fruitful area of research, opening up questions that are only touched on in *The Charitable Crescent*: such as relations with other Faith Based Organizations and the international aid system; changes in the interpretation of Islamic doctrine; gender relations; and the pros and cons of 'cultural proximity' in the delivery of aid. This sudden growth of a new research topic is welcome. A gap in *The Charitable Crescent* – the near absence of quantitative data – has yet to be rectified, for the work of Islamic charities is still almost entirely omitted from the analysis of international aid flows.

The Charitable Crescent has been charged by some Muslim readers with bringing to bear on Islamic charities an excessively political approach. Yet we aspired to be even-handed: on p.155 will be found sharp criticisms of Western humanitarianism, and due tribute is paid to the strength of the charitable imperative in Islamic teaching (e.g. pp.89, 156). Furthermore, as soon as any charitable activity goes beyond individual giving or helping, it is likely to become politicized. Like any organization, charities are subject to competition for their control, and this is compounded as they build constituencies in the delivery of aid. Even the International Red Cross and Red Cross Movement, which strives to keep away from politics and calls for universality, has been affected by political rivalries among nations. It took years of diplomatic efforts for the Movement to find a compromise over the politicized issue of its emblems, with the adoption in 2005 of a third emblem, the red crystal, and with the full admission to the Federation in 2006 of the (Israeli) Magen David Adom and the Palestine Red Crescent Society.

While it would be naïve to overestimate the power of private philanthropy to resolve the world's urgent problems, development practitioners are increasingly recognizing the power of Faith Based Organizations to reach out to vast civil society networks. Scant recognition was given until recently to the Muslim tradition, though the spiritual and moral values embodied in the ancient institution of zakat surely have great potential to promote social justice and respond to emergency needs. Solidly based, impartial research is now called for to build on the findings that are already available.

2008

Selected articles published by the authors since 2003

Bellion-Jourdan, Jérôme. 2007. 'Are Muslim charities purely humanitarian? A real but misleading question' in M. Feher (ed.) *Non-Governmental Politics*. Cambridge, MA.: Zone Books.

Benthall, Jonathan. 2006. 'L'humanitarisme islamique', *Cultures et Conflits*, no. 60. Available free online: www.conflits.org/index1928.html
----2006. 'Islamic aid in a north Malian enclave', *Anthropology Today*, August, 22.4.
----2007. 'Islamic charities, Faith-Based Organizations and the international aid system', in J. Alterman and K. van Hippel (eds), *Understanding Islamic Charities*, Washington, DC: CSIS Press.

Note
In March 2008, Jérôme Bellion-Jourdan was Political Officer, European Commission Technical Assistance Office for the West Bank and Gaza Strip, East Jerusalem. Jonathan Benthall was an adviser to the Swiss Federal Department of Foreign Affairs, Political Division IV (Montreux Initiative). Both authors write here in a private capacity only.

PREFACE

The war against Saddam Hussain's Iraq in spring 2003 was a striking example of the mixing of military and humanitarian action. As the United States administration made clear, the military campaign aimed at bringing down the regime was to be accompanied by the delivery of humanitarian aid to win the hearts and minds of Iraqi people and make them accept the occupying force. Hence the relevance of our chosen topic to a war that all commentators, of whatever opinions, agree was a historical turning-point.

Humanitarian relief has been a pressing issue in wartime for a century and a half, but never so much as in this war, with its continuous media coverage. During the initial stages of maintaining basic services and supplies, only a few front-line independent agencies such as the ICRC had a role. The main humanitarian responsibility was that of the occupying forces, which at one point were so overstretched as to be unable even to protect hospitals and aid offices – the American-British war plan having resulted in the collapse of all Iraq's civil administration in the cities. As the high-intensity conflict wound down and the Iraq war gradually gave way to other headline news, sharp disagreements arose over the respective future roles of the United States military, the United Nations and Iraqi politicians in coordinating aid delivery and post-war reconstruction. Voluntary agencies from many countries were preparing to complement the efforts of intergovernmental agencies in meeting the relief and reconstruction needs of this devastated, though potentially well-to-do, country. It was feared that factionalism and violence would persist in the new political vacuum.

Given the US policy of opposing Muslim charities suspected of being linked with 'terrorism', it seemed to us that the tighter the control that the US government decided to maintain over Iraq, the more limited would be the opportunities for external Islamic charities to intervene. But intervene they would certainly set out to do. The case-studies in this book describing humanitarian intervention by Islamic agencies in Afghanistan in the 1980s (Chapter 4) and Bosnia-Herzegovina in the 1990s (Chapter 7) may be of special relevance to post-war Iraq.

Wesley Clark, the American general who had led Nato forces during the Kosovo campaign, predicted in the press that Iraq was likely to prove a fertile ground for Al-Qa`ida recruitment via Islamic charities in the war's immediate aftermath: 'both Shia and Sunni extremists will be embedded in international Islamic charities, and some will be recruiting for their own purposes.' He added that among the precautions that would have to be taken against such recruitment would be identification and background checks on charities, and monitoring of the mosques (*The Times*, 3 April 2003). Yet at the same time, evangelical Christian charities from the United States were poised behind army lines to bring in relief aid and to seek to convert Muslims. These included the influential Southern Baptists, and an organization named Samaritans' Purse that was led by Billy Graham's son, the Rev. Franklin Graham, who was avowedly anti-Muslim (*The Times*, 19 April 2003).

Crude as may be the Huntington 'clash of civilizations' model (discussed in the Conclusion to this book), it is all too easy to imagine this becoming a self-fulfilling prophecy, when Manichaean world-views are adopted by both Christian and Muslim militants and expressed in the form of offering aid to the vulnerable. Yet one should avoid over-simplification: since the 19th century, charities in the Muslim world have often developed in a mixed relation of contention with and imitation of Western agencies. This is the case of the development of Red Crescent societies within the Red Cross movement (Chapter 3) but also of international Islamic charities.

Among the points made in this book is that Islamic charities in countries such as Sudan (Chapter 6), and even more in countries such as Britain with sizeable Muslim minorities, are seeking common ground with secular aid agencies and aiming at high professional standards. Yet there are always differences of style and emphasis. A recent example is the reactions of the two major British Islamic relief agencies to the Iraq war. Both Islamic Relief and Muslim Aid launched appeals at the start of the war. The more Establishment-oriented Islamic Relief had already joined a number of other British agencies in September 2002 to warn against the humanitarian consequences of war against Iraq. By January 2003 it was able to set up an office in Baghdad, and in March it launched an appeal for € 10 million in the House of Commons. But Muslim Aid, addressing its own public more directly, went further and protested that the war 'lacks legitimacy' (source: web-sites, April 2003).

Those charged with regulating relief and reconstruction in Iraq need to bear in mind both the diversity of objectives that Islamic charities bring to bear, and the diversity of their funding sources. Some are awash with funds from Gulf States' oil. Others represent the fruits of zakat contributions from ordinary Muslims all over the world (as analysed in Chapter 1), or what has been described in another context as the 'philanthropy of the poor'.

A new development in the link between business and Islamic charities (discussed in Chapter 2) is for Muslim entrepreneurs to launch products for the Muslim market that have the quadruple aim of pleasing the devout, challenging the dominance of American companies, making profits, and passing on a proportion of them to charity. Named after the well at Mecca, Zamzam Cola, which used to be a partner of Pepsi-Cola in Iran until 1979, was taken over by one of the large Shi'ite foundations and now employs 77,000 people. The idea was recently copied in France by Mecca Cola and in Britain by Qibla-Cola (*qibla* is the direction that Muslims face when making the ritual prayer towards Mecca). On Mecca Cola bottles, a picture of the Dome of the Rock in Jerusalem is accompanied with a slogan explaining that 10 per cent of net profits will be funding projects for Palestinian children: 'No more drinking stupid, drink with commitment, drink Mecca Cola'. So far, the Coca-Cola Company remains unperturbed. But Islamic colas may foreshadow further efforts to mobilize the economic power of the Muslim *umma* for humanitarian purposes.

2003

INTRODUCTION*

'Islamic philanthropy: does it exist?' we have heard this would-be-witty rejoinder several times from Westerners when we have mentioned our topic. Since the attacks on New York and Washington, reportedly by members of Al-Qaʿida, on 11 September 2001, it has even acquired some notoriety in newspaper headlines; for some politicians and journalists have drawn the conclusion that a number of Muslim charities were using humanitarian programmes as a cover for 'terrorist' activities.

We argue that the topic of Islamic philanthropy is pivotal, bringing together the richness of Islamic studies with an almost virgin field for academic research – the traditions of voluntary aid that fall outside the normal category of presumed Western largesse. We will supply detailed analysis of Islamic charity in political context, with readers in mind who may be able to make practical use of such findings in their work. But we will also touch on general questions such as the following. How can one form a true picture of Muslim ethical values and traditions, in all their variety, without being trapped by media caricatures of fundamentalist Islam or by their opposite – a sentimentalized oleograph of Muslims as akin to Quakers in jellabahs? To what extent does a legacy of Judaeo-Christianity underpin the supposedly universal humanitarianism that originated in the West? Is there one humanitarian tradition or several, each moulded by its cultural past? The principles of human rights may seem self-evident to many, but will a decline in religious observance, such as may be observed in many Western countries, chip away at our deep-seated sense of a common humanity, on which the humanitarian tradition depends?

'Does Islamic philanthropy exist?' Only an elementary knowledge of Muslim history is needed to make the question redundant. What is true is that the representation of Islamic organized charity in the Western mass media has been extremely muted until recently, when it became for the most part negative.

Western aid agencies at the international level engage in a symbiosis with the mass media, providing access in exchange for exposure. It had been uncommon for a television reporter for NBC or the BBC to interview a field officer from one of the Red Crescent Societies, or one of the large international aid agencies funded by Gulf States, on the occasion of an earthquake or a refugee exodus. But in the Afghan conflict of the 1980s, then the Balkan conflicts of the 1990s, the Western media became more alert to the existence of Islamic aid agencies on quite a large scale. The assumption was often made that the role of these agencies was purely instrumental

* by Jonathan Benthall and Jérôme Bellion-Jourdan

to the interests of Muslim governments or movements. A typical episode was in 1996, when a US federal judge allowed Israel to extradite Mousa Abu Marzook, a senior member of Hamas, one of the grounds for his decision being that he believed money raised by Mr Marzook in America for hospitals, schools and mosques in the Middle East was actually being used to buy weapons for Hamas, the principal Islamist movement in the Occupied Territories in Palestine.[1] Since the revived Intifada in Palestine in September 2000 and military strikes by Israel, the Israeli authorities have further increased pressures to stop financial support to Hamas and other militant groups. At an international level, after 11 September 2001, the funds of a number of international Islamic aid agencies were frozen by the USA and other governments, on suspicion of abetting Al-Qa`ida.[2]

At the domestic level within Muslim[3] countries and among Muslim communities in non-Muslim states, social welfare programmes carried out by voluntary Islamic associations came to the West's attention over the same period, when it was realized how effective they were in mobilizing political support in countries where state support cannot satisfy welfare needs and demands. Some organizations, such as the idiosyncratic but widely supported Edhi Foundation in Pakistan, have stuck to a traditional charitable last. But the Society of Muslim Brothers in particular, founded in Egypt in 1928, had developed a kind of dual identity, as both a political and a social welfare movement, which has provided a key strategic model for other countries in the Arab-Islamic world as well as Egypt. Few of the Western relief and development agencies working in Muslim countries show any inclination to try to work with Islamist associations as sub-contractors or partners, partly because these associations are usually at odds with their governments and partly because of suspicion of their political or religious aims. But these associations' success in responding to grass-roots needs can only be seen as an admonition to centralized regimes that have failed to earn popular trust.

This book does not attempt a comprehensive survey of Islamic charities. Rather, we have sought to explore the relations between local and transnational dynamics, and to contextualize our findings against wider debates: including those about humanitarianism and aid agencies, civil society and volunteering, the supposed clash of religions, Islamic fundamentalism and modernizing movements, transnational institutions as they relate to local ones, and the 'market' in suffering and its relief.

There is already a substantial academic literature on the institutions of 'political Islam', but very little on the social welfare aspects of these institutions.[4] By the same token, the more general politics of humanitarian aid and philanthropy have attracted a body of trenchant analysis in recent years, but rarely with an emphasis on those donors who do not fit the pattern of the West patronizing the Rest. We have drawn on a variety of relevant scholarly sources combined with first-hand data in order to open up a new field for investigation. With this in mind, we have not tried to define terms such as 'aid', 'charity' and 'humanitarian' too closely – words which are not only somewhat elusive to pin down in European languages, but also do not necessarily translate precisely into a non-European language such as Arabic.

This book is the outcome of two independent, but complementary, research projects.[5]

Benthall's point of entry to the topic was his attempt to apply insights from cultural anthropology to the study of aid agencies, in which he has a practical as well as an academic interest. A study of the semiotics of the Red Cross led him to note that nearly thirty countries have a Red Crescent instead of a Red Cross national society, but that these societies were almost undocumented. Interviews with officials of the International Committee of the Red Cross (ICRC) in Geneva in 1994 made him aware that its relations with the Islamic world were a matter of considerable concern to them, while Islamic apologists were disseminating a heady rhetoric promoting the ideal of an Islamic society based on zakat that would somehow transcend both capitalism and communism. He undertook field research in Jordan and the Palestinian territories in 1996, and during a short period held useful communications with officials of the International Islamic Relief Organization, based in Jeddah, at a time when this organization was keen to develop its external relations. In order to deepen his understanding of the dialectic between religious ideology and practice, he has also ventured into another field, Quranic studies – 'where angels fear to tread'.

Bellion-Jourdan's interest in the topic first arose when he was conducting research on young Muslims in France. In an Islamic congress in Paris in 1993, he noticed the visibility of Secours Islamique, a branch of the UK based Islamic Relief Worldwide, mobilizing support for the victims of the Bosnian conflict. Far away from Paris, during a visit to Sudan in 1995, he realized the increasing role played by Islamic humanitarian agencies, both Sudanese and international. Officials of the international relief agencies and leaders of the local churches were objecting to this competition with their own programmes, which raised the sensitive and burning issue of who should provide aid to the displaced populations surviving in camps on the outskirts of the Sudanese capital. Since then, Bellion-Jourdan has undertaken field research in Sudan, Pakistan, Bosnia, Egypt, France and England with the aim of helping to fill a gap in the research literature on both Islamism and humanitarianism, where international Islamic relief agencies were hardly mentioned. As an empirical political scientist, his approach has been driven by a willingness to understand, rather than judge or evaluate, the emergence and development of Islamic relief institutions and their interaction with the international humanitarian scene.

Though wishing to provide the reader above all with an adequate body of documentation, including entry-points to all the relevant ongoing debates in our chosen field, we have also given consideration to a fundamental question: the tension between universalist morality and more relativistic viewpoints. Absolute moral relativism is not, we imagine, a position that many of our readers will hold. But we take it that many will be concerned by the ease with which a vocabulary of universal morality and rights is so often used to impose a view of Western moral superiority over the rest of humanity, or to make national or economic interests appear more respectable. One example of this tendency is the concept of 'humanitarian war', which was first floated by some Western governments during the Kosovo conflict of 1999 and has since been used to justify the US-led attacks on the Afghan Taliban regime in late 2001. Whatever justifications may be advanced in support of these campaigns against oppressive regimes, the phrase 'humanitarian war' seems a contradiction in terms, devaluing the laborious achievement of the Red Cross and other organizations in gaining acceptance for humanitarian principles. An opposite tendency is for some regimes to dissociate themselves from the growing international consensus on universal human rights by claiming a cultural exception – for instance, on the rights of women or of those accused of crimes.

The path of anthropological and political analysis should help to disentangle some of these knots. We would start from the premise that the act of charity, whether based on some religious precept or merely on the human recognition of another human being in need, is best characterized as a bodily act: the offering of firstfruits from an orchard to hungry people, or the extending of a hand by the Samaritan to a stricken traveller. Such acts do not result in the foundation of organizations, and they are therefore immune to political analysis. However, they are realities only in a utopian sense.[6] Even the existence of an orchard implies territorial rights, while the story in St Luke's Gospel about the Samaritan conceals a latent message of anti-Jewish sentiment. Great efforts have been made to ring-fence areas of charitable activity as being distinct from political activity: examples are the Charities Acts in England, the French Law of Associations of 1901, and the development of Geneva Law since the foundation of the Red Cross.

These efforts at boundary maintenance aim to give charitable and philanthropic institutions a kind of secular sanctity. However, it has become uncomfortably clear to the managers of international aid agencies that they are often viewed from outside, and specially by their recipients or presumed beneficiaries, in different ways: as agents of Western power and influence, as providers of enviable employment opportunities, sometimes as carriers of Christian evangelism or post-Christian godlessness. Similarly, even apparently blameless Islamic charities have been accused by critics, such as Daniel Pipes, of dissimulating their real subversive motives under a veil of philanthropy; and the existence of an Islamic tradition of *taqiya* – the right to conceal one's faith when one is in danger – can give some plausibility to this charge (Ghandour 2002: 200, 210).

One response has been to recognize that no charitable organization is in fact immune to political analysis, and that humanitarian and development aid in particular has an inescapable political dimension. What Alex de Waal has called the 'humanitarian international' has begun to be subjected to searching examination in recent years. Two recent articles in *Humanitarian Affairs Review* are specimens of current thinking. David Rieff asks what is left of the idea of independent humanitarian agencies after the war in Kosovo, when they fell into the role of sub-contractors to NATO (Rieff 1999). Michael Pugh asserts: 'Like it or not, humanitarians *are* political'. They compete for an annual global aid budget of about $3 billion; their policies are moulded by states; their actions can inadvertently fuel conflicts or sustain genocidal movements; they can provide a fig leaf for the inefficacy of politicians (Pugh 2002).

Another response in the aid world has been to turn the focus from Western or international aid agencies to home-grown or local movements, 'civil society', or the 'grassroots'. Naturally, this shift of emphasis has stimulated new varieties of opportunism. Local movements in themselves are clearly not enough to satisfy all humanitarian and developmental needs. And a current debate is asking how to foster the most constructive collaboration between international agencies and these local movements – a question which needs to be addressed by both Western and Islamic international aid agencies.

The especially interesting point about Islamic institutions is that not only do they have an extensive popular outreach, but they have developed international programmes sustained by an alternative form of universalism to that of the Judaeo-Christian West. Islam has been a proselytizing religion just as much as Christianity, and its origins in Arab tribalism have long been massively outweighed by its global and non-racial aspirations. Indeed, Islam originated as a critique of Christianity and Judaism, and has reinvented itself over the centuries in opposition to a succession of real or perceived threats: the Spanish, the Crusaders, European empires, Hinduism, Zionism, communism. A large number of Muslims today see the USA and what it stands for as an ideological enemy, though the sentiment is in fact probably more one of 'love-hate' than enmity, except in the case of a small minority.

In a well tried manoeuvre of anthropology, and increasingly one of political science as it seeks to reduce its tendency towards ethnocentrism, we offer the results of our research in no spirit of apologetics either for Islam or for any other religion or ideological system, but in the hope that these results will supply a fresh perspective for considering the politics of global humanitarianism through the exercise of 'decentring', or unsettling of prior assumptions.

Structure of the book

Chapter 1 examines how the injunctions in the Quran on charitable giving have been interpreted and implemented, both in the past and in the present. It concludes more speculatively by suggesting how the Quran's references to firstfruits, as the epitome of charity, might offer a 'green' alternative to the symbolism of animal sacrifice which dominates mainstream Islam.

Chapter 2 reviews how two key institutions relating to Islamic charity, the *waqf* (charitable endowment) and Islamic finance, are both part of a ductile religious tradition whose consistency over time has often been exaggerated. It examines the financial resources available to contemporary Islamic charities.

Chapter 3 considers the efforts of the Red Cross and Red Crescent Movement, initially rooted in Christian culture, to be true to its non-denominational principles while accommodating the presence of a large Muslim constituency. Long-standing controversy over the religiously loaded symbolism of the two emblems has been accompanied by substantive differences of view relating to the principle of 'universality'. The Red Crescent National Society in Jordan is chosen as the principal contemporary case-study.

Chapter 4 focuses on the new international Islamic charities that have emerged since the 1980s. Explanation of the ambiguities in the key Islamic concept of jihad leads to analysis of the different motivations within this movement: charitable relief, religious militancy and military involvement. In a number of countries such as Saudi-Arabia, Egypt and the United Kingdom, since the time of the Afghan conflict of the 1980s, charitable organizations were mobilized to serve the duty of Islamic solidarity at the level of the *umma* (community of believers) but were often in competition with one another. Some of these decided to adapt to the world of international humanitarianism.

Chapter 5 outlines the growth of studies of NGOs and civil society over the last twenty years, and argues that there has been a close link between Western philanthropy and the Judaeo-Christian tradition. Similarly, the religious constituent in Muslim charitable traditions should not be ignored, appropriated as these may often be by politicians and militants. Evidence is offered of the effectiveness of 'social Islam' in countries without adequate state welfare provision. The voluntary sectors in Algeria and Jordan are discussed as case studies, with an emphasis on Islamic charitable associations and their particular characteristics. It is argued that despite successes at the grassroots, a lack of accountability is widespread – except in countries with strict laws on auditing – and disastrous for the reputation of Islamic charities as a whole. The Lebanese Hizbullah is a prime example of combining extensive welfare provision with a radical religious, political and military agenda.

Chapter 6 analyses competitive relationships in humanitarian aid in Sudan, where Islamic agencies in the North such as Da`wa Islamiya ('Islamic Call') have been launched since the 1980s to compete with Western NGOs. Western NGOs have been charged with attempting to impose their activities on Sudanese society in the style of Christian missionaries. In turn, Islamic agencies are accused of 'islamizing' the beneficiaries of their programmes. The two decade long conflict between the authorities in the North and the rebel movements in the South has made the humanitarian field particularly tense.

Chapter 7 takes Bosnia since the 1992-95 war, to illustrate the strategies of Islamic charities and movements to develop their activities in the Balkans. Most of the Muslim agencies were concerned to maintain Muslim populations in place, as opposed to the United Nations High Commissioner for Refugees' perceived policy of encouraging an exodus. However, the 'Islamic cause' concealed manifold tensions at the international and local levels, and was eventually disowned by Bosnian Muslim leaders.

The book ends with a brief Conclusion, followed by a key to abbreviations and a glossary of Islamic and Arabic terms.

1

FINANCIAL WORSHIP*

The special status of the Quran

We shall consider in Chapter 5 to what extent religious doctrine may be considered an independent determinant when we try to understand Islamic charities. We must make due allowance for the self-interested motives that underlie much charitable giving – whether in expectation of an earthly or a heavenly reward, or both – and for the universal ability of human beings to preach one thing and do another. However, an exclusive emphasis on donors' self-interest and hypocrisy can yield repetitive and excessively narrow explanations. It is sensible, then, to begin with an enquiry into what the Quran teaches, and above all into how this teaching has been varyingly interpreted.

Supporting evidence for the religious determinant in Islamic charities might be adduced from the strength of the *waqf*s or religious foundations in Islamic history – to be given extensive treatment in Chapter 2 – or from the early history of the Muslim Brothers (Mitchell 1969). However, the Quran itself is of fundamental importance.

Little in the Sunna – the sum of the actions and judgments (*hadith*s) of the Prophet, from which precedents and guides for later Muslim practice were derived – would contradict what is to be found in the Quran on these matters. But there are several reasons for concentrating on the Quran itself in this chapter, so that when *hadith*s are cited, they are among the well-known ones that are affectionately and selectively repeated by devout Muslims, whereas the references to the Quran are grounded in the text. First, studying the Sunna is a branch of knowledge where distinguishing the more from the less authentic requires almost a lifetime's devotion (Burton 1994), whereas the Quran is a standard text with only minuscule variant readings. Second, the mainstream of Muslim scholars contends that, though the Sunna illuminates the Quran, the Quran has ultimate precedence. It is, after all, considered the eternal and immutable speech of God, primary revelation as opposed to secondary revelation such as Christian doctrine holds most of the New Testament to be. And third, there has been a renewed emphasis on the Quran in the twentieth century Islamic revival. Sayyid Qutb, the influential Egyptian ideologue, argued that

* by Jonathan Benthall

the Quran contained all the necessary answers to the world's problems (Carré 1984). And I shall not forget a discussion with a devout Berber schoolteacher in a village in Morocco in the spring of 1997. In a context of economic crisis and widespread disillusion with the government's claims to be moving towards more democracy and freedom of expression, he claimed with pride that all over the Muslim world ordinary people are now reading their Qurans and discovering that its teaching is at variance with the reality of regimes that claim to be Islamic. This recalls the part that the Bible once played in the growth of literacy and radical politics in English or French history. An Act of 1543 'for the advancement of true religion and for the abolishment of the contrary' forbade reading of the Bible by the lower orders (Williams 1961: 159, see also Eickelman 1992: 643).

This chapter will first outline the Quranic injunction to almsgiving and some variations in interpretation, and then consider how it is attended to in a number of Islamic states. All Quranic studies have to be carried on in a setting where even abstruse details can acquire heated political overtones, a kind of Jerusalem of the intellect where scholars behave like guests at a diplomatic reception, some of them quietly ignoring the existence of others (cf. Berg 1997). Whereas a number of anthropologists have analysed the use of Quranic verses and *hadith*s in ethnographic context (e.g. Antoun 1989, Bowen 1993, Fischer and Abedi 1990), there is no reason why textual analysis of the Quran itself should not also be attempted, in emulation of the long established contribution of social anthropology to studies of the Bible. An excursus into textual analysis inspired by the anthropologist Mary Douglas concludes the chapter.

The grounding of zakat in Quranic interpretation

Present-day interpretation and present-day practice
My approach in this section will be to review present-day teaching on zakat through the prism of interpretation, which is interwoven with present-day practice. The reader is invited, whatever may be his or her position on religious belief, to adopt provisionally for the sake of argument the viewpoint of the devout believer who accepts the authority of the Quran as a guide to life. Does this excursion into theological interpretation risk taking us too far from the emphasis on politics in the present book's title? I think not, first – a general point – because of the extensive historical overlap between theology and politics, in Islam as in Christianity. And second, more specifically, interpretative nuances of Islamic teaching today have direct practical relevance to the lives of millions – ranging from injunctions on women's dress, through prohibitions on financial speculation, to the admissibility of non-Muslims' presence on territory held to be sacred. A contrary view, which we might call 'neo-Kemalism' after the founder of modern Turkey, contends that theology should be de-linked from all public and political issues. Whatever one's personal position may be with regard to religious belief and its place in the polity, it is indisputable that religious dogma, ultimately founded in a belief in supernatural revelation, seems likely to hold much of its spiritual force for the short and medium term in the Muslim world.

In contemporary Muslim societies we see a spectrum between complete incorporation of zakat by the State and its marginalization to the individual's private conscience. An example of the first is Pakistan, where it is collected by the State Bank and deposited in a federal zakat fund from which it is redistributed first to provincial zakat departments, and subsequently both directly to institutions such as schools and hospitals, and to some 40,000 local zakat committees. Examples of the second are Oman and Morocco, or Muslim communities in non-Muslim countries. But there are a number of intermediate solutions. Jordan has established a directorate of zakat under the Ministry of Religious Affairs, but local zakat committees are also allowed to raise and distribute charitable funds. In Malaysia and Kuwait, Islamic Councils closely linked to the governments are responsible for administering it (Weiss 2002). Problems of lack of popular trust in centralized zakat systems seem to be widespread.

However, zakat's importance is entrenched since it is the third of the Five Pillars of the Religion (*arkan ad-din*) which are recognized by all branches of Sunni Islam, and it means the religious duty to give up a fixed proportion of one's wealth for specified good causes.[1]

Zakat derives from the verb *zaka* which means to purify (also with the connotation of growth or increase).[2] The meaning is usually taken to be that, by giving up a portion of one's wealth, one purifies that portion which remains, and also oneself – through a restraint on one's selfishness, greed and imperviousness to others' sufferings. The recipient, likewise, is purified from jealousy and hatred of the well off. Thus the action of giving alms has this moral function as well as fulfilling needs. The traditional proportion required is one-fortieth of one's assets per year, but there is a great deal of scholarly literature which sets out different proportions for different kinds of wealth. Muslims with wealth below a certain fixed threshold (*nisab*) do not have to pay zakat. In addition, there is an annual requirement on everyone to pay a small zakat *al-fitr* (*fitr* = breaking of the fast) or *fitrah* to the needy at the end of Ramadan. This is supposed to correspond to one bushel, or about 2.2 kilos, of the local staple food, or the equivalent in cash. There is wide agreement about the general principles of zakat. It is a kind of 'financial worship', and without its observance, the efficacy of prayer is negated. It is closely associated with prayer in many verses of the Quran. During Ramadan, the exercise of fasting is supposed to remind believers of what it would be like to be poor and hungry, and they are called on to be more than usually generous. Alms given during Ramadan are said to be seventy times more meritorious than at other times of the year. We are merely vice-regents or trustees over the resources available to us. Whatever we have must be used to bring us closer to God. A *hadith* warns that he who sleeps with a full stomach while his neighbour goes hungry will be deprived of God's mercy; and there are numerous stories of good rulers such as the second Caliph, Omar, who used go round Mecca at night with a sack of flour making sure that everyone had enough to eat. Zakat as a religious duty is to be distinguished from *sadaqa*, which is the giving of alms more voluntarily. The two terms are, however, closely associated throughout the Quran, so closely that in the key verse of the Quran (9. 60), which specifies the permitted beneficiaries of zakat, the word *sadaqa* is actually used in the text but it is generally interpreted as referring to zakat.

Who should benefit from zakat? The distribution of zakat funds is a matter for choice only within specified limits. There are eight permitted classes of beneficiaries of alms, listed as follows (9. 60):

1. The poor (al-fuqara').

2. Al-masakin: usually interpreted as the needy or very poor, a word paraphrased in Q.90. 16 as 'those down in the dust' (dha matrabatin).

3. 'The officials appointed over them' (al-`amalina `alayha), usually interpreted as the people appointed to administer the zakat and negotiate with outlying groups.

4. 'Those whose hearts are made to incline [to truth]' (al-mu'allafati qulubuhum), interpreted as being to help those recently or about to be converted, and/or to mollify powerful non-Muslims whom the State fears, as an act of prudent politics.[3]

5. Most Islamic commentators seem to have thought that 'captives' means Muslims captured by enemies who needed to be ransomed, but Décobert argues (1991: 226) that it means men from other tribes enslaved by the early Meccans and Medinans.

6. Debtors: particularly, argues Décobert, because those who cannot repay their debts lose rank and become clients of their creditors.

7. Those in the way of God, that is to say in jihad, teaching or fighting or in other duties assigned to them in God's cause.

8. 'Sons of the road' (ibn as-sabil) i.e. travellers.

As with the other world religions, Islam encompasses a great deal of disagreement between authorities about matters of interpretation, and this verse of the Quran is a good example of the different readings that have arisen. I shall give some instances of these, as well as of consensus where it can be found, without attempting to cover the whole topic thoroughly.[4]

It is often stated that the recipients of zakat must be Muslims (e.g. by the Egyptian scholar `Uthman Hussayn Abd-Allah, quoted by Abu-Sahlieh 1994: 261), but this proposition is as frequently rebutted today. Abdul-Aziz Al-Khayyat, a leading Jordanian Islamic scholar, told me that it is clear that the phrase al-fuqara' must mean in Arabic 'all the [category of the] poor', and therefore it must include the non-Muslim poor. The difference of view is reflected in the respective policies of two major British Muslim relief agencies: Islamic Relief extends zakat funds to non-Muslims in Africa, while Muslim Aid restricts its aid (with some occasional minor exceptions) to Muslim beneficiaries only.

Abd-Allah proposes the following sub-groups of poor: orphans and foundlings, widows and divorcees, prisoners and their families, the unemployed, students, the homeless, those who cannot afford to marry, disaster victims, and those in need of free medicines or dignified funerals. Al-Khayyat (1993: 184) stresses a distinction between the poor (category 1) and the very poor (category 2). The very poor are people deprived of any kind of ownership who are not even able to evaluate their own needs. The merely poor may just not be able to meet their expenditure out of their income, and account must be taken, in assessing their need, of their obligations to their families and of their social status.

Category 3, the zakat administrators, now allows charitable institutions to receive zakat provided they are set up to help one of the permitted classes of beneficiary. This provision has sometimes given rise to a large proportion of zakat being applied for State purposes by certain rulers, in a way that would now be considered abusive. But that was generally in states where no other taxes were levied by governments – as in the Ibadate imamate of Oman in the late nineteenth century, where zakat became more like a type of Danegeld than a form of religious alms (Wilkinson 1987). The practice may still be flourishing today in a country like Pakistan, where following zakat's absorption into the State taxation system in 1980, a measure of official corruption has been diagnosed (Roy 1991: 179ff., Novossyolov 1993). The Taliban at the height of their power in Afghanistan were reportedly levying a 20 per cent zakat tax on the value of all truckloads of opium (Rashid 2000: 118). The allocation of zakat funds for administration of NGOs has been criticized by one British sheikh, Omar Bakri Muhammad, leader of a radical movement, who has gone so far as to attack Muslim Aid and Islamic Relief as 'the False 'Aamileen A'liyha ... the so-called collectors' (Weiss 2002: 29).[5]

Category 4 is interpreted by Al-Khayyat (1993: 185) as applying to anyone sympathetic with Islam. Abd-Allah, however, contends that this category applies to missionary education, propaganda to combat secularism or communism or Zionism or Christian missions, assisting new converts to Islam, and assuring the support or neutrality of people in power. Some interpretations allow the building of mosques as an object for disbursal of zakat funds.

Abd-Allah adopts a sharply political interpretation of category 5, the captives, claiming that this function of zakat includes helping Muslims in their struggle against colonialism and supporting Muslim minorities living in non-Muslim tyrannies. This point of view is controversial and would squarely place such donations outside the category of 'non-political charity' in a country such as Jordan where this distinction is insisted on by the State. Similar interpretations have been offered for category 7, 'those in the way of God'. Since the term jihad is deeply equivocal, as argued elsewhere in this book, category 7, like 4 and 5, clearly allows considerable leeway for the application of zakat funds in ways that non-Muslims might criticize.

'Debtors' (category 6) has been restrictively interpreted by some as meaning only those debtors 'who by financing good works have become impoverished' (Schimmel 1992: 35). 'Travellers' (category 8) seem to Abd-Allah to include the sub-category of refugees; Al-Khayyat admits youth hostels, and adds that even if a traveller is rich in his own country, as long as there is a need he is eligible for a share of zakat (1993: 186, 181).

Opinion is moving in parts of the Islamic world towards what might be called a liberalization of the definition of eligible beneficiaries. Traditionally, it seems that zakat donors have expected to try to meet local needs before looking farther afield, and this practice is still the norm in many Muslim communities. However, with the growth of the mass media and organized relief agencies, some Islamic scholars have ruled that it is permissible and indeed desirable to spend zakat funds wherever the need is greatest. This is the principle that results in large Saudi zakat funds being disbursed overseas by the International Islamic Relief Organization (IIRO), which now reportedly has an annual expenditure of some $33 million. (In Saudi-Arabia, as a substitute for tax, individuals and in particular businesses are officially invited, but in effect required, to contribute to zakat funds about the time of Ramadan.) Similarly, the UK based organization Islamic Relief disburses all its income, much of which derives from zakat, overseas, except for central administration and fund-raising costs. This reflects the dominant view among British Muslim donors that true poverty is not to be found in industrialized states with their welfare safety nets. Pnina Werbner, an anthropologist who undertook fieldwork with Pakistanis in Manchester in the 1970s, wrote that she was frequently told that, living in Britain, she could not imagine real poverty. No Pakistanis in Britain were willing to define themselves as poor and take the remains of the meat-sacrifice, known to them as *sadqa*, offered on the occasion of someone's escape from a bad accident – on which occasion all the remains of the sacrificial victim were supposed to be given to the poor – or the third part of the meat which was supposed to be given to the poor on the occasion of the *qurbani* or festive sacrifice (Werbner 1988: 86-90).

Islamic scholars have reviewed the question that has troubled European organizers of charity for centuries: should charity be designed to help all the poor, or only the 'deserving poor'? The consensus seems to be that Islam calls on all people to work, and the characters and reputations of poor people may be taken into account in deciding whether they deserve help. Schemes for relieving unemployment are eligible for zakat subsidy (Al-Khayyat 1993: 181). People who are unable to work deserve to be helped (see e.g. Quran 51. 16-19, 70. 24-25).

How should zakat be collected? The categories of beneficiary are mentioned in the Quran, but the way it is to be collected only in the Sunna. Al-Khayyat says (1993: 180f.) that this was because God foresaw that there would be new forms of money, and wanted to ensure that there was flexibility. 'If the Quran had specified the sources of income, a lot of awkwardness would have arisen.' In his book, he devotes many pages to a review of the different rates that should be levied on livestock, trees and crops, minerals, factories, dwelling houses, stocks and bonds, even silk-worms and bee-hives.

There is general agreement that possessions required for the owner's basic needs – including a house, clothing, tools and consumables – are not zakatable. Also, zakat is not payable until an asset has been held for one year.

The argument for flexibility in calculating zakat percentages rests on the principle that the lesser the amount of labour exerted and capital invested, the greater should be the levy. For instance, a *hadith* states that when a plot of land is watered by rain or natural springs, the rate of zakat on the product will be one tenth, whereas when the land is watered by wells the rate should be one twentieth (Mannan 1986: 255). The zakat on treasure trove should be as much as one fifth because it has incurred no labour (ib.: 257).

Present-day examples of zakat in action

These niceties must be seen in perspective: with very few exceptions such as Saudi-Arabia and Pakistan, zakat in modern Muslim countries amounts to a voluntary or optional payment, sometimes a fund-raising vehicle. The British based organization Islamic Relief has cut through some of the complexities, after taking due advice from learned authorities, and has published a simplified 'Everything you need to know about Zakah' in its newsletter (*Partnership*, Winter 1996, p.3) Modern necessities such as a family car and business furniture are not zakatable. Investment property is.

The original threshold for zakat (*nisab*) set by the Prophet was 88 grams of gold. Islamic Relief calculates this as the equivalent of £740. According to the British advice, this obligation is over and above any liability to state taxes. This view is supported by Al-Khayyat but disputed by other experts. The issue is complicated by the provision in Islamic law for a special tax to be levied on non-Muslims in return for their protection by the state (*jizyah*, to which was later added *kharaj*, which is in effect a land tax).

Zakat is often described in devout literature as mandatory, but there are no penalties set out in the Quran or the Sunna to enforce payment or impose discipline on defaulters. Gradually reliance came to be placed on the believer's sense of responsibility and fear of God (*taqwa*) – a process accompanied by the secularization of the State as Muslim countries came under Western influence and control. In those Muslim countries where zakat has become an entirely private matter, stress is laid on those verses in the Quran that set store on disbursal of alms in secret (e.g. 2. 271).

Extensive evidence suggests that almsgiving is emphasized by preachers throughout the Muslim world. For instance Richard Antoun, who did ethnographic fieldwork in a village in northern Jordan during a number of stays between 1959 and 1962, analysed the themes addressed by the local preacher in his Friday *khutbas* or congregational sermons. This young sheikh, who was independent-minded but on the whole non-political, did not ignore questions of ritual and theology, but gave the strongest emphasis to questions of local-level ethics. Of the sample of 26 sermons analysed by Antoun, over half had an ethical orientation of some kind, and of these, three were concerned specifically with alms and charity. Sermons on zakat were given annually before harvest time and at the end of Ramadan, but the same topic might be addressed at any time of year in response to a day-to-day event, for instance the miserliness of a particular local individual (Antoun 1989: 90- 94). What Antoun calls 'normative Islam ... the message of Islam as it is rendered every Friday in mosques throughout the Muslim world' needs to be understood if we are to interpret adequately the late twentieth century Islamic revival.

My own research in Jordan and the West Bank in early 1996 gives evidence of some Jordanian and Palestinian zakat committees working with apparent effectiveness in the context of an active and varied voluntary sector. Jordan's middle path (see above) gives state recognition to zakat but does not enforce it. In 1944, a law was passed making it obligatory, but this was repealed in 1953 (Al-Khayyat 1993: 91ff.) Payments are now voluntary; tax relief is obtainable for this and indeed for all donations to recognized charities.

The *nisab* (threshold) was set in 1996 at 500 Jordanian Dinars (1 JD = about £1) per year, which effectively removed the obligation from about half the adult population. In 1994, JD 1 million was apparently collected by the central zakat fund, run by the Ministry of Awqaf (Religious Affairs) and JD 2 million by local committees.[6] The central fund supported educational and income-generating projects, old people's homes, rehabilitation projects for handicapped people, soup-kitchens etc. Recently, the Ministry has decided to revamp the work of the kingdom's 166 zakat committees by initiating a gynaecological hospital in Amman and many other new projects, with the support of substantial private donors including Jordanian expatriates in the USA.[7]

The most impressive zakat-funded programme that I visited was in Nablus, the historic town in the Palestinian West Bank which has suffered particularly from the Arab-Israeli conflict over many years. This had been run since 1982 by a committee that has drawn support from Jordan and other Arab countries. Large sums i.e. up to £10 million had been raised. The committee had bought buildings – a cow farm, a sheep farm, a dairy for pasteurization – and also invested in land and real estate to bring in income. It had founded one of the best equipped clinics in the West Bank. About 3,500 income payments, at a minimum of $50 per month, were paid out, and grants to 750 students at secondary and university level. *'Id* (festival) gifts were presented to 7,500 families. According to my informants, the Nablus committee made a point of being non-political and not giving any preference to devout Muslims.

I also visited the Jordanian branch of the International Islamic Relief Organization (IIRO), which is mainly funded by Saudi zakat contributions. The Jordan branch is only a small part of this major organization. The annual budget was about JD 2 million spent on orphan centres, JD 600,000 on health services, and JD 20,000 on assisting 43 overseas students in Jordan at university level. The IIRO sponsors *iftar*s (Ramadan evening breakfasts); and the distribution of frozen carcasses of sacrificed sheep, imported from Australia, to poor families on the occasion of the annual 'great feast' (*'id al-kabir*) (cf. Brisebarre 1993). IIRO also sponsors about 80 orphans every year to go on the lesser pilgrimage (*'umra*) to Mecca.

Spending the month of Ramadan in Jordan in 1996, I discussed the question of zakat with a wide variety of Jordanians ranging from the pious to 'nominal Muslims', and from the rich to the poor. It became clear that for a large proportion of them, when they hear the word, assume it to refer to the zakat *al-fitr* (see above), a practice which is widely observed among believers and only a trivial financial commitment for well-to-do families – though not trivial for a poor man with many children. Many people will make gifts during Ramadan to poor people in their immediate neighbourhood or social circle, ignoring the zakat committees. Others hold that in a modern state such as Jordan with a tax system, the zakat obligation is obsolete. One of the prominent royal charities, the Hashemite Fund for Social Development, has instituted a kind of secular zakat system during Ramadan.

I also visited members of a zakat committee in the south of Jordan (the town of Wadi Musa) where most of the population of settled Bedouin are poor and the question of paying on assessment of wealth does not arise. Money is however collected from shopkeepers and owners of sheep and goats, and distributed locally.

Ethnographic study of the actual collection and distribution of zakat in a Muslim community would be a worthwhile project, but its difficulty and sensitivity should not be underestimated. One aspect is that beneficiaries are often unwilling to disclose that they have been helped, for fear of compromising their eligibility for public welfare benefits. Another is that special religious merit is gained by giving alms in secret. Indeed, the Christian adage from Jesus's Sermon on the Mount, 'When you do some act of charity, do not let your left hand know what your right hand is doing' (*Matthew* 6. 3), is also well-known to many Muslims within the corpus of prophetic *hadith*s. Students of charitable giving in the West have noted that there are practical as well as spiritual advantages to be gained from anonymous giving, such as not wanting to appear wealthy or to attract requests for gifts (Schervisch 1993).

Zakat in modern Islamic doctrine

Zakat is a major support in the standard Islamic case against the evils of both capitalism and communism. It 'draws the sting of Marxism', Kenneth Cragg writes, depriving it of a legitimate argument against private property, and property of any scandalous features; it turns the main contradiction in capitalism into a happy spiral of redistribution, and it answers with clarity the communist denial of the right to possess. It solves the problem of poverty by leave of the rich, and punishes those who hoard and monopolize and try to corner markets (Cragg 1956: 153). Under the ideal scheme that wide observance of zakat would make possible, the rich do not become poor, but the poor cease to be poor. Zakat is a reminder that all wealth belongs to God; but there are several verses in the Quran that tolerate economic inequalities even though the dignity and fundamental equality of all human beings as children of Adam are also recognized. Islam accepts – so the argument runs – that there are inevitably differences among human beings that will in nearly every society result in economic inequalities. Wealth is to be cherished in moderation, but not to be (as we might say today) fetishized. The Quran condemns the emulous multiplication of wealth (102. 1-2, see also 104) – and deprecates ostentation: according to ancient tradition, Muslims should have no table utensils of gold or silver, and males should wear neither gold nor silver. Provided that believers obey the rules enjoined, there is no need for them to feel guilty about their inability to measure up to an ideal morality: there is no need for the well-to-do either to give away all their wealth, or to feel guilty about not being poor. Nor would Islamic teaching commend, as does the Christian Gospel, the widow who gives away her last farthings.

This point of view is put in a somewhat parodic form by a contemporary Pakistani Islamic economist, who writes that a Muslim's 'capacity for contribution to social welfare ... is to be measured by the amount one is able to spare after enjoying the standard of living which is commonly enjoyed by men of one's rank and station in life' (quoted by Kuran 1989). Put like this, the precept is not inspiring, but it is at least an accurate sociological observation of how members of the upper and middle classes in all stratified societies do in fact engage in alms-giving, with rare exceptions.

The Quran does not downgrade money in the style of many passages of the New Testament. It is crammed with injunctions about the right spending of money. Over one hundred verses of the Quran deal with these matters (e.g. 2. 195, 70. 23-25). Islam is the only one of the three Abrahamic religions that explicitly urges the believer not only to be generous in alms-giving but also to persuade others to be charitable (Q. 107).

We might presume to speculate how the pillars of Islam could be interpreted if there were equivalents in Islam to those Christian theologians who have in various ways approached Christian doctrine as a set of moral constructs, rather than in its aspect of supernatural revelation. It is often argued that Islamic theologians today have not adapted to modernity as keenly or effectively as their Christian counterparts. But a comparable approach to that of present-day 'Christian ethics' may be found in one of the major works of the eleventh century Islamic scholar and religious judge Al-Mawardi. Mawardi, in his Book of Right Conduct in Matters Worldly and Religious (*kitab adab ad-dunya wa ad-din*) set on one side the more purely religious significance of the pillars of religion, leaving us with their pragmatic moral content (Arkoun 1977: 259ff.). Prayer, he wrote, is to maintain a desirable mood of fear and ardour. Fasting is to help us have pity on the poor, so that we want to feed them; also to tame the body's appetites, which are lowering to human dignity. Pilgrimage to Mecca stimulates repentance for sins, and also through the rigours of the journey reminds us of the comforts of home and the goodwill which we ought to extend to travellers. Finally, zakat was prescribed to comfort the poor and thus free them from hatred, isolation, despair and envy. Furthermore, generosity leads to respect for rights.

Mawardi does not try to define the level at which wealth ceases to be necessary and becomes superfluous, and he does not seek to challenge existing social structures. Rather, he seeks to set out how each citizen should behave, given his condition – whether poor, medium or rich. Poor people are excluded, by definition, from the virtue of generosity, and are obliged to depend on the benevolence of the rich. Virtue for them lies in not becoming humiliated – for instance, in laying themselves open to refusal from a miser. They should seek help only when it is really needed, and then only from people known for their wealth and liberality, and for the discretion with which they dispense alms. Those of middle condition, neither poor nor rich, are freed from the paralysing anguish of the poor, without being exposed to the risks of wealth. They can achieve a solid morality, but without the éclat that magnanimity brings. The rich must give, to be purified of their possessions, which otherwise enslave them. They must also know how much to give, when to give and to whom. They should not wait for an open request; a hint should be enough. They should give willingly and whole-heartedly, and keep promises of help. They should not give for the sake of a reciprocal benefit, and should not remind people of their generosity or boast.

These precepts conform at least to a theoretical pattern of how Muslims are supposed to behave many centuries later. From the point of view of poor people, begging is probably less stigmatized in Islam than in the West. From the point of view of the well-to-do, the question of intention or *niyyah* is important. These and other ideas have been incorporated into a somewhat idealistic literature on zakat (e.g. Al-Khayyat 1993) that presents it as almost a panacea for the world's ills, allied with Islamic economics and the prohibition of bank interest or *riba* as the opposite of zakat (Carré 1984: 155) – a connection which will be thoroughly explored in our Chapter 2. Zakat's importance seems to be one principle on which all devout Muslims are united.

The striking claim was made by Sayyid Qutb that zakat was a superior concept to the Western concept of charitable alms. Qutb maintained that zakat had nothing to do with charity, which was a non-Islamic concept (Carré 1984: 151, Mitchell 1969: 253). Though repudiating socialism as also non-Islamic, Qutb held that Islam disapproved both of people being in need and of class distinctions. Zakat was 'the outstanding social pillar of Islam', enabling individuals' efforts to be steered towards a common goal. By contrast, a gift provokes the hatred of the recipient towards the donor.

A similar idea, but outside the Islamic social context, was articulated earlier in the century by Mauss, the sociologist, in *The Gift*: the unreciprocated gift, while bringing moral credit to the donor, actually wounds the recipient (Mauss 1990 [1925]). Islamic apologists argue that the poor can accept their due with no loss of dignity.

It is often claimed that the doctrine of zakat, insofar as it was ever realized, introduced the first codified (as opposed to informal) system of social security. In ancient Rome, a system of monthly sale of corn to citizens at subsidized prices had been introduced by Caius Gracchus in 123 BCE, resulting in conservative senators accusing the system of encouraging indolence and depleting the public treasury

(Garnsey 1988). But no code of social welfare so far-reaching was to be proposed in the West until Bismarck's reforms in the 1880s as part of a campaign against socialism. The principle that all citizens have a right to the services of the Welfare State, rather than having to beg for alms, is considered (even if under pressure today) a hallmark of modern industrial society.

It is difficult to see how in any modern society the one-sidedness of alms – the absence of Maussian reciprocity – can be avoided. According to the cultural self-image still adhered to by many Arabs, their society still has a 'face-to-face' aspect; and as a corollary, it is widely contended by them that Western communities have become atomized and lacking in spiritual values. The needy beneficiary of largesse can reciprocate by means of services and homage to patrons. Many Muslims believe that by their good acts they are preparing for themselves a place in Paradise. The prayers of the beneficiary are also, in Islam as in Judaeo-Christianity, a possible way in which the benefactor receives a return. When a righteous man has given to the poor, according to *Psalms* 112: 9, 'his horn shall be exalted with honour'. Likewise, Al-Khayyat says in his book on zakat that the poor are always praying that they will get help; and if you are the person who gives help, then the benefit of the prayer will go to you and your family and even to your wealth itself (Al-Khayyat 1993, 13-14). Weber pointed out that the blessing of the poor on their benefactors was the obverse of the curse uttered by the unjustly treated (Weber 1952: 259, *Deuteronomy* 24. 13-15).

Henri Lammens, the early twentieth century Roman Catholic scholar of ancient Arabic literary sources, was impressed by the repayment given to the benefactor in the form of poetic praise as the 'father' or 'refuge' of orphans and widows:

> 'Gifts come and go', said the Caliph Omar, 'but praise remains'. It remains engraved on the nomad's tenacious memory. That is how Bedouin custom seems to have resolved the problems of income and tax and public assistance. Unfortunately this solution presupposes the spreading of a poetic gift. Thus did the poets show themselves not embarrassed, but rather proud of seeing themselves enriched by the munificence of others. … In this free exchange of gifts and dithyrambs, the Arabs thought they recognized not a proof of venality but a transaction, a kind of commercial operation: *do ut des* [Latin: 'I give that you may give'] (Lammens 1914: 236).

Looked at in historical context, the claim that zakat is fundamentally different from Jewish and Christian charity sounds like special pleading. In particular, the doctrine that all wealth belongs to God seems to be Jewish in origin, and adopted by both Christianity and Islam, though there may well have been common historical roots in ancient Near Eastern cultures. Similar rules apply in Judaism about not shaming the recipient. Maimonides, the twelfth century Jewish philosopher exiled to the Egyptian court, was to lay the foundations of modern principles of enlightened charity by asserting that the highest form of giving was to help the poor to rehabilitate themselves, thus encouraging self-reliance.

However, as a matter of degree and emphasis it is a fair claim that 'Among sacred books, the Quran seems to be the only one in the world which sets out precisely [in 9.60] the basic principles of the budget and expenses of the state' (Hamidullah 1959: ii. 617). It is doubtful too whether any other religion has an equivalent to the Islamic

principle that hungry people have the right to share in the meal of those who are
well fed. If one is refused, then one has the right to use force and, should one
happen to kill one's adversary, one is considered innocent as one was struggling for a
legitimate right (Boisard 1985: 101). Similarly, thieves may plead in defence that they
have been forced to steal out of necessity, and the penalty should then fall on
whoever has allowed them to fall into such dire need (Carré 1984: 149). This
principle is adduced today by moderate Islamists, such as the Muslim Brothers in
Jordan, as an argument against introducing the rigours of Islamic criminal law, which
predicates a more equitable society.

The theory of zakat is raw material ready to be picked up and made use of by
Islamic reformists. Potentially, it might even suggest a way out of some of the
contradictions of Western charity, whereby Western aid workers are represented in
the mass media as heroic bearers of magical fixes to problems. The Islamic notion
that a poor person in the community is, or ought to be, a source of public shame is
one that could be fruitfully built on; and is in tune with some of the fund-raising
approaches adopted by Western charities such as Oxfam since the 1960s.

But in practice, zakat has been marginalized. Not a single Islamic state exhibits it
functioning as it should, as a system of automatic redistribution. Prince Hassan of
Jordan's often repeated proposal for an international zakat system, whereby the
richer Muslim states would help poor Muslims, remains on the table and has not
been taken up by Jordan's richer neighbours. There are great inequalities, and a
serious measure of chronic poverty, in Jordan itself; and even greater inequalities in
the Islamic world in general – though of course economic disparities are by no
means confined to the Islamic world.

One of the most impressive instances today of Muslim charity, even though it is
idiosyncratic and has excited some controversy, is the Edhi Foundation, built up
from nothing in Pakistan by Abdul Sattar Edhi (Edhi 1996). It is now a prominent
national and international agency specializing in emergency relief, medical care and
refugee aid, with branches in New York, London, Tokyo, Sydney and Scarborough
(Ontario). By the early 1990s its property and investments were claimed by the
founder to be valued at 1,000 million rupees (ib. 310). Edhi was born into a family of
small farmers in Gujarat, India, left school at the age of thirteen, and migrated with
his parents to Pakistan as refugees at the time of Partition, when he was in his early
teens. He started by opening an independent dispensary and maternity unit in
Karachi, funded by zakat and *sadaqa* donations, and by such fund-raising ploys as
asking people to donate the skins of goats sacrificed at *'Id* and selling them (ib. 56-7)
– which was later developed into a meat processing industry (ib. 283). With a flair
for the dramatic, Edhi also made a practice of rescuing bloated corpses from the sea,
roadsides or drains. Like a number of other markedly successful reformers in history,
Edhi refuses material comforts and inveighs against all kinds of extravagance,
including the building of mosques (ib. 177, 261) and the personnel costs of Western
NGOs (ib. 216). Edhi has a low opinion of modern Muslims' observance of tithing,
finding on a visit to Mecca that only one in 340 Hajjis had marked the occasion by
giving zakat. He condemns the Gulf States' misuse of the oil given them by Allah,
and holds up Denmark and Norway as examples of countries that have put the zakat
principle into practice (ib. 141, 188-9). However, his work is permeated by a
specifically Muslim piety, asserting that giving ought to be motivated by compassion

and not with a view to 'personal rewards, to forestall punishment, erase sins, assuage bad consciences and make impressions' (ib. 99). 'Call it what you like, the Islamic system is a welfare system. It is heart of Islam as well as the basis of all religions and the only answer to world peace' (ib. 357). His foundation reputedly attracts considerable support from all sections of Pakistani society, being seen as an alternative to corrupt official institutions.

By contrast, many other reformers in Islamic countries are impatient with religious rhetoric and see the only solution in secularization and the adoption of Western values, broadly following the precedent of Kemal Atatürk in Turkey, and contemplating with a sense of envy the ability of a number of East Asian countries to adapt successfully to the modern globalized economy.

Islamic charity in history, and its possible Arabian roots

There is no firm evidence either to support or to discredit the traditional view of the early Caliphate under Omar as a golden age of social equity. Some recent historians have addressed the issue of poverty and charity in later periods of Islamic history, compared to other civilizations at similar periods. Sabra, for instance, has studied records from thirteenth to fifteenth century Mamluk Egypt and concluded that the elite was far less concerned by *rural* poverty than were their contemporaries in medieval Europe and medieval China, since their main concern was for political stability in the cities. However, the Sufis' embracing of poverty as a choice preceded the development in Europe of the Christian mendicant orders; and it appears that private almsgiving was an important social practice in Mamluk Cairo and throughout the medieval Middle East, though less institutionalized than in either Europe or China (Sabra 2000: 169-77). Before the Mamluk period in Egypt, zakat was rapaciously collected by the state, and those refusing to pay it had been severely punished, but the Mamluk rulers decided to leave zakat a private matter for individuals (ib.: 39-40).

More evidence about the history of Islamic charity will be found in the section of our Chapter 2 dealing with the institution of *waqf.*

How does the Islamic injunction to charity compare with others? All the great religions lay stress on almsgiving (Parry 1986: 467). The Jesus of the Gospels gave general and warm support to the Hebraic teaching on almsgiving, but with no precision: indeed, on one occasion teasing the Pharisees for their tithing of cooking herbs – mint, dill, rue and cumin – and neglect of truly spiritual duties (*Matthew* 23. 23, *Luke* 11. 42). In English and some other languages since the sixteenth century, confusion has been caused within Christianity by two senses of the word 'charity' – spiritual love or (in Greek) *agapē*, and almsgiving.

As for Islamic charity, there was a clear debt to Hebraic ethics and laws of tithing, but this does not exclude the possibility of independent Arabian sources. Orientalist scholars may have underestimated the extent of institutions for providing mutual aid in traditional Arab societies. For instance, we find in the 1938 *Encyclopaedia of Islam* the following words under the entry for Sadaka: 'Care for the poor is a characteristic of the Semitic peoples, but the Arabs were not troubled by the feeling of pity. ... Alms are not a feature of Arabia before Islam'.

Modern scholars view this kind of generalization with suspicion. It is impossible to settle the issue by studies of contemporary Bedouin societies, especially after many centuries of islamization. But it may be noted nonetheless that compassion for the weak has been observed in traditional Arabs by a number of modern field-workers. Emanuel Marx, ethnographer of the Bedouin of the Negev in the 1960s, saw a number of what he called 'displaced persons' who were looked after by what he calls the 'voluntary charity of friends', sometimes moving from the hospitality of one camp to another; men who had quarrelled with their kinsmen, men who were blind or hunch-backed and too poor to marry (Marx 1967: 89). Wilfred Thesiger observed among the Marsh Arabs of southern Iraq in the 1950s that 'the tribesmen were especially kind to the afflicted', such as a boy paralysed with polio or another born totally deaf, so that 'among them a major physical disability was perhaps less of a handicap than in some other parts of the world' (Thesiger 1964: 168). Examples from ethnographies of African societies, too, not yet either islamized or christianized, could be multiplied. Maybury-Lewis quotes strikingly from an elder of the Gabra people, pastoral nomads in northern Kenya: 'Even the milk from our own animals does not belong to us. We must give to those who need it, for a poor man shames us all' (Maybury-Lewis 1992: 85, based on fieldwork by A. Kassam).

To look further back, Doughty, writing of his travels in Arabia between 1875 and 1877, noted that the Bedouin were ruthless in refraining from coming to the help of destitute pilgrims who fell by the wayside on the *hajj* road to Mecca (Doughty 1936 [1888] 1: 91). Yet he also praised Bedouin hospitality both to their own destitute people (ib. 1: 330) and particularly to strangers. On the arrival of his party near a Bedouin camp, one of the lads milks a camel for them: 'This is *kheyr Ullah* ("the Lord's bounty"), not to be withheld from any wayfaring man, even though the poor owners should go supperless themselves' (ib. 1: 256). ' "Be we not all, say the poor nomads, guests of Ullah?" Has God given unto them, God's guest shall partake with them thereof: if they will not for God render His own, it should not go well with them' (ib.1: 269). Doughty found the hill-Bedouin he visited ignorant of scriptural Islam to the extent that they had not even heard of an after-life; yet they did practice *sadaqa*, glossed by Doughty as 'the willing God's tribute and godly kindness of an upright man, spared out of his own necessity, to the relief of another' (1: 493). And A.H. Layard writes in his account of the British Museum expedition to Mesopotamia in 1849: 'In times of difficulty or scarcity ... the whole [of a Bedouin] tribe frequently expects to be fed by [the chief], and he considers himself bound, even under such circumstances, by the duties of hospitality, to give all that he has to the needy' (Layard 1853: 289).

Alois Musil, in his ethnography of the Rwala Bedouin in the 1920s, wrote that there were no beggars among them: an impoverished man was helped by his kin, his clan, and the chief. Beggars from other tribes were helped 'partly from love of Allah ... partly because they like to hear the beggar's thanks and hope that their charity may be extolled elsewhere'. (Musil 1928: 452-3). Musil also records that dervishes who could not keep up with the *hajj* caravan to Mecca were abandoned by their fellow-pilgrims, but added that the Bedouin would look after them 'passing them on from tribe to tribe'. A popular theme of the Bedouin poetry that he transcribes is the lot of a man beset by misfortune (ib. 326-7).

Père Lammens came to the implausible conclusion that the Bedouin was an extreme individualist: 'Never did he succeed in raising himself to the dignity of a social animal, *politicon zōon*. Hence the absence of devotion and sacrifice in the common interest: the whole train of beneficial social virtues, softness above all, humanity, the charms of this earthly life, are lacking in him' (Lammens 1914: 187, translated from the French). It is true that some of the literary data that he examines describe women prisoners of war being led like camels. But Lammens also wrote of the ancient Bedouin as holding 'an odd mixture of Christian and communist theories', a rich man being 'a simple depositary, a momentary holder of his own fortune. His mission is to distribute it to the needy of his tribe, to use it to exercise hospitality, to buy back prisoners and pay the blood price' (ib.: 235). Lammens saw Bedouin benefactors as being repaid by praise and panegyrics from their clients.

There is a danger, in all such retrospective musings, of reconstructing the past in order to make a point about the present. Steven Feierman points out, in a discussion of reciprocity and assistance in precolonial sub-Saharan Africa, that where traditions of mutual aid are based (as in Africa) on kinship and clan membership, they prove weakest just at the time when they are needed most: when a kinship group is withering away, or when individuals are separated from their supporting relatives. Kindly help, in precolonial Africa as in the modern philanthropic West, is double-edged: 'a peculiar combination of caring and dominance, of generosity and property, of tangled rights in things and in people, all in a time and place where the strong would not let the weak go under, except sometimes' (Feierman 1998: 4).

Zakat in the ideological system of foundational Islam

The remainder of this Chapter will adopt a more direct and analytical approach to the Quranic texts, on the working assumption that they represent a 'deep structure' or ideological system encapsulating the concepts, assumptions and practices of foundational Islam. It will consider in more detail how the Quranic teaching about charity relates to its Jewish and Christian equivalents.

Christian Décobert takes as his starting-point the *hadith* according to which when the Prophet died he left no worldly estate except a mule for travelling, his weapons for fighting and a small plot of land to be held in charitable trust – on which institution this book will have more to say in Chapter 2. The devout Muslim is a fighter who has given up his goods and travelled from his kin and land in the 'way of God', so that he has come to depend on the work of others – whether booty or alms. Every Muslim thereby recapitulates the flight of the Prophet and his Companions from Mecca to Medina, and those who give generously on leaving the mosque are participating in this ideal circle (Décobert 1991: 370). Alms are a 'loan to God' (Q. 2. 245). The share given to others facilitates their enrichment so that they can proceed to reimpoverish themselves (Décobert 1991: 241).

Here it is enough to make the obvious point that in the Quran as in other historically successful religious texts, a great deal of suasion and retrospective justification is at work, so that – except for those who make a jump of faith – it cannot easily be read as the straight representation of an actual historical society.

Offering the firstfruits: a green parable

The Quranic parable of the People of the Garden is told in the Surah called 'The Pen' (Q. 68. 17-33) which is thought to have been one of the earliest revealed to the Prophet Muhammad, at a time when he was confronting detractors in Mecca. God tells how he tested a group of men who resolved to collect the fruits of a garden in the morning, but they failed to make the reservation 'If it be God's will', *In sha' Allah*. A terrible storm came down at night and destroyed the garden while they were sleeping. At dawn, they called out to one another, 'Get up early if you want to gather the fruits', and they set off with confidence, whispering furtively to one another that no paupers must be allowed to break in on the garden and claim any of the fruit that day. When they saw the dark and desolate garden, they said 'We've surely lost our way' and then 'We're dispossessed!'. But one of them, a relatively just man, said 'Did I not say to you, why don't you glorify God?' They all said, 'Glory to our Lord! We have really done wrong!' Then they started to blame each other. They said 'Alas for us! We've behaved outrageously. Maybe our Lord will give us in exchange a better garden than this, for we turn to him in remorse'. The Surah goes on to state that the punishments of this life are nothing compared to the punishments in the hereafter, whereas gardens of delight are reserved for the righteous.

Though the parable does not explicitly mention firstfruits, I will follow Décobert who says it must refer to them (1991: 196). They are certainly fruits which the owners of the garden intended to pick first thing in the morning, which is considered an auspicious occasion throughout the region (Westermarck 1926: ii, 252-253, Jaussen 1948: 364-365). According to Hebraic teaching, which deeply if often obscurely underlies the Quran, the firstfruits, like the firstborn of a family and the firstlings of animals, belong to God and are subject to sacrifice.[8] Another passage in the Quran says that 'dues' (*haqq*) must be paid on the day of harvest (6. 141).

Fruits are frequently mentioned both as signs of God's abundance on earth and as the principal sustenance in the gardens of Paradise. Like the bad gardeners in the parable, the people of Saba'[9] or Sheba were once surrounded, according to 34.15-16, by gardens, but they turned from God and he flooded their gardens so that only bitter tamarisks and thorny lote-trees would grow there.

Discursive fields of ritual giving

In the Hebraic Pentateuch, the three themes of ceremonial sacrifice (whether of animals or vegetables), tithing, and provision for the poor seem to occupy discursive zones that hardly overlap. Ilana Silber has proposed a more general tripartite comparative classification – gifts to gods, gifts to religious officials, and gifts to the needy – which seems to correspond to this specific biblical pattern (Silber 2002).[10] Many injunctions in the Pentateuch provide for the poor, but the only overlap with tithing is to be found in *Deuteronomy* 14. 28-29 and 26. 12-15. Whereas the annual tithes went to the priests, Levites (members of a priestly tribe) or to fund ceremonial feasting (*Numbers* 18. 21-27, 28. 26-27, *Deuteronomy* 12. 17-19, 14. 22-27; 18. 4; *Nehemiah* 10. 38-40), also singers and doorkeepers (*Leviticus* 13. 5-15), a special triennial tithe was prescribed for Levites but also for widows, orphans and resident aliens. Otherwise, the right to annual gleanings provided for these beneficiaries, and owners of fields and orchards were enjoined not to strip the entire crop (*Leviticus* 19. 9, 23. 22). As for sacrifice, the Pentateuch provides for a rich variety of sacrifices and offerings – some simple gifts with no presentation at an altar, others involving complex cooking and rituals (Marx 1994, Rogerson 1980), with a preference for Abel's offering of ovine firstlings over Cain's arable produce (*Genesis* 4. 1-7). But tithing seems to be a separate matter.

In the Quran, by contrast, the three fields are thematically connected. Let us take first the major sacrifices of camels and cattle which are retained in Islam, even though some minor rites – such as the dedication and loosing for free pasture of a she-camel after someone has recovered from an illness – are condemned as pagan superstitions (Q. 5. 103). It is clear that the Great Feast or Feast of Immolation is not only a ceremony but a practical means of providing for the needy: 'Then eat thereof and feed the distressed ones in want' (Q. 22. 28). Again: 'When [the camels] are down on their sides [after slaughter], eat ye thereof, and feed such as [beg not but live in contentment], and such as beg with due humility' (Q. 22. 36) – the point being that the most importunate beggars are not necessarily those most in need.

As for the Quranic tithe or zakat, this is aimed to benefit the poor far more emphatically than the Hebraic equivalent. The connection between zakat, mentioned many times, and animal sacrifice, mentioned sparingly, is not made explicitly, but both are closely associated with prayer: zakat frequently and sacrifice occasionally, e.g. 108: 1-2: 'To thee we have granted the fount [of abundance]. Therefore to thy Lord turn in prayer and sacrifice'.

The main references to animal sacrifices seem, as we would say today, to accept their materiality (no question of converting it into mere metaphor) while asserting that they are 'symbols' – sha`air – of God (Q. 22. 32, 22. 36). For 'It is not [the camels'] meat nor their blood. that reaches Allah: it is your piety [*taqwa*] that reaches him: He has thus made them subject to you, that ye may glorify Allah for his guidance to you' (22. 37).

In many parts of the world, Muslims still perform the sacrifice of a camel, sheep, cow or goat on the day of the Great Feast, `Id al-Kabir, to commemorate Abraham's sacrifice of the ram instead of his son (Q. 37. 99-106, Bonte 1999, Brisebarre 1998). According to a dominant Muslim tradition, the son was Isma`il, his eldest by Hagar, who in the Genesis narrative (16: 16, 21:5) was 14 years older than Isaac. (An alternative Muslim tradition identifies Isaac as the son; cf. Bonte 1999: 23, Dagorn 1981: 357). Abraham and Isma`il are held to have founded the Kaaba in Mecca and to have been Muhammad's ancestor, while Isaac was the forefather of the Jews. Some Muslim commentators argue that the biblical version (*Genesis* 22: 1-18) must be an erroneous overlay because Isaac was never the only son of Abraham, whereas he is so called in verse 2 (`Ali 1989: 1148-1151). In both versions, Abraham's intention to carry out the sacrifice satisfies God, and finally an animal replaces the son. However, in the biblical version, Abraham seeks (at least on a naive reading of the text) to deceive Isaac when he asks where the sacrificial beast is, saying that God will provide it, whereas in the Quranic version the son, who has reached the age of working with his father, consents to the proposed act. Later rabbinic traditions assert that Isaac was told by his father that he was to be the sacrificial victim and assented (Hayward 1980). Abraham's interrupted sacrifice deeply underpins the theology of all three Semitic monotheisms, so deeply that we have had to wait till 1998 to read a thoroughgoing critique, by the feminist anthropologist Carol Delaney, of the patriarchal values that she claims have legitimated this disturbing narrative over more than two millennia. Why, she argues, cannot love of God be expressed through love of one's children, rather than in spite of it? And she argues that Freud was unable to analyse the Abraham narrative clearly, displacing it by a dubious palaeontological story of the sons stoning their father to death, and claiming universality for the

Greek myth of Oedipus which but for Freud would have remained within the preserves of classical scholarship (Delaney 1998, cf. Benthall 1999).

The Parable of the Garden brings the three themes together. Christians are also enjoined in the New Testament to say 'If it be the Lord's will' before embarking on a project, but Arabic theology has a special name for the reservation, *istithna*, deriving from this passage (Q. 68. 18).[11] The gardeners' first error is therefore to forget the firm principle, Quranic but shared by the other two Abrahamic monotheisms, that all wealth belongs to God. Their second error, if we accept Décobert's interpretation, is to refuse to offer the firstfruits. And their third is to seek to exclude needy people from the gleanings.

Purity and danger in the Quran

Décobert also makes a connection between a key Quranic term zakat and Mary Douglas's theorizing on purity (based on her early *Purity and Danger* rather than her later work on the Bible) – for it is derived from the Hebrew-Aramaic *zakūt* (Décobert 1991: 198ff.), which had connotations of purity, rectitude and thriving, but not of alms. Here we must be careful. Many students of the Quran have made much of the etymological and philological approaches to which Arabic, with its system of derived forms of root verbs, so readily lends itself. However, the same cautions must apply to Arabic as to other languages: that arguments based on etymology are often merely reviving dead metaphors or in other ways underestimating the element of historical contingency in all language. The 'root fallacy', exposed as such by Barr (1961: 100ff.) in his critique of interpretation of the Hebrew Bible, must surely be also one that the Arabist can succumb to: that is to say, the assumption that there is for every root a meaning which is effective through all the variations given to the root by affixes and formative elements. Furthermore it is often hard to determine when a given Arabic word is being used in the Quran in what was a normal sense, and when it should be deemed to have been divinely 'transferred' (*naqala*) as a technical theological term (Izutsu 1965: 69). To these caveats must also be added the point that meaning inheres in the things that writers say in sentences, not the words they say them in (Barr 1961: 270). But it is surely legitimate to build up an analytical pattern of semantic fields of force cumulatively.

Mary Douglas's extensive publications on the Hebrew Bible are developments of her key insight that: 'The Bible classes together defilement of corpses, idolatry and all lies, deceits, false witness and bloodshed' (Douglas 1993: 152). Again:

> One may think of it like a rift in existence: on the one side there is God and everything he establishes, on the other side, inevitably and necessarily, there is impurity. For the Bible, and in the whole region, the destructive effect of impurity is physical, like a lightning bolt or disease. Nothing less than divinely instituted rites of purification will defend against it. (ib., 23).

The same may be said of the Quran, but we can also invert the signs and group together the opposite of these categories: ritual purity, acknowledgment of the Oneness of God and Islam, and faithfulness to promises. As Décobert has argued, there is a clear semantic overlap between the idea of alms and that of rectitude via the word *sadaqa* (1991: 199ff.), which is closely associated with zakat and combines the two connotations.

The unfortunate gardeners confess to *tagha*, which means breaking boundaries like a swollen river. In the same Surah we find others castigated for calumny, arrogance, mocking of the Prophet, denying the Oneness of God, and other violations that we may see as interrelated.

Décobert argues that zakat is fundamentally a way to conceptualize the lineage – for relatives are entitled to much more than alms: *nafaqa* or 'expenditure' includes support or maintenance of kindred as well as *sadaqa* or alms (ib.: 216- 227). He contests the claim by Watt (1953: 165-169, and see Izutsu 1959: 190) that Muhammad's teaching succeeded in the transfiguring of pagan taboo-thinking into a supposedly higher conception of ethical sincerity. According to Sunni orthodoxy, zakat purifies both the donor's wealth and his or her own state of mind. Islam as it developed was certainly founded on the idea of lineage, but this aspect was held in tension with the principle of voluntary election and openness to all candidates.

In this respect, the Quranic principle of purity is similar to what Douglas finds in *Leviticus* and *Numbers*, that is to say, contagion comes from the body or from moral failure, not from contact with foreigners or the lower classes as in many societies studied by anthropologists. Indeed, just before the Parable of the Garden we read a blistering attack on one of the Prophet's slanderers who despite his 'wealth and numerous sons' (v.14) will soon be branded on the snout like an animal.

Contagion also emanates from idolatry, on which much has been written in the tradition of Jewish scholarship. For instance, Halbertal and Margalit (1992: 215) explore a marital metaphor of God as husband, and idols as lovers. Kochan (1997: 5) states that worshipping gods other than the God of Israel is the only transgression that can be committed by a mere verbal expression of intent as opposed to action.

The Quranic concept of *shirk* is related – also explicitly associated with the sin of adultery or fornication (Q. 24. 3) – but different. Whereas this word – 'association', from a root that means 'sharing' – is often glossed as a synonym for paganism or polytheism (e.g. Glassé 1991: 370), modern scholarship suggests that this is imprecise.

Kister has argued that 'the Jahiliyya [pre-Islamic, literally time of 'barbarism' or 'ignorance'] tribes cannot be said to have been straightforward polytheists; they were *mushrikun* [from the root *shirk*], i.e. while accepting and admitting the existence and supreme authority of God, they associated other deities with Him' (Kister 1990: I.48, see also Henninger 1981: 12).

More recently, Hawting has suggested that the accusation of *shirk* is part of an intra-monotheist polemic, directed against groups who regarded themselves as monotheistic, and that it provides us with no evidence of the actual beliefs of the pre-Islamic Arabs (Hawting 1999).

In an article entitled 'The pure religion', Ringgren analyses the term *mukhlis*, applied several times in the Quran to followers of Islam and meaning 'pure and spotless': he argues that the primary figurative meaning in the Quran is that of exclusive devotion to the One God (Ringgren 1962, see also Izutsu 1959: 189). Wansbrough too sees the underlying motive of Islamic 'election history' as a 'reaffirmation and restoration of original purity', that of the original theophany and Islamic community. This is a reversal of biblical salvation history, which was essentially anticipatory and teleological (1978: 147-148).

Faith and works in Islam

Some Western students of Islam have argued that the religion insists on 'orthopraxy' (correct conduct) as opposed to orthodoxy (correct doctrine), and it is true that in some versions of Islam, the theological debate focuses more on practice than on belief, as perhaps it does more generally in Judaism. Malcolm Ruel, in an important anthropological paper which claims that the concept of 'belief' is specific to the Christian and post-Christian tradition (Ruel 1982), concedes that the Islamic concept is similar. The Quran repeatedly emphasizes *iman* or inner conviction, and, whereas analysis of the various modalities of belief in different religions must be left to philosophical anthropologists, it would be perverse to read the Quran without acknowledging its interest in mental states as well as actions. During the early history of Islam, a sectarian dispute arose which broadly, if not in detail, foreshadowed the later disagreements in Christian theology as to the relative importance of faith and works (Izutsu 1965). The Murji'ites held that serious sins are offset by faith, and that good works (`*amal*) are secondary. The Kharijites downgraded faith and held that major sins forfeited salvation. So salient are the Quran's injunctions to good deeds on the one hand, and its celebration of God's attributes, especially mercy, on the other, that it is not surprising that mainstream Islam settled down to teaching that faith and works are mutually intertwined. Zakat is therefore both an act of social solidarity and an affirmation of faith. The famous *hadith* or prophetic utterance 'Actions are according to their intentions' [*niyyah*], inscribed over a gate at Al-Azhar University in Cairo, is well supported in the Quran (e.g. Q. 37. 5). Actions and thoughts are integrated in the Quranic terms for piety and God-fearing, *birr* and *taqwa* (Q. 2. 177 and cf. Izutsu 1959: 210 ff., 1965: 73-74), while hypocrisy and lip-service are excoriated with the terms *fisq* and *nifaq*. The Quran developed late-antique traditions of piety, but did not shun the world as did the Christian and Manichaean ascetics – rather, piety was enjoined within the context of this world – and it also urged Believers to adopt an activist or militant stance in promoting piety around them (Donner 1998: 71-74).

> The emphasis on being godly and God-fearing thus appears in the Qur'an in many guises, and is such a persistent theme that we must conclude it to have been the very essence of Muhammad's message. It is far more prevalent, for example, than any emphasis on Muhammad's role as prophet, although that is also present. To judge from the Qur'an, then, Islam began as a movement of uncompromising, indeed militant, piety, perhaps initially inspired by Muhammad's fear that the Last Judgment was imminent (ib.: 75).

Problems of interpretation

A number of the scholars I have cited have tried to improve our understanding of the ideological system underpinning the rise of early Islam. This is similar to Mary Douglas's anthropological aim in her study of the Bible, and she considers the society represented in *Leviticus* and *Numbers* as a type of egalitarian enclave (not, of course, egalitarian as regards gender relations).[12] A similar argument could be advanced about the early Meccan period before Islam developed immense expansionary ambitions. The difficulty is that there is very little external, that is to say non-Muslim, historical or archaeological evidence relating to the origins of Islam until the end of the eighth century C.E. or about 150 years after the traditional date for the Prophet's death in 632 (Waines 1995: 268-279). One of the new school of revisionist Western scholars arrived at the conclusion that the Quran itself as we have it was compiled not by the Caliph `Uthman less than twenty years after the Prophet's death, as tradition tells us, but by the Prophet himself (Burton 1977). Another however has contended that the Quran was assembled over time in a milieu of Judaeo-Christian sectarian polemics, with such a strong element of post-rationalization that it can bear no weight at all as a factual historical source (Wansbrough 1977, 1978; see also Berg 1997; Madigan 1995). The existence of two contrasted literary styles in the Quran is undisputed, but the assignment of one set of Surahs to the early Meccan period and the other to the late Medina period is no longer. A consensus now seems to be emerging that extreme versions of sceptical revisionism rely on some hypotheses for which there is no evidence, such as the existence, in the community of Believers, of an orthodox authority sufficiently centralized to promulgate a unitary doctrine (Donner 1998: 25-31).

Great sacred texts cannot be analysed simply as material from which information about the societies that generated it can be read out. The founders of each of the successful religions of the Middle East must have been cultural anthropologists *avant la lettre*, engaged in a project to make the new system acceptable; as Wansbrough puts it, selecting appropriate 'insignia' of confessional identity from the 'monotheist compendium' which included rites, membership rules and catechisms (1978: 99-100). History is crammed with examples of sectarian movements that did not make it. Mary Douglas contends that much of the Pentateuch is cast in a rustic or pastoral idiom by compilers who were in fact versed in the learning of ancient civilizations (1993: 90-91). It is possible that some of the more prominent features of the Quranic text may have been intentionally injected into it in order to provide a kind of primordialist local colouring. What could have been more anthropologically sensitive than the Quranic revelation's careful hierarchization of celestial entities or angels, and wayward local spirits or jinns, within the overarching 'chain of being' of *tawhid* or monotheism? or than the qualified toleration of the Jews, Christians and Sabians? If *shirk* was held in such horror this was perhaps because it was a categorical anomaly defying this hierarchy, as well as because the new Islamic community's survival depended on suppression of the traditional forces which threatened it. Meanwhile, the animal sacrifices were preserved but transmuted into symbols of piety and unselfishness. The same themes can be found in some passages in the Old Testament, such as *Psalms* 51: 16-17 – 'My sacrifice, O God, is a broken spirit; a wounded heart, O God, thou wilt not despise' – but their interpretation is controversial (Rogerson 1980: 52). The Jews ceased to offer sacrifices around 70 C.E., while Pauline Christianity claimed that God's sacrifice of his Son made further sacrifices redundant except for the recapitulation of God's sacrifice in the Eucharist.

'Thematic interpretation'

A current, if not undisputed, trend among Muslim scholars is towards 'thematic interpretation' (Hanafi 1996), according to which the fact that all textual interpretations are inevitably geared towards the reader's current agenda is embraced rather than repressed. Among some Christian theologians, the Sermon on the Mount and some of Jesus's parables now stand out as a universal message of Christianity, whereas the narrative of his torture and execution, made to bear an immense burden of sacrificial meaning in traditional doctrine, is conceded to be a historical contingency and/or fulfilment of prophecy. Perhaps the Parable of the Garden and similar passages in the Quran are the Islamic equivalent of the Sermon on the Mount? Might it point the way towards a more 'vegetarian', 'herbivorous' Islam than we are accustomed to – that is to say, a form of religious doctrine that actively eschews symbolic violence against fellow-creatures, but encourages economic redistribution and the conservation of natural resources? It is highly relevant that the Quranic Paradise is a garden, and *al-khudra*, the place of greening, a synonym for Paradise.

Such topics are still inflammatory. A number of Islamic scholars have recently been killed (since as Mahmoud Muhammad Taha in Sudan in 1985) or forced into exile (such as Nasr Abu Zayd in Egypt in 1995) as a result of their re-examinations of the Quran and Sunna. A recent compendium of scholarly essays representing the revisionist approach to the history of early Islam, and edited by an Indian ex-Muslim, had to be published by an obscure American publishing house and under a pseudonym (Ibn Warraq 2000).

2

WAQF AND ISLAMIC FINANCE*

Two resources for charity

Waqf and Islamic finance have been linked in this chapter because both institutions are grounded in Islamic tradition but both have shown considerable versatility. Whereas the tradition of waqf was rediscovered at various points in the history of Islam and has had a limited resurgence during the period since the 1967 Six Day War, which we may take as a historical watershed date, Islamic finance has developed almost *de novo* during this period, and with considerable speed and visibility. It has also become a considerable resource for supplying the charitable sector, and at least potentially a resource for assisting in its field operations.

In our analysis of such institutions, we follow such scholars as Fred Halliday who stress the historical ductility of Islam (Halliday 1996: 58). It is a characteristic of most religious doctrines, especially when they veer towards fundamentalism, to emphasize continuity and permanence. Viewed analytically, however, a façade of timelessness invariably masks continual adaptation. For instance, Hamas's claim that the whole of Palestine is waqf in an extended, figurative use of the term (Milton-Edwards 1996: 190-3) would have been unintelligible before the conflict with Zionism.

Waqf: tradition and rediscovery

The *waqf* (Arabic plural *awqaf*) or pious foundation has a long and extensive history in Muslim societies. We shall summarize this history and its various interpretations by modern scholars, and will then examine how it is made use of today by Islamic charities as part of a repertoire of Islamic motifs supplementary to zakat and *sadaqa*.

Some survivals of traditional waqf

In the Sultanate of Oman, which has only been a modern state for some thirty years, hundreds of waqfs are administered by the Ministry of Awqaf. Some are mosques and schools, but they exist for many other purposes such as funerals for poor people and washing of the deceased. People give property such as farms as well as money, and some waqf holdings have been converted into prime commercial property in

* by Jonathan Benthall and Jérôme Bellion-Jourdan

order to improve the income. The Ministry owns two buildings in Mecca, one for the accommodation of pilgrims and the other rented out.

So many citizens in Oman wish to fund the building of mosques that (in 1996) the Ministry was trying to make a law that there must be a distance of one kilometre between each mosque, or two kilometres between big mosques. The religious authorities believe that regular meetings of Muslims in a neighbourhood for prayers enable them to know one another and so facilitate the solving of problems and the reduction of potential conflict.

Owing to the absence of written records until recently in Oman, almost all waqf property is held on trust by word of mouth tradition. According to informants (who admittedly one must assume were intent on conveying a favourable impression to a visiting researcher), the whole society is based on trust and this tradition continues even in the modern state, though gradually the legal status of waqf property is being formalized. Disputes over such matters are apparently very rare.

Another example of a traditional waqf is the 550-year-old Takiyat Khaski Sultan soup-kitchen in the Old City of Jerusalem. It still serves vegetables to about a hundred people a day, and meat to about a thousand people a day during Ramadan.

These are, however, atypical survivals, made possible by particular political conditions: in Oman, a benevolent autocracy where no voluntary associations of any kind are allowed; in East Jerusalem, an ongoing conflict over heavily sacralized territory where every traditional right is closely guarded.

Characteristics and origins of waqf

The institution of waqf, the Islamic equivalent of the charitable trust or foundation, known alternatively as *hubs* (Arabic plural *ahbas*, French *habous*) in North Africa, dates back virtually to the founding of Islam. With its legal status consolidated in the eighth century, it spread over almost the whole of the Islamic world, so that, for example, between a half and two thirds of the lands of the huge Ottoman Empire were waqf at the start of the nineteenth century (Barnes 1987: 83). The great exception was sub-Saharan Africa, in whose history waqf is mentioned only in a limited area around certain cities such as Timbuktu: west African largesse tended to be personalized in prestigious individuals (Feierman 1998: 19), and wealth was concentrated in moveable property such as cattle. During the nineteenth century, centralizing states were already chipping away at the independence of local waqfs. In Egypt and some other countries, all waqfs have been nationalized as state assets and the term is often popularly understood as referring only to mosque properties. Since the 1960s the institution has been given new life in some countries, partly as an Islamic response to the worldwide upsurge of voluntary organizations, but sometimes with a strong admixture of political motivation.

In many ways it is comparable to the European tradition of church property (Schacht 1964: 19), except that first, it allowed more scope for private interests to combine with charitable objectives, and second, there was no equivalent in Islam to ecclesiastical ownership and corporate personality.

Since the word means literally 'stopping' or 'tying up' (from the root *waqafa*), it was tempting for Western observers to blame waqf for the alleged 'immobilism' of Islamic economies – and indeed, there is evidence of its abuses having been locally satirized (Bilici 1994: 10). A waqf is in Western legal terms a 'perpetuity', which came to be opposed by English courts after money rather than land became the basis of a market economy, so that in the late nineteenth century this became a source of tension between Muslims and the ethnocentric legal authorities of British India (Kozlowski 1985: 148). The British courts were concerned to promote efficient markets in property. Not only colonial rulers but also some historians of Marxist tendencies have interpreted waqf negatively. For instance, waqfs in the Ottoman-ruled Balkans have been interpreted as an economic link between town and country that enabled a quasi-feudal hierarchy of family beneficiaries, administrators and religious officials to extract a surplus from the land, with more concern for maintaining rents than for developing the rural asset base (Vesely 1995).

But other historians – while noting the openings that waqf offered to particular interest groups for self-advancement, and the grave problems that often arose as a result of inadequate supervision of administrators – have shown appreciation of durability and suppleness of waqf. It has been hailed as a key institution in early Islamic history in facilitating interaction between the religious and the economic spheres (Décobert 1984: 124), and as giving openings during the colonial period for small-scale entrepreneurship and resistance to imposed institutions (Hathaway 1998: 123, Bilici 1994: 6). Some scholars have argued that it is unhistorical to overemphasize the private dimension of many waqfs in their heyday. For instance, the observatory organized by the great astronomer and poet, Omar Khayyam, was in strict law a private endowment, founded by the powerful and philanthropic Nizam al-Mulk (d. 1092), first minister of the Seljuk empire in Baghdad. However, there is little doubt that this institution, as well as the many schools, hospitals and mosques that he founded, were in fact public policy measures (Arjomand 1998: 117).

The same word is used for the legal deed setting up the trust and the thing whose use is 'tied up' for future beneficiaries. What things could be established as inalienable or *mawquf* (the correct term for the asset itself)? First of all, mosques and schools; but also libraries, hospices for travellers, hospitals, fountains and wells, cemeteries, gardens, windmills, public transport facilities, and services for the needy or disabled. Religious and cultural obligations were also catered for by waqfs: for instance, in nineteenth century Tunisia, waqf revenues were pledged for special clothing for circumcision ceremonies, and for consultations to declare young girls' virginity for those unable to meet the cost themselves (Qasim 1994). Some 15 per cent of waqfs under the eighteenth century Ottoman Empire remitted their revenues for prayers to be said for such purposes as the salvation of souls, the happiness of the Empire and the victory of the Turkish army (Yediyildiz 1985: 83). As in the case of British charities, waqfs were also set up to benefit animals as well as humans. In Morocco, the stork is traditionally a protected bird, and a substantial waqf is said to have existed in early nineteenth century Fez for the nursing of sick storks (Westermarck 1926: II. 330).

Most of these things and services incurred maintenance costs including employees' salaries. A second category of waqf included working assets that bore revenues, rather than absorbing them, to support the good cause: farms and vineyards and gardens, dwelling-houses and shops and industrial plant. Revenue yield or 'usufruct' was essential to the institution of waqf. Bare ownership remained with the founder. Waqfs seem to have been generally exempt from the Islamic prohibition of taking interest on financial capital. (In this however and in many other details, variations are to be found both in local historical contexts and according to the different schools of Islamic law.) Some objects of waqf such as water supply were seen principally as a common good, but could also be used as income-generating assets.

An important distinction must be made between the 'public' and the 'private' waqf. The public waqf (*khairi* or `*ami* or *shar`i*) or *hubs kubra* ('greater *hubs*') was entirely charitable, all benefit being given to the final object – except the prestige accruing to the donor. The private or customary waqf (*ahli* or *khass* or *dhurri* or `*adi* or *al-awlad*) or *hubs sughra* ('lesser *hubs*') benefited a category of intermediaries, usually the donor's descendants or his clients, before going to its final object when the lineage dies out (at which point it became public). There were refinements such as the shared (*mushtarak*) or semi-private waqf, which came to be the dominant form in the Ottoman Empire.

Scholars disagree as to the historical origins of the waqf, the early written sources being silent on the subject (Cahen 1961, Barnes 1987). Neither waqf nor *hubs* are mentioned in the Quran, but many other references to almsgiving and the 'way of God' (*sabil Allah*) are held to prefigure and authorize it. Islamic tradition ascribes its origin to the patriarch Abraham's having created the Kaaba (sacred cubic building) in Mecca; and the Prophet is said to have told the second Caliph, Omar, to sequester a piece of land and have its revenues given to the poor. Modern historians have sought its origins variously in the pagan sanctuaries of the pre-Islamic Arabs, in the Islamic concept of lands subject to tribute, and in ancient Babylonian law. One coherent theory (Barnes 1987) is that the early Islamic community wanted both to be charitable and also to revert to pre-Islamic custom and evade the Quranic rules on inheritance, which required a share of the patrimony to be bequeathed to female descendants. Abu Hanifah (d. 767), the founder of the Hanafi school of law, which came to dominate in the Ottoman Empire and India, actually tried to curtail the development of waqf, asserting that it was essentially revocable and that ownership remained with the founder (*waqif*). But two of his disciples – perhaps yielding to aristocratic pressures – adopted the more liberal view, which became standard: that waqf property is kept in God's possession irrevocably, so that the profit can be assigned to his creatures (Barnes 1987, Yediyildiz 1985).

A prevalent theological metaphor – with clear parallels in Christianity, and resonances explored in our Chapter One – asserted that good works (*khayrat* or *hasanat*) are grains sown in the fertile soil of the earth to last for centuries, so that their fruits can be collected both in this world and in the world beyond. Preparation for the after-life was an essential constituent, which resulted in a close connection between charitable giving and rituals associated with death such as visits to tombs (Sabra 2000: 97). The preamble to a typical early waqf might begin 'This old world lives in the midst of nothingness'. According to a *hadith*, when a man dies, only three things survive: perpetual alms, science which benefits others, and the prayers of a pious son (Yediyildiz 1985: 9-10 citing medieval deeds). Thus waqf allowed for multiple aspirations: obtaining divine grace through supererogatory *sadaqa*, leaving a name behind, gaining prestige, securing the fruits of one's labour by tying up the asset to reduce the risk of confiscation, and benefiting one's heirs and clients. A further outcome, whether or not intended originally, was an accumulation of power among the administrators (*mutawallis* or *nazirs*). The aim of permanence till the Day of Judgment was not achieved: the majority of waqfs suffered in practice from fragmentation, neglect, diversion to other beneficiaries, or confiscation; and they were often a cause for bitter dispute. But a few proved durable, such as the large cruciform hospital founded in Cairo by Sultan al-Mansur Qalawun in 1284 – perhaps to atone for the deaths of many innocent commoners when his Mamluks put down a riot – which continued to function till well into the nineteenth century (Sabra 2000: 69). Another was the waqf supporting the shrine of Ali, the Prophet Muhammad's son-in-law and the fourth Caliph, at Mazar i-Sharif in what is now Afghanistan (McChesney 1991).

Minority communities in Islamic lands, mainly Christians and Jews, were allowed to found waqfs as family foundations or to support their own places of worship. Like the fully Islamic waqfs, these often became focuses of conflict between religious hierarchs and the administrators. For instance, a power struggle arose in Mount Lebanon during the eighteenth century over ownership and control of the Sayyidat Bkirki Monastery, a Maronite Christian waqf (van Leeuwen 1995).

Waqf under the Ottoman Empire

As many as 6,000 waqfs were founded in the Ottoman Empire during the eighteenth century (*vakif/evkaf* in Turkish), 90 per cent by the ruling class. They were legally charitable and provided widespread benefits to society at large, including the provision of many basic services such as education, health care, water supply and the maintenance of bridges and roads (Yediyildiz 1985: 45-46). However, they also became – with some deviation from the prescriptions of classical Islam – a device for tying up the huge patrimony of the founders and their descendants, subject only to weak government control. Much of this property consisted of state lands whose revenues had been made *vakif* by former sultans. Religious *vakif*s were often put in the hands of unsuitable *mutawalli*s such as the corps of imperial halberdiers. High state personages such as the grand vizier or the chief black eunuch of the palace were entrusted with the inspection of the endowments (Barnes 1987: 43-44, 83). The process of decentralization was reversed by Sultan Mahmud II, who founded a Ministry for Imperial *Evkaf* in 1826 that soon assumed full control of all the religious foundations and supervision of the revenues of the familial landed estates. This Ministry functioned independently during the subsequent decades of political reform (*tanzimat*), struggling unsuccessfully to impose sound administration. All *mutawalli*ships were consolidated into a powerful central office. The revenues of the then powerful dervish fraternities were cut off.

The effects of this central control on the administration of *vakif*s such as mosques, bridges, fountains and inns were probably on the whole damaging and degrading (Barnes 1987: 118-27, Yediyildiz 1985: 204); 'the abuses committed by individual mütevellis are not to be compared with the fleecing of Islam by the state....' (Barnes 1987: 127). Others have suggested that, at least in the provinces far from Istanbul, the attempts to impose its jurisdiction resulted in relatively little actual change until the twentieth century (Deguilhem 1995: 51). The ministry's responsibilities were transferred to the Imperial Finance Ministry in 1868. In 1924, after the abolition of the sultanate, empire and caliphate, the Grand National Assembly in Ankara set up a new ministry to administer all aspects of the Islamic faith including the *vakif*s.

Other Muslim countries which nationalized all waqfs included Syria and Egypt. In Algeria, too, the French state's control of waqf followed a logical progression. In 1830, all Algerian public *hubus* were declared state property; as from 1844, the perpetual revenue or usufruct of the private *hubus* was made redeemable; as from 1873, only French law was applied to all *hubus* management. However, the policy of suppressing and controlling waqf was common to the whole Arab region, rather than a special feature of European colonialism (Décobert 1984). In pre-colonial Tunisia, waqf endowments for education were independent of government until the advent of the French protectorate in 1881 and the policy of secularizing modernization, which was followed through after independence in 1956 when the new government seized all waqf property (Al-Ghannouchi 2000: 107-9).

Rediscoveries of waqf
Though the most striking and widespread revival of waqf took place in the twentieth century, there were precedents.

It was not until the tenth and eleventh centuries that waqfs were first used by state officials as an instrument of policy, and some adjustments had then to be made to the law in order to allow property belonging to the public treasury to become *mawquf*. During the Mamluk period of rule in Egypt after the mid thirteenth century, waqfs proliferated with the result that by the time of the Ottoman conquest in 1517 most of Cairo's buildings and nearly half of Egypt's agricultural land were waqf (Sabra 2000: 71-2). The 'mixed' waqf (*mushtarak*) was specially favoured by the Mamluk military elite in Egypt. It enabled them both to endow a pious cause such as a school or mosque, linking their family names to a highly prestigious asset, and also to make sure that there would be a surplus of income available to their family heirs – thus evading a regulation that their property was confiscated after their deaths. During the final period of Mamluk rule, around 1500, the sultan began successfully to raid the income of these endowments (Berkey 1992: 130-46). In medieval Damascus, too, ruling elite households were able to combine a legacy of meritorious works with looking after their own economic and political interests, including the setting up of family tombs integrated into Islamic schools: 'A ruler or amir or one of their intimates, buried in a madrasa-tomb, was assured of having attendants in the form of Qur'an-reciters, often on one of the prime pieces of real estate in the city, the tomb chamber overlooking a main street' (Chamberlain 1994: 55).

In fourteenth century Morocco, the Marinid dynasty introduced an ambitious programme of social welfare centred on the *zawiya*, an institution that combined the functions of hostelry and mosque, usually on a burial site. The state was trying to compete with the established network of Sufi *zawiya*s or lodges, borrowing the same name from these independent philanthropic institutions, run by mystical brotherhoods, which had flourished for more than a century – providing many services such as communal granaries, sanctuaries for outlaws, and poverty relief. The Sufi orders in general have been described as making a major historical contribution by providing 'warmth and security against the coldness and formality of orthodox Islam' (Layish 1994: 147). Sultan Abu `Inan, who ruled Morocco from 1349-59, sought unsuccessfully to co-opt Sufis into officiating at the state-run *zawiya*s, but the policy failed. Later, in the fifteenth century, the claims of the Sufis to monopolize the privilege of giving charity went to their heads, and their lodges became powerful political institutions manipulating dependent groups (Rodriguez-Mañas 2000).

Many of the important *hubs* set up in Morocco under the Almohad (1130-1269) and Marinid (1269-1471) dynasties came to be pillaged and ruined under a succession of predatory sultans. The great Arab geographer Leo Africanus (c. 1485-1530) records this process in a vivid vignette of Fez:

> Formerly the pupils were fed and clothed in colleges for seven years, but at present they have no benefit except their lodging, because on account of the wars of Saïd [Sultan Abu-l-Hassan As-Saïd] many of the colleges' possessions, whose revenues were reserved for that purpose, were despoiled and there is only a small fraction left ... so that the colleges are frequented only by some foreign students that are maintained through the charity of the city and its territory. ... There are in Fez hospitals and colleges of unsurpassed beauty. But during Saïd's wars the king found himself very short of money and was advised to sell their revenues, which the people opposed strongly, but a royal procurator was so articulate and persuasive that the possessions belonging to these hospitals were sold with their rents' (Leo Africanus II. 77, Milliot 1918: 39-40)

Much later, in British India, private waqfs became a focus of dispute between Muslims and the courts, which tried – with the supreme appellate authority of the Privy Council in London – to enforce a rigid distinction, between family settlements and charitable foundations, that had no basis in Muslim law. British attempts to invalidate private waqfs were eventually unsuccessful. However, it is noteworthy that only public waqfs seem to have existed in pre-British India (Kozlowski 1985: 40).

As for Morocco, in the 1960s (some six years after the end of the French protectorate) when Clifford Geertz and some American anthropologist colleagues studied Sefrou, an old walled town at the foot of the Middle Atlas Mountains in the northern interior, the bazaar economy was still shaped by the institution of *hubs*. It was the largest property owner by far in the town. Under one form or other of public *hubs* ownership were many shops and ateliers, as well as ovens, *funduq*s (hostels for caravans), public baths, granaries and a slaughterhouse; and, in the surrounding countryside, many gardens, wheat-fields and orchards. The original donations dated back to the mid-17th to early 19th centuries, and were systematized in *al-mujallad al-mubarak*, 'the blessed bound book', in the early nineteenth century at the behest of Sultan Mulay Sliman. 'In Sefrou, the religious institution ... does not merely sanction trade: it engages in it'. *Hubs* income went to maintain religious properties and employees. Geertz noted that, though these pious endowments had been nationalized under the Ministry of Habus, in practice it still had little control over essentially local policies, including the setting of rents in the bazaar at extremely low and stable rates. During the first three or four decades of the twentieth century, almost all commercial property had been in *hubs*, and the institution had been crucial in facilitating the emergence of a recognizable commercial class (Geertz 1979: 151-4, 242).[1]

In the twentieth century, a revival of waqfs may be analysed as a way of opposing centralization, though sometimes also as a means for governments to escape parliamentary control. In Turkey since 1967, legislation inspired by both Islamic and American law has facilitated the founding of 'new waqfs' with precautions against administrative abuse of the kind that occurred in the past (Bilici 1985: 12). An example of this is the Koç Foundation set up in 1969 by a Turkish tycoon, the late Vebhi Koç. It was worth some $20 million in 1988. Its policy is to adhere 'rather closely to the Atatürk tradition of putting Islam to the service of nation building'. Its focus is on building medical, educational and cultural facilities with a strong nationalist bias (Kozlowski 2000: 291-2).

In Israeli-occupied East Jerusalem, waqf still survives and flourishes, having been rediscovered for special political reasons – as a tool for promoting the cohesion of Muslim society. A large proportion of the Old City is said to be waqf – including many of the Christian monasteries and churches – and this is likely to be a major bargaining point during any final status negotiations with Israel. The extreme position is that the whole of Palestine, having once been conquered by Muslims, is *fai'* – the right of all Muslims – a theological riposte to Zionism (Layish 1994: 163, see also Dumper 1994). On the other hand, where one might expect to see a revival of waqf one does not always find it: most of the powerful foundations in Iran (*bonyad*s) created from confiscated property after the Islamic revolution in 1979 are, legally, modern corporations whose constitutions do not draw on the Islamic waqf (Arjomand 1998: 127, Maloney 2000: 150). Though the large Saudi foundations describe themselves as waqf in Arabic language publications, they would more recognizably be characterized as 'parastatals' or GONGOs (Government Organized Non-Governmental Organizations). It seems to be only recently that Saudi charities such as Al-Haramain have begun to invest donations in waqf projects. The first of these, in Riyadh, has been named after Abdul Aziz Abdullah bin Baz, the conservative and controversial General Mufti of Saudi-Arabia from 1962 until his death in 1999. Another large waqf is planned by the same Foundation to provide for the care and protection of children all over the Islamic world.

The integration of waqf into Western-style fund-raising was pioneered on a large scale in the United States, which has a Muslim population of some six million. It was developed in the United Kingdom in the 1990s by Muslim Aid and Islamic Relief. (In neither country does it have any special recognition from the law.) Islamic Relief now offers a Waqf Bond offering donors the choice of special waqf funds devoted to Relief and Emergency, Orphans, Educational Projects, Water Projects, *qurbani* [annual feast of sacrifice] and Health Projects. Each bond costs £700, from which £70 is deducted at once for administrative costs. The remaining £630 is invested in accordance with *shari`a*, in real estate and monetary instruments, separately from the rest of Islamic Relief's accounts. About 80 per cent of the profits are spent on the beneficiaries – for instance, providing health care in Sudan, or flood relief in Bangladesh; 10 per cent is reinvested to preserve the fund's value against inflation; and 10 per cent is applied towards administrative costs. An annual report is sent to each donor ('Waqf Future Fund', Islamic Relief, n.d.).

Waqf in conclusion: between immobility and adaptation
It should not be surprising to us that an institution whose explicit ambition was to elude the necessity of mortality should have survived (to the extent that this can be said of it) only by means of an adaptability that is the exact contrary of the idea of immobility which gave waqf its Arabic name. In the above short historical summary, it has been impossible to do more than hint at the extent of change over time that

the institution has known. A final example shows how diverse the use of the contemporary notion of waqf can be.

In present-day Turkey, as we would expect from a Muslim state that has attempted to de-link religion from core social institutions, the tradition of waqf/*vakif* has been incorporated into the banking system with no reliance on Islamic law. The *Vaqiflar Bankast* was founded in 1954, endowed as to 75 per cent by nationalized waqf funds and as to 25 per cent by private investors. It has 326 branches in Turkey and eight overseas offices, providing a range of normal banking services as one of the country's leading banks, and pledging much of its profits to the restoration and maintenance of historical monuments which were formerly constituted as waqf, and also to educational programmes.

The Turkish Vaqif Bank is a direct successor to monetary waqfs that developed in the Ottoman Empire since the fifteenth century and were allowed to lend their capital at interest. These, because of their acceptance of the principle of interest, were almost unknown in the Arab or Persian worlds. Hence the Vaqif Bank is an exception in the Muslim world (Bilici 1994, Arda 1994). It is, however, typical of a more general resort to Islamic concepts in the contemporary finance system, as will now be demonstrated with a survey of 'Islamic finance' and its connections with the charitable sector.

Islamic finance and its claim to morality

Before exploring the links between Islamic finance and Islamic charities, we will trace how Islamic finance seeks to distinguish itself from the conventional banking system and how it has now spread to involve some 150 institutions working in more than seventy countries (Maurer 2001: 8).

The Quranic prohibition of riba and the islamization of finance

In every publication that sets out the essentials of Islamic finance, the prohibition of riba or usury is recognized as the main principle justifying a break with the banking world that depends on interest. This prohibition is mentioned in the Quran:

> Those who devour usury will not stand except as stands one whom the Evil One by his touch hath driven to madness. That is because they say: 'Trade is like usury', but Allah hath permitted trade and forbidden usury. ... Allah will deprive usury of all blessing, but will give increase for deeds of charity. ... (Q. 2. 275-6)

Its scriptural grounding is therefore strong.

However, what was new was the reappearance of this theme in the rhetoric of late twentieth century Islamist movements, combining a socializing denunciation of inequalities with an appeal to the inauguration of an Islamic system founded on the principle of justice. The practice of usury has come to be seen as a factor that aggravates inequalities. The thought of Sayyid Qutb, who was imprisoned and executed on the orders of Nasser, was particularly uncompromising. Apart from his major publication *Social Justice in Islam*, Qutb set out in a tract that was to become a handbook for several Islamist movements, *In the Shade of the Quran*, his fierce opposition to 'the *riba* society' and expressed his nostalgia for a society ruled by the 'principle of zakat' (Carré 1984: 153). Private property was not called into question, but was held to be subject to automatic redistribution.

For Qutb, the carrying out of zakat is:

> the payment of Islam's social tax (*daribat al-islam al-ijtima`iyya*) established by God as a right of the poor over the wealth of the rich, by virtue of (*bi-hukm*) his being Master of all goods which he has entrusted as property by means of a contract (`*aqd*) one of whose conditions is the carrying out of zakat (Qutb 1978: 161).

In this perspective, zakat is the opposite of *riba*, representing the gift as an 'ethic of generosity pure and simple', literally the contrary of the practice of paying a reimbursement of a debt with interest (Carré 1984: 152).

Reliance on this type of thought led to the prohibition of bank interest, which numerous Islamic banks and other financial institutions have embarked on since the 1970s in order to promote a form of Islamic economy (*al-iqtisad al-islami*). The first modern banking venture adhering to the tenets of Islamic law was founded in the late 1950s in a rural part of Pakistan (Roy 1991: 428).

Three principal factors led to the emergence of this sector in the 1970s.

First, the shock caused by the defeat of Arab armies by Israel in the June 1967 Six Day War rekindled a determination to close ranks in the face of what was seen as a common enemy. Pan-Islamism had not led to the founding of a unified Islamic political system, any more than pan-Arabism had resulted in Arab unification (with the exception of Egypt and Syria's abortive three-year union in 1958-61).

Might it be that the real function of Islamic economics and Islamic solidarity was to palliate this failure of the political project? In the face of the impossibility of political union, the transnational dimension of Islamic finance and practices of solidarity stepped in to maintain the utopia of the unity of the Muslim world. Often, the project strayed outside the framework of economics and had an undeniable political aim, as may be seen from this extract from an internal bulletin published by the Dar al-Mal al-Islami group:

> Given the Islamic nature of the enterprise and the desire to promote unity within the *umma* of Islam, the founders earnestly hope that Dar al-Mal al-Islami will become as soon as possible a company governed by the laws of a Muslim state, with its headquarters in Mecca as a sign of its pan-Islamic character (quoted by Galloux 1997: 102).

Second, the promoters of Islamic economics were keen to develop an alternative third way between capitalism and socialism, at a time of confrontation between the United States and the Soviet economic models. Among many publications on this topic since the 1970s, Ismail Sirageldin of the Kuwait Institute for Scientific Research holds that 'the ethical system of an Islamic society may be located between the two extremes', namely 'market capitalism' and 'materialist socialism'. The Islamic system aims at 'an equilibrium between motivations and freedom of the individual on the one hand, and social obligations on the other hand' (Sirageldin 1996: 1).

A third reason was the favourable economic situation. The explosive growth in the price of petroleum after the Ramadan/Kippur war of October 1973 resulted in a considerable financial windfall: 'petrodollars' were available to be banked or invested in financial institutions. We will consider the character of these institutions before reviewing their relationship to the charitable sector.

The emergence of powerful institutions

State or public banks may be distinguished from private banks. The first of its kind, the Islamic Development Bank (*bank al-tadamun al-islami*, IDB) was founded in October 1975 by 22 states. The idea for its foundation went back to the 1960s, when King Faysal ben Abdul Aziz ben Saud keenly promoted the idea of the founding of an Islamic bank within the framework of the inter-governmental Organization of the Islamic Conference (OIC). At a conference of finance ministers of countries belonging to the OIC held in August 1974, the constitution of the new IDB was approved, with a view to its headquarters being set up in Saudi-Arabia. The bank is an institution independent of the OIC but works closely with it. It is an inter-state bank, of which in 1989 all members of the OIC except Iran and Nigeria were members, with the launch capital being provided initially by the Saudi and other governments.[2] The IDB is the only Islamic bank authorized to operate within Saudi-Arabia, which, though it was 'the principal inspiration behind the islamization of banking' (Carré 1992: 60), continues to tolerate the practice of paying interest on loans in the normal way. The IDB may be considered to be 'an instrument of Saudi proselytization, for external use, which does not call in question the country's internal financial arrangements' (Galloux 1997: 204) – a similar logic to that which underpins the World Islamic League in the sphere of Islamic politics.

Two principal private banking groups emerged, the Dar al-Mal al-Islami and Al-Baraka. The fruit of private Saudi initiatives, these two groups include a vast international network of institutions – banks, insurance companies and investment houses. The Dar al-Mal al-Islami Trust was founded in 1981 in the Bahamas by Prince Muhammad al-Faysal al-Saoud. A son of King Faysal, who had been a keen promoter of the idea of creating Islamic companies and an Islamic bank within the OIC, Prince Muhammad resigned in 1977 from his post of financial advisor to the Saudi government to devote himself to Islamic banking. In 1977, he founded the International Association of Islamic Banks as its chairman. Islamic banks in Egypt and Sudan were affiliated to the DMI group in the late 1970s. The Al-Baraka Company for Investment was founded in 1982 by Sheikh Salah Abdullah Kamel, a business-man from an important Saudi family.

Despite some divergences, one can discern 'an emerging toolkit' (Maurer 2001: 9) common to professionals in Islamic banking. The banking operations are of various types and aim at financing projects and investment without recourse to *riba*. Among the most commonly found techniques are *mudabara* and *musharaka*. *Mudabara* – like the Western 'sleeping partnership' – is a form of business contract between two parties, one of which (the Islamic bank) provides the capital, and the other (the entrepreneur) the effort. The profit is divided between the two parties by mutual agreement: in case of loss, only the capital provider (*rab al-mal*) takes the responsibility, whereas the entrepreneur (*mudarib*) gains no recompense for his work. *Musharaka* is an agreement whereby the depositor is a partner and, setting aside a remuneration for management, shares in the profits but can also share in the losses.

Not strictly linked with the Islamic banking system, *hawala* – literally, a note of exchange – has become a widespread vehicle for financial transfers. It permits a debtor to charge a third party to reimburse his debt to his creditor, in return for becoming indebted to the third party. This facilitates the settling of accounts without any physical transfer of funds. We may note that the term *hawala* was used during the Abbasid period of early Islam, when the public treasury could not honour its debts to creditors; these were invited to occupy a territory for a given period and reimburse themselves through taxing the population directly.[3] This means of transferring funds attracted public attention during the financial investigations that followed the attacks in the United States on 11 September 2001. The *hawala*, it was alleged, enabled funds to be circulated in order to finance the attacks, bypassing the standard banking institutions.

In order to verify and guarantee the legitimate character of these banking operations from an Islamic viewpoint, there is appointed to each Islamic bank a supervisory religious council (*al-hai'at al-`amma li-raqabat al-shara`iya*) composed of *ulama*. According to the supreme religious authority of the International Association of Islamic Banks (IAIB), for a bank to be considered Islamic it must have a council consisting of at least 13 Muslim *ulama*, entrusted with overseeing adherence to *shari`a* (Hosny 1995). So in practice Islamic finance is by no means a refusal of modernity, but reflects a desire to give an Islamic legitimacy to the financial system. Some commentators therefore see in these modes of finance a mere cosmetic difference, a disguised pursuit of traditional banking practice. The cleric, it has been observed by one scholar, 'does not seek to replace the technocrat but to islamize him' (Carré 1992: 61).

Yusuf al-Qaradawi: militant guardian of morality

One man's career may be summarized here because it illustrates well this interpenetration of the logics of business and charity, under the supervision of intellectual figures in the movement of Islamic militantism. Yusuf al-Qaradawi was elected in 2001 'Islamic personality of the year' by an international committee. His role in both Islamic finance and Islamic charity has been a central one.

Born in 1926 at Seft at-Turab in Egypt, al-Qaradawi lost his father at the age of two and was brought up by his uncle. He began his education in the village *kuttab* or Quranic school, before going on to a religious institution in Tanta for his primary and secondary education. He studied in the faculty for the foundations of religion (*usul ad-din*) in the University of Al-Azhar, Cairo, earning a degree in 1953 and a further degree in the Arab language faculty in 1958. He pursued his studies of the Quran and Sunna at Al-Azhar, obtaining a doctorate in 1974 for his study of '*zakat* and its influence towards resolving social problems'.

Al-Qaradawi has been close to the Muslim Brothers since his student days. He was influenced as a boy by their founder, Hassan al-Banna, and later while studying at Al-Azhar he was sent by Hassan al-Hudaybi (the brotherhood's second-in-command) to undertake *da`wa* in various governorates of Egypt and in Syria, Lebanon and Jordan. On campus, he was responsible for students who were members of the brotherhood. His thought is marked by his reading of ancient authorities such as Ibn Taymiyya, the thirteenth to fourteenth century 'literalist' and precursor of Wahhabism, the strictly scriptural school of Islam that now prevails in Saudi-Arabia, and by the influence of contemporaries such as Sayyid Qutb and Muhammad al-Ghazali.

His political activities had him arrested several times under the reign of King Farouk and after the 1952 revolution. In 1961, he immigrated to Qatar and he founded successively in 1973 the department of Islamic studies in the University of Qatar, in 1977 a faculty of *shari`a* in the same university, and in 1990 a centre for research on the Sunna and the Life of the Prophet. Among his many other appointments, in 1985 he was one of the revered sheikhs imported by the Algerian government to head an Islamic university in Constantine in an attempt to educate a new generation of imams sympathetic to the regime; however, he paid only lip-service to the government while encouraging the 'Islamic awakening' in Algerian society (Kepel 2002a: 165).

Al-Qaradawi's authoritative, 1,800-page monograph on *zakat* (Al-Qaradawi 1994) has been only the starting-point for numerous publications on such topics as 'the problem of poverty and how Islam resolves it' and 'the role of moral values in the Islamic economy'. His expertise in the field of Islamic finance has resulted in his being invited to take part in most of the big conferences on the subject. Above all, he has taken part directly in the creation and supervision of Islamic financial institutions. He has been a member of the religious supervisory board for the Dar Al-Mal Al-Islami Trust in Geneva and other banking organizations, and he is still believed to be a member of similar boards for the Islamic Bank of Qatar, the al-Taqwa Bank in the Bahamas and also banks in the Al-Baraka group.

According to the biographical profile published on the occasion of his nomination as Islamic personality of the year,[4] from which we draw this information, Al-Qaradawi ascribes 'special importance to social work and charity', and reproaches the Islamic revival for having invested too much time in political activity. The Islamic revival should not be limited to words but must pass to action. To return Muslims to their faith, the 'appeal to Islam' (*da`wa*) must be undertaken 'under the cover [*sitar* = curtain or screen] of social services and charitable activities' (p.27), through the building of schools or hospitals. It is reported that Sheikh Qaradawi was specially alerted by Christian missionary projects which used poverty and illness to spread the Gospel, alluding to a conference of missionaries that took place in Colorado in 1978 at which they announced their intention of investing a billion dollars to convert as many Muslims as possible all over the world.

Qaradawi then decided to put together on his side a similar sum to preserve the faith of Muslims through developing projects of charity and *da`wa*. He launched the slogan: *idfa` dollaran w tunqidh musliman* – 'pay a dollar and save a Muslim'. And this idea was basic to the launching of the International Islamic Charitable Organization (*al'hai'at al'khairiyat al-islamiyat al`alamiya*), which was founded in Kuwait and charged with collecting these funds and working for the protection of Muslims everywhere in the world. Qaradawi was the inspiration behind this society's foundation and he is still a member of its board. His record is no less impressive in the field of charity than in Islamic finance: in Qatar, he founded the Qatar Islamic Fund for Zakat and Sadaqa, for the benefit of the needy both in the Emirate and abroad. The financial holdings of this fund were held in the Islamic Bank of Qatar, where he was a member of the supervisory board, until the Minister of Waqfs introduced a public zakat fund in its stead.

Qaradawi may be found on the boards of numerous Islamic institutions: the Islamic University of Islamabad, the Islamic University of Medina, the Oxford Centre for Islamic Studies, and the European Faculty of Islamic Studies (France); he advises the World Islamic League on Islamic law and has many other responsibilities.

Finally, he has his own web-site (*qaradawi.com*) and has founded a bi-lingual site, in Arabic and English, 'Islam On Line'.

The career of this key figure illustrates an interpenetration between different fields: religious militancy, intellectual expertise in Islamic law and zakat, business and social work considered as essential for the revival of Islam. It remains for us to consider how in concrete terms business and social work go in harness to promote the revival of the Islamic *umma*.

Islamic banks funding the charitable sector

The principle of solidarity is essential in the arguments for Islamic finance. For instance, it is apparent in the concept of *takaful* – mutual assistance on the basis of the principles of insurance, but also inter-Muslim solidarity (Sadiq 1995). The connection works by means of the circulation of two types of funds – zakat moneys and moneys which are said to be 'reconverted'– between the banking and the charitable sectors. As regards the zakat moneys, they are generated by means of a percentage – 2.5 per cent, to simplify a little – which is levied annually by Islamic banks on depositors' accounts. The mechanism is fairly simple to understand.

Less easy to understand are the moneys which are reconverted, in the sense that they are generated from moneys that from the point of view of Islamic finance are illegitimate. Islamic banks, operating in the context of a financial system where loan interest remains dominant, are obliged to enter transactions that involve interest, both with non-Islamic banks and with entrepreneurs. In order that the bank's operations should remain consistent with the prohibition of *riba* and so maintain its Islamic legitimacy, the religious supervisory council requires that the funds deriving from interest should be reconverted for the benefit of charitable works.

Let us take an example from the Al-Baraka bank. A boat on the point of being sold is put in dry dock for a survey. The vendor needs to be assured of the sale, and so the purchase moneys are collateralized in a bank with a high rate of interest ('overnight rate'). The moneys are freed after thirty days but there is 30 days' interest payable. To legitimize this transaction, the 'shari`a board' has this sum of interest extracted from the accounts and placed in a special fund. This fund is used to resource the Iqra Foundation, which sends humanitarian gifts – medicine for Bosnia, financing of a school of Islamic law, etc.[5]

In the case of the Islamic Development Bank, the council of governors, meeting in Kampala, decided in 1979 on the creation of a special fund resourced by interest deriving from credits held in foreign banks. According to S.A. Meenai, a former executive director of the IDB, the idea of using these funds was the subject of consultation with the *ulama*, who gave their authorization, invoking the 'principle of necessity' so that the poor in both member and non-member countries could 'maintain their Islamic identity and legitimate rights' (Meenai 1989: 195). Hence a process of halalization (making *halal* or legitimate) has arisen to religiously launder, as it were, funds deriving from illegitimate transactions.[6]

Thus zakat and halalized moneys have provided considerable recurring income for the charitable sector. Data published by the Islamic Faysal Bank since its founding in August 1977 in Khartoum will give an idea of the scale. For 1984 alone, the total of zakat donations amounted to 1.159 million Sudanese pounds, while other types of donation from the bank (recorded as 'charitable donations') amounted to 4.462 million Sudanese pounds.[7] As for the Islamic Development Bank, the special fund mentioned above was able on its own to finance, between 1979 and 1988, 350 projects for a total sum of $168 million in order to help Muslim communities in non-member countries – projects ranging from relief aid after natural disasters to the establishment of religious and cultural centres (Meenai 1989: 152f.)

The financing of relief and development projects by Islamic banks may be undertaken either indirectly or directly. Indirectly, when the bank works through an intermediary institution that uses the funding to initiate a project. This, for example, is the regular practice of the IDB, which is a regular supporter of programmes undertaken by the International Islamic Relief Organization.[8] But banks may also make their own arrangements to fund charitable or developmental projects, as in the case of the Al-Baraka group which funds health programmes and also has its own foundation, the Iqra Foundation, which is active in education and professional training. The IDB has intervened directly in Africa during periods of drought that struck the Sahel at the beginning of the 1980s, and set up a programme for emergency aid to member countries in the Sahel.[9] Since the renewal of the Intifada in September 2000, the IDB has made several financial contributions to support the Palestinians. In January 2003, its director announced that Saudi-Arabia had contributed an additional $7 million to a special fund, the Al-Aqsa Fund. This is said to have reached a total of $692 million, aimed at financing development projects in Palestine and showing support for the Palestinian people's determination.[10]

In some cases (see the previous Chapter) zakat funds may be used to stimulate people in need to become economically self-supporting, and here the link between zakat and investment is considered fundamental. According to Qaradawi and some other authorities, zakat funds may be used to help an individual set up his own business (Cizakra 1995: 157).

And so there can be a shift from charitable aid to supporting the launching of small and medium-sized businesses. Through engaging with the funding of micro-economic programmes, Islamic banks can become agents for development alongside Non-Governmental Organizations. Some observers recognize the capacity of these development projects to combine a commitment to tradition with a measure of economic effectiveness, following the successful and pioneering precedent of the Grameen Bank in Bangladesh (Hours 1993). In Sudan, 'the extension of "Islamic" credit into small-scale agriculture and artisanship has fused traditional mechanisms with the insights of recent development anthropology' (de Waal 2002: 260). This connection between finance and development at the micro level has attracted the attention of international funding agencies such as the World Bank (African Rights 1997: 211).

We have shown how the world of business and profit and the world of social solidarity and altruism interpenetrate. Islamic relief and development programmes provide a guarantee to underscore the legitimacy of a system of Islamic economics that can never openly transgress its founding principles. At the technical level, with its 'halalization' of capital and investments, Islamic aid is seen as a guarantor of the morality of financial practices. At the ethical level, by offering the possibility of credit to those in need, Islamic banks attempt to compensate for the inequalities produced by economic activity, by means of the moral – and Quranic – principle of the rights of the poor over the rich. The rich must not just help the poor, but also give them the means through economic micro-projects to get out of their dependency so that they are integrated in the system. One might suggest a comparison with Max Weber's thesis on the link between Protestantism and the rise of capitalism, especially with regard to the emphasis on work. The Islamic ideal model is one of circulation of wealth, through business and solidarity functioning together. Solidarity allows the poor to be encouraged to set themselves up in business. Doing business generates funds for charitable works.

Conclusion

The institutions of waqf and Islamic finance should be seen historically as far more flexible and indeed opportunistic than is often recognized.

The rich heritage of waqf remains available today as an ideological 'tool-kit' for building new Islamic institutions. As for Islamic finance, its operational distinctiveness in reality as opposed to ideology has often been questioned; and sceptical observers will continue to note how regimes in need of political legitimacy are willing to fund movements rich in religious symbolism in order to cultivate an image of piety (Kuran 2001). However, Islamic finance is likely to maintain its salience as the conventional banking system displays its shortcomings. It has an ideological contribution to make in encouraging the questioning of some of the assumptions of Western economics.[11] Since *riba* and zakat are conceived as linked together in binary opposition, Islamic finance and Islamic charity are interdependent in forming a circle of seamless discourse.[12]

3

RED CRESCENT POLITICS*

If the International Red Cross and Red Crescent Movement has a seemingly permanent 'image problem', this is mainly because few people except those with a direct interest in its activities are aware of its peculiar structure. It is not widely known that there are two Red Cross organizations, both with headquarters in Geneva, linked by an overarching Standing Commission. However, the Movement also experiences particular problems of a chronic nature in its relations with the Muslim world, which have not been covered in such general histories as Caroline Moorehead's *Dunant's Dream* (Moorehead 1998).

My own study of charities originated with an attempt to understand how every Non-Governmental Organization (NGO) is involved with the 'merchandising' of its services and hence of representations of the suffering that it seeks to alleviate: a process of which the worldwide dissemination of the red cross emblem provides a striking historical example (Benthall 1993: 139-155, 242-243). But complications set in soon after the foundation of the Red Cross movement in the 1860s, and these were initially due to the antipathy of Muslims to the cross as a symbol. This chapter will focus on the still frustrating 'question of the emblem' as an entry into some of the wider issues that the Movement faces in an Islamic context.

The International Red Cross and Red Crescent Movement

The founding body of the International Red Cross and Red Crescent Movement is the International Committee of the Red Cross (ICRC), a private institution incorporated under Swiss law that draws authority from the Geneva Conventions (and Additional Protocols). As a neutral intermediary in conflicts and disturbances, both international and internal to nation-states, its primary role is to provide protection and assistance to the victims – essentially, protection to those who have lost their normal protection by a state. It also tries to prevent suffering by promoting and strengthening humanitarian law and universal humanitarian principles.

The International Federation of Red Cross and Red Crescent Societies (founded in 1919 but known as the 'League' until 1991) also has a headquarters in Geneva but is managerially more or less independent of the ICRC. Its job is to contribute to the

---

* by Jonathan Benthall

development of the humanitarian activities of the Red Cross and Red Crescent National Societies in some 180 countries; also to coordinate their relief operations for the victims of natural disasters, to care for refugees outside areas of conflict, and, in so doing, to promote world peace.

The supreme policy-making body of the Movement is the International Conference of the Red Cross and Red Crescent, which usually meets every four years and which includes not only the above organizations but also the States Parties to the Geneva Conventions. A Standing Commission is trustee of the conference between two conferences. The loose expression 'International Red Cross' may therefore refer either to the whole movement, or to the ICRC, or to the Federation. The ICRC uses only the red cross as its emblem, but the Federation uses both emblems together, because thirty of the National Societies use a red crescent instead of a red cross.[1] There is, however, no such organization as the 'International Red Crescent'.

The division of labour between the ICRC and the Federation used to be that the ICRC concentrated on conflict situations, the Federation on natural and technological disasters, and this remains the guiding distinction today. Only the ICRC engages in protecting and assisting prisoners of war and political prisoners, but recently the line has become blurred. The ICRC has occasionally undertaken programmes of agricultural and veterinary 'rehabilitation' in the aftermath of conflict: it is not equipped to engage in long-term development aid, but sometimes attempts to bridge the gap between emergency assistance and development aid, which can take years to get established. After the Cambodian war, for instance, the ICRC imported agricultural tools and seeds over a period of six months, arguing that the alternative would be to have to feed the population for years. And in the 1990s, the Federation was committed to sending regular emergency relief to Baghdad in the form of food and medicine via Jordan, to alleviate the acute suffering that resulted from the oil embargo imposed on Iraq – a disaster, but one directly connected with conflict.

For the ICRC, confidentiality and discretion are an important part of its values, and it traditionally recruits among the young Swiss educational elite, some of whom spend a few years in the ICRC before passing on to other careers. It is still governed by a small executive board of eight to ten Swiss members. The Federation is larger, more cosmopolitan, not nearly as old, and more like other international organizations. Such a structural relationship between two components in a whole – not unknown in other institutions such as universities or armed forces – inevitably results in some friction, which is, however, kept in check by a sense of mutual dependence as well as respect for the primacy of helping the victims of disasters. Increasing tensions and duplications, arising from rapid expansion, led the Movement to negotiate the Seville Agreement in 1997, designed to harmonize all its components and thus optimize its effectiveness. A key concept is that of the 'lead agency', a coordinating function entrusted in each emergency situation to one organization in the Movement. For instance, it was decided at a meeting of 21 National Societies, held in Ankara in October 2001 as a result of the Afghan crisis, that the ICRC would lead the Movement's activities within Afghanistan, while the Federation would coordinate the international relief operations of National Societies in the neighbouring countries – though it has been speculated that not all of them will consider themselves bound by the declaration (Hazan 2002). The Movement's new overall strategy formalized in 2001 emphasizes the priority of 'reaching vulnerable people with effective humanitarian action throughout the world'.[2] Its seven Fundamental Principles are: humanity, impartiality, neutrality, independence, unity, universality and voluntary service – all of which concepts are open to debate in changing circumstances, and some of them we will have cause to comment on later in this Chapter.

The single emblem

The story has been often told of how Henry Dunant, a Geneva businessman, happened to witness the sufferings of the wounded after the battle of Solferino in northern Italy in 1859. Not only did he do his best to help the wounded of both sides on the spot, but in 1862 he published his historic appeal for a new humanitarian organization, *A Memory of Solferino*; and he succeeded in forming a committee, soon to become the ICRC after international meetings in Geneva in 1863-4 and the ratification of the first Geneva Convention.

The committee intended the treaty and their activities to have universal appeal. They conceived the masterly idea of choosing a single emblem to protect ambulances and hospitals, an emblem that would be recognizable at a distance, universally accepted and backed by law. Louis Appia, one of the original committee members, argued that 'the sign should arouse a sort of reflex of respect' (Bugnion 1977: 12). If they had been even more far-sighted, they would have picked an emblem, possibly a red heart, less burdened by centuries of religious connotations; this[3] was in fact suggested as a replacement by the delegate of the Ethiopian Red Cross at a conference in 1975 (ib.: 55), in the course of a long-running international debate about the emblems which has not yet been resolved.[4]

The red cross on a white ground was a reversal of the national flag of Switzerland, but it also happened to be similar to the arms of the Knights Templar which had once been widely adopted by the Crusaders. One Geneva expert has suggested to me that the original committee may have deliberately intended their choice of emblem to bear the connotation of Christian supremacy over the 'infidels' (on the grounds that Dunant knew the Arab world and might be presumed to have had some foreknowledge of the problems which the choice of the cross would cause)[5], but it is more likely that this choice was merely a result of unconscious ethnocentrism.

The Red Cross Movement spread quickly as a result of the continued frequency of wars. The choice of emblem undoubtedly helped in the global expansion of the Movement, but also became an irritant as early as 1876, during the Serbian war, when not only was a local committee secretary, Luka Popovitch, killed after capture by Turkish soldiers, but his arm carrying the white 'brassard' was cut off and chopped up, and the red cross shredded. The committee's bulletin noted that:

> The source of the evil ... is attributable, we think, to the religious antagonism between Muslims and Christians, or rather to the inveterate hatred of Muslims for Christians. The Quran does not, admittedly, instruct its partisans in a duty to massacre and make martyrs of infidels, but rather recommends them to live in peace with them; but the Prophet's precepts have given way to a traditional animosity, which has already left only too many bloody traces in history. If the Cross is an emblem which speaks to the heart of Christians and commands their respect, it

arouses, by contrast, wild passions in the Mohammedans, and their instinct brings them to aim blows against it. It is even a little difficult to understand that the Sultan [of the Ottoman or Turkish Empire] consented, when he signed the Geneva Convention, that the red cross would be officially flown and worn within the ranks of his army; this bold innovation must have elicited much discontent. So it is not surprising that the commitment to using the red cross has not been adhered to, and that this sign has never been seen next to the national flag with the crescent, as the Convention provides.

It would seem, then, that one must despair of seeing the treaty of 1864 faithfully observed by the Muslim peoples, and notably by the sovereigns of Turkey and Persia, whose sovereigns agreed to it. However, even if the Turkish nation in general holds a hostile prejudice against the red cross, it does possess an elite of men who are well disposed to associate themselves with the charitable views of Christians. Even if it is supposed, as has been said, that the Sultan only signed the Geneva Convention out of pure courtesy, and with the intention of ignoring it, the same suspicion ought not to hover over the founders of the Ottoman Society for Relief to the Wounded, who were in no way obliged to put themselves in the firing line in this way. Their initiative has been all the more laudable in that they were under no illusions with regard to the lack of sympathy which their compatriots would extend to a project which had the cross as its symbol; but their lack of success, at a time of full peace, is clear evidence that the circumstances inherent in wartime are not the gravest obstacles to the implementation of the Geneva Convention.

Today, an attempt is being made ... to replace this ineffectual society with another, which hopes to have better success. How will it overcome the repugnance of Mohammedans for the red cross? That is what we do not know. We keenly hope that it will succeed in doing so, but we have no suggestions as to how.

There is one suggestion, however, which several of our correspondents have made and which seems worthy of attention. This is that, for the Turks, the cross would be replaced by a crescent on the flags and brassards of the relief service. The presence in the Turkish army at Nisch of people wearing red crescent brassards has already been drawn to our attention, and we know of no evidence to contradict this assertion. In any case, the Turkish government clearly has no right to substitute the crescent for the cross on its own authority, without the consent of all the other States who are signatories to the Geneva Convention; or, if it does so, it must not expect its adversaries to respect this sign in the same way as that adopted with the agreement of all the Powers. [6]

The uniqueness of the emblem diluted

The mutilation of Popovitch was one of a number of similar incidents.[7] On 16 November 1876, the Sublime Porte in Istanbul wrote to the President of Switzerland that the cross 'wounded the feelings' of the Muslim soldier, and that the Porte had authorized the introduction of ambulances, in conformity with the Geneva Convention, with white flags and brassards but a crescent instead of a red cross. The request for approval was supported by England and Montenegro.

But Russia soon objected that there could be confusion between the Turkish national emblem and the new emblem of neutrality:

Would it not be inappropriate to make a contrast between the Cross of Geneva [red cross], in which the Muslims wrongly see a religious emblem, and the Crescent, which is another religious emblem? Ought not such a contrast to be avoided, especially in a war when the fanaticism of races and beliefs will necessarily be overheated to the maximum? Already the Sultan has announced a holy war under the flag of the Caliphs; and if one is to believe the claims of Montenegro, the sight of the white flag with the red cross flown by a convoy of the wounded was enough, last October, to attract cannon fire from the Turkish forts, which went silent when the emblem was lowered.

If such is the fate of those who think themselves protected by the emblems of neutrality, it is certain that the suppression of these signs would be preferable to the present state of affairs.

Despite these comments by Russia, the International Committee gave permission in June 1877 for the Ottoman Empire to use the crescent instead of a cross, but as a stopgap measure with no intention of creating a precedent and despite the reservations of the Committee, which saw strong arguments for maintaining the single emblem (Bugnion 1997: 18)

At about the same time, there were problems with Japan, where Christianity was unacceptable, and two parallel horizontal rectangles were substituted by the national authorities.[8] However, Japan was eventually to accept the red cross emblem (Bugnion 1997: 21), whereas the adoption of the crescent by the Ottomans was to lead to many national societies using the crescent today.

A British imperial episode

The British Red Cross Society was one of the earlier National Societies, founded in 1870, and has flourished since. For a short period however, between 1912 and 1920, there was actually a British Red Crescent Society as well. It was set up to start a field hospital for the relief of sick and wounded Ottoman soldiers, and later provided help for Indian Muslim soldiers in Flanders and elsewhere through an 'Indian Troops' Comforts Account', and worked to alleviate Muslim distress in Tripoli and Turkey. Its founders wished to promote cooperation between 'Englishmen and Englishwomen on one side and Moslems on the other in a great work of mercy, a solidarity of sympathy between two component elements of the British Empire'. All donations were listed in the official report, down to sixpence worth of postage stamps from Brighton, but the scheme seems to have been principally a device to tap donations from wealthy Muslims such as the Nizam of Hyderabad and the Aga Khan (who subsidized the London office).

A report to the subscribers in November 1913 from the British Red Crescent Society's Surgeon-in-Charge, Dr William E. Haigh, on relief work in Bulgaria and Adrianople, reads as follows:

> I found that the 'Red Crescent' emblem was a constant source of difficulty, and often prevented the accomplishment of the best work, because of obstacles which were purposely not removed or smoothed away, and more especially in Adrianople. The Bulgarian officers of lower ranks and ordinary soldiers did not understand its significance, just in the same way that I found antipathy amongst Mussulmans to the Red Cross brassard.

Haigh wore the red crescent for eight months and included the following 'Note on the Use of "Red Crescent" Emblem' in his report:

> Because of the ignorance in the armies as to the innocuousness of both [cross and crescent] emblems, my experience leads me to believe that they are calculated in

some measure to defeat their objectives, to reflect upon their wearer, and may even lead to personal discomfort if not worse. This campaign has made the demand for some reform more urgent, and any suggestions are worth considering which really aid the humanitarian armies of both sides.

I hereupon call the attention of the Geneva Convention to this and beg to suggest as a modification the use of a horizontal bar and a vertical crescent crossing the bar at right angles, this combining both the present emblems, the colours to remain the same, and that this should be made the universal emblem.[9]

After off and on discussions, the Movement finally agreed at its Conference in 1929 to allow two alternative emblems in addition to the standard emblem of the cross: the red crescent, and the red lion and sun, the latter to meet the wishes of Persia (Iran). After the fall of the Shah, when Iran changed to the crescent, there are now only two emblems in use, though in theory three are recognized.

The waxing of the red crescent

The Ottoman Red Crescent continued to lead the way among the Muslim countries. In 1922 it organized collections on religious holidays throughout the Muslim world, for the benefit of needy Muslims.[10]

Today, some of the Red Crescent National Societies are very active and play important national roles. Some have also played a major part in the development of the Movement and in particular in nudging it towards policies that take account of the perspectives and aspirations of non-Western countries.

Documentation on the growth of the Red Crescent National Societies is sparse. But a report published in Geneva in 1986 describes the short history of the Mauritanian Red Crescent, which was recognized in 1973. It has been a pioneer in income generation projects (*'réhabilitation par le travail'*) and has given special attention to marsh agriculture and reforestation. The Swiss chronicler's view is of a nation relatively unmarked by French colonization:

> Everywhere, the National Society resembles Mauritanian society: strongly structured – some would say hierarchical – radical in its decisions, rigorous in its options, jealous of its autonomy, but extremely welcoming towards people of goodwill from outside, provided one does not claim to be giving them lessons ... Among the countries of the Sahel, the Mauritanian Red Crescent is one of the organizations which has showed the way forward for what could be the building up of a Red Crescent National Society in the Third World without any inferiority complex. Particular problems in this part of the world require particular solutions which the Mauritanian Red Crescent has managed to devise at every level.[11]

An example of a strong National Society – indeed, one of the largest of all the Movement's National Societies – is the Iranian Red Crescent, which has special expertise in responding to earthquakes and flash-floods in one of the most disaster-prone countries in the world. It has over 200 branches with a central office in Teheran and regional offices. Originally founded as the Red Lion and Sun Society, and acquiring much influence and prestige under royal patronage, it was managed by members of the Shah's court, and at one time was running over two hundred hospitals and was a major part of the national health care system. After 1979, the name was changed to the Red Crescent and it became smaller, the Department of

Health taking over responsibility for health services. The Iranian Red Crescent is still responsible for imported medicines and medical equipment, provides orthopaedic and physiotherapy services and has managed a number of refugee camps. It also runs a large Youth Department, and most of its offices provide social services. It was active in Bosnia (see Chapter 7). Recently it has embarked on expansion plans, including quasi-commercial activities such as manufacturing tents for sale.

The Bangladesh society has accumulated skills in disaster-preparedness to confront the frequent cyclones and floods that plague the region. Some Red Crescent National Societies, such as that of Morocco, were the successors to Red Cross societies introduced by the former colonial power – in this case, France. The Moroccan Red Crescent took a lead in the relief operation of 1959-61 after olive oil was criminally polluted with engine oil and caused 'flaccid paralysis' in victims; sixteen other Red Cross and Red Crescent Societies joined with WHO to help rehabilitate paralysed patients. In 1964 – an early example of regional organization within the movement – a conference was organized in Algiers of North African Red Crescents.[12] At that time Morocco was out of line in that all appointments to the national committee were made by the King. Now, however, virtually all National Societies follow democratic election procedures.

The 'question of the emblem' today

As the ICRC's official emblemologist has observed, the decision reached in 1877 'was hardly logical. It opened a door to the emblems proposed by Turkey, Persia and Egypt [which like Turkey sought approval for the crescent], and then quickly slammed it shut' (Bugnion 1977: 34). No further dilution of the semiotic power of the red cross emblem has been allowed. Most Muslim countries have gradually adopted the crescent instead of the cross for their National Societies, two of the latest being Uzbekistan and Turkmenistan in 1995. But some countries with majority Muslim populations still use the cross, such as Nigeria and Indonesia. These are all countries with no popular memory of the Crusades. Even in Nigeria the red cross does not escape suspicion in Muslim-dominated provinces, partly owing to its religious connotations but also because of memories of British colonialism. Malaysia changed from the cross to the crescent in 1975.

Other non-Christian countries such as India, Japan and Thailand use the cross without any serious problems arising, though a number of alternatives have been proposed over the years such as a red wheel for India, red cedar-tree for Lebanon, and even a red rhinoceros for Sudan (Bugnion 1977: 57-70). The Lebanon national society uses a red cross, though some of its ambulances use the crescent in Muslim areas, or frequently both. (The Lebanon Red Cross was the only organization that operated continuously throughout the seventeen years of the war.) The cross and crescent are used together by the International Federation; and were formerly used together in the days of the Soviet Union by its own internal federation, the Alliance of Red Cross and Red Crescent Societies of the USSR, though each republic used either a cross or crescent alone according to the group which composed the majority of the population in each case (Bugnion 1989: 418).

The ICRC continues to use the cross only. Serious problems relating to the emblems remain unresolved in two political contexts. One of these is in a few states which depend on Islamic imagery to legitimize state institutions: particularly Saudi-

Arabia, where any display of the Christian cross is forbidden: there are recent signs that this rule is being slightly relaxed, but it would appear that during the 1990-91 Gulf War the red cross emblem was not used (Ghandour 2002: 314). The ICRC has also been accused of Christian proselytization in Somalia, Sudan, Pakistan and Afghanistan (Bitter 1994: 74, 2003; see also Chapters 4 and 6).

The other political context is that of Israel. Since the foundation of the State of Israel in 1948, it has used neither cross or crescent for the emblem of its National Society, but the Red Shield of David (Magen David Adom or MDA), that is to say the six-pointed Jewish 'star of David'. The ICRC has never been empowered to recognize the Israeli relief society, for it does not use one of the three recognized emblems. No satisfactory solution has been found despite regular discussions.[13] This legal difficulty has not prevented the MDA society from developing effectively, cooperating in practice with the Movement though it is officially still a National Society in the process of formation.

The non-recognition of the Red Shield of David annoys Israel and its supporters, some of whom have protested articulately. It was argued on their behalf in 1949 that the shield 'was a sacred symbol dating back three thousand five hundred years and, after having marked the Jewish victims of Hitlerism, had become the symbol of life and charity: few emblems were so ancient and so widely known' (Bugnion 1977: 41). The cross is as little likely to be acceptable to Israel as the crescent, on account of the centuries of oppression and marginalization of Jews by Christians in Europe.

There is anxiety within the Movement that, if a concession were made to Israel and the Shield of David accepted, two undesirable consequences would follow. First, there would be a proliferation of proposals for new emblems, thus detracting from the 'unity' and 'universality' of the Movement, which are two of its seven Fundamental Principles: above all, perhaps, from that 'reflex of respect' for an emblem originally stressed by Appia. Second, it could be a pretext for a number of Muslim countries – especially those such as Iran that are strongly opposed to Israel – to seek to renegotiate their whole relationship with the Movement. This risk is taken seriously because relations between some of the Red Crescent societies and the headquarters in Geneva – particularly the ICRC – are not always entirely harmonious, for various reasons to be discussed.

Semiotics of the red cross and red crescent
As was foreseen in the 1870s by some of those who opposed recognition of the crescent, the undesired religious connotations of the cross creep back in as soon as it is either replaced by the crescent or juxtaposed to it. The ICRC adopts the only course currently open to it, which is to insist as an article of faith that the cross is simply a geometric device. As for the Federation, it uses the two devices together, and discourages any tendency to think of the Red Crescent societies as forming a bloc or sub-movement.[14] From time to time, the thought of replacing the two emblems by a new one has been entertained and it recently came almost to fruition. Apart from the particular sense of injury experienced by Israel over its exclusion from the Movement, the present dispensation gives more generally 'an impression of a bias in favour of Christian and Moslem countries, and of discrimination against those of other faiths' (Bugnion 1977: 71, see also Sommaruga 1992). In the heated atmosphere of conflict associated with religious affiliation that has marked the

beginning of the twenty-first century, the work of the Movement's staff and volunteers can be impeded by the unwanted religious symbolism, and their personal safety may be put at unnecessary risk.

There is a semiotic asymmetry between the cross and the crescent. The cross was not the earliest symbol of Christianity[15], but it became so dominant a symbol that every Christian church building, at least in the major denominations, is marked by the presence of a cross. Though educated Muslims respect Jesus as a great prophet, they consider the doctrine of his Crucifixion to be an historical aberration or archaic survival (Glassé 1991: 208-9). The cross as the banner of the Crusaders is still part of the folk memory of the Arab world, and the Arabic translation of 'cross' in 'Red Cross', *salib*, refers not to a mere geometric device but to crucifixion. There are legends, possibly founded in fact, that when European generals in the twentieth century entered Jerusalem or Damascus, they likened themselves to victorious Crusaders.

By contrast, the crescent (*hilal*) is less important to Muslims. It is associated theologically with determining the dates for pilgrimage and for the beginning and end of the holy month of Ramadan, since Islam is based on the lunar calendar. The motif of the crescent has been prominent for many centuries in decorative and heraldic art and in architecture. But it did not become an official Ottoman emblem till the late eighteenth century, when it was used for the imperial flag: it was adopted by Turkey when it became a republic in 1923. Tunisia followed and now the Crescent is used by most Muslim countries for their flags and postage stamps (Ettinghausen 1971: 381-5). A crescent is not an indispensable part of the design of a mosque. It is more a political than a strictly religious symbol.

Visual symbols are, in fact, tools of political persuasion – in this case, tools of humanitarian politics. Folk memories of the Crusades are not passively transmitted from one generation to another, but mobilized by Arab-Muslim leaders to articulate a *current* complaint against the West. Long-standing differences of opinion over the red emblems have masked more recent substantive differences over ideology and policy which are only now coming to be articulated and discussed more directly and frankly.

The threat of an 'Islamic Crescent'

Since the late 1960s, the Arab members of the Federation have gradually succeeded in organizing themselves more effectively than before, when it was dominated by Europeans. The Federation, which has a regional delegation in Jordan and sub-regional delegation in Tunisia, organizes regular conferences for National Societies in the MENA region. But the Conference of Arab Red Crescent and Red Cross Societies has a secretariat in Jeddah (including Lebanon as the only Arab national society which uses the red cross), and this grouping is independent of the Federation. It works at having an active share in the Movement as a whole, and fights for such issues as having Arabic included as a fourth language of the Movement in addition to English, French and Spanish, and for having National Societies in the region represented in elections to major positions in the Federation.

In June 2001, the 30th Conference was held in Rabat under the chairmanship of Princess Lalla Malika, Chairwoman of the Moroccan Red Crescent. King Muhammad VI of Morocco took advantage of the occasion to send a message urging Arab Red Crescent and Red Cross societies to extend further backing to the Palestinian people and in particular to their rights to an independent state with Al-Quds (Jerusalem) as its capital. He also underlined the importance of volunteering and 'social solidarity action', to whose promotion he had committed himself since his succession to the Moroccan throne in 1999.[16]

Even less dependent on the Movement itself is an organization, launched in 1982, known as the Islamic Committee of the International Crescent. With a secretariat is in Benghazi, Libya, it comprises a number of National Societies in the Middle East and North Africa (including Lebanon, and the Palestine Red Crescent) and four in Africa (Sudan, Somalia, Mauritania and Djibouti), with the General Secretariat of Arab Red Crescent and Red Cross Societies as an observer. It meets on the premises of the Organization of the Islamic Conference (OIC), but has not yet been able to muster quite the quorum of members (fourteen) which would enable it to be officially adopted.[17] The original plan was to develop humanitarian functions similar to those of the ICRC within the Islamic world, for instance mediation between two countries or repatriation of prisoners, but to date there are no programmes in operation.

When I first undertook research on the Movement in 1994, the view could be heard that the Islamic Crescent was building up to face the ICRC with significant competition, with the aim of eventually displacing it from Islamic countries and removing about one quarter of its global mandate. Its aspirations were not only to operate in Islamic countries, but also to assist Muslims in difficulty everywhere.

A glance at the rhetorical keywords used by the Islamic Committee suggests that they would seek to eliminate the Geneva principles of 'unity' (only one National Society per country) and 'universality' or global responsibility, and would substitute the principle of 'justice'.[18] This is significant because justice is often considered the central ethical value of Islam, whereas the leaders of the Red Cross have never deemed it to be a necessary component in their set of principles – though in recent years there has been an appreciable move towards integrating the concept of human rights with that of humanitarianism.

A contrary interpretation of the Islamic Crescent plan was shared by the majority of my informants in 1996, and seems to have been vindicated: the view that it is completely unrealistic in the current and immediately foreseeable state of relations between many Muslim states, which are tense and competitive. In many Arab countries, travel restrictions imposed on those who hold passports from other Arab countries are more stringent than are those imposed on Europeans. Regional cooperation in other spheres such as commerce is not particularly harmonious. Arab and Islamic governments have an even weaker record than the UN in preventing regional conflicts. One Swiss informant has told me he had been in Amman during the killings of September 1970 – 'Black September' – when the Jordanian army bombarded the Palestinian refugee camps. He said that Palestinians and Jordanians did not at that time trust one another, and in that extreme situation the red cross was a more effective protective emblem than the crescent – 'even if it was worn by a Swiss'.

It would seem likely that the Islamic Crescent plan is in actuality, if not in its original intent, a bargaining counter with which sections of the Arab world seek reforms from the Red Cross and Red Crescent Movement and from the ICRC in particular (the Federation is less exposed to criticism). The OIC is particularly keen to prevent Israel from having its Red Shield of David recognized alongside the red crescent and red cross.[19]

The criticism of the ICRC, at its most blunt, is that it is a Geneva charity whose senior managers are exclusively Swiss. Even its critics concede that this enables it to be a more tightly run organization than any UN-style organization can hope to be. But few observers from developing countries believe that the ICRC is genuinely independent from the Swiss government, with which many of its senior figures are closely linked through their connections and earlier careers. The ICRC and Western humanitarian aid in general are likened to the sugar round the pill – the pill being politics, and particularly foreign policy, increasingly dominated by the United States.

The ICRC adapts – within limits

The ICRC is perceived by its Islamic and Third World critics as a deeply conservative body. In fact, it has been impelled to adapt quite sharply during the last thirty-five years in response to criticism, to pressures from the mass media and to competition from brasher agencies such as Médecins Sans Frontières. For instance, a substantial minority of its permanent staff are now non-Swiss. It has openly acknowledged that in retrospect its role during the Second World War in not denouncing the Nazi murder camps was excessively legalistic and cautious. It now speaks out more publicly against certain blatant violations of the Geneva conventions, when the private pressures that it traditionally prefers have failed. It has adopted a generally more open policy towards journalists and researchers than previously. Its international media campaign against the manufacture of anti-personnel mines has been a success.

More specifically, the ICRC makes available a manual of advice, for staff about to take up appointments in Muslim countries, counselling respect for religious tradition. Among its senior officials in the Middle East region is a Tunisian Muslim who is a Quranic scholar. It has commissioned a number of internal reports on various aspects of its relations with Muslim societies. In 1994, it held a videotaped meeting with representatives of Hizbullah including Lebanese Islamic scholars, who challenged the ICRC on problems arising from its Christian background and claims to universality; the meeting also dwelt on ways of using cultural tradition to try to restrain the conduct of hostilities. In the Palestinian Territories, the ICRC now holds regular discussions with Hamas and other militant groups on questions of military ethics, focussing on three issues of principle: attacks on civilians, the training of children in camps, and the treatment of collaborators including extra-judicial killings.

The ICRC's detractors complain that when the ICRC denounces, it is 'too little, too late'. The ICRC defends its position by reminding us that its effectiveness depends on maintaining the confidence of governments and on behind-the-scenes persuasion. The ICRC denounces so rarely that when it does denounce, its complaints are taken seriously. There are many cases of serious atrocities that it has known about but not denounced, for whatever reasons. Operational neutrality is frequently in conflict with human rights advocacy (Bradbury 1995: 23), but the latter is not seen as the ICRC's primary commitment. Nor does the ICRC see fit to adopt any position condemning capital punishment or corporal punishment in those nations, whether Muslim or other, where they are part of the penal code.

To revert to the issue of 'justice', 'neutrality' is a difficult enough principle to maintain, and the ICRC does so as well as any other organization, but the concept of 'justice' is vacuous without reference to a judicial authority. The laws of war are notoriously fragile and depend greatly on their implementation at the behest of the victors in war and/or compliant superpowers or international bodies. Justice in war is often the fickle travesty of justice dispensed by the mass media. The ICRC's core commitment – expanded though this may have been by other demands on its resourcefulness – remains the defence of certain minimal rules of conduct, as set out in the Geneva Conventions, as impartially as possible. Neutrality as perceived from Switzerland certainly has limitations, but the case in favour of the ICRC is that its sense of neutrality is more likely to be generally acceptable than justice as defined by a religiously based organization, whether the Islamic Crescent or any other.

Toothing-stones and cracks in the edifice

A display near the entrance to the International Museum of the Red Cross and Red Crescent in Geneva, teaching us that wolves do not polish off their enemies once they have secured submission, has now been removed after further reflection caused the Museum to doubt the value of drawing such lessons from the animal kingdom. The permanent exhibition now begins with a series of showcases by means of which it is argued that modern International Humanitarian Law (IHL), especially in its restraints on violence during armed conflict, is prefigured in the teachings of Islam, Confucianism, Buddhism and other ancient traditions.

This section of the Museum is indicative of an effort that the Red Cross has made over many years to show that the Arab-Islamic world, in particular, has made its own contribution to humanitarian law. In 1969, the Imam of the Geneva Islamic community was invited to write for the *International Review of the Red Cross* about Quranic teaching on Muslims' duties towards their fellow-creatures and about the injunctions to be found in the Quran on the treatment of non-combatants, prisoners of war and the like (Ereksoussi 1962). Another article eleven years later, by a Tunisian law professor, adopted a more historical point of view, pointing out the huge difference between the seventh century CE and the present day as regards military technology and the concerns of governments: therefore, only a loose argument by analogy is possible, but he concluded that 'nothing in the Koran or Sunnah seems to be in direct contradiction to international humanitarian law' (Ben Ashoor 1980).

The content of the Islamic law of war was drawn up two or three centuries after the Prophet's death, but there is considerable evidence that from the earliest days the religion did impose restraints on the behaviour of soldiers. For instance, Abu Bakr, the Prophet's close friend and the first Caliph, instructed his soldiers not to let their victory be stained with the blood of women, children or old people; not to cut down palms or fruit-trees; not to burn down houses and crops; only to kill cattle for food; to stand by treaties; and to spare men of religion and their monasteries (Hamidullah 1945: 300, Boisard 1985: 259). Elaborate attention was given to the proper treatment of combatants and prisoners of war, which is one of the sharpest issues in International Humanitarian Law today (Zemmali 1997). A concern for what we now call conservation runs through the early teaching of Islam, for survival in the desert is only possible by means of discipline and foresight. Also, Islam set an example of religious tolerance in its provisions for protection of the People of the Book or 'scriptuaries' (also called *dhimmi*s) – that is to say, principally Christians and Jews.

In recent years, as well as founding the new museum, the ICRC has published some booklets, lavishly illustrated with illustrations from medieval Islamic manuscripts, arguing that Islamic law is one of the sources of the universal cultural heritage whose principles and ideals are codified in International Humanitarian Law (e.g. ICRC 1993). We read for instance of the correctness and magnanimity with which Saladin, the twelfth century Muslim hero of the Third Crusade who took Jerusalem, is recorded as having treated prisoners of war.

There is certainly merit in showing respect for a great, often neglected non-Western religious and cultural tradition, with the aim of persuading Muslims that they 'own' International Humanitarian Law as much as Westerners do. However, the exercise as conducted by a Swiss agency has only a limited cogency.

First, it is often possible to find statements in the Quran and *hadith*s which contradict a given reading or interpretation. The process of renewed interpretation in each generation (*ijtihad*) is a vital part of Islam but is never uncontroversial.

Second, the technique adopted is to pick a revered historical figure such as Saladin and argue that he anticipated the Red Cross. Indeed, the ICRC has made clear that it is actively searching the corpus of non-Western religions to find common ground on which to engage in humanitarian dialogue. Jean-Nicolas Bitter, in his study of how Western humanitarian agencies should engage with the Islamists, has argued that this 'parade' derives historically from the Christian missionary theology of 'toothing-stones', the projecting stones left by builders at the end of a wall to allow its continuation; according to this strategy, one should seek motifs in local traditions compatible with the metropolitan message and only waiting for the arrival of missionaries to be realized (Bitter 1994: 88-9). When humanitarian agencies adopt a like strategy towards Islam today, he claims, they ignore what feeds the anti-colonial motivation of radical Islamist movements, and they may actually aggravate the problem (see also Cockayne 2000).

Bitter is alluding to the Islamists' critique of what they see as the 'intellectual attack' (*al-ghazw al-thaqafi*) by the West on Islam. 'Its so-called perpetrators', writes Yvonne Haddad, 'are accused of not being satisfied with military and political domination, but of aiming at the eradication of Islamic culture, civilization and intellectual output in the effort to obliterate the religion of Islam' (Haddad 1995).

Moreover, returning for educational purposes to the historical sources of the Islamic religion and Quranic revelation cuts both ways. An inescapable element of combativeness runs through the texts: more precisely, perhaps, an acceptance of conflict as inescapable. According to some analysts, the Christian injunction to turn the other cheek and love one's enemies is alien to Muslims (Boisard 1985: 242) – though the actual belligerence of Christians in history has often been pointed out as incongruous, and non-violent Gandhi-style movements are not unknown in Islamic history (Banerjee 2000). Islamic combativeness is balanced by a strong commitment to justice, magnanimity and mercy. But whereas the status of the People of the Book was guaranteed in Islamic law in return for payment of a head tax, the status of 'polytheists' (adherents to traditional non-written religions) has always been uncomfortable within Muslim jurisdictions. Tensions on some topics such as the rights of non-believers are likely to remain and cannot be ignored.[20] Furthermore, some practices such as hostage-taking are forbidden by International Humanitarian Law, but taken for granted in the traditions of local welfare in some Muslim societies, for instance in central Asia (Delorenzi 1999).

The principles of universality and neutrality are under strain in some Islamic quarters of the Red Cross and Red Crescent Movement. For instance, nearly a hundred nurses and doctors were sent by the Algerian Red Crescent to Iraq after the 1990-91 Gulf War, with particular zeal because Saddam Hussain had posed as a Saladin fighting the 'evil America'; but they insisted on withdrawing their services when they saw his destruction of holy cities. And some of the Red Crescent societies, for instance in the Emirates, make uninhibited use of religious texts and imagery in their fund-raising (Ghandour 2002: 179). However, the problems of maintaining the principles of the Movement are not specific to the Red Crescents. For instance, the American Red Cross was slow to support the ICRC's campaign in the mid-1990s against anti-personnel weapons, because it conflicted with the current US government policy, and some other societies interpreted this as showing a lack of independence. The British Red Cross made an (uncharacteristic) error in associating itself too closely with the ruling Conservative Party's political interests in 1991 after the Gulf War, in a grandiose fund-raising campaign on behalf of the Kurds (Benthall 1993: 50-2).

Despite the tensions between the ICRC's humanist representations of Islam, and Muslims' insistence on the distinctiveness and originality of their religion, the common ground is enough to permit cooperation. Perhaps the ICRC's strongest card is that it is eminently practical, attempting primarily to restrain foul conduct, mitigate aggression and supply essential relief to victims, rather than put into effect ambitious projects for social change.

The tensions that exist between the Red Cross and Red Crescent Movement and the Islamic world probably derive less from any clash of abstract principles, than from the institutional forms and tacit assumptions that have grown up as an outcome of centuries of domination by the Christian West. Rather than merely scan the Quran and Islamic history for texts that buttress the humanitarian principles of Geneva, it is possible to use the standard practice of anthropological distancing to see how other societies – in this case, Muslim – perceive Western humanitarian agencies.

These agencies certainly secure wide deference in poorer countries partly for their practical help, but also for the apparatus of power and technology they bring, for the foreign exchange they import, and for the local employment they finance (de Waal 1997). Among many intellectuals, deference towards the agencies has turned to criticism: they point out the lack of accountability to the 'consumer' (though recently Western NGOs have given much attention to this problem, as in Oakley 2001).

The Red Cross's principle of 'universality' is sometimes impugned as a veil for neo-colonial power and a prolongation of religious missionary activity in a new form (Bitter 1994: 100-1). In fact, 'universality' is defined by the Movement as the principle that all national societies 'have equal status and share equal responsibilities and duties in helping each other'. Since it is plain that in reality the huge American Red Cross and the tiny Djibouti Red Crescent do not have equal status (except in voting at conferences), this must be a statement of belief and principle rather than practice. Such an affirmation of universalism – if it is not to be a dead letter –

necessitates a wish to escape from parochialism, and an effort to see the other's point of view. This means not looking for toothing-stones to add on to, but looking for cracks in one's own edifice, which can be openings for understanding. Geneva has opened up to a considerable extent.

The brief case-studies which follow illustrate some of the above themes, but also the specificity of each national society's position within the movement.

The Jordan National Red Crescent Society (JNRCS)

This information is largely based on a two month stay in Amman from January to March 1996, as part of a wider study of the voluntary sector in Jordan.

The Jordan Red Crescent was founded in 1948. The King is its Honorary President and Princess Sarvath, wife of the present King's uncle Prince Hassan, is Honorary Vice-President. It is the general practice for all the National Societies in the Movement to have this level of official support. In fact, though the National Societies are required under the statutes of the Movement to be independent so that they can always act in accordance with Red Cross principles, they are also 'auxiliaries in the humanitarian services of their governments': thus, they are not really Non-Governmental Organizations and their 'independence' is always qualified.

The flagship of the JNRCS is its general hospital in south-east Amman, founded in 1953 near the Al-Wihdat Palestinian refugee camp in one of the poorest quarters of the city. It had recently been expanded to 150 beds, with specialist facilities such as an X-ray department and new operating theatres donated by the Japanese and German Red Crosses; this expansion was the JNRCS's main contribution to the national effort required to absorb the Palestinian returnees from Kuwait in 1991. Poorer patients are treated completely free of charge, but there are some private wards which generate revenue from paying patients. For these rooms, the policy is to charge lower rates than the private profit-oriented hospitals. The hospital incorporates a blood bank and medical laboratories, and runs an emergency department for motoring and other accidents. Priority is currently being given to the care of Palestinians recently wounded in the West Bank.

Originally when the Society was founded there were two committees, a men's and a women's. The men's committee was less successful than the women's committee, which started the hospital. Shortly afterwards, in the name of integration, the two committees were merged into one. As might perhaps have been predicted, the executive committee is now dominated by men.

One of the most striking features of the society is its claim to a membership of 1.2 million, which would be nearly half the adult population of Jordan and would make the Jordan Red Crescent the mother of all grass-roots organizations. However, in fact this is the schools membership. Under an agreement with the Ministry of Education, every school pupil is considered a member of the Red Crescent and paid a nominal sum of 150 *fils* (about 15 pence) per year. Ten per cent of this sum, I learnt, is taken by the Ministry of Education to pay for some fifty Red Crescent holiday camps, and the remainder stays within each school to pay for first aid cabinets, and for some of the expenses of poorer pupils such as clothing, stationery and books. In every school, a Red Crescent committee made up of three pupils is elected by the pupils, a teacher and the principal. Efforts are made to disseminate knowledge of first aid and of the Movement. This scheme is unique in the world, giving the Red Crescent a potential outreach into every home where there are children.

Branches and funding

As well as the headquarters in Amman, there are also eleven branches, of which I visited two. The first was at Salt, 30 km. north-west of Amman and one of the oldest towns in the kingdom. The Red Crescent branch has 75 members, ten of whom form the executive committee, and there are 100 volunteers. Apart from a boy-scout group, the main commitment of the branch at Salt was a small residential orphanage for girls, which was started in 1965; it is described elsewhere in this book on p.103.

The branch at Madaba was the oldest, founded in 1952. Madaba was a town of about 55,000 people with a 36 per cent Christian population and a tourist trade. This branch now had to compete with some 28 other voluntary committees, so the competition was strong. The committee happened to be all-woman at the time of my visit, and most of them happened to be Christian. Their main commitment was running a general medical clinic, founded in 1970. The charge per patient was only about 250 fils, which was waived when the patient could not afford even this. The clinic supplemented a government hospital in Madaba (as well as a private hospital for paying patients). The branch also ran a training centre in the same building, for women to learn sewing and other skills. The branch committee, supported by a general assembly of about 180, was planning to build a house for old people. Another need that had been identified in Madaba was for children's playgrounds, and there was the possibility of funding from other sources if a branch could put together a good proposal. For instance, the Netherlands Red Cross had just provided the funds for a health centre further south, in Ma'an.

Both branches had their own buildings and some land. Both were survivors from the period before the explosion of the voluntary sector in Jordan and the availability of international funding. Both betrayed some signs of neglect by headquarters, and this is clearly because the leadership until recently was more interested in the JNRCS's international role than in domestic activities. This trend was being actively corrected in 1996 by the dynamic Dr Muhammad Al-Hadid, now President, who stressed the need to build up the society as a stronger institution within Jordan itself, integrated with the Federation's ambitious international development plan to 'improve the situation of the most vulnerable'.

Unlike other Red Crescent societies – nearly always de facto dependencies of government, the officers typically being retired civil servants – the JNRCS had traditionally been subsidized by wealthy individuals. Under the rule of the last President, H.E. Ahmed Abu-Goura, who resigned in 1993, the Executive Committee used to face a deficit at the end of every year, amounting to perhaps JD 10,000, and this was met through each member of the committee making a personal contribution. Both Dr Abu-Ghoura and Dr Al-Hadid, his son-in-law, were wealthy individuals. (This is similar to the way a number of small to medium size British charities used to be run up to about 30 years ago, and probably a few small ones are still funded like this.) Dr Al-Hadid became Vice-President in 1987 and introduced more orderly financing of the Society. One major donor, a Circassian lady, had given a donation of JD 500,000 shortly before my visit. She was given a gold medal by King Hussain, and a new sewing and typing centre in Amman was named after her.

The government supplied the JNRCS with only enough funds to pay the required annual subscriptions to the ICRC, the Federation and the Arab secretariat in Jeddah.

By contrast with a typical Western voluntary organization, where branches help towards head office expenses, in Jordan the branches have to be subsidized from the centre. Despite a formal commitment to democratic procedures, Al-Hadid, who had given up his personal career as a clinical chemist to work as a full-time volunteer for JNRCS, openly used his power to postpone branch elections or abolish branches if he suspected that they were being politically infiltrated – the current pressure coming from the Islamists. He insisted to me that the JNRCS was set up to alleviate suffering, not to express political views. Al-Hadid was proud of being a Bedouin, and asserted that as such he was willing to help anyone who came to him and asked for his protection. The relationship between branches and head office is similar, I suggest, to that between client and patron tribes, the relationship of *wala'*. It was said of a powerful Arab prince of the early part of the twentieth century that he 'resembles a long branch to which smaller twigs are attached' (Musil 1928: i. 439), and the same could be said of Al-Hadid. To which it must be added that having Bedouin forebears now carries some glamour in urban Jordan, like descending from a Highland clan for the Scots. Dr Al-Hadid regularly entertained visiting Red Cross dignitaries, JRCNS staff and other friends at his farm on the outskirts of Amman, serving a lavish lunch in a convincing replica of a Bedouin tent.

Since the 1990-91 Gulf War

The great challenge for the JNRCS came in 1990 and 1991 with the Gulf crisis. This put it on the map and gave it a stronger starting-point for future development, though no similarly acute crisis has yet afflicted the kingdom since that date.

One of the consequences of the invasion of Kuwait by Iraq in August 1990 was the evacuation of many thousand Asian workers – mainly Bangladeshis, Indians, Sri Lankans and Filipinos. A normally very quiet post on the Iraq-Jordan border, Rweished, which normally had no more than fifteen people passing through it per day, now had 20-30,000 people stranded in the no man's land between the two countries. With only twelve toilets at the border, people were using the desert to relieve themselves, and in the intense heat there was a risk of cholera or typhoid. There was not enough water, and no medicines.

Supported by the ICRC and the Federation, the JNRCS played a major role in accommodating the evacuees and arranging for the airlift to their home countries. Out of 700,000 evacuees, some 140,000 passed through the Red Crescent camps, each spending between two and seven nights, and not a single life was lost (Girod 1994).

Jordan adopted a neutral policy during the 1990-91 Gulf crisis, when the government refused to support the anti-Iraq coalition (arguing that an 'Arab solution' should be pursued). This gave the JNRCS other opportunities to demonstrate the Movement's impartiality. On Thanksgiving Day in November 1990, Al-Hadid arranged for turkeys to be bought at the Safeway store in Amman and flown to the American hostages in Baghdad. This opened the door to the American Red Cross, and in March 1991, at the end of the short war, he advised the American Red Cross not to visit Kuwait only, but also the Baghdad Red Crescent. He accompanied senior officials of the American Red Cross to visit facilities in Baghdad and Basra, and the American Red Cross made a substantial donation to the Iraqi Red Crescent. Al-Hadid was voted 'man of the year' by the American Red Cross in 1992; in the same year he received the gold medal of the Iraqi Red Crescent; and he is currently a member of the Standing Commission of the Movement.

It was said that the Federation was offered its new Middle East regional headquarters in Bahrain on attractively subsidized terms, with the support of other Gulf states, but the Federation insisted on opening in 1993 in Jordan. This was mainly to support the major relief operation to Iraq that was coordinated from Amman, but also partly because of the relative stability of the country and its good communications, and no doubt partly because of the good record of the JNRCS. Other observers complain that, in common with some other National Societies, the JNRCS is too concerned with prestigious projects and not enough with the more humdrum side of the Movement, particularly dissemination of humanitarian principles; and that little effort is made to develop the JNRCS into a genuinely grass-roots organization.

Many of the National Societies all over the world have to struggle with the tension between their role as auxiliaries to their governments and the strategic aim of building up grass-roots networks. It is particularly difficult for them to successfully identify the needs of the most vulnerable in societies where governments enjoy little public trust – which is the case in nearly all Arab-Islamic states today.

The Federation's development plan

The Federation adopted in 1993, in Birmingham, a Strategic Work Plan for the Nineties whose stated 'challenge' was 'improving the situation of the most vulnerable'. This was a massively ambitious programme in principle, for the 'most vulnerable' include women, children, the elderly, people living in earthquake and flooding areas, refugees, those affected by HIV, and many other categories. Each National Society would contribute a national profile and these would be consolidated into a 600-page 'development book' which would be used by the Federation for cross-national fund-raising. It was proposed that each branch of each National Society should undertake a vulnerability analysis. Already the branch in Salt had done so in its fashion, by keeping a register of local families considered most likely to be in need.

In recent years, a new Strategy has been endorsed for the whole Movement, and the cumbersome plan for a 'development book' has been replaced by the Internet.

Jordan, because of the National Society's specific top-down organization and the whole country's conspicuous lack of a middle class, is unlikely to be the copybook example in the Middle East. The Federation points rather to Iran (see above) or to Syria, where there is a strong branch network and successful local fund-raising – for which the Syrian Red Crescent has permission from the government which is granted to no-one else (no doubt for fear of Islamist penetration). Affluent Syrians give a proportion of their olive harvest (5 or 10 per cent) to Syrian Red Crescent offices for collection and distribution to the poor.

However, throughout the Middle East the president of each national society does tend to be the be-all and end-all, and the issue of democratic procedures has to be played down. Cancelling the elections of a local branch would be headline news in, say, Scandinavia or Britain, but is normal in the Middle East. Yet this is perhaps more a matter of cultural style than substance. In Europe and America, too, charities can be vehicles for the expression of personal ambitions, whether on the part of retired public servants or wealthy private individuals; and a theoretically democratic structure can be of less practical import than the authority exercised by a powerful chief executive over communications and appointments.

Jordan's part in the International Movement

A significant part in the history of the Movement in the late twentieth century was played by Ahmed Abu-Goura, who was Secretary-General of the JNRCS from 1951 to 1964, then President until 1992, and also for a time President of the Standing Commission of the Movement.

When I interviewed Senator Abu-Goura, a radiologist by profession, he was living in retirement in the Jordan Valley, having handed over the Presidency to his son-in-law, Al-Hadid. He had been specially identified with the gradual inclusion of the cumbersome but equitable reference to the Red Crescent in the full names of the International Movement and of the Federation. For many years, the Red Crescent and the Red Lion and Sun had been referred to only in brackets. In 1981, Jordan represented by Abu-Goura pushed through the inclusion of the Crescent in the name of the International Conference. The inclusion of the Red Crescent in the names has resulted in some new problems, but has had a symbolic value in making a point against the ethnocentrism of the West. The name of the museum in Geneva, too, was changed at Abu-Goura's instigation to include the Red Crescent. Abu-Goura was also instrumental in founding the Secretariat of Arab Red Crescent and Red Cross Societies, which has helped to change the balance of elections to senior positions in the Movement.

Abu-Goura spoke critically of the ICRC in particular, not on account of its retention of the Red Cross alone in its name, but on account of its general resistance to change over the decades. He portrayed the ICRC as having a record of being against reform. It opposed, first, the use of the red crescent in the 1870s by the Ottoman Empire; second, the foundation of the League of Red Cross Societies in 1919, which was only made possible through pressure from the United States Government; and third, the inclusion of the Red Crescent in the name of the Movement. He was concerned that the ICRC is not able to undertake humanitarian acts freely, but has to ask permission from governments. That, according to him, is the weakness of the Movement, and is why other bodies such as Médecins Sans Frontières have risen to prominence over the last thirty years. He also contended that the ICRC has been much too late and cautious in protesting about flagrant violations of human rights, even when it had incontrovertible evidence – one example being the massacres of Palestinians at Sabra and Chatila by Christian Phalangists, with the connivance of the Israeli army, in September 1982. He contended that there was a serious question-mark over the ICRC's neutrality.

Abu-Goura's successor, Al-Hadid, was also critical of the ICRC but paid tribute to the high quality of its Swiss delegates, which he said was due to ICRC's being able to pay high salaries. The ICRC used to distance itself from the National Societies but was now reviewing this policy; it needed their support, partly because in the constitution of the Movement the ICRC has only one vote, as does each of the 169

National Societies. He also charged the ICRC with having a subconscious bias in favour of Western interests.

Abu Goura seemed to me clearly by temperament a master of the techniques of caucuses and committees, but less attuned to the practicalities of managing such a large and sensitive organization as the ICRC. It must be said that whereas the charge of bias against the Arab countries is regularly levied against the ICRC, there are also Israelis who maintain that the ICRC has a strong historical bias against the State of Israel. In defence of the ICRC, its task is so delicate as to make it unavoidable that it will sometimes make what are seen in hindsight as errors of judgment. Moreover, there is every reason to applaud that other organizations such as UNHCR and Médecins Sans Frontières should have grown up to respond to pressing humanitarian needs, provided that the special responsibilities of the ICRC are both properly carried out and also understood by governments and others. Most vitally, the ICRC is changing.

The Jordanian delegates may be seen as having performed a valuable service to the ICRC in representing the Arab point of view over the years, but in a fair and loyal way, respecting the fundamental ethos of the Red Cross and Red Crescent Movement. They have thus prepared the Movement and in particular the ICRC for criticism which was inevitable and which, but for them, might have been articulated from less moderate Islamic states in a harsh and destructive way – borrowing, for instance, from the rhetoric of the Sudanese Islamist, Hassan al-Turabi:

> ...The world today does not lack charitable organizations and missionaries who sometimes have no consideration for religion: for such people, their work is just a career with no connection with true charitable objectives and is simply a means to realize their personal objectives. Certain NGOs conspire against Islam in the name of charity.[21]

The Green Crescent Society

As already observed, the active role of the JNRCS in international committee rooms resulted in some neglect of its domestic tasks. Just as the Islamic states hatched the idea of the Islamic Crescent as an international complement or alternative to the Red Cross, so a group of Islamists in Jordan has founded a Green Crescent Society which is a challenge to the domestic position of the JNRCS. Its first president, the late Ahmed Qutaish Al Azaideh, and the current president, a prominent parliamentarian named Hamzah Mansour, have both been members of the Muslim Brotherhood.

This still tiny organization was launched in 1990 when a number of moderate Islamists set up the Islamic Relief Camp near the border camp between Iraq and Jordan, to provide basic services and medical aid for evacuees displaced from Kuwait and Iraq. It is claimed that 96,000 evacuees from many nationalities were helped. The camp workers set up a small clinic and put a flag on top of the tent, choosing a green crescent to distinguish it from the neighbouring Red Cross and Red Crescent clinics. Green is an evocative colour in Islam, associated with the gardens of the Paradise and also with the Prophet. Soon after the Gulf War, in April 1991, the Green Crescent Society was registered officially with the Ministry of Social Development. Its aims are to provide relief aid, educational bursaries and medical facilities. For instance, in March 1991, in collaboration with one of the international Islamic aid agencies, it organized relief for those in need after floods that struck the provinces of Tafilah and Karak; and it has sent relief aid to Bosnia. I visited the Green Crescent clinic in a back street of the small provincial town of Wadi Musa, near the tourist site of Petra.

The Green Crescent of Jordan has started partly because of the domestic weaknesses of the JNRCS and the country's chronic welfare needs, but also because of the Red Cross and Red Crescent Movement's commitment to non-confessionality. On the latter issue, a difference of view is inevitable between the Red Crescent's leadership and the Islamists. If any Red Crescent national society were to allow itself to be substantially influenced by Islamists, it would be at variance with the rest of the movement founded by Dunant, so that Al-Hadid's policy of secularism is the only logical one to follow. Yet for the Red Cross and Red Crescent Movement as a whole, the small clinic in Wadi Musa represents a new type of interlocutor throughout the region: and a change which the ICRC and the Federation are far-sighted enough not to belittle.

The Palestine Red Crescent Society (PRCS)

The earliest Red Crescent society in Palestinian territory was the Jenin branch, founded in 1948, but the name Palestine could not be used till 1968. When I visited in 1996, efforts were being made to mould a fragmented wartime-oriented organization into a genuine national body in the making, and it has indeed since then become one of the stronger National Societies, in the context of the intensifying conflict between Israel and the Palestinians. Half of the population of the Autonomous and Occupied Territories – some 3 million, 65 per cent in the West Bank and 35 per cent in Gaza – is registered as refugees, and a third live in refugee camps. Over the years, the PRCS headquarters were successively in Amman, Beirut, Cairo and Jericho, but now it has moved to Al-Bireh, north of Jerusalem, and there are twenty branches in Palestine – including East Jerusalem – as well as corresponding offices in Egypt, Syria and Lebanon that serve the interests of Palestinian refugees. Political importance is attached to the name Palestine rather than Palestinian. Efforts are made to maintain the society as a focus for cooperation between Muslims and Christians, and to promote an enthusiasm for voluntary work that had previously been strong in Palestinian society but was eroded during the Occupation.

The main commitment is the emergency and medical service. At the time of my visit in June 1996, there were still less than thirty ambulances for the whole of the West Bank with a population of 1.7 million, and radio control had only recently been introduced. Other priorities include youth development, primary and secondary health care, and rehabilitation of the handicapped. The programme includes a recognition of the importance of art and heritage in Palestinians' lives, as for instance in a project to preserve the tradition of embroidery which also has commercial potential.

In Gaza, next to one of the poorest refugee camps in Khan Younis, the PRCS has built the imposing Al Amal City (City of Hope) Abilities Development Centre, offering a range of services and facilities including a hospital, theatre, conference facilities, and Internet café and music and art workshops. It is described as an 'oasis in the bleak surrounding landscape', offering some symbolic as well as practical alleviation of Gaza's intense political and economic crisis aggravated by an exceptionally high birth-rate, with devastating repercussions for health and welfare. The PRCS cooperates extensively with overseas agencies, for example in youth exchange schemes with several European countries. As well as receiving support from abroad, it has itself provided relief aid to Sudan, Yemen, Iraq, Egypt and even one European territory, Kosovo, where the PRCS sent out a team of 18 medical professionals to set up a field hospital in cooperation with the Norwegian Red Cross.

Humanitarian politics in Palestinian relief aid today
The President of the PRCS was until recently Dr Fathi Arafat, Yasser's younger brother, and its development has been marked by local power struggles. Before the recent growth of the society, the ICRC had to protect it from threats of domination by both the Israelis and the Jordanians.

The PRCS has played a dramatic part in helping victims of the current Israeli-Palestinian conflict. On 3 April 2002, its president, Younis Al-Khatib, and eight other PRCS rescue workers were ordered out their ambulances by Israeli soldiers, strip-searched, handcuffed, blindfolded and detained under a freezing downpour for seven hours before they were released. Some PRCS paramedics have been killed while on duty, and many more injured. Justly or not, at the time of writing the Palestine Red Crescent has lost some credibility – most importantly, with the American government – after explosives were found in one ambulance. This reportedly gave the Israeli army a pretext for frequent seizing of ambulances and use of their crews as human shields, which is forbidden by the Geneva Conventions.[22] Cooperation between the Israeli MDA National Society and the PRCS is now inevitably under considerable strain, though in recent years the MDA has provided such expertise as training programmes for Palestinian ambulance drivers, and a memorandum of agreement was drawn up between the two societies in December 2000 agreeing on the importance of assistance for the wounded and sick.[23]

The ICRC set up that meeting, and it appears to have generally maintained the confidence of both sides during the heightening of conflict since September 2000. This has prompted it to embark on a strategic programme which it hopes may help it to overcome creatively a long-standing problem: the mismatch between the Movement's principle of universal humanitarianism and the principle of solidarity between Muslims, to which many of the National Societies in the region are probably more strongly committed than they are to the non-confessionality required by the Movement. The ICRC is also committed to disciplined evaluation of relief needs, as opposed to immediate reactions in response to media enthusiasm, and to doing as much as possible to defuse political tension by means of even-handed logistical effectiveness.

They have devised a 'voucher programme', initially funded by large generic grants to the ICRC from western governments, which has identified 20,000 specially vulnerable families in the Occupied Territories, with a list of strict criteria for eligibility such as single-parent households, handicap or advanced age, the list being drawn up by the Ministry of Social Welfare and local emergency committees, with built-in 'checks and balances' to minimize the risk of abuse. The value of each voucher is $90 per month, which can be converted into essential supplies such as food. Though weaknesses in the scheme may yet emerge – notably, the risks of vouchers being counterfeited, or of shops refusing to honour them – the ICRC's new scheme might be described as 'smart aid' since it is designed to bypass the political authorities and parties which always tend to make use of humanitarian aid for political purposes. At the time of writing, however, response from the National Societies in the region has been parsimonious: they have done little to supplement the funding provided from the West.

Why? There is still a lingering suspicion of the Cross as representing the West. More concretely, the ICRC's scheme offers the wealthier Arab states an alternative to the funding of welfare networks such as those provided by the Palestinian Authority or by Hamas – but one that would undercut a long-standing relationship of patronage and dependence. Some donors too would prefer the ICRC to go back to its 'core mandate' rather than carrying out aid operations.

Maintaining the integrity of the Movement

Contraventions of the ideals and principles of the Movement by National Societies are not exclusive to the Arab-Islamic world. They have occurred in Britain (see above) and domestic controversy has also afflicted the American[24] and French[25] Red Crosses. However, a new spotlight has fallen on Islamic charities since the attacks of 11 September 2001. The Red Crescent societies have not escaped this attention entirely.

The most specific of the allegations about abuse have been directed against the Saudi Red Crescent's activities between 1984 and 1992. It is undisputed that the American CIA bought arms for the Afghan resistance against the Russian army and that they were transported to Afghanistan by the Pakistani Inter-Intelligence Service. Allegedly, the Saudi Red Crescent was made use of to facilitate the transport of arms within Afghanistan itself, by providing a channel of finance for various Afghan political parties (Rubin 1997: 191[26], Rashid 2000: 131).

These allegations have never been formally considered by the ICRC or the Federation, and indeed it is not clear that any constitutional procedure exists for disciplining an errant National Society – short of expulsion by its peers, which has never been carried out. However, both the ICRC and the Federation have responsibilities for protecting the integrity of the Movement, and the issue came to the fore in the mid-1990s with the publication of a paper called 'Characteristics of a well-functioning National Society' and guidelines for regular reporting and self-assessment. As ever in the Movement, the preference is for dialogue rather than denunciation. Issues such as misuse of funds, or conflicts of interest affecting National Society leaders, are now more regularly ventilated than before, when questions of integrity were almost taboo.

The issue of protecting the integrity of National Societies is likely to press harder on the Movement in future.[27] The Saudi case does seem to be anomalous because there is no pretence at democratic procedures, and all the Society's funding is supplied by the government. The Saudi Red Crescent is in effect a sub-department of the Ministry of Health, with special responsibilities for overseeing the *hajj* and a close link with national security. The election in 1999 of its president, Dr Abdul Rahman A. Al Swailem, to membership of the Movement's supreme Standing Commission[28] is typical of the tensions that have grown up and the compromises applied to defuse them.

Conclusion

During the last decade or so, as an indirect result of regional conflicts, more Red Crescent societies have been willing to cooperate with the ICRC, whereas before there was a tendency to put religious solidarity first. Geneva officials are aware that the Movement's activities in the Arab-Islamic world are hampered by the region's deficits in mass education, in political freedom and participation, and in understanding of the value of intercultural dialogue and critical approaches. However, the Movement's relations with the region are considerably better than with much of the Southern Hemisphere. Two factors are of specially positive value: first, the huge money flows emanating from the Gulf states, and secondly, cultural traditions of generosity and empathy – now at risk of being undermined by the spread of intolerance, prejudice and religious fanaticism.

Tensions within the Movement do not abate. In October 2001, the Federation was obliged to instruct its Western representatives in Pakistan to keep the lowest possible profile in the towns of Quetta and Peshawar, since they were targets for anti-Western hostility. The summit meeting organized by Geneva with National Societies from Islamic countries, held in Ankara in the same month (see p.46 above) was not attended by some key countries (Egypt, Jordan, Lebanon, Syria, Saudi-Arabia and Bahrain), while for diplomatic reasons neither the Afghan Red Crescent nor the American Red Cross were invited (Hazan 2002). The failure to resolve the 'question of the emblem' contributes to the tensions. However, it would be naive to imagine that even when the Movement's name is changed to the 'Red Crystal', as may happen in the course of time,[29] the political tensions will automatically be resolved, for they run much deeper.

The ICRC and, in a more limited way, the Jordan Red Crescent have both played prominent parts in the 2003 Gulf War, which has still not been concluded as this book goes to press.

4

HELPING THE 'BROTHERS'

The medic, the militant and the fighter

The medic, the militant and the fighter

A cartoon is printed on the first page of Issam Daraz's book on the 'veterans of Afghanistan' (Daraz 1993). In the foreground: a bearded man in a dark *jallabiya*, a kalashnikov in position; close behind him, another bearded man holding the Quran in his right hand, apparently preaching; in the background, a third man, his beard trimmed like the others, carrying a doctor's case. The fighter, the militant and the doctor: these roles are presented as emblems of the commitment of individuals from Muslim societies who came to support the Afghan resistance after the Russian invasion in 1979. These forms of commitment are undertaken in the name of 'Islamic solidarity' (*al-ta'awun al-islami*) between Muslims as members of the *umma*, the community of all believers – though let us recall that the term *umma* is polysemic, and can also be used in the Arab world to refer to a nation in the modern sense of the word (Jadaane 1992, Bensaid 1987). 'Islamic solidarity' is neither mechanical, nor natural, but the result of the mobilization of governments or groups that invite Muslims to help their 'brothers' in religion, in the name of defence of the community. 'The body of believers is one, and when a part of it is unwell, it is the whole body that suffers': in the past two decades, this *hadith* has been repeated like a slogan to justify the mobilization of support for the Muslims of Afghanistan, Kashmir, Bosnia and Chechenia.

At the heart of these three types of engagement, 'Islamic relief' has developed as one of the manifestations of 'Islamic solidarity'. 'Islamic relief' is a translation of the Arabic term *ighatha islamiya* as used in the names adopted by several charitable organizations founded at the end of the 1970s and in the course of the 1980s: *haiat al-ighatha al-islamiya al-`alamiya* (International Islamic Relief Organization or IIRO, set up in 1979 in Saudi-Arabia); *haiat al-ighatha al-islamiya al-`ifriqiya* (Islamic African Relief Agency, set up in 1981 in Sudan); and again *al-ighatha al-islamiya* (Islamic Relief, set up in Britain in 1984). These organizations, which must be distinguished from the equally active Red Crescent Societies (see Chapter 3), have become established participants in the various fields of 'humanitarian crisis'.

* *by Jérôme Bellion-Jourdan*

These organizations represent a form of transnational militancy[1] at the contemporary interface where militant mobilization in the name of Islam meets international humanitarian action. More precisely, 'Islamic relief' is a mobilization of agencies in the Muslim world that refuse to leave the field of humanitarian action to agencies that are 'Western' or considered to be so (NGOs and international organizations), specifically in situations where the victims are identified as Muslims. This reaction to humanitarian agencies justifies the use of human and material resources to bring aid to victims, sometimes by means of a reappropriation of contemporary forms of humanitarian action. 'Islamic relief' both contests and reappropriates. And hence this reappropriation is not an imitation: these agencies ground their work in an Islamic tradition of commitment to those in need, which they mean to revive.[2] This commitment should not be too hastily characterized as 'charitable', in the Judaeo-Christian sense with its connotations of spiritual love, for the terms in which it is justified and defended by the agencies are grounded less in the sentiment of charity than in the desire for and need for justice (Boisard 1985: 436, and for a militant view see the works of Qutb summarized in Carré 1984).

During the two decades since the foundation of the first organizations of Islamic relief, the types of commitment and ways in which it is justified have developed to turn Islamic relief into one of the varieties of contemporary humanitarian action. (This Chapter is concerned with the international level of activities; for the work of Islamic associations at the domestic level see Chapters 1 and 5.) But initially, relief activities were part of a wider commitment in the name of 'Islamic solidarity': *ighatha* was a support activity only weakly differentiated from *da`wa* (militancy) or jihad. The latter term we will translate in this context as 'military action', though (like *umma*) jihad is a polysemic term referring to any 'effort' in the way of God (*fi sabil Allah*), military action being only one form of this effort; and it is imprecise to translate it as 'holy war'.[3] Thus the period of commitment during the first phase of the war in Afghanistan was marked by complementarity and a weak differentiation between medicine, militancy and military action. This was the period before the turning-point of April 1992 when the *mujahidin* (those who devote themselves to jihad, singular: *mujahid*) arrived in Kabul, and the war turned into a civil war among former allies (Rubin 1995, 1996).

Thereafter, whether by design or under constraint, some relief agencies were led to adopt a demarcation, if only partial, between relief activities on the one hand and *da`wa* and jihad on the other. Which raises the question of whether, in line with the trend observed in many international NGOs, Islamic relief agencies may have passed from the model of commitment or militancy to that of a humanitarian 'trade' marked by increased professionalization. As humanitarian action was professionalized, was it also depoliticized, and was its ideological content weakened? This phenomenon of differentiation from militant and para-military organizations marks the period of commitment on behalf of the victims of the war which broke out in Bosnia in April 1992, when some 'Islamic relief' agencies sought to conform with the dominant conceptions of humanitarian action.

Islamic relief agencies during the 1980s Afghan conflict in the service of jihad

The war in Afghanistan was a catalyst in the creation and development of these agencies. After the continent of Africa, it was the first great cause that mobilized support for Muslims in need. In Africa, the main concern had been to undertake relief and development programmes to bring *da`wa* to Muslim and non-Muslim populations. Such was the priority at the time of the founding in Khartoum of the Islamic African Relief Agency in 1981, as the humanitarian branch of the Islamic Call Organization (*munazzamat ad-da`wa al-islamiya* – see Chapter 7).

Private initiatives and political strategies
After the invasion of Afghanistan by the Soviet Union in 1979, the Afghan war was the object of considerable mobilization in the Muslim world: different agencies worked to make this war an 'Islamic cause' (*qadiya islamiya*). In Aghanistan itself, some of the resistance groups used the notion of jihad to justify the resistance of Muslims to the *kafir* (infidel) Soviet enemy. Seven Sunni parties were recognized among the *mujahidin* in Afghanistan. The more radical of them appealed for the support of the Muslim world: for instance, the Islamic Party (*Hizb i-Islami*) led by Gulbuddin Hikmatyar and the Islamic Union Party (*Ittihad i-Islami*) led by Abd al-Rabb Abd al-Rasul Sayyaf. In different parts of the Muslim world, and among Muslim minorities in Western countries, the appeals for support for the Afghan resistance were reinforced.[4]

One example from 1985 points up the transnational dimension of this mobilization. Yusuf al-Qaradawi, an Islamist intellectual of Egyptian origin teaching in Qatar (see pp.40-2), proclaimed in an interview published in Peshawar by the journal *Al-Jihad* that all Muslims were obliged to commit themselves, medically or militarily, in support of the Afghan resistance: 'Jihad is *fard 'ain* [an obligation for individuals, as opposed to *fard kefaya*, a communal obligation] for military and medical experts or anyone with a special skill that the *mujahidin* need. They should help the *mujahidin* in the field of their competence and capacity. In general, it is incumbent on all Muslims to provide material and intellectual help in order to live with them in the heart even if they cannot live with them in the body.'[5] Thus different types of commitment were appealed for: the doctor's, to care for bodies; the fighter's, to resist the enemy; the militant's, to ensure that the support is not merely material but aims at people's minds as well. This was the set of rationales that sparked off the origin and growth of the Islamic relief agencies.

The initiative came largely from private agencies whose mobilization in the Afghan cause was tolerated, even encouraged by certain Middle Eastern states that sought to make use of the cause to further political or strategic aims. At that time, Saudi-Arabia was seeking to counter the regional ambitions of revolutionary Iran. As it had already done when it created the World Islamic League in 1962 to counter Nasser's Egypt, Saudi-Arabia was compensating for the weak legitimacy of a Wahhabite Islam (Schultze 1990). This is the version of Islam developed by Abdul Wahhab (1703-87), limited as it is to the Saudi kingdom, which it is used to legitimate (Salame 1987, Fraser 1997). The Saudis sought an alliance with Islamic movements that have an international audience, in particular movements such as the Muslim Brothers in Egypt and Jama`at i-islami in Pakistan – inspired by nineteenth century Salafi reformism, which they altered significantly. Numerous differences separate the Wahhabi and the Muslim Brothers, but they have in common an allegiance to the strict school of Hanbalism, rejecting the difference between juridical schools of Islam and also, most importantly rejecting both Shi`ism and popular forms of religiosity (Roy 1998).

In addition to the Saudis' facilitation of arms supplies for parties of the Afghan resistance, by agreement with the United States (Rubin 1997, Yousaf 1991, Yousaf and Adkin 1993), the Saudi commitment was of three types. First, the creation of para-public structures of aid to Afghanistan, such as the Committee for Support for Afghanistan directed by Prince Salman, governor of Riyadh, and brother of King Fahd who had acceded to the throne after the death of King Khaled in 1982. Second, support from the World Islamic League (*rabita al-`alam al-islami*) and its humanitarian branch (IIRO) for the activities of Islamist movements in the region. And finally, encouragement of private initiatives of support for the Afghan jihad, as in the case of the Saudi, Usama bin Laden.

The context was doubly favourable for the financing of charitable activities. On the one hand, the sharp spurt in the price of oil at the time of the Ramadan/Kippur war in 1973 provoked a spectacular increase in the disposable revenue of producer countries. On the other hand, the emergence of 'Islamic economics' released considerable sums that had to be distributed. Islamic financial institutions were founded on the principle of forbidding *riba* (usury) and converted illegitimate funds into charitable works (see Chapter 2). Many ways were found to collect zakat (see Chapter 1). Even if the interpretations relating to the categories of beneficiaries of zakat are not unanimous, zakat can be used to support the activities of *ighatha*, *da`wa* and jihad.

Finance was thus guaranteed. Organization was provided mainly by Islamist movements, and first of all the different branches of the Muslim Brothers (*al-ikhwan al-muslimin* – see Chapter 1 p.64, Chapter 5 pp.88-9). In Kuwait, it was the Association for Social Reform (*jama`iat al-islah al-ijtima`i*), the social welfare branch of the Kuwaiti Muslim Brothers, which formed an international subsidiary to collect funds to help the Afghans: the Committee for the Islamic Call (*lajnat ad-da`wa al-islamiya*).[6] In Egypt, it was within the medical doctors' professional association (*niqabat al-atibba'*), largely controlled by the Muslim Brothers, that the pro-Afghan initiatives emerged. To start with, this association recruited and sent doctors to work in the various medical services of Islamic organizations on the Afghan-Pakistan border. Later, a specific agency was formed to organize relief, the Committee for Humanitarian Relief (*lajnat al-ighatha al-insaniya*).[7] The Egyptian authorities tolerated mobilizations of solidarity with the Afghan cause in so far as they channelled militants from the domestic political opposition into an external cause. Initiatives came too from agencies that mobilized populations of Muslim origin living as minorities in Western countries. Thus, in 1985, a collective of British associations founded the organization Muslim Aid.

As for Iran, it may be noted here that it produced no equivalent to the Islamic NGOs. It did support factions of Shi`a Afghans to stand up to Sunni groups, but Iranian commitment in the field was limited to the sending of *pasdaran* (Guardians of the Revolution) and the activity of some foundations (*bonyad*).[8]

Weak differentiation of roles

The group of organizations that were set up in Pakistan at the beginning of the 1980s aimed at supporting the jihad of Afghan resistance. The organizations were of three types. First, the *da`wa* organizations, which had a precise ideological mission: disseminating their conception of Islam among the Afghan refugees who flowed into the camps of the North Western Frontier Province (NWFP), especially in the outskirts of Peshawar. Sometimes in collaboration with the Afghan resistance parties or Pakistani Islamist movements (notably Jama`at i-Islami), these organizations had the role of spreading ideology among the refugees – all of them potential combatants in a war where the distinction between civil and military was being shattered. That was the case of the Saudi-based World Islamic League, the Kuwaiti-based Committee for the Islamic Call (which worked at first through an NGO of Canadian origin, Human Concern International), and the Organization for the Renewal of Islamic Tradition (*jama`iat ihya' al-turath al-islami*) – a Salafi association originating from Kuwait. There was frequent inconsistency between the organizations' different interpretations of Islam, particularly with regard to divergences between the Muslim Brotherhood and contemporary Salafi interpretations. Moreover, the *da`wa* of the 'Arab NGO' militants was often in conflict with local Islamic concepts and practices (Daraz 1993).

Then came the paramilitary organizations that were directly involved in the support of the Afghan combatants. This was notably the case of the Office for Services to the Mujahidin (*maktab khidamat li-l-mujahidin*) founded in 1984 by Abdallah Azzam, a militant Muslim Brother of Palestinian origin and doctor of jurisprudence at the University of Al-Azhar[9], who was to be killed in a booby-trapped car in November 1989. This Office was supported financially by Usama bin Laden, who had a diploma in economics and management from the University of King Abdul Aziz and was one of the sons of the construction magnate in Saudi-Arabia, head of the Ben Laden group of companies (Hubley 1997, Rashid 2000: 128-40). Convinced very early of the importance of supporting the Afghan resistance, the Palestinian and the Saudi joined forces to enable hundreds of young Muslims from different backgrounds to commit themselves to fight beside the Afghan *mujahidin*: those who were later to become known as 'freedom fighters' or 'Arab Afghans'. Based in Peshawar, but with branches in the United States and other countries, this Office was able to arrange logistics for the Muslim volunteers who came to join the front in Afghanistan. Volunteers were often housed in Martyr Houses set up as part of humanitarian programmes of the Ben Laden Foundation run by a Frenchman of Algerian origin (Ghandour 2002: 13). The volunteers mainly joined the ranks of Hekmatyar's *Hizb i-Islami* and Sayyaf's *Ittehad i-Islami*. Abdallah Azzam and bin Laden were initially close but seem to have separated following disagreement as to whether the Arab volunteers should be separately organized or fight alongside the Afghan *mujahidin*. It was this disagreement that led bin Laden to found his own organization, Al-Qa`ida.[10]

Finally, relief (*ighatha*) organizations developed their activities mainly in the medical field: installing hospitals and medical clinics, supplying medicines and medical equipment, and so forth. The Kuwaiti and Saudi Red Crescent societies were specially active from the beginning of the 1980s, mainly in Peshawar and Quetta. Subsequently, NGOs originating from Saudi-Arabia (IIRO), Sudan (Islamic Relief Agency), Egypt (Human Relief Agency) and Britain (Muslim Aid) opened offices in Pakistan and ran hospitals and clinics on the Afghan-Pakistani border. Like Western organizations, they worked with foreign staff in leadership and management roles, with recourse to local recruitment, Pakistani or Afghan, for the other posts. The administrative positions were therefore filled by expatriates, mainly from Sudan, Saudi-Arabia, Algeria and Syria. Most of the medical posts went to Egyptians. The main beneficiaries of these organizations' work were the Afghan refugees who had fled their country and settled in the refugee camps near the Afghan-Pakistani border. Combatants wounded at the front were also cared for in the medical facilities provided by these organizations.[11]

The distinct character of the three types of commitment (*da`wa, jihad, ighatha*) must be qualified. For one thing, most of these organizations fell under a coordinating body, the Council for Islamic Coordination (*majlis al-tansiq al-islami*). Planned by the Saudi and Kuwaiti Red Crescent societies, ISRA (the name used by the Islamic African Relief Agency for its network of offices outside the African continent), and the World Islamic League, this body was formed in 1986 and united most of the Islamic organizations supporting the Afghan jihad, regardless of their form of support.[12] Moreover, there was no real specialization of tasks. A *da`wa* organization also did *ighatha*: the *Lajnat ad-Da`wa al-Islamiya* built hospitals. An organization for supporting jihad intervened in the field of *ighatha*: the *Maktab al-Khidamat* organized food convoys that went inside Afghan territory to join the front lines. Finally, a relief organization such as ISRA invested in *da`wa* projects to incite Afghans to support jihad actively. Thus, in a 'memorandum on the future of teaching in Afghanistan' outlining the 'danger of leaving teaching to the agents of Moscow in Kabul or to Western religious organizations', the director of ISRA's office in Peshawar justified the commitment of his organization in the education sector, writing that 'teaching is the strongest weapon, after faith in God, in the sacred struggle'.[13] The militant training of minds was considered, above and beyond material relief, as a tool necessary for military victory. 'Islamic relief' was not merely an action of relief for victims, but part of a total commitment to the support of a political cause with a strong religious component.

Relations with Western NGOs: defiance and competition

During the 1980s, relations between the 'Arab NGOs' and the Western ones were marked by defiance. The Islamic NGOs, and the Islamist parties of Afghan resistance, condemned the activities of the Western humanitarians, attributing to them activities they considered harmful to Afghan society. In a conflict characterized by an intense 'politicization of humanitarian aid' (Baitemann 1990), the Western NGOs were accused of supporting the most moderate political parties: the French NGOs, for instance, were considered to be supporters of Ahmed Shah Masood. On the cultural level, the Western humanitarians were suspected either of missionary activities or of introducing norms and practices that were illegimate as regards Muslim Afghan populations. In one of these writings on jihad published in the 1980s in Peshawar, Abdallah Azzam, director of the Office for Services to the Mujahidin, denounced the work of missionary organizations. In a section devoted to the question of the health of Afghan refugees, Abdallah Azzam asks: 'Who is facing this dramatic situation? It is the missionaries, because wherever poverty, ignorance and illness are to be found, missionaries are there. And so groups of missionaries (*al-mubashirun*) bearing different names have come to settle in Peshawar'.[14] The image of the humanitarian remained that of the missionary. Lack of understanding, even hostility, ruled between the two 'humanitarian' worlds, which ultimately communicated little with each other (Bitter 1994).

In *Le Malheur des Autres*, the book published by the prominent pioneer of humanitarianism 'without borders', Bernard Kouchner recalls that he could not understand how certain Afghans, invoking their cultural traditions, prevented Western doctors from coming to the sick-beds of Afghan women (Kouchner 1991).

At the international level, a body had been formed to federate and encourage initiatives in the field of *da'wa* and relief: the World Islamic Council for Da`wa and Relief (*al-majlis al-`alami li-l da`wa wa-l-ighatha*). Founded in Cairo in 1988 at the height of the Afghan war, this Council was characteristic of the overlap of governmental and non-governmental Arab organizations in the support of Islamic activities outside the Arab world. The membership included the Ministries of Religious Affairs of several Arab countries such as Saudi-Arabia, Kuwait, the United Arab Emirates, Qatar and Egypt, and para-statal organizations such as the International Islamic Relief Organization (IIRO), but also organizations close to Islamist movements such as the Sudanese Da`wa Islamiya, close to the National Islamic Front; the Human Relief Agency, close to the Muslim Brothers of Egypt; and several Kuwaiti organizations either close to the Muslim Brothers (the Committee for Islamic Da`wa), or to the Salafi movement (the Organization for the Renewal of Islamic Tradition). One of the founding principles of this coordination system reads: 'the foundation of a wide communication network connected to a unified direction center so that this center shall duly become a pressure source for supporting such Islamic causes as Palestine, Bosnia and Kashmir and others [...]'[15] In a sense, the World Islamic Council was to be an equivalent of the Peshawar-based Islamic Coordination Council but with a scope extended to the world.

In their activities in Afghanistan, the Islamic NGOs were not completely isolated and there were some attempts at coordination on the ground. Thus, the director of the Sudan-based Islamic Relief Agency (ISRA) took part actively in setting up a body coordinating different humanitarian agencies: ISRA was part of the organizing committee for the Afghan Coordination Body for Afghan Relief (ACBAR) – though, admittedly, that was as far as cooperation went. Moreover, several Islamic NGOs have worked in partnership, on specific projects, with international organizations such as UNHCR (the UN's High Commissioner for Refugees), WHO (the World Health Organization) or WFP (the World Food Programme).

Cooperation in the field could often be inhibited by the negative attitudes to Westerners shown either by local workers or by their managers in headquarters. On the other hand, some heads of Islamic relief organizations and some Afghan Islamist militants have acknowledged the professionalism of Western NGOs. The experience of the Afghan war led to a recognition of the ineffectiveness of Islamic organizations by comparison with their Western equivalents: though decried for their political activities or their missionary dimension, Western 'humanitarians' were respected for their effectiveness. Thus there was acknowledgment of the commitment of Médecins Sans Frontières who did not hesitate to go forward and take risks inside Afghan territory, whereas the Islamic agencies remained concentrated on the Afghan-Pakistani border.[16]

Progressively, the Islamic relief agencies began to aim at professionalism and effectiveness. At the beginning of the 90s, and perceptibly at the time of the Bosnian war, this option in favour of professionalism resulted in a demarcation from militant and military activities. From now on, some Islamic NGOs foregrounded the image of the medical doctor: the images of *da`wa* and jihad did not disappear, but could no longer figure at the heart of organizations that were seeking recognition and legitimacy as 'humanitarian'.

Islamic relief agencies since the 90s: a problematic move towards 'humanitarianism'

The start of the 1990s marks a turning-point in the history of 'Islamic relief'. A succession of events during 1990-92, though not apparently linked to humanitarian action, had consequences for Islamic relief organizations. Two main developments may be traced from that period: a policy to demarcate them from political or paramilitary activities, and a wish to professionalize and accept effectiveness as an indispensable condition of recognition for any 'humanitarian agency'. These two developments did not apply to every organization, and often they provoked tensions and resistance within organizations as much as in their environment. Specialization in humanitarian action and in aid to victims came sometimes to be perceived as an abandoning of the commitment to support 'Islamic causes'.

Restriction to relief activities as opposed to militancy and militarism

Several factors obliged the relief organizations to demarcate their field from political and paramilitary activities. Local processes led to global political reorientations that, in turn, had repercussions for the organizations in their different sites of intervention. Thus, during the period of the 1990-91 Gulf War, there was an upset in the relationship between the principal states of the Middle East and certain Islamist movements: the latter denounced the participation of Muslim countries such as Saudi-Arabia and Egypt in the coalition led by the United States to repulse Saddam Hussain, whose troops had invaded Kuwait in August 1990. Saddam's appeals to jihad did not succeed in winning over many Islamists who knew his Ba'ath party to have little time for religion, but nonetheless the Gulf War was a period of crisis for the informal alliance between the United States, Saudi-Arabia and the Islamist movements (Piscatori 1991). Symptomatic of this upset was the personality of the *mujahid* Usama bin Laden, that former right hand of Saudi-Arabia in Afghanistan who became the chief instigator of the campaign against the Saudi monarchy on the grounds that it had allowed the land of the two Holy Places (*al-haramain*, Mecca and Medina) to be violated by infidel foreign troops.[17]

Within this regional development was a local dimension too. After the entry into Kabul and the victory of the *mujahidin* in April 1992, the Afghan conflict turned into a civil war between factions that had been allies. Disappointed by the way that jihad turned out, numerous Arab combatants left the front and considered the question of their redeployment. The redeployment of the former combatants took three main forms. Some left Afghanistan to join other fronts of the jihad, such as Tadjikistan, Kashmir and Bosnia. Others embarked on small businesses such as beekeeping and selling honey. The third group were employed by Islamic organizations in Peshawar.

The former 'freedom fighters' were again seen as political militants capable of sustaining the internal opposition in their countries of origin. Moreover, a new generation of militants came to be trained, ideologically and militarily, in the training camps on Afghan soil.

States in the Arab world (mainly Saudi-Arabia, Egypt and Algeria) used the redeployment of former combatants into humanitarian action for their own purpose: to justify an increasing control over charitable organizations. During this period, the fear of an Islamist takeover, the so-called 'Islamic threat', has been used by Arab regimes to deepen their system of repression in order to remain in power (Leca 1997, Salame 1994). Internally, the authorities have cracked down on Islamist or alleged Islamist militants in an attempt to silence an opposition likely to threaten the ruling elites. On the international scene, they have exerted pressure on other states to have the militants abroad forcibly returned to their countries of origin. From now on, these were praised no longer for their noble support for the Afghan jihad, but condemned – whether justly or not – for giving cover to political or 'terrorist' activities. (In the Middle East, as elsewhere, the term terrorist, in Arabic *irhab*, carries a highly evaluative connotation, for the 'terrorism' denounced by one may be another's 'political struggle'. An organization such as Hamas in Palestine has been variously characterized as 'terrorist' or part of a 'resistance movement' at different times and from different viewpoints.)

These pressures from Arab Ministries of the Interior resulted in two forms of control. The first, a time-honoured one, was a temporary decrease in the public funding of charitable organizations, followed by a policy of stricter control over their funding. Hence at the time of the Bosnian war, the Egyptian authorities accused the Human Relief Agency of acting as a front, through its international network, for the activities of the Egyptian armed group Al-Jihad (Shaqiq 1995).

The second means of pressure was the recourse to massive arrests, which often came to be seen as abusive. Hence, from 1992 onwards the Pakistani government of Nawaz Sherif yielded to the injunctions of Arab states and the United States (converted henceforth to the same 'anti-terrorist' policy), by making a number of arrests among the staff of the Islamic organizations on the Afghan-Pakistani border. As part of a campaign to check up on the activities of the NGOs in Peshawar and Quetta, a hundred individuals of Arab origin linked to the NGOs were arrested in April 1993.[18] The protests of the Pakistani Islamist parties were not enough to mollify the Pakistani authorities. On the contrary, they followed through their policy of repression, which finally forced several organizations to scale down their activities or leave Pakistani soil, as in the case of Muslim Aid in July 1993.[19] The counter-offensive after the 11 September 2001 attacks allowed US forces to enter Afghanistan and take the lead themselves in a massive crackdown on possible 'terrorist' suspects. They disposed of the Taliban regime, which had acted since 1996 as a protector of Arabs, including Usama bin Laden, in Afghanistan. Simultaneously, US forces proceeded to arrest hundreds of foreign nationals, including Arabs who used to work for Muslim charities. Some have been detained in Afghanistan and others deported to the 'X-Ray' camp at the US base of Guantánamo Bay, Cuba. The fate of Usama bin Laden, key target of the United States, remains unknown at the time of writing.[20]

As a consequence of these pressures, the Islamic organizations which intended to carry on had to prove the strictly 'humanitarian' character of their activities. They had to come terms with the dominant conception of 'humanitarianism', a form of action that seeks to be distinct from both the political and the military. And so they adopted the standard discourse of international humanitarian action, common to NGOs and international organizations, which mentions only relief (*ighatha*) and 'development'. *Da`wa* and jihad are terms which disappeared from the forefront of leaflets and reports of those organizations that, from now on, sought recognition on the international scene. Pressures coming not only from Arab but from Western authorities encouraged certain organizations to play this humanitarian card. (Yet some organizations, presenting themselves often as exclusively charitable, also pursued political activities, as in the case of the Maktab al-Khidamat in Peshawar, whose weekly publication *Sada al-Jihad* showed how active this body remained in supporting various 'Islamic causes' affecting the Muslim world.)

Up till this point, only a few organizations had sought this international recognition: a notable exception was Islamic Relief Agency, which, thanks to its President's career, had tried since the 1980s to be recognized as a humanitarian agency (see Chapter 6). It was this idea, till then peculiar to ISRA, that in the 1990s was adopted by several Islamic relief organizations. The British-based organization Islamic Relief is a striking example of the importance which was now to be given to 'humanitarian' recognition.

This organization, founded in 1984 in Birmingham,[21] had a particular period of growth at the time of the Bosnian war. Islamic Relief adopted a twofold identity, Islamic and humanitarian, which allowed it to combine different forms of support. The Islamic aspect emphasized a communitarian spirit at two levels. On the one hand, it made use for fund-raising of Muslims' obligation to give zakat and, according to their means, the voluntary gift of *sadaqa* and also *qurbani*, the money which makes possible the distribution of sacrificed meat on the occasion of the annual `id al-adha or `id al-kabir. On the other hand, the organization collected funds for Bosnia to help the Bosnian Muslim community, members of the *umma* who had become victims of Serb aggression. Simultaneously, Islamic Relief developed a humanitarian discourse with a universal dimension. It took part, in the same way as British organizations such as Oxfam or Save the Children, in fund-raising campaigns launched by the London daily newspaper *The Independent*; it stressed that its aid was distributed to all communities without distinction, benefiting Muslims but also Serbs and Croats. Thus the agency was presented in the British press as working for 'the deprived of all races and all religions'.[22] This Islamic relief organization foregrounded the universal reach of its programmes, a fundamental principle of contemporary humanitarianism.

Islamic Relief as well as other British-based Islamic charities have become partners of the authorities in the implementation of humanitarian programmes. With the support of the Department for International Development (DFID), Islamic Relief, Muslim Aid and the Muslim Council of Britain have launched in November 2001 *Target 2015: Halving World Poverty* marketed as something more than a 'soundbite' but a project that is 'part of a broad strategy to eradicate poverty and achieve greater global justice through economic growth, development assistance and advocacy for international, financial and trade rules that favour the poor in developing countries'. The glossy brochure further presents the project as 'a shared vision of reducing world poverty – British government and British Muslim charities working to realise the common good'. In the Summer 2002 issue of Muslim Aid's newsletter, *In Focus*, a photograph of Clare Short, Secretary of State for International Development, with two trustees, Tanzeem Wasti and Chowdhury Mueen-Uddin, provides the organization with a good asset to publicize Muslim Aid's recognition by the authorities as a partner in humanitarian and development activities.

The professionalization of organizations

Since the beginning of the 1990s, certain Islamic relief agencies undertook a policy of professionalization. We must relate this to a parallel development across the whole field of humanitarianism; if during the 1970s and 80s it was a commitment, it was progressively changed into a career or trade. Intention was no longer enough: the professional humanitarian was evaluated by results. For organizations such as Islamic Relief or Muslim Aid, professionalization was justified on the one hand by the proven ineffectiveness of certain operations and the wastage of human and material resources, and on the other by the need to adapt to the demands of the donors that funded programmes whose effectiveness had to be demonstrated.

Professionalization meant a demand for effectiveness and cost-benefit analysis. Islamic relief agencies had to face a widespread criticism of charitable organizations, which was that the costs of administration were too heavy, given their aim of bringing relief to those in need. Organizations were reproached for having excessive salary bills, which could be reduced by means of using volunteers. Replying to a criticism which alleged that the Muslim charities spent too much on administrative costs, Fadi Itani, then manager of the English office of Islamic Relief, defended the employment of professionals in the following terms in 1998: 'Have you ever seen a company run professionally exclusively by volunteers? Surely, when it is a charity which is working to save people's lives and responding to emergencies as they arise, it is even more important for it to be run professionally ... Therefore, we employ the minimum of staff needed to keep the charity running in an organised fashion which ensures that all the donations are utilised in the most efficient way possible'.[23]

This trend towards professionalization led to the setting up of policies on staff recruitment. In the profiles that the agencies were looking for, the emphasis was on the competence of candidates, not only on their commitment. This is borne out by the job advertisements and newsletters published by the Muslim charities based in the United Kingdom. Thus, Islamic Relief announced in its autumn 1995 newsletter that it was looking for enthusiastic staff and volunteers who wish to work in its Community and Training Centres in Albania, Bosnia and Sudan, with expertise in at least one of the fields of management and administration, information technology, teaching, social work and professional training. The candidates were invited to send a *curriculum vitae* and letter of application to the project leader in the Birmingham headquarters. Applicants for such work were more and more considering it as professional experience with a view to a career in the humanitarian field or, more generally, in an international organization. Thus, when I met him, the development officer with Muslim Aid, who had a master's degree in development studies, considered his job in the London organization as a step towards an international career in the United Nations.

And so militant commitment was no longer enough to become a participant in Islamic relief. But this policy of professionalization did not avoid all obstacles. For instance, Mahmood al-Hassan became executive director of Muslim Aid in 1993,

and, with his training and experience, wanted to make it an effective agency run by
qualified and competent people. A Pakistani by origin, he had obtained a master's
degree in Business and Administration (MBA) in 1982, supplemented after his arrival
in Britain by an MA in management at Imperial College, London. Having worked in
the banking sector, he had some experience first in Islamic Relief before becoming
director of Muslim Aid: his commitment to the organization was not 'purely to help
the poor', but, as he put it, 'I do it as a job'. Stressing this point, Mahmood al-Hassan
acknowledged during the interview that his activity had little to do with the kind of
commitment shown by a personality such as Edhi, the extraordinary Pakistani
philanthropist (Edhi 1996 and see above, pp.18-19). In 1998, he had been striving
for two years to reform the organization through recruiting professional staff. There
were two difficulties, one external and one internal. One of the difficulties was the
short supply of suitably qualified candidates among British Muslims. To this external
factor was added an internal factor that put a brake on, or even blocked, the process
of professionalization. Within the organization, al-Hassan was not free in his actions,
for a board of trustees had oversight of it and defined its broad strategy. This dual
control was a source of tension because, while he defended his policy of
professionalizing the agency, he came up against trustees who had no qualifications
in the relief and development field.[24]

For the most part, the trustees are not humanitarian professionals, but dignitaries
or leaders of the British Muslim community, who owe their positions to their having
taken part in the launch of the organization Muslim Aid. The profiles of the two
chairmen since its foundation illustrate this point. The first, between 1985 and 1996,
was the former rock singer, Cat Stevens. After his conversion to Islam at the end of
the 70s, Cat Stevens – now known as Yusuf Islam – embarked on the development
of a system of private Islamic schools in the United Kingdom, and was very active in
generating support for Afghan jihad, to which he devoted some songs such as
'Afghanistan, Land of Islam'. Then he took the lead in the committee that founded
Muslim Aid. In 1996, Yusuf Islam resigned from the chair to devote himself to the
development of the network of Islamic schools in the United Kingdom. He was
succeeded by Suhaib Hassan, who had a different profile but was just as remote
from humanitarian action: born in Pakistan, he studied at the Islamic University of
Medina. Having taught in a *madrasa* in Kenya, he settled in Britain in 1976 and there
he founded the Al-Qur'an Society, taught the Quran and wrote brochures.

Thus a singer converted to militantism was succeeded as head of Muslim Aid by
an intellectual working on religious education in the heart of the British Muslim
community. In an interview given to the weekly *Q-News* after his appointment,[25]
Suhaib Hassan himself admitted he was not in the best position to be chairman of a
charitable organization such as Muslim Aid; he said he had confidence in the
executive director to develop the organization's policy. Nonetheless, the board of
trustees often had a contradictory approach to the running of the organization. The
good intentions of the trustees – that the proceeds of donations should go to the
deprived – would tend to minimize the organization's running costs, and in
particular the salaries; such a policy would conflict with the pragmatism of the
professional, for whom too low a level of salaries would prevent the recruitment of
competent staff. As a direct consequence, Muslim Aid found it impossible to fill five
posts advertised as part of a recruitment campaign in 1997. This internal conflict

between militant founders and professional managers is symptomatic of the development of 'Islamic relief'. Does professionalization mean the end of militant commitment? Professionalism and militantism are not necessarily contradictory, for professionalism can be a tool in the service of militantism, a militantism transformed. Yet the result is that the legitimacy of these organizations is questioned both within them, and by others who have remained committed to the support of 'Islamic causes'.

A 'job' obeying 'humanitarian principles'?
The depoliticization and professionalization of Islamic organizations that were initially committed to forms of solidarity with Muslim victims has evidently not been without difficulties. The tensions resulting from this transition from 'Islamic solidarity' to 'Islamic humanitarianism' has been at two levels. Within the agencies themselves, there has been generally a lack of consensus as to whether to halt or continue projects for Islamic renewal in the regions concerned, such as the building of mosques or Islamic schools, distribution of Qurans and religious literature, and *da`wa*. Some staff in the agencies would have been ready to give up this type of activity to concentrate their funds on projects that were strictly humanitarian: the distribution of rations and medicines, and the setting up of health systems. In reality, the Islamic relief agencies continue to pursue religious activities. They serve as intermediaries for philanthropists who give the money necessary to build a mosque. Above all, their programme of material aid has often retained a strong religious dimension: distribution of the zakat *ul-fitr* (or *fitranah*) at the festival which marks the end of Ramadan (`id ul-fitr*), and distribution of sacrificed meat in the ritual of *qurbani* at the end of the Feast of Sacrifice (`id ul-adha). Without a doubt, the programmes of Islamic relief agencies retain a strong communitarian character, symbolically binding Muslim donors and beneficiaries. Yet the agencies campaign to rebut any allegations that they support political activities, defending their position as strictly humanitarian.

When some British organizations were suspected of supporting the Palestinian movement Hamas, their leaders responded sharply, asserting that they only supported welfare programmes such as hospitals in Palestine.[26] It is not uncommon for Muslim relief organizations to launch legal proceedings against media groups that have asserted that these charities are a cover for political or military activities. During the Bosnian conflict, the Birmingham-based Islamic Relief accused the French monthly magazine *La Vie* of having done the organization harm. At stake was a photograph showing Bosnian beneficiaries under a streamer labelled 'Islamic Relief', the caption stating that 'certain Islamists use food to blackmail' (6 August 1993). *La Vie* conceded a right to reply, which Islamic Relief used to portray itself as an 'international humanitarian organization' committed to helping the poor and relieving distress worldwide without any distinction of race or nationality' (22 June 1995). More recently, in the aftermath of 11 September 2001, Muslim relief organizations launched many libel cases against newspapers after they made allegations about links between charitable and 'terrorist' activities. Whatever may or may not remain of links with political or military activities, these legal cases are evidence that humanitarianism has become the norm of reference.

In turn, this development of the agencies towards the 'humanitarian' leads to internal problems and lands them in a critical situation with regard to their traditional bases of support, and more generally with regard to other militant Islamic organizations, as will be shown especially in Chapter 7. With this position of promoting humanitarian action and distancing themselves from military action, they ran the risk – for example, during the Bosnian war – of being assimilated to the policies of both Arab governments (Saudi-Arabia and Egypt) and Western ones (the United States, Britain, France). In fact, for a considerable period after the war broke out, the Western governments did little more than provide humanitarian aid to the Bosnians. Their lack of political, let alone military, involvement, shaping the policy of the United Nations (Weiss 1994: 21-2), was heavily criticized. Similarly, Muslim humanitarian agencies faced strong criticism from militant and para-military Islamic organizations that considered humanitarian programmes to be a weak form of commitment. These organizations criticized the policy of *ighatha* and called for a military commitment on behalf of the Bosnian Muslims against the Serb aggressor.

That was true of the Muslim Parliament of Great Britain. From 1992 onwards, the Muslim Parliament, which leaned towards the Iranian cause and was led at the time by Kalim Siddiqui, struck a position of support for armed jihad in Bosnia and criticism of organizations and states that limited themselves to humanitarian programmes. During the Bosnian crisis, the Muslim Parliament tried to mobilize an ultra-minority of Muslims dissatisfied with 'humanitarian' commitments, arguing that food and medicines were not enough to defend oneself with: 'Help Muslims to defend themselves!' In a special session of the Muslim Parliament on 19 June 1993, it decided to create an 'Arms for Bosnia' fund. [27] The British authorities decided to ban the purchase and transportation of arms for Bosnia, whereupon the Muslim Parliament decided to replace the Arms for Bosnia Fund by a Jihad Fund, which could not be attacked under English law because jihad has not only its military connotations but also refers to any effort carried out 'in the way of God'.

The image of the combatant was stressed because it made it possible to conceive of putting an end in the medium term to aggression and hence to its humanitarian consequences. The image of the medic was discredited as merely providing a short-term palliative to the suffering of the victims of an ongoing aggression. Thus, the organizations that abandoned the multidimensional conception of jihad which had prevailed during the Afghan war had to manage the tension between their militant heritage and their humanitarian programme. Playing the card of humanitarian recognition on the international scene, and defending the principle of universality in aid provision, ran the risk of criticism from militant Islamists, who continued to analyse political situations in a dichotomy of friends versus enemies, Muslim victims versus non-Muslim aggressors.

Cultural exceptionalism versus universal humanitarianism?

The depoliticization of some Islamic relief NGOs does not imply that they now imitate their Western counterparts and that they have abandoned their claim to be specific. In fact, these organizations tend to use their recognition in the international humanitarian system as a way to promote a specific form of humanitarianism, presumably rooted in the Islamic tradition of almsgiving and charitable activities.

The operations of Islamic humanitarian organizations are now often similar to those of Western humanitarian organizations, but they also intentionally compete with their Western equivalents in taking up the same types of project. Most of them take up the discourse of universal aid 'without distinction of nationality, race, religion or ethnicity', which had become a leitmotif in the international system of humanitarian aid. But their understanding of universality remains relatively different from the contemporary vision endorsed by secular human rights and humanitarian law and principles.

In the Islamic NGOs' vision of the world, there is a distinction between Muslims and non-Muslims; but that is not necessarily inconsistent with a universal conception of aid, which could be summed up as helping 'brothers' (Muslims) and 'potential brothers'. Working often in areas where Muslims and non-Muslims still live together, the Islamic agencies have practices that derived from debates about the legitimate use of zakat, the mandatory tithe. For some, zakat was collected from Muslims and could only be disbursed for Muslim beneficiaries, whereas *sadaqa*, the voluntary gift of alms, could be disbursed for anyone in need. For others, non-Muslims could be considered as the fourth legitimate beneficiary of zakat as laid down in the Quran: those whose hearts can be rallied (to Islam). That is the meaning of the fatwa delivered in September 1992 by Sheikh Abdul Aziz Abdullah bin Baz in Saudi-Arabia, to legitimate gifts from the Saudi High Committee for Somalia and Bosnia, an umbrella structure raising funds for relief in the war torn Somalia and Bosnia, notably financing the Saudi High Committee in Bosnia-Herzegovina (see Chapter 7): 'One finds in Somalia and Bosnia those who are not Muslims, but who are victims of disaster. It is licit to disburse zakat to them because they are those whose hearts can be rallied [*al-mu'allifa qulubuhum*] and therefore rightful beneficiaries of zakat'.[28] The quid pro quo for this entitlement was that the beneficiaries should receive an invitation or call (*da`wa*) to join Islam.

In a situation such as Bosnia, practical arrangements and theoretical justifications thus allowed Islamic humanitarian agencies to distribute their aid to non-Muslims. Yet practice in the field varied. Some agencies turned the Bosnian situation to their account by showing the universal character of their aid. For instance, the British branch of the Sudanese agency Islamic Relief Agency displayed, as an example of Muslim-Christian cooperation, a programme of support for a centre for the protection of women at Tuzla, organized in conjunction with the Methodist Church's Fund for Relief and Development.[29] On the other hand, other agencies reverted to the Islamic reading of the conflict – Muslim friends against non-Muslim enemies – to justify giving aid to Muslims only, the Serbs and Croats being treated as enemies. Thus, the Malaysian relief centre refused to undertake any work with the Croats and Serbs of Bosnia.[30] The intermediate position was that of organizations that came to the help of non-Muslims, but in order to improve their chances of converting them to Islam.

Developing within the international system of humanitarian aid, the Islamic NGOs often foreground their adherence to the principle of the universality of aid. And indeed, their own conception of aid allows them to conform to this principle, since helping Muslims as a priority does not prohibit giving help to non-Muslims. In a similar way, certain Islamic NGOs use their status as humanitarian organizations to act as defenders of Muslims' rights, sometimes with the credibility of being active in areas where personnel of other humanitarian agencies prefer not to take risks (Ghandour 2002: 333). They call on United Nations agencies and Western NGOs to recognize these rights as part of their programmes; but this defence allows them to reintroduce the idea of an Islamic norm incumbent on all Muslims. From 12 to 14 November 1994, in the middle of the Bosnian crisis and a few months from the Peking conference devoted to the rights of women, the Saudi International Islamic Relief Organization organized at Sharjah in the United Arab Emirates an 'international conference on uprooted Muslim women'. Under the co-direction of the UNHCR, this conference set out to 'defend the religious and cultural identity' of such women. The conference's recommendations sounded an attractive defence of the rights of Muslim women; but in reality, they revealed the set of Islamic duties which Islamic organizations sought to impose, or at least to spread, such as the (undefined) *shari`a* (Islamic law), Islamic dietary rules, religious rituals and Islamic teachings.[31]

Therefore, by no means should the evolution of Islamic relief organization be perceived as a process where depoliticization and professionalization would lead automatically to secularization. As pictured in a CNN programme broadcasted on 31 August 2002, the Birmingham-based Islamic Relief Worldwide is now described as a charitable organization as opposed to radical movements such as Omar Bakri's Al-Muhajiroon. The programme gave an overview of the activities of Islamic Relief, including its recent relief programmes in Afghanistan after the strikes by the American-led 'coalition against terror'. Here we have an organization praised for its humanitarian work, and there is no more talk about jihad and *da`wa*. What comes through clearly is the Islamic character of the organization, with images of staff fulfilling their religious obligations. In the same programme, the humanitarian legitimacy of the organization was further supported by footage of Prince Charles visiting the premises of the organization in London, and by an interview with a Charity Commission official who regretted that allegations are often made against such charities because they are 'Muslim' and most of the time without evidence.[32] This recognition by one of the most powerful international media represents without doubt a victory for Islamic Relief Worldwide. What remains to be seen is the strategy that Islamic relief organizations will adopt in negotiating their religious commitment within the international humanitarian system.

At least three scenarios can be envisaged: confrontation, integration or cooperation. The scenario of confrontation would lead to the promotion of an Islamic alternative to a universal humanitarianism, with a strong claim that secular humanitarianism should be challenged for its lack of cultural sensitivity and replaced by a communitarian approach based on the so-called 'cultural proximity'. The scenario of integration would imply that organizations continue to adopt and agree on universal and secularized principles, as some organizations have done by signing since 1994 a Code of Conduct for the International Red Cross and Red Crescent Movement and Non-Governmental Organizations (NGOs) in Disaster Relief.[33] Finally, cooperation would mean Islamic relief organizations' seeking to undertake joint activities, with other NGOs or international organizations such as UN agencies, on an ad hoc and pragmatic basis, without necessarily a firm agreement on principles. Strategies will continue to vary depending on the organizations and, as important, the context. Scenarios can be also linked: a phase of cooperation can lead to ultimate integration; strategic integration can be a preliminary stage for the ultimate aim of confrontation.

5

NGOs IN THE CONTEMPORARY MUSLIM WORLD*

Doing without NGOs?

Systematic communism and even its softer-edged sister, socialism, are in general retreat today, whereas in the Arab-Islamic world they have never attracted a high level of popular support. Almost certainly, these movements will be rediscovered in new formulations, but for the time being it is the hour of consumerist capitalism – challenged by only ill-coordinated protests. Hard-line state socialists opposed charity as a ploy to legitimate the undeserved privileges of the rich and reduce the pressure on politicians to promote redistribution (hence, in the idiom of Marxism, to slow down the inevitable proletarian revolution). This must be taken seriously as a tenable interpretation of much charitable activity as sponsored by some of the elites in the Arab-Islamic region; but in fact, they merely carry out these activities with less subtlety of style than their counterparts in the West.

To push this line of argument to its logical conclusion and outlaw all charity is, however, to place all power in the hands of the state. This was the policy of the former Soviet bloc since the earliest days of the Bolshevik revolution. The network of Russian charitable organizations was as far as possible abolished by the Soviets as inimical to the principles governing human relationships in a socialist state (Madison 1960: 536). Serious welfare crises and famines later forced the Communist regime to call on Russian and foreign philanthropic organizations for help, and after Stalin's death in 1953 official hostility towards philanthropy somewhat abated (Lindenmeyr 1998). The socialist government of Algeria followed a similar state policy for some twenty years after it won its independence.

I know of only one government in the non-Communist world that has until recently outlawed all independent charitable bodies, and that is the Sultanate of Oman. In that country, although the tradition of charitable giving by individuals to individuals is vigorous, not even a Red Crescent National Society – which in other neighbouring countries is invariably a conservative organization with close links to government – is yet allowed. An Omani informant told me that this is because the

* by Jonathan Benthall

political troubles in the late 1960s were initially ignited by charitable organizations. Whatever the truth of this, the fear of charitable agencies' potential involvement in politics is a reasonable one, in the regional context, for the Sultanate to entertain. When I visited Oman in 1996, a leading businessman had just succeeded in getting permission for the first charity in Oman to be founded, principally for the relief of poverty in rural Oman but also for disaster relief. It is a sign of the sensitivity of the issue that this charity, the Omani Organization for Charitable Works, was to be presided over by the Minister for Legal Affairs and managed by five other government nominees and six members from the private sector – so that its independence is evidently limited.

In virtually all other countries today, it is recognized that private charity has a legitimate and necessary function complementary to the services provided by the state. To an earlier generation of radicals, the drawbacks to private charity – the way it can aggrandize the donor and humiliate the beneficiary – sometimes seemed decisive objections. Nowadays, its offsetting advantages are widely recognized – especially its pluralism, and the personal commitment it can draw from individuals. Therefore doing without NGOs (Non-Governmental Organizations) is rarely considered a realistic option for governments today – even in a nominally Communist country such as Vietnam.[1]

Religious and secular charities in the West
No commitment to charity derives from the logic of shareholder capitalism. An older, more paternalistic tradition of stakeholder capitalists believed in a commitment to the wider community, and this has recently been revived in the new guise of abbreviations such as CSR (Corporate Social Responsibility). But Western charity emerged from a diffused civic or humanist morality. Many social theorists would argue that this depends on fundamental ethical principles such as 'do as you would be done by', enlightened self-interest, the greatest happiness of the greatest number, or universal human rights. All these principles can be traced back to the Enlightenment in the European eighteenth century, which was in many ways critical of religion. But they all have in common an assumption about the primacy of the individual soul or spirit which is deeply Judaeo-Christian, and which has in many ways survived the radical questioning of the definition of humanity prompted by Darwin's major works. On this reading, the anti-humanist atrocities conducted in the twentieth century in the names of Marxism-Leninism and Nazism were a direct result of two different attempts to supplant the European religious tradition: by, respectively, the atheist state and a form of neo-paganism.

The Christian faith has been an instigator or cause of aggression and war in the past as much as any other religion, despite the pacific message of the Gospels. However, it may be that some of the Western humanists who turned away from religious commitment, either because it seemed inconsistent with the findings of the natural sciences, or in a rejection of its exclusionary propensities, may have underestimated the extent to which a deep-seated Judaeo-Christian culture has underwritten the more civilizing Euro-American values. Raymond Firth the social anthropologist and humanist wrote, after a lifetime's reflection on these problems, that 'To profess a religion is no guarantee of a moral life. ... Morality can rest upon social foundations, without a concept of divine validation.' Yet he conceded. '...

[T]he creation of a moral system, which many individuals have managed for themselves, is nonetheless not an easy matter' (Firth 1996: 209, 211). A set of moral rules acceptable to philosophers is not the same as a set of rules that a broadly based community can accept and act by.

Many Western charitable institutions derive directly from historic religious sources, especially the schools, orphanages and hospitals founded since the Middle Ages (Moe 1961). Some of the most important international charities operating today are explicitly Christian (Caritas, Christian Aid, World Vision, Order of Malta) or strongly influenced by Christian values (Oxfam, Save the Children Fund, the Red Cross – on which last see Chapter 3). But one can go further and argue that the entire Western tradition of charity, resulting in today's enormous NGO sector, has historically deep religious roots that are not always noticed.

What would be left of the charitable tradition, it may be asked, if its religious vestiges were effaced? Would we be left just with charity balls for the rich, and state lotteries for the poor? Formal religion is still a powerful influence in organized charity in the West; but in many Western countries, despite vigorous local manifestations of religious revival, there is an overall trend towards progressive secularization (Payton 1989). The United States seems to be an exception to some extent, but even there social researchers have diagnosed a sharp drop in charitable giving and volunteering during the last third of the twentieth century, and a more self-interested and controlling motivation in current philanthropy – with the striking exception of the Jewish-American community (Hamer 2002: 169-86, Ostrower 1995). One response by charities to secularization is for their fund-raising to become gradually a branch of consumer merchandising in which the various motives for charitable giving are skilfully played on (Benthall 1993, Chapter 2).

To some extent, formally religious traditions of morality have been replaced by principles of humanitarian aid, human rights, women's rights, children's rights, labour standards and so forth, which are intended to be universally acceptable. However, when these are analysed they turn out to be heavily loaded with ideological assumptions (cf., from the point of view of the Arab-Islamic region, Dwyer 1996, and for a collection of essays disputing the fallacies of naïve 'secularization theory' in a Middle Eastern context see Tamimi and Esposito 2000). These non-confessional, universalizing sets of principles are the best we have and are available for strategic use by campaigners all over the world. When they are rejected by non-Western governments as being Eurocentric and one-sided, this is often because they are challenging to these governments' policies (Mayer 1999). On the other hand, universalistic principles are often invoked to legitimate Euro-American *Realpolitik*. Moreover, one would not expect them, being relatively recent in history and formulated by cosmopolitan elites, to have a deep grounding in popular culture.

Hence the interest of examining the charitable traditions of the world religions other than Judaeo-Christianity. Historians have given considerable attention to European charities and attempts to relieve poverty since the Middle Ages (e.g. Geremek 1994), but are only beginning to extend this attention outside Europe.

The religious determinant in Islamic charity

A prominent early twentieth century anthropologist aptly wrote that 'Real progress is progress in charity, all other advance being secondary thereto' (Marett 1935:40).

Progress in the comparative academic study of charity has been slow; for an attempt at synthesis we have to go back to as early an anthropologist as Westermarck (1908). Historians of colonization have also made stimulating contributions. For instance, Sanjay Sharma's monograph on famine and philanthropy in early nineteenth century northern India shows that the British authorities, in the process of adopting new interventionist policies to confront numerous scarcities and famines, systematically depreciated as 'ostentatious' or 'superstitious' the indigenous traditions of philanthropy, both Muslim and (especially) Hindu, which were in fact deeply embedded in Indian society. One result, which endured into the period after Indian independence, was to sharpen the distinction between the 'deserving' and 'undeserving' poor; another was that formal voluntary associations gradually took the place of more personalized practices. This reflected a similar policy of institutionalization of charity that was implemented in Britain itself (Sharma 2001: 135-92).

The present book addresses in particular the politics of charity in Muslim countries. A specific reason for studying Islamic organized charity is that, as is well known, the Islamist movements, especially in the Middle East and North Africa, have achieved their salience and popular support through blends of religious, political and welfarist activism. While some intellectuals and activists who reject the priorities of Islamism see secular politics as the only hope for the region, others reject this as a 'mirage' and identify the true political challenge as being that of trying to capture the symbolic imagination of the same populations who are targeted by the militants (An-Naim 1996: 125-6). This may still be a useful inference to draw from the current political crisis in the region, even though political Islam has probably been weakened through withdrawal of support for the cause by the devout middle classes, alarmed by the activities of its violent wings (Kepel 2002a).

In southern Lebanon during the 1980s when the state collapsed, Hizbullah stepped in to provide a wide range of social, educational and health services for the Shi`ite community. Studies of Arab Israeli villages (Israeli 1993a) and of the voluntary sector in Egypt (ben Néfissa 1995, Ibrahim 1988, Rugh 1993, Sullivan 1992) testify that, relatively speaking, Islamist voluntary associations are capable of delivering effective welfare and relief services in certain contexts where the state has been unable or unwilling to provide them. After a serious earthquake in Cairo in 1992, killing some 500 people, the Muslim Brothers took a leading role. Again, when Egypt was hit by serious floods in November 1994, the government's response was slow and ineffective. It was the Muslim Brothers and similar organizations which gave refuge in the mosques to families who had lost their roofs (Ayeb 1995). In the late 1990s, at least half of all welfare associations in Egypt were Islamic in character, often based on mosques built and controlled by the people rather than the state, providing services to millions. 'It is widely agreed that such Islamic community activities often outdo their secular counterparts' (Bayat 2002: 12), as well as stimulating other voluntary organizations and the state sector to do better. After a national disaster in February 2002 – a serious railway accident at Al-Ayatt, 70 kilometres south of Cairo – the Muslim Brothers were reportedly forbidden by the Egyptian government to raise funds or organize help for the victims.[2]

This is not to deny that in some Muslim states such as Iran, Saudi-Arabia and Algeria there is almost certainly extensive financial abuse in the philanthropic sector owing to accumulations of capital in its hands – an issue touched on in our Introduction. However, at the Islamic grass-roots in a number of countries an analogy may be drawn with the South American Christian 'base communities', that is to say, groups of marginalized people who start by coping with small local issues and work their way slowly up to larger ones (Sullivan 1992: 8, 157-158). The analogy should be pushed too far, however. Though some apologists for social Islam such as Roger Garaudy have likened it to the Latin American 'liberation theology' (Kepel 1987: 340-1), in fact Islamism in the Middle East is not based on any theology of liberating the poor but aims rather at the broad political objective of establishing an Islamic order. Social Islam is characteristically paternalistic, supported by marginalized professionals as much as by the poor, and with a strong emphasis on service provision rather than galvanizing disadvantaged communities (Bayat 2002: 13).

There seems to be quite a widespread view that, to quote a French sociologist, the founding Muslim Brothers were 'more inspired by the methods of Leninism than by Muslim tradition' (Badie 1992: 171), and I have heard this said of present-day Islamists by U.S. State Department spokesmen, despite the hostility of Marxism-Leninism to private charity which we have noted above. Granted, Islamist organizations are sometimes taken over by demagogues and militants, but so are popular movements of nearly all descriptions. The religious injunction to give aid to others should not be neglected as an independent determinant of Islamist movements, or more generally of all forms of charitable giving by Muslim communities. In this book we refer frequently to ways in which the institutions of charity are used to benefit the donors, but an exclusive emphasis on their self-interest yields repetitive and excessively narrow interpretations. Pnina Werbner strikes the right balance, in one of her studies of Manchester Pakistanis' voluntary associations, when she writes 'Fundamental moral ideas draw an ethnic elite into public action' (Werbner 1985: 285). There is some evidence among Muslims, just as among Christians, of a correlation between generosity in donating to aid organizations and a personal commitment to religion. This presumed correlation is made use of by the marketing professionals responsible for mass fund-raising on behalf of Muslim as well as Christian charities (Ghandour 2002: 156-7).

Coverage of Islamic charities would be incomplete without mention of the strong tradition of philanthropy built up by the transnational community of Ismaili Muslims. Its best-known representative is the Aga Khan Foundation, which, though formally a non-denominational development agency, has deep roots in the Ismaili community. Founded in 1967 as a private foundation under Swiss law, it is specially active in Asia and East Africa and is highly regarded by development professionals, with an annual flow of funds of about $100 million.

NGO and civil society studies

Information on the voluntary sector in Algeria or in Jordan, the two countries to be specially considered in this chapter, is of value in giving a comparative edge to the growing field of 'NGO studies', which until recently has tended to be rather ethnocentric. 'NGO studies' is not an academic discipline in itself, but a problem area to which a number of disciplines have contributed insights. Though NGOs are far from constituting a homogeneous category, the frequency of use of this term today reflects an increasing attention to the significance of the non-profit sector (sometimes known as the 'third sector') which itself is part of a wider and indeed somewhat ill-defined field known as 'civil society' – broadly speaking, all the associational forms in society other than the state and the market (Clayton 1996, Benthall 2000).

Social anthropologists have begun to make a distinctive contribution to these debates, introducing a much needed comparative flavour. It had long been noted that traditions of voluntary or quasi-voluntary redistribution have often been applied with a politically conservative effect. Within economic anthropology, a significant literature inspired by Marshall Sahlins (1958) sought to identify redistribution as an essential function of chiefdoms. It was this kind of insight, as well as the lingering influence of state socialist theory with its opposition to private charity, which may have inhibited anthropologists from following up Westermarck's interest in comparing the more positive aspects of traditions of charity. However, a long-standing theoretical anthropological interest in voluntary associations (Caulkins 1996) has recently been rekindled, with the growing salience of NGOs and a new political attachment to 'civil society' as a counter-balance to nation-states (de Waal 2002).

The boom in NGOs and NGO studies since the 1980s has now provoked an intellectual reaction, drawing attention to the inescapable and irreplaceable responsibilities of national governments, to the complex relationships between NGOs and governments (through, for instance, funding, tax privileges and diplomatic assistance) and to the complexity of all the institutions that mediate between self and society, including many not formal enough to be recognized as civil society organizations by external NGOs (Hann and Dunn 1994).

Self-criticism within the aid profession has followed a trajectory that parallels post-colonial self-criticism within academic anthropology – where the challenges advanced in the 1970s by Talal Asad, Dell Hymes and Edward Said appeared subversive to the establishment of the day but have now been absorbed as part of received wisdom. I remember a conversation in about 1972 with one of the founders of the London Technical Group, then an influential ginger group in the world of aid agencies. He criticized aid agencies for having so many retired military officers in management posts. At that time, Save the Children's overseas committee was chaired by the redoubtable daughter of a Viceroy of India, whose connections used to enable her to have a problem solved by getting straight through on the telephone to a government minister in Whitehall. In the aid agencies as in the academic world, work was done, however effectively, with less reflection and soul-searching than today. One of the achievements of the last quarter-century, in both the aid agencies and anthropology, has been to disturb the self-satisfaction of the expeditionary from a white metropolis confronting a feminized and unsophisticated Third World, assisted by unobtrusive local ancillary workers (for a recent study of NGOs that represents this change, see Mawdsley et al. 2002).

A major change in the NGOs has been to appreciate and examine the role of non-Western or local voluntary organizations in providing welfare and other services to vulnerable populations. It is clear that all societies, rich and poor, have developed systems of mutual aid to at least mitigate social suffering. These can of course be eroded, whether as an incidental result of prolonged conflict or shortages, or by the intentional policies of governments whose ideologies seek either to stamp out spontaneous grass-roots activities, or to discourage what they see as passive dependency on welfare provision. However, voluntary associations can show surprising resilience. The most thoughtful Western relief and development agencies now seek to encourage and support local-level organizations in the non-West with judicious subsidy and also by providing such services as training. Religious organizations are often among the most effective in mitigating social suffering. This has enabled the London based Christian Aid to become one of the most effective in its campaigning – with its emphasis on troubling the conscience of the affluent West – while becoming almost entirely 'non-operational', i.e. confining its field activities to selecting locally inspired projects for grant-aid and then monitoring and auditing them. Many of these local initiatives are run by Church organizations, especially in highly christianized regions such as Latin America and sub-Saharan Africa. Western agencies are now developing similar links with Christian associations in the former Eastern bloc. An important current trend is for Western governments to give serious consideration to direct funding of local initiatives in developing countries, thus making less pivotal the traditional intermediary function of the metropolitan relief and development agency, though also introducing a number of new problems such as the rise of a new class of local NGO organizers more or less dependent on foreign aid (INTRAC 1998). This point has been put with particular harshness by Olivier Roy in his criticisms of the efforts of foreign NGOs in post-Soviet central Asia; he charges them with seeking local mirror-images of themselves and 'professionalizing' potential opposition politicians, thus inhibiting efforts towards political reform (Roy 2001). It has also been suggested that secular local NGOs in the poorer Muslim countries tend to avoid basic humanitarian aid and to gravitate towards issues that are of special interest to elites – such as culture, the environment, women's rights, the protection of consumers (Ghandour 2002: 175). Many countries that have only small Christian minorities, such as India and Indonesia, are nonetheless richer than is usually recognized in voluntary associations of every kind, including ones with religious affiliations other than Christian. An injunction to help the socially disadvantaged is one of the hallmarks of all the world religions. Roger A. Lohmann has attempted to assemble evidence from Buddhist traditions in China, Japan and Korea in order to refute the hypothesis that a 'third sector' did not exist in Asia before the introduction of Western-style not-for-profit organizations after the Second World War (Lohmann 1994). Studies of south Asian and other traditions of philanthropy are beginning, belatedly, to unsettle the Eurocentric assumption that philanthropy is a European monopoly (Ilchman et al. 1998).

Some observers of the Arab-Islamic world, such as Ernest Gellner, have concluded that it suffers from a paucity of civil society. This view has been robustly challenged in, for instance, Sheila Carapico's study of civil society in Yemen (Carapico 1998; see also Norton 1995). A more interesting difference of opinion in the study of civil society in the region has emerged: between those who emphasize the importance of NGOs, trade unions, the media and the 'public sphere' on the one hand, and on the other hand those for whom these elements are external, 'top-down' impositions – missing that essential element in productive human association, which is the trust and cooperation available from informal, vernacular or grass-roots practices, such as tribal traditions of conflict resolution. The latter approach indeed digs deep into the texture of society, inviting sensitive ethnographic fieldwork. Scholars such as Richard Antoun and Chris Hann are quite justified in being suspicious of rhetoric about the contribution of NGOs, which is often exaggerated. But whatever the shortcomings of NGOs, they are a major point of connection between the West and countries dependent on aid, and they are often effective in stimulating progressive trends such as women's and children's rights, or better care of disabled people. By contrast, traditional systems of cooperation based on kinship and clientage can undermine the growth of meritocracy and reinforce reactionary tendencies (Antoun 2000, 2001, Benthall 2001). Religion-based associations such as mosque and zakat committees, and the more local and small-scale Islamic charities, would appear on the whole to satisfy the criterion of cultural embeddedness more than do NGOs constructed after Western models.

Just as the international Christian relief and development agencies habitually work through local churches in christianized communities in Africa, benefiting from the grass-roots support and trust to which they have access, so there are opportunities for international Islamic agencies to work through local religion-based associations in Islamic communities. An example of such an intervention working with apparent success may be found in Mali, west Africa, a Muslim country. Islamic Relief, based in Birmingham, has undertaken for some years a pioneering project of community reconciliation after a civil war early in the 1990s, in the district of Gourma Rharous in northern Mali, one of the most disadvantaged districts in one of the world's poorest nations. The project also involves setting up cereal banks, artisans' and food marketing cooperatives, school rehabilitation projects and literacy centres. A special feature of this programme is that the local partners are Islamic associations.[3] This contrasts with the history of external aid to Mali in recent decades, which has frequently spurned and sought to marginalize Muslim networks. Louis Brenner, a historian of west Africa, writes that during the 1980s, 'many of Mali's aid partners, particularly certain French and Americans, … either officially or personally (or both) were deeply suspicious of anything "Islamic", despite the fact that they were meant to be assisting in the "development" of a Muslim society'. By contrast, agencies associated with the United Nations 'have consistently been more prepared than most national and international aid agencies to offer support and assistance to Muslim institutions like schools' (Brenner 2000: 257, 281). Islamic Relief's initiative in Mali, which seeks to adapt the best technical practices of Western development agencies to Muslim networks of local association, could point the way towards opening up channels of effective aid elsewhere in the Muslim world that would be inaccessible to either Christian or secular international NGOs. This would bring to the fore all the issues of competing political interpretations of Islam which are discussed in Chapter 4 of this book. (A comparable scheme is the Aga Khan Foundation's Madrasa Pre-School Programme in East Africa, launched in 1986 in Kenya as part of its Early Childhood Development Programme and now extended to Uganda and Zanzibar.)

Some of these issues are brought out in the following case-studies of Islamic aspects of the voluntary sectors in Algeria and in Jordan.

Algeria

Our first case study will be present-day Algeria. 'During our visit yesterday to the premises of the Islamic Charitable Association in Belcourt', one of the poorer suburbs of Algiers, wrote a reporter for *El Youm*,[4] the Arabic language Algiers daily, on 25 November 2001,

> they were almost deserted by the families that used to come and go there a great deal, especially during Ramadan. Calm reigned over the place, except for the voices of children repeating the letters of the alphabet, and this preparatory class is threatened with closure following the recent decision to freeze the operations of the association for a period of six months – with a drift towards its eventual dissolution.

The decision coincided with a major flood disaster at Bab El-Oued, after which the Association had been forbidden by the government to provide relief aid. It had been operating without problems for thirteen years.

The reasons given for closure of the Association were that it had allegedly collected donations in mosques or shops without a government permit, and that it had been advertising for donations. In an interview, the director, Sheikh Chemseddine Bouroubi, denies the first charge, and pleads in his defence against the second charge that there is no law in the world to prohibit charities from advertising for their projects:

> it is odd that we can read every day, in the pages of our newspapers, advertisements for cars and fashions, even for various breeds of dogs, so how is it that advertising for orphans and widows is forbidden? This decision is not reasonable, and with regard to us it is illogical. For one thing, it depends on a number of regulations, such as the State of Emergency, which permit the freezing of organizations whose activities constitute 'dangers to public security'. Does this apply to helping victims of disaster or the unemployed? I cannot see how a Ramadan hamper constitutes a 'danger to public security', nor the circumcision of orphans, nor the distribution of medicines.

The interview is of relevance to our theme for various reasons.

First, Chemseddine takes the moral high ground claiming that his association is totally non-political, and appealing to God as well as to all available judicial authorities:

> We live in a country where they have politicized everything, even the water taps. ... Others destroy but I build; others divide but I unite. I will continue to be a peace-loving Muslim who appeals for the Good, and unites the people to his cause. I shall not form a party and not be with the powers-that-be or against them, nor with the Opposition or against them. And I have sworn to God that I will only be on the side of the orphan and widow. ... In the present situation, I am not happy about the future for charities. Indeed, I fear for them, as I fear that – in the face of the adversity that afflicts the life of our citizens, with the last of the doors of hope being closed, that is to say our charitable societies – that indeed our citizens will behave as the river-beds did in the Bab El-Oued flood [i.e., rise up]. ... I only seek from the State that it should leave me and my brothers and sisters who are people of charity, to get on with our work; and I have a great hope in the head of the Government that he will look on us with a merciful eye, for we are first and foremost Algerians and sons of the fighters [i.e. freedom-fighters], and the people have a need of us – so be kind.

It is likely in fact that, though the Association complies formally with the law that charities should be non-political, Chemseddine has an informal link with one of the legal and moderate Islamist parties such as the Mouvement de la Société pour la Paix (MSP). The immediate provocation for governmental action appears to be that the Association got involved with the highly sensitive issue of Kabylia, the region of Algeria where most of the Berbers come from, by providing relief aid after a fire.

Second, the portfolio of programmes that was closed shows some distinctly Islamic features. The Association was, according to Chemseddine, providing benefits for 36,000 orphans per year, and one of the projects frozen by the governments was to present *'id* [religious festival] clothes to about 10,000 orphans. We will consider the specifically Islamic concern for orphans later in this Chapter in the context of Jordanian and Palestinian charities.

Freezing of the association, says Chemseddine, will mean letting down 7,000 young men wanting to get married and provision for 400 brides. The Association had offended the government by trying to raise a million signatures in support of a national fund for young people to get married, thus in the government's eyes appearing to try to set up a national institution without authorization. An advertisement for the campaign states that (out of a total national population of some 32 million) some nine million women in Algeria are not married, three million of them over the age of 30.

> The situation is serious and worrying! Half the population of Algeria has not been able to marry, and the result is: spreading of drugs, suicides, rapes, abortions, madness ... and psychological disorders, young people running away from home, the spreading of sorcery and charlatanism, prostitution ... single mothers ... more than 3,000 children conceived in sin each year. It is important to find a scientific and rational solution. If you are a defender of marriage, if you are against bad traditions, [then subscribe...]

This programme was sharply criticized by a Spanish newspaper in 2001 for discriminating against those who preferred to remain unmarried (*El Mundo*, 19 August 2001). However, such a programme would find favour in many Muslim societies that remain socially conservative, and on the face of it has nothing to do with Algeria's notorious Islamic extremism.

At the time of the closure, the Association was also planning to provide 1,500 Ramadan *iftar*s or evening meals, and to give funds for the circumcision of 200 boys. Boys are usually circumcised around the age of seven, but the ceremony calls for expensive celebrations and is sometimes not performed among poor families. Other programmes run by the Association have no specifically Muslim content, such as vocational training for young women in such skills as sewing.

Chemseddine claims in his interview to *El-Youm* that when his Association was suspended, hundreds of other associations closed their activities through fear of the consequences. It is a fact of considerable embarrassment to the Algerian government that, as a team of British consultants concluded as a result of a commissioned survey in 2000, the Islamist charitable associations throughout the country are well connected politically, adequately funded for their needs, and 'almost without doubt the strongest NGOs in Algeria'.

Islamic charities and the Algerian voluntary sector

Though other Islamic countries such as Egypt and Iran have experienced civil violence in recent decades, Algeria is exceptional in the savagery of the 'black years' (or in Arabic *sinawat ul-fitna*, years of discord) since the 1990s and in the extremism of its armed Islamist movement, which has had less in common with traditional Islam than with millenarian cults, the Cultural Revolution in China or European fascism. At the end of the 1990s, it seemed that the current Bouteflika government was leading the way among its neighbours in its active encouragement of the country's 'associative movement' or voluntary sector. The government saw this as a major ingredient in relieving poverty and social exclusion and reinforcing the policy of *concorde civile*: that is to say setting out to let bygones be bygones and reserving punitive retribution for the most extreme of the armed Islamist groups.

During a visit to Algiers in the spring of 2000, I interviewed the Minister for National Solidarity, a medical doctor. He admired the British tradition of voluntary associations, which he saw as having deeper and broader roots in communities than their French equivalents, because ever since the French Revolution and Napoleon the French had become used to expecting the State to provide for almost all needs. However, shortly after my visit a huge national conference on voluntary action was convened; other government ministries intervened with attempts to gain political advantage; and the Ministry of National Solidarity was dissolved amid a general atmosphere of disappointment that the policy of *concorde civile* was not able to heal the country's wounds effectively. It has seemed to many observers that the apparent freedom of the press and civil pluralism were in fact illusions fabricated by the army to disguise its dominance over the civilian authorities.

Well before the colonial period, the region that was to become Algeria was marked by immemorial Arab-Islamic traditions of mutual aid, in particular by *touiza*, the rural practice of local cooperation. Shortly after the Second World War, Algerians created new forms of voluntary organizations directed towards cultural, sporting and other associational objectives, under the French law of 1 July 1901. These were few in number and largely urban, but they played their part in safeguarding the sense of national identity.

Two very different associations that were both influential in the national movement were the Association des Oulémas (religious scholars), founded by Sheikh ben Badis in the 1920s, and the Scouts Musulmans Algériens, founded in 1936 by another national hero, Mohamed Bouras. However, according to new research (Arous 2000) there were about one hundred active associations. The first Islamic charity was the *jam`iyat ul-iqbal* ('society for concern), founded in 1940.

Historians look back on the Association des Oulémas as having provided the liberation struggle with a cultural component to complement the political struggle. The Oulémas' motto was 'Algeria is my fatherland, Arabic my language, Islam my religion'. But it was not until the late 1930s that they abandoned their loyalty to France, with the result that their association was marginalized by the more radical Front de Libération Nationale (FLN). Secular Algerians in the 1990s accused the Islamic extremists of having grossly exaggerated the contribution of the Oulémas to the war of liberation (Labat 1995: 59-62).

Algerian voluntary associations crumbled during the war of independence against the French. But shortly after the Algerian victory in 1962, they revived in the fields of culture, sport, youth and social action, in a very brief flowering for one year only, comparable to the rather longer period at the beginning of Soviet rule in Russia. In 1964, the government undertook an exhaustive enquiry to stop subversive associations (Babadji 1991). The ruling FLN policy of 'unity of action and thought' led to their replacement by 'mass organizations' following the Eastern European model. The Islamic movement went underground, making use of the national associations set up by the government and also using mosques to pursue their aims, in a way comparable to the Catholic church in Communist Poland. Muslims drew on the Shi`ite tradition of *taqiya*, that is, dissimulation of one's religion under duress. This situation prevailed until new legislation in 1987 and 1990, which encouraged a rapid growth in the foundation of associations. 'Free mosques' were now built outside government control and in defiance of planning regulations, and the Muslim Brotherhood movement from Egypt began to exert influence.

Concentrating on some of the more impoverished urban areas, the Islamists began by cleaning up housing estates, planting trees and rosebushes, marking out soccer fields and clearing away rubbish. A multi-party political system was allowed in 1989, allowing activists from the Front Islamique du Salut (FIS) to work within the framework of mosque associations and bring political ideas into the neighbourhoods. In October 1990, the government's response to an earthquake in the Tipasa region of northern Algeria was condemned as callous, contrasting with 'the devotion and effectiveness of the FIS-inspired doctors, nurses, and rescue teams who arrived in ambulances bearing the party's insignia' (Kepel 2002a: 169). This process culminated with the FIS's victory in municipal elections in 1990. Elected FIS officials gave a good impression of civic virtue, and their control of municipal budgets enabled them to multiply welfare activities on behalf of the poor (ib.: 170). The resulting political crisis led to the military coup in 1992 and to the civil war (Rouadjia 1990, Bekkar 1997, Verges 1997).

The number of national non-profit associations, which have to be approved by the Ministry of the Interior, stands at some 800, and there are said to be as many as 53,000 local associations, regulated at the level of the 48 provinces. This type of statistic, commonly published by governments in the Arab-Islamic region, needs to be taken with a large grain of salt. Some 32 per cent of this impressive total are school parents' committees. The remainder cover a wide variety of activities. The majority are entirely non-confessional. The tiny but well respected Roman Catholic Church in Algeria runs effective charitable programmes, some of them focused on children with the cooperation of Unicef.

The large quantity of associations registered in Algeria is by no means yet matched by a proportional contribution to national life. Despite its keenness to encourage the voluntary sector, the government is also keen to control it both from unwelcome international infiltration and from the militant Islamic factions. Among the most successful associations would seem to be a handful of private associations launched by small professional groups in response to the challenge of the 'black years'. A good example is the Fondation Mahfoud Boucebci, launched by the family of an admired psychiatrist who was murdered by armed Islamists in 1993. Headed by his widow, it is devoted to a range of medical, scientific and cultural activities at a professional level. One project is to build a clinic and research centre in order to give psychotherapeutic help to victims of violence. The fact that the therapeutic model envisaged is Freudian analysis is an indication of the approach that tends to be adopted by the francophone professional elite.

A number of reasons are given for the hitherto feeble contribution of voluntary associations. Among these are: the novelty of voluntary associations in Algerian life; lack of experience and resources; the use of associations by leaders to realize personal ambitions, sometimes of a political nature, while not departing from the letter of the law; sometimes, too close links with political parties; the lack of grass-roots participation; and an endemic preference for talk over action. Algerian society as a whole does not yet accept the notion that disadvantaged people can be actors in the development process, rather than being merely the objects of charity. A possible exception is the Fondation Touiza – aptly named after the traditional rural institution mentioned above – which has for some years, among other things, undertaken micro-projects for vocational training for young people both in the city and in rural areas, where on the whole poverty is more severe.

Arous's sociological research on the Islamic voluntary associations concludes that some of them are performing good work with deep roots in the communities they serve. His view contrasts with the establishment view in Algeria, which is that all the Islamic voluntary associations are highly politicized, and in some cases morally compromised. Since 1994, the government has tried to encourage a revival of the Sufi *zawiya*s or brotherhoods, which it had formerly opposed, as a counterbalance to the fundamentalist threat (Ghandour 2002: 92).

In the spring of 2000, I met with Mr Aissa Benlakhdar, head of Irchad Islah ('guidance and reconstruction') which has an explicit connection with the Mouvement de la Société pour la Paix (MSP), mentioned above, the moderate Islamic party formerly known as Hamas (but with no connection to the Palestinian Hamas) which is led by the prominent politician, Sheikh Mahfoud Nahnah, once the Muslim Brothers' representative in Algeria. (No political party is now allowed to include the word Islamic in its name.) Irchad Islah's founder, Sheikh Mohamed Bouslimani, was kidnapped by armed Islamists in 1993 and found dead two months later with his writings left on his chest; his only offence had been to refuse to give the Groupe Islamique Armé (GIA) a fatwa declaring that their crimes were a holy jihad. Founded in 1989, Irchad Islah is now a large association with branches in all 48 provinces. It incorporates a human rights programme, as well as religious instruction, social development, education and health. There seems little doubt that Irchad Islah is at the hub of a national network of charities which provide a base for MSP's electoral machine nearly as effective as that of the FLN, the former single party. Mr Benlakhdar was planning in 2000 to start a new centre for helping children who have suffered psychologically from the 'years of discord' – known as 'severely affected children' (*al-atfal ul-musdumin*). He was critical of projects to impose European models of psychotherapy on Algerian patients, on the grounds that they do not resonate with traditional ways of drawing on a community's resources for helping individuals in distress. This viewpoint needs to be taken into account by external humanitarian agencies that seek to make their interventions in such a country as sensitive as possible.

Algeria faces a problem of cultural identity in that almost the entire population remain Muslim, Christianity is associated with the colonial past, state socialism was tried and failed dismally, yet large numbers of Algerians have drifted away from religious institutions, disgusted by the excesses of the armed Islamist factions. Some Muslim leaders such as the late Abdelmadjid Mesiane, president until his recent death of the Haut Conseil Islamique, are joined by a few colleagues from overseas such as Soheib Bencheikh, an Algerian mufti prominent in Marseilles, in attempting to formulate interpretations of Islam more consistent with modern life than those currently dominant; but they are rather isolated voices.

A widely held view among the francophone elite of Algeria is that Islamism is an indivisible movement and even its moderate adherents are not to be trusted. Thus the editorial in the Algiers newspaper, *La Liberté*, on 27 April 2000: 'Current developments give one the impression that Algeria is in the same situation as a person who is not quite convinced that AIDS is lethal, and who in order to be convinced asks to be injected with the virus'.

On my visit in 2000, I was slightly misled by the impression of intellectual freedom conveyed by the press. On reflection, it became clear that its tradition of outspoken criticism and even flamboyant polemic is confined within limits set by the military authorities, while television is totally government controlled. Though a liberalizing tendency within the government can be identified, it has shown itself incapable of following through a declared intention of allowing more freedom to voluntary associations. Their development is likely to be slow, and confrontation between the authorities and the Islamic charities is likely to continue.

Jordan: the voluntary sector

Jordan, which I will take as a second case study, is the site of a rich variety of voluntary agencies, new and old, indigenous and international. Over 650 voluntary societies are registered there, serving a population of about 5.25 million. (In Egypt, with a population of some 70 million, the number of voluntary societies is said to be 12,000 to 14,000.) Islam is enshrined in Article 2 of the Hashemite Kingdom of Jordan's Constitution ('Islam is the religion of the State and Arabic is its official language') and some 90 to 95 per cent of the population are Sunni Muslim. Whereas in some other Muslim states the Islamist revivalists have been excluded from legal recognition, the Muslim Brothers have for political reasons been accepted for many years as part of the social fabric – albeit with a perhaps increasing reserve on the part of the government authorities. This 'policy of inclusion', as it is called, has resulted in the Muslim Brothers' adopting pragmatic and moderate policies in Jordan. Charitable work plays an important part in their blend of social, religious and political activity.

Jordan is a kind of seismograph of the political convulsions of the Middle East. Its prominence in regional politics has given it a salience exceeding its economic power, through a deliberate strategy adopted by the Hashemite leadership. Also, Amman has become a centre for numerous regional offices of international agencies. Some of these moved from Beirut during the Lebanese civil war, and have stayed.

The country has considerable domestic and humanitarian needs. Some 37 per cent of the population is estimated to live below the accepted poverty line, and public health is declining in the poorer areas, especially in the southern governorates. Jordan is a host to a number of so-called camps – in fact, strictly regulated townships which only in theory are regarded as temporary – for Palestinian refugees which are still in part the responsibility of the UN Relief and Works Agency (UNRWA). The country is poor in natural resources and in water. Its economy was severely hurt by the outcome of the 1991 Gulf War, since it had become dependent both on trade with Iraq and on aid from Saudi-Arabia and Kuwait, aid which was to be withdrawn for some years as a punishment for its non-alignment during the Gulf War. Jordan succeeded in absorbing some 300,000 Palestinian 'returnees' from Kuwait (or nearly 10 per cent of the previous population of Jordan) after the Gulf War, but at considerable economic cost. In common with many other Arab countries, the birth-rate is high: some 41 per cent of the population are under the age of 15. It imports 70 per cent of its food, some of this in the form of grain donated by the United States and the European Union. Urbanization is taking place rapidly, but political tribalism is only slowly declining in importance (Freij and Robinson 1996: 14, 29). Among the other dominant tensions in Jordanian society today are the acute divisions between rich and poor (with the relative lack of a middle class), the uneasy balance of power between the Palestinian majority and the Transjordanians, and gender inequality. Potential civil turbulence lurks beneath a surface calm, held in check by an efficient state intelligence service. Tensions in the country have not been eased by the war in neighbouring Iraq in 2003.

Many elements in the voluntary sector in Jordan today have little if anything to do with Islam. The national lottery is a clear example. In the early 1970s, leaders of the voluntary movement in Jordan looked around for alternative sources of revenue to government funding, on which they were at that time dependent. Some 80,000 tickets at JD 2 (£1 = 1 JD approx.) are now sold twice a month. Of these proceeds, 40 per cent goes to the General Union of Voluntary Societies (GUVS), 20 per cent in commission to the sellers, and 40 per cent to the winners – the maximum prize being about JD 100,000. With the proceeds inflated by periodic special lotteries with higher ticket prices, the gross proceeds are JD 5 million per year, yielding JD 2 million for GUVS to distribute. The Government takes nothing of this, aware that GUVS is satisfying needs which would otherwise fall on the public exchequer. Only rarely is there an article in the press attacking the lottery on the grounds that it is forbidden by Islamic law (*haram*). However, as many as 85 per cent of the tickets were (in 1996) sold in Amman, which has about 33 per cent of the population; one reason being that in some governorates such as Maan in the south, the selling of lottery tickets is looked down on as an undignified occupation, and a second being that people in rural areas are more prone to consider the lottery *haram*.

GUVS is an entirely secular organization. Voluntary associations began in Jordan (then Transjordan) in the 1930s, when immigrant groups such as the Syrians set up societies to help their own members in need. The Christian churches were also active. The Circassian Charitable Association has the distinction of being the oldest association (it was founded in 1932) which is still active. It has eight branches with some 3,000 volunteer members, and runs a kindergarten and youth centres as well as helping poor families. Its policy is to try to breed new leaders for this influential Muslim minority.

Government institutions began to grow during the 1930s, and by 1948, with the influx of refugees from Israel, new concepts of social work, and a minimum standard of subsistence for all refugees irrespective of ethnic origin, began to be introduced. The government introduced laws on voluntary associations in the 1950s, and in 1958 GUVS was set up as an umbrella organization to coordinate and control the voluntary movement. It is an elected body, but the Ministry of Social Development ultimately controls the whole voluntary movement through its right (subject to judicial appeal) to veto appointments to the governing committees of all voluntary societies.

Government subsidies began in the 1960s. In 1970, the country was deeply shaken by what was in effect a civil war, settled in 'Black September', when some 7,000 Palestinians were killed by King Hussain's troops. This disaster resulted indirectly in expansion of the voluntary sector as the government tried to heal the country's wounds. Expansion has also followed on from economic belt-tightening in the early 1990s and from the influx of returnees after the 1990-91 Gulf War.[5]

A report by the President of GUVS (Khatib 1994) claimed credit for the voluntary sector's effective management of resources, but also underlined Jordan's pressing social needs and the limited funds available to meet them. The most favoured forms of activity for NGOs within the framework of GUVS are kindergartens, vocational training, health centres and clinics, scholarships and loans for students, care for the handicapped, and care of orphans. Recent work has focused also on the role of women in development, income-generating projects and child care. With regard to women, it is recognized that though traditional training in sewing and knitting gives women a potential source of income that can be combined with domestic duties, this does nothing to challenge gender stereotypes and can actually widen the gap between educated and 'traditional' Jordanian women.

GUVS's biggest contribution to Jordan, as of 1996, was a much needed cancer treatment centre in Amman. Substantial funds (I was told the equivalent of $10 million) had been raised for this through a telethon. This, like the lottery, is an example of Western fund-raising techniques successfully transplanted.

All but a handful of privileged associations are legally required to be members of GUVS. Two of these are characteristic of Jordan in that they are patronized by prominent members of the Royal Family. One is the Hashemite Fund for Social Development, formerly Queen Alia Fund (after one of King Hussain's earlier wives who was killed in a helicopter accident in 1977 while travelling home from a visit to a hospital), and now presided over by Princess Basma, the late King's only sister. The second is the Noor al Hussein Foundation, founded in 1985 and named after the late King's last wife. These are sophisticated operations, attracting extensive sponsorship from governments and international agencies. The former is perhaps best known for its network of community centres, the latter for its projects to encourage and develop traditional crafts in rural areas of Jordan.

The Young Women's Muslim Association was, in 1996, not a membership organization but a vehicle for the charitable projects of Princess Sarvath (wife of the the then Crown Prince, Hassan). One of these projects was a day-care centre near Amman for mentally handicapped children, which has done much to stimulate reform of the treatment of such children in Jordan. Conventionally, they were regarded by their families as a source of stigma and often hidden. The children in this centre, often with multiple handicaps, are enabled to acquire skills and confidence, and many of them progress to a sheltered factory and even to compete in the normal job market. The charismatic director, Ghusoon Diab Al-Kareh, brings to the work her up-to-date professional training in the USA, but also her religious conviction that handicapped people are specially blessed.

Though no doubt modelled on the practices of twentieth century British royalty (Prochaska 1995), the involvement of the Royal Palace in charitable works is far more active than one would find in a Western monarchy. An Arab monarchy does not stand back from the political fray, but is typically engaged in face-to-face interaction with the various interest-groups on whose support it depends. Critics of the status quo maintain that the Palace's participation in charity goes further than energetic benevolence, and is actually a means of controlling and limiting the growth of grass-roots organizations. At the time of my visit in 1996, this argument was being voiced specially on behalf of the women's movement, for Princess Basma chaired the Jordanian National Committee for Women and made frequent speeches in support of women's groups. Certainly the immunity of royal activities from public criticism means that there is little unfettered debate about the effectiveness of the leading charitable organizations in Jordan. Unflattering critics call these royal foundations 'parallel organizations' or GONGOs (Government Organized NGOs) rather than voluntary organizations in the proper sense. It is an open question whether they contribute more in professionalism, influence and éclat than they take away by smothering grass-roots initiatives with official control.

By comparison with other countries in the region and given the harsh political and economic shocks it has had to endure, it is remarkable that Jordan enjoys reasonable internal stability and in particular that Transjordanian ethnonationalism has not already taken a more virulent form. Much of the credit is generally given to the political charisma of the late King Hussain and the preaching of humanistic tolerance and inclusiveness – for instance, with regard to the small Christian minority. Significantly, the Palace has also taken every opportunity to support a humane and tolerant interpretation of Islam. Islam frequently becomes co-opted by patriotic states, of which Jordan is one, and in this case it is fused with a concept of enlightened monarchy borrowed from the West (Massad 2001: 212-13). But the universalistic message of Islam – within the confines of fellow-Muslims and 'people of the Book' – is a powerful counterbalance against ethnonationalism, when skilfully adapted. The Hashemite leadership even speak of the possibility one day of a federation of Abrahamic states that would include Israel.

I have heard it argued that the whole of Jordan's voluntary sector is informed by Arab-Islamic values of social solidarity. This claim must obviously be qualified, given that the society is deeply stratified, but an element of truth seems to remain in such an assertion – to do with the strength of face-to-face relationships, family ties and other bonds of reciprocal obligation which anthropologists generally regard as analytically prior to indicators based on money. It is related to the fact that the ideal of communism, which depends on the workers subsuming their personal identities in a common solidarity of economic class, has never found favour in Arab states.

The Muslim Brothers in Jordan, *al-ikhwan al-muslimun*, and various affiliated associations, have been extremely active in what they call *at-tarbiyat al-ijtima`iya* or 'social training', which includes both relations among members of the fraternity and also injunctions to serve the public and assist the ill-fated. As well as the Green Crescent (Chapter 3), too small to be much more than a token, and extensive educational programmes, the *ikhwan* are associated with a large and important Islamic Hospital in central Amman, and various organizations for poverty relief. It is hard to research the *ikhwan*'s activities, for the procedures, rigorous training, forms

of organization and members' names are in principle secret. They have a saying
sirriyyat at-tanzim wa `alaniyyat ad-da`wa: 'secrecy of the organization and openness in
its mission' (Roald[6] 1994: 111, 147-9).

One of the founding principles of the Muslim Brothers was 'avoidance of the
domination of notables and important men; since rising movements attract them and
mean riches and benefits for them' (Husaini 1956: 43). It would seem that moderate
Islamist organizations in the Middle East have impressed many recent researchers,
including some ideological enemies (Israeli 1993b: 32, 35), with their personal
modesty, dedication and even accessibility. Their enemies would say that they were
merely putting on a show of humility in adverse circumstances. Here again we can
refer back to the Quran, with its stress on *niyyah* or intention, and its theological
insistence on human dignity. In keeping with the Islamists' more general critique of
what they see as objectionable features of Western domination and Arab
governments, the Jordanian and Palestinian zakat committees that I mentioned in
Chapter 1 claim to be seeking to build up communal trust (a word I heard repeated
many times when I met them) through door-to-door welfarism. Radical Islamism
has many fierce critics – and its sociological interpretation is an academic
battleground (Milton-Edwards 2002). Among other things, it strives to reject the
ossified and autocratic political styles that mark the regimes of the area. The
effectiveness and integrity of this rejection have, however, been compromised, in the
eyes of many, by the support it has received from Saudi-Arabia, which appears to
have 'exported' radical Islamism as a price to be paid for maintaining its domestic
status quo. Moreover, Arab regimes are adept in co-opting the insignia of Islam.
While in Jordan certain Islamist intellectuals have been tempted to adjust their
position from critics into official ideologues, in Egypt the rising middle class has
been courted away from religious militancy so that the *hijab* and the beard now turn
up commodified as style accessories, and free Ramadan dinners are given on tables
in front of modern offices (Kepel 2002a: 298, 339-41; 2002b: 104-5).

Two projects to support orphans in Jordan

We have mentioned above some popular types of programmes such as Ramadan
hampers and funds to help young men to marry, as well as the educational
programmes which are much favoured by Islamic charities, based as they are on the
*madrasa*s or mosque schools which have flourished since their foundation in
medieval times (Ghandour 2002: 56). Another favourite cause, relief aid to refugees,
is rooted in the story of the Prophet Muhammad's *hijra* (exodus) from Mecca to
Medina. And one of the most favoured objects for Muslim charitable works is the
care of orphans. There is a theological reason for this, for Muhammad was an
orphan himself: his father died either just before or just after he was born, and his
mother died when he was only six and he was taken into the family of his paternal
uncle. If one speaks of orphans to a pious Muslim, he or she is likely to make a
gesture of crossing two fingers, which alludes to a saying of the Prophet that
whoever looks after an orphan will be 'like this' with him in Paradise. The Prophet
also said, 'I am he who takes care of the orphan'. Several passages in the Quran
condemn those who misappropriate orphans' property (e.g. 93. 9, 107. 2). The result
is that there can be few Islamic welfare organizations that do not include orphans
among their beneficiaries, and emotive appeals on their behalf are distributed to the

public. For instance, the British-based charity Islamic Relief supports 4,000 orphans in over ten countries. 'Orphan' is generally defined as a child who has lost his or her father, i.e. the family breadwinner; the loss of a mother is not seen as so disastrous. The term 'orphan' is also sometimes used as a euphemism for a child born out of wedlock who is rejected by a family. Considered in a long historical perspective, a concern for the welfare of orphans may be seen as part of a strategy for extending and consolidating the domination of Islam.

I visited a small residential girls' orphanage during a visit to Salt (see above, p.60). It was administered by the local branch of the Red Crescent society, which is secular and non-denominational, though its day-to-day operation was overseen by a devout Muslim, Hajja N., a full-time volunteer, an affectionate and cordial lady in late middle age. It had space for twenty girls, whose ages ranged from one-and-a-half years to seventeen. The original aim when the orphanage was started in 1965 was to accept children from four years up, but they cannot refuse younger children. I had coffee in the Hajja's office, and she led in a little girl, only eighteen months old and clinging to her. An even younger boy was brought in, but he had been accepted just for a short time and would soon go to an orphanage in Amman. The older girls help to look after the younger ones, and some of them go on to higher education. The small size of the orphanage made it relatively easy to take care of, I was told, especially because the Hajja and her husband have no children themselves and make the orphanage like a large family. Though most of the bigger children were out at school during my visit, I could see that the living spaces were rigorously ordered: the children sitting in bare side-rooms with all the toys in a cupboard in the Hajja's office (possibly tidied up for my visit); a communal cupboard of children's clothes in the dormitory.

I also visited an orphans' day centre in Amman, run by the Saudi-based International Islamic Relief Organization (IIRO). This was just outside the Jabal Al Husayn refugee camp, the oldest of the Palestinian refugee camps. Two hundred children up to the age of 15 were looked after here, just over half of them boys. Most of them came from the refugee camp, but some from up to 5 kilometres away. The primary aim of the centre was to enable the families to become economically self-sufficient, and there were courses for the mothers in straw handcrafts, ceramics, knitting and other productive activities that can be carried on in the home. (In 1996, the IIRO was cutting back, in deference to the government of Jordan's wishes, on funding projects to benefit Palestinians in Jordan, in favour of the South of the kingdom where poverty among many Transjordanians was even more serious. The manager in Amman told me that the IIRO had not intended to offend the Jordanian authorities by favouring Palestinians, but had been unaware of their wishes.)

Boys and girls, on alternate days, attended Quranic instruction and extra classes. On the morning when I visited, it was the girls' day. The women teachers were all fully veiled, and the girls had their heads veiled. On request, one of the girls recited some verses from the Quran, with only a little prompting from a teacher. The class then rose to their feet, I was invited to sit down together with the Saudi manager, and the girls then chanted some verses in Arabic, accompanied by one of the teachers with a tambourine. The meaning of the two rhymes was 'Welcome to guests of the IIRO' and 'Don't forget the rules for reciting the Holy Quran'.

I was then invited to the office of the head of the day centre, Basma Sharif, and asked her some questions. She had graduated from Jordan University in 1985 after studying *shari`a*, then did a postgraduate course in school administration. She had worked with UNRWA as a teacher, the UN body with responsibility for Palestinian refugees, and subsequently as a supervisor in an orphan centre like this one. She was in favour of non-residential orphan centres, and of the sponsorship of orphans within their extended families rather than building up institutions; and she contended that this tendency is envisaged by Islamic principles. She played an active role in community work outside her paid employment, and was clearly a strong personality of some influence. Basma Sharif was strongly in favour of local initiatives rather than big international agencies, and stressed the importance of Islamic volunteering without reward. She stressed the principle in Islam that poor people have the right to assistance, quoting a well-known Quranic passage: '[They will be blessed] in whose wealth is a recognized right for the [needy] who asks and him who is prevented [for some reason from asking]' (Q. 70. 24-5). Therefore, there should be no loss of dignity in receiving assistance.

According to traditional Islamic education, children would memorize the Quran before going on to formal schooling. The emphasis is still on memory, until the children start reading at the age of eight or nine. A few children of this age in Amman, as in many other places in the Muslim world, are still trained to memorize the whole of the Quran.

The Jabal Al-Husayn orphan centre represents an approach to the care of children that accords with current expert Western thinking in seeking to strengthen family bonds through day centres, rather than board children in institutions. The apparent imposition of rigid gender roles by means of dress is harder to reconcile with the policies of progressive NGOs, though the issue is subtler than is always realized, and women's clothing is not necessarily a reliable indicator of psychological or economic independence. Many Western educators deprecate rote-learning of the Quran, by contrast with Western education which sets a high value on the encouragement of original problem-solving and creativity. The defence within Islamic cultural terms is that these children are being educated in a knowledge of what is for them their priceless religious heritage: a guarantee of human dignity for the child victims of a grim power-game which has left the Palestinian refugee community disinherited and unassimilated for fifty years in 'temporary' housing. Critics of this form of instruction, which Saudi-Arabia has done much to encourage and facilitate in other Muslim states, argue that it can engender a blind submission to authority.

A different view to Basma Sharif's was that which I encountered a few months later, on visiting the active and energetic zakat committee in Nablus, the historic town in the West Bank – which had built up an effective complex of medical services, income-generating projects and the like, all from Muslims' contributions. It had set its heart on building a huge residential orphanage in a walled compound, an architect's vision of which appeared as the frontispiece of the committee's glossy annual report. As in the West, prestige projects have a great appeal for many heads of charities.

Special characteristics of Islamic voluntary associations

Another feature of traditional Islamic organized charity seems to have been a strong emphasis on giving preference to Muslims rather than non-Muslims. This has been challenged in recent years by the more liberal theologians' interpretations of Islamic doctrine (see Chapter 1), and by the desire of the more internationally minded voluntary agencies to harmonize with the worldwide humanitarian network with its manifold opportunities for funding. The issue has not arisen as a critical one in a country like Jordan with a very large Muslim majority and minorities – Orthodox, Catholic and Protestant Christians – that each have a strong sense of group identity such as is characteristic of the history of the whole Middle East.[7] Many Islamic charities are concerned with furthering the Muslim cause as well as benefiting already committed Muslims. This is consistent with a major element in much traditional Islamic doctrine, the refusal to acknowledge a distinction between aspects of life which other religions tend to separate; the contention that Islam is a seamless whole in which religion, politics, economics and morality are interfused. To what extent this corresponds to lived reality is debatable, though an otherwise informative recent article on Islamic NGOs in Africa accepts it as a fact (Salih 2003).

The Christian churches often adopted a similar position before the Enlightenment, but since then the principles of separation of Church and State, and of freedom of conscience, have gradually won wide, if still not complete, acceptance within the Christian world. One outcome is that the mainstream Christian philanthropic agencies are today strongly opposed to the combining of humanitarian aims with proselytizing. It is now condemned as unethical – by churches that belong to the World Council of Churches – to try to effect religious conversion of someone who is hungry, sick or otherwise disadvantaged. This was not always so, from the early centuries of Christianity up to the colonial period when many Christian organizations, such as the Mission to Lepers, sought to combine evangelical and humanitarian aims, and some, such as World Vision, still do. There are signs that some Islamic charities are moving towards a similar approach to that of the modern Christian agencies, but the doctrine of what I have called Islamic 'seamlessness' still provides resistance.

A related characteristic of the Middle Eastern voluntary sector is the conspicuous permeability between charity and politics. The Society of Muslim Brothers in Egypt is now denied registration either as a political party or as an NGO, but continues to enjoy success, popularity and leadership, pursuing its dual goal of socio-economic development and political influence. Founded in 1928 by Hassan al-Banna, the organization was concerned among other things with public health and it was active in cleaning up villages and responding to crises such as epidemics. In 1945 it was required by the Egyptian Government to split into two: a section concerned with politics and a section concerned with welfare. The latter had 500 branches all over Egypt by 1948 (Mitchell 1969: 36, 289-91). Similarly, both Hamas in Palestine and the Shi`ite Hizbullah (Party of God) in Lebanon are composed of a militant faction prepared to use violence and a broadly-based faction which prefers negotiation. Each has built up a formidable network of welfare services to support their respective causes. Documentation of Hamas shows that its schools, libraries, youth clubs, hospitals and welfare organizations are not merely devices to gain political support, but also the result of a conscious policy to build up Islam as the basis for a sense of community to replace the sense of nation shattered by the occupation, which is seen as a new Crusade against the *umma* or community of Muslims (Legrain 1991, 1996).[8] Thus the religious rhetoric of political Zionism is turned against the Israelis. Palestine is conceived by Hamas as waqf until the end of days. Jewish zealots in Israel have achieved their present position of political influence by means of welfarist strategies analogous to those of Islamists elsewhere in the Middle East. A study by two Israeli social scientists carried out in the late 1990s concluded that, contrary to the prevailing image of Hamas as ideologically intransigent and rigid, it is essentially 'a religious movement involved in a wide range of social activities, ... deeply rooted in the Palestinian society in the West Bank and Gaza Strip', able to transcend social fragmentation and class division and 'to maneuver within the prose of political reality while never ceasing to recite the poetry of ideology' (Mishal and Sela 2000: vii-viii, 12, 21-3).

It has been estimated in Western and Israeli intelligence-gathering circles that financial support for Hamas has recently exceeded $100 million per year, with some 90 per cent of this total going towards social service programmes and 10 per cent to Hamas's military wing Izz al-Din al-Qassam (named after a Syrian-born resistance leader shot dead by British troops in 1935 near Jenin). Whereas since 11 September 2001, 147 countries have frozen more than $100 million in alleged Al-Qa`ida and Taliban assets, it has proved more difficult to stop the flow of funds to Hamas because of its wide support throughout the Arab world, although Hamas has been declared a 'terrorist organization' by the USA since 1995, and in December 2001 President George W. Bush froze the assets of three entities on the grounds that they were Hamas-controlled. Regular funding and logistical support for Hamas are still provided secretly through Iran, Syria, Jordan, Qatar and Saudi-Arabia, in addition to some $2 million annually from British Muslims and nearly $20 million from the USA. Couriers and middlemen are used, and the tri-border area between Paraguay, Brazil and Argentina is thought to be a special focus for financial transfers. The USA has tried to put pressure on a number of Middle Eastern states to stop facilitating this funding. However, Hamas's food distribution, schools, youth camps, scholarships and programmes for the elderly have given it the local reputation of being the most trustworthy provider of social services to Palestinians (Eshel 2002, Roule 2002). The ICRC's new programme of 'smart aid' in the Occupied Territories seems to be deliberately aimed at providing an alternative source of effective support, but it is as yet unproven.

So the Islamic voluntary sector covers a wide political spectrum from official quasi-governmental bodies, pejoratively described as 'parallel organizations', to popular movements of a radical and even politically violent tinge. The privileges of charities are manipulated on all sides. For instance, a Jordanian zakat committee for Palestinian relief which I visited seemed on all the evidence to raise funds successfully for a variety of projects in the West Bank for sponsorship of orphans, income generation, medical care and the like. They used a picture of the Dome of the Rock – that potent symbol of Islamic claims to Jerusalem – superimposed on a map of the whole of Israel/Palestine, as a logo, and a plastic model of it as a collecting-box.[9] Thus they adapt Western fund-raising techniques to the local context. However, when their fund-raising leaflets routinely savage the 'Satanic' Israelis[10] – at a time when the Jordanian Government is trying to support the Peace

Process – it becomes clear that charitable operations just will not fit into a segregated, politics-proof container. Rather than merely note the permeability of charity and politics in the Middle East, we should also ask how intellectually and practically sustainable is the sharp distinction between the two that the Euro-American law of charities strives so hard to enforce.

Problems of accountability

Despite successes at the grass-roots which are well attested, it would be a mistake to idealize the voluntary sector in the Islamic world, for a serious lack of accountability is widespread. It would seem that in some cases Islamic charities in the Arab world have been used simply as fronts for organizing political violence. Another extreme example is the huge charitable foundations (*bonyads*) set up in Iran under the direction of religious leaders after the Revolution, on the orders of Khomeini. The biggest is the Foundation for the Oppressed and the Self-Sacrificers, which was created in 1979 with a view to taking over the wealth of the Shah and those connected with the court, including the highly politicized Pahlavi Foundation. It is private but exempted from both taxes and reporting requirements. It is now said to control assets of $12 billion with an estimated 400,000 employees, its interests including manufacturing, importing, hotels and even real estate in Manhattan. Some published reports about these foundations are damning, drawing parallels with the Philippines under Marcos or to the Communist Party under Soviet apparatchiks. They have strengthened the Islamic Iranian state while undermining its ability to impose its will on the economy (Waldman 1992, Maloney 2000).

Nonetheless, between two and four million refugees (Afghans, Iraqi Shi`ites and Kurds) are looked after in Iran, for which the country receives little recognition from the outside world. But public accountability is absent. Hence, when Islamic charities are accused of laundering funds on behalf armed extremist groups, as some of them were in the aftermath of 11 September 2001, it is difficult to know the truth. This seems not to apply to organizations such as Islamic Relief and Muslim Aid that submit to the United Kingdom's stringent reporting and auditing requirements.

In a country such as Saudi-Arabia, by contrast, charity is generally regarded as a matter concerning only the donors. Fund-raising videos – *Tariqu l'amal* ('the path of hope') and *as-sab`a sanabil* ('the seven seeds')[11] – distributed by the IIRO in the mid-1990s emphasized the sufferings of Muslims all over the world, especially in the former Communist states, and the need to defend the religion. Horrific scenes of misery and destruction alternate with footage of formal conferences attended by Saudi dignitaries, and of high-tech medical equipment. But hardly any concrete information is supplied, and I have found it impossible to obtain an official report since 1996.[12]

Narratives of misery in the poorer countries are exported to the West – subject to unpredictable shifts of consumer fashion, to political manipulation, and to control of the channels of aid by Western intermediaries. Unsurprisingly, the larger Islamic charities such as IIRO now use fundraising techniques borrowed from the West, if in a brasher and more lurid idiom. I have suggested elsewhere (Benthall 1993: 81, 234) that a major aspect of fundraising by charities, as opposed to their operational departments, belongs to what anthropologist Simon Harrison (1992) has called the luxury or prestige modality of social action.

Genuine accountability in the Middle East voluntary sector is aimed at by some of the more progressive large organizations in their published annual reports, but the kind that is accepted by the people at large is more likely to be the personal trust built up by small face-to-face groups.

Western NGO specialists see considerable scope in the region for supporting sustainable local-level initiatives, and injecting technical skills and accumulated experience of managing projects. A most important principle to disseminate is that of public accountability and transparency. Some also argue that even more crucial to the promotion of social development in the Middle East is the necessity for articulate 'pressure from below' through advocacy organizations, which have hitherto been weak in the region (Bayat 2002: 24).[13] It is clear that merely calling for better reporting is not enough, for one of the most lively current debates among development professionals focuses on the excessive reliance on paper documentation that is indulged in by the 'new managerialism' with its 'auditing culture', so that workers at the grass-roots are made to feel that 'activities not at our desks are invisible' (Townsend 2002, Mawdsley et al. 2002).

The Lebanese Hizbullah

Mention has already been made of Sunni organizations that are both political and charitable, but one of the most important of this type is Shi`a. 'Hizbullah', the Party of God, is a name that has been borrowed by a number of groups from two Quranic verses, one of which says that the Party of God are 'the victors' (Q. 5. 56); but the best known of them is the Lebanese Shi`a organization, founded after the 1979 Iranian revolution and still a major element in Lebanese politics. Its astutely planned provision of social services is now extensive enough to be accepted by the Lebanese government as saving costs that would otherwise fall on the state (Jorand 2002: 34).

The Arabic nouns *hizb* and *shi`a* both mean 'party'. Whereas nearly all other Muslims are Sunnis, Shi`ism is the minority 'party' of those Muslims – about 10 per cent of the total – who recognize Ali, the Prophet Muhammad's son-in-law, as his rightful successor. It is the official branch of Islam in Iran, and Shi`as form an important minority in some other Arab countries and in Pakistan and Turkey, and a majority in Bahrain and Iraq. Shi`as have another religious tax in addition to zakat, known as *khoms* (one-fifth), levied annually on net income and wealth and paid to their religious scholars (*ulama*). These contributions are applied towards the expenses of religious institutions but also for hospitals, poverty relief etc.

In the National Pact that lasted for forty years in Lebanon after 1943, Shi`a Muslims had taken a back seat (among fifteen other religious confessions), the driving seats being taken by the Maronite Christians and Sunni Muslims; but the Shi`as' birth-rate was higher and many of them were migrating from the countryside to the poor southern suburbs of Beirut. A social uprising was organized in the 1960s and 70s, spearheaded by the Movement of the Deprived (*harakat al-mahrumin*) whose militia was known as AMAL – 'hope', also A*fwaj al-Muqawamah al-Lubnaniyah*, Lebanese Resistance Battalions). Their leader, Imam Musa Sadr, disappeared in Libya in 1978 and became a posthumous cult hero. However, in 1982, after years of regional conflict, AMAL veered towards a reformist Shi`a nationalism rather than Islamic radicalism, though a splinter group called Islamic AMAL was also formed – later to be absorbed by Hizbullah. During the late 1980s, Hizbullah and AMAL were at times fighting one another other rather than the common enemy (Esposito 1992: 140-50, Jaber 1997: 34-5).

Hizbullah was founded in 1982 under the inspiration of the Iranian revolution and with the support of the Iranian state and encouragement from Syria. Its leadership has been based on mosques and militias. It is marked by the Shi`a doctrines of self-sacrifice and martyrdom that generated, in the early 1980s, the first suicide bombings in the region. Hizbullah claims that its 'martyrological will' (*irada istashadiyya*) gives it an edge over its Israeli and other enemies (Saad-Ghorayeb 2002: 128). Its passionate commitment provided an effective resistance to the Western military presence but also helped to undermine the ideals of pluralism and tolerance in Lebanon, allowing Syria to dominate the area. Hizbullah makes skilful use of the press, radio and television. It also manages a formidable network of hospitals and other welfare and educational services. Typically, the southern suburbs of Beirut, once a middle-class residential district, had come to be known as the 'belt of misery', disfigured by sewage from burst pipes and piles of garbage: Hizbullah with Iranian help was able to build a comprehensive welfare infrastructure surpassing anything set up by its rival AMAL (Jaber 1997: 145-7).

Among Hizbullah's institutions are the Shahid ('martyr') Foundation, set up to support casualties of the war with Israel and their families, and also to promote – with considerable success – the ideology of martyrdom. 'Museums', in fact converted apartments, have been set up throughout Hizbullah areas, to display relics of martyrs such as bloodstained clothes, photographs in combat uniform, and their handwritten testaments which follow a standard form. In one of Beirut's Hizbullah fiefdoms, Dahhyat, it has been estimated that almost every family has some kind of affiliation to the Shahid Foundation (Danawi 2002: 29-68). Another institution is Jihad al Bina ('construction' – also the name of a major Iranian foundation), which aims to improve conditions in areas of Lebanon devastated by the war. Its policy stresses the importance of co-operation and self-reliance, using the analogy of a healthy immune system to explain how society can stand up to an enemy attack. Hizbullah's Relief Committee, spanning a wide variety of humanitarian and educational functions, has branches in eight regions of Lebanon, and is theoretically at the service of poor people whether or not they are Shi`a, though in practice few non-Shi`a avail themselves of the facilities. Indeed, there is evidence that families that do not vote for the Party at elections are excluded from Hizbullah's benefits Danawi 2002: 58-60). As well as subsidies from Iran, Hizbullah raises funds from Shi`a in Lebanon and elsewhere, and has interests in real estate and in commercial enterprises such as textile exports (Jaber 1997: 148-52). Through these and other initiatives, Hizbullah has won a powerful political base, shelving its original ideal of setting up an Islamic state and instead, in 1992, entering the electoral process. One of its strengths is a sophisticated committee structure, with no mass membership organization but a large pool of supporters, allowing it to present different faces to different publics. Women are prominent in Hizbullah's social programme but excluded from its political and military activities (Jorand 2002: 21). Like other Islamist movements, it is internally split between moderate and radical factions. It has been the only significant success in Iran's effort to export its Islamic revolution, and has had an influence beyond Shi`ism (Kepel 2002a: 130). In particular, it maintains an uncompromising stand against the state of Israel's right to exist, fanning the fire of Israeli-Arab conflict by extending its anti-Zionism (which it shares with all other Islamist movements) to include a comprehensive anti-Judaism that seeks its grounding in Quranic lore (Saad-Ghorayeb 2002: 134-86). Israel's decision to withdraw from nearly all of southern Lebanon in May 2000 was widely interpreted as a victory for Hizbullah, which has increased its regional prestige.

Hizbullah replicates the same pattern we have noted in Egypt and Algeria, whereby flagrant gaps in social provision by government are filled by Islamist private enterprise. One dramatic episode was the acute shortage of water in parts of Beirut after General Michel Aoun launched a war in 1989 against the Syrian presence in Lebanon, when his government turned off water and electricity supplies in an attempt to force the Muslims into submission. Hizbullah's Jihad al Bina opened an office to import hundreds of water tanks into Lebanon, adorned with the Hizbullah slogan, the Iranian flag and pictures of Iranian ayatollahs. Through such initiatives Hizbullah's leaders are able to claim that the organization is something 'larger than a party, yet smaller than a state' (Jaber 1997: 154-5, 168). Recently commentators have begun to speculate as to whether Hizbullah, with the experience of two decades of operating as a paramilitary in war conditions, would find it easy to adapt to conditions of peace and become an ordinary political party and/or development agency (Gerges 2002: 26).

An immediate outcome of the 2003 war in Iraq has been for the United States administration to apply intense political pressure on Syria, one of its complaints against it being the support given to Hizbollah and other organizations that the United States characterizes as 'terrorist'.

6

WESTERN VERSUS ISLAMIC AID?*

International Muslim charities and humanitarian aid in Sudan

'The missionaries in Africa have brandished the motto that says "Give up the religion of Islam, and we will free you from hunger, poverty, fear and sickness" ... Armies of missionaries have crossed Africa with food in their left hands and crosses in their right hands.'[1] It was in these terms that the Sudanese organization Da`wa Islamiya depicted, in its 1995 report of 15 years of activities, the missionary danger, in order to justify the activity of *da`wa*, the call to Islam. The play of events in Sudan has strikingly illustrated the relationship between the politics of aid and the religious question. Since the end of the 1970s, the country has been the victim of serious 'humanitarian crises': it has been a refuge for the crowds of exiles who have fled from neighbouring countries at war, but it has also been at war itself since the resumption in 1983 of hostilities between the Southern Sudanese rebels – principally, the Sudanese People's Liberation Movement/Army (SPLM/A) – and the government in the North.

Before going on to analyse the question of aid in Sudan, we must dispose of two misunderstandings that have a wide currency. The first is that it was after the coup by Omar al-Bashir in June 1989, and the setting up of an Islamist regime directed by Hassan al-Turabi, that the Islamic question emerged as central to political debates in Sudan. On the contrary, Islam had had a strong presence in Sudanese politics since the nineteenth century, when the Khatmiya and the Mahdi movement had been rivals in the mobilization of religious symbolism for political ends. The Khatmiya was an order founded by Muhamad Osman al-Mirghani (1793-1853), inspired by the teaching of the Idrissiya order of the Hijaz in Arabia. This order, which supported the Turko-Egyptian regime, actively opposed the Mahdist revolutionary movement, opening up a political rivalry that was slow to burn out. The Mahdist movement also dates back to the nineteenth century. Muhamad Ahmad al-Mahdi, who came from a family belonging to the Samaniya fraternity, launched a revolutionary movement against British rule in 1881, and developed an autonomous movement of *ansar* (as in

* by Jérôme Bellion-Jourdan

the 'helpers' of the Prophet Muhammad in Medina) or partisans. Since the 1950s and 60s, forms of political Islam evolved to build influence on the credit of these movements with their strong roots in the society.

The other misunderstanding is to characterize the war as simply one between the Muslim North and the Christian and animist South. First, while it is true that the various parties to the conflict make use of a rhetoric that borrows from religion (Hassan and Gray 2002), we must not forget the material motivations that have generated and fed the conflict, especially the desire to control the petroleum resources in the South. Second, strategic alliances and political manœuvres to seek a solution to the conflict show that self-interest can often win out over ideological considerations. Let us remember that one of the reasons for the arrest of the Islamist leader, Hassan al-Turabi, in February 2001, on the orders of his former ally, President al-Bashir, was that he had signed a memorandum with the Southern rebels calling for a lasting solution to the conflict and the 'constitution of a new society which would not allow the discrimination between citizens on the basis of religion, culture, ethnicity, gender or region'.[2]

As will be shown, the question of aid is at stake because its exploitation is mutually suspected by both sides of conveying elements of a religious idea, indeed a religious ideology used for political aims. In Northern Sudan especially, Islamist denunciations of 'Christian' or 'Western' intentions – the two are sometimes conflated – have been used to support a strong investment in the alternative arrangements of an 'Islamic' aid. But these elements of ideological mobilization should not be allowed to mask the fact that all parties to the conflict are capable of a pragmatic attitude.

The Islamist denunciation of the missionary past

A study by a Sudanese author, Hassan Makki, of the influence of the missionary factor on the political and cultural integration of the Sudan, indicates the elements that are taken up in the Islamist critique of humanitarianism. Published by the UK-based Islamic Foundation, which is close to the Pakistani Islamist movement Jama`at i-Islami, this analysis of missionary activities from 1843 to 1986 leaves no room for doubt about the reality of a 'Christian design' on Southern Sudan. According to Makki, Christian missionary organizations were traditionally abettors of the policy of Western influence over the Sudan. This was already so at the end of the nineteenth century, in the campaign against the Mahdi's revivalist movement: the Catholic mission in the Sudan provided a channel for foreigners to have arms conveyed in order to defeat Mahdism. This author likens the activities of these missionaries to the Crusaders, for they allowed the European powers to put the last touches to their preparations for the conquest of the Muslim state of the Sudan (Makki 1989: 31-2). According to Makki, the Catholic missionaries, considered as agents of European powers, facilitated the British tutelage of the Sudan, which was formalized by the setting up of an Anglo-Egyptian condominium in 1899.

Makki claims that the link between missionary and political projects continued into the twentieth century. Under the Condominium, missionary activities intensified in the South; for instance, a cathedral was built in Juba in 1920 which became the headquarters of the Gordon Memorial Southern Sudan Mission (ib.: 60f.). Seeds of conflict were sown which were to explode between the South and the North after

Sudan became independent in 1956. The elite that had been created by Christian missionary education was relegated to second place in independent Sudan, and became a critical factor in the dispute with the North which led to the conflict. After independence, the activity of missionary societies was controlled by the Missionary Societies Act of 1962. But Makki contends that Western and Christian influence has continued, this time in the form of NGOs – aid being used as a weapon to impose Christianity or Western secularism on the populations of South Sudan (ib.: 117). Interviewed in 1996 in Khartoum, where he was director of a centre for research and translation in the African International University, the author of *The Christian Design* emphasized this historical perspective on the emergence of the Islamic NGOs. He recalled with pride the pioneering role of the Islamic Relief Agency in the conception of an international activity of 'Islamic relief' connected to a system of financial institutions and businesses.[3]

The development of an Islamist alternative to meet Christian competition
The historical reality is no doubt more complex than the above picture of the missionary record in Sudan would indicate. Memories of the missionary past are inevitably selective, but the point here is that they have been used to justify the launching of counter-programmes. Africa is considered a strategic zone for the expansion of Islam, and the location of Sudan is especially important. Different methods have been used to ensure the Muslim presence on the African continent. During the 1960s and 70s, the emphasis was on education and *da`wa*. From the beginning of the 80s, the strategy was adopted of penetrating the charitable sector so as not to leave African populations exclusively in the hands of Western organizations. But as we shall see, the relative consensus over the necessity of opposing Western projects did not lead to any unity of action, but resulted in competition among Muslim organizations: appeals to the principle of unity (*tawhid*) did not stand up to a reality that was fashioned by rival ambitions.

Investment in charitable organizations was one means towards this competitive penetration, but not the only one. In the 1960s, some states supported networks of Sufi fraternities in order to maintain influence in Africa; for instance, Egypt under Nasser built up close links with the Tijaniya fraternity, which was strongly entrenched in west Africa and whose leader, Ibrahim Niasse, was received by Nasser several times in Cairo.[4] It has been suggested that this link enabled the Egyptian president to increase his popularity in west Africa. In order not to be left out, and although its Wahhabi ideology was opposed to Sufi Islam, the Saudi state also supported these networks through offering educational and research bursaries (Kane 1997: 55-6).

From the 1960s onwards, Saudi-Arabia was active in seeking to develop networks favourable to itself on the African continent, particularly in East Africa, which was considered an 'Islamic frontier', the limit of the *umma* (Brenner 1993: 15). The Saudi influence was particularly manifest in the activities of the World Islamic League in education and *da`wa*, and in the support given to launching a number of Islamic institutions (Constantin 1993: 48-53).

Another step to further the interests of the Gulf States was the founding in 1967 in Khartoum of an African Islamic Centre, designed to mould an African elite as a counterweight to the Westernized or Christianized elites. Its activity was interrupted after the coup which brought Jaafar Numayri to power in May 1969, but it was reopened in 1971 under the control of the Ministry of Religious Affairs and Property, and then in 1972 turned into the Institute of Islamic Education. With its headquarters ten kilometres south of Khartoum, it was funded by Saudi-Arabia, Kuwait, Qatar, the United Arab Emirates, Egypt, Sudan and Morocco. In 1977, this centre welcomed about sixty students from Tanzania, Kenya, Uganda and Sudan, but by 1987 the number had risen to 780. Meanwhile, the centre built up four departments: education, da`wa (from 1980), research and publications (from 1982) and social services – the last-named of which was responsible for material aid to various Islamic institutions in Africa. After the coup of June 1989, the new regime decided, as part of a reform of education, to turn the centre into the International African University (Grandin 1993). When I visited it in 1996, the university was still very active and full of students from all over the African continent. Many received support from Islamic organizations such as Da'wa Islamiya. According to an employee, it supported the university financially and enabled African students to attend by providing them with flight tickets, housing and monthly scholarships.[5]

Da`wa Islamiya and the Islamic African Relief Agency

Gradually the charitable sector was penetrated. The idea was to combine support for African Muslim populations with da`wa. The Islamic African Relief Agency (IARA) was started as a branch of the Organization for the Islamic Call (munazamat ad-da`wa al-Islamiya or MDI) in Sudan. These two organizations were to play a very active role on the African continent, contributing to an increasing presence of Islamic NGOs in Africa, and thus to what Salih has called the 'promise and peril of Islamic voluntarism' (Salih 2003). The founding of IARA illustrates how 'Islamic relief' was initially thought of as part of a broader project of commitment to Islamic renewal through da`wa – a project which has provoked strong competition both at the national and the international levels. The decision to found Da`wa Islamiya was taken at an international conference on da`wa organized in Khartoum in 1980 at the invitation of Jaafar Nimayri, who was keen to give his regime some Islamic legitimacy. This conference agreed to the creation of an organization to specialize in the call to Islam on the African continent.

The aims for which it was launched in May 1980 were to work towards 'the propagation of Islam as faith [`aqida] and as law [shari`a] in non-Muslim communities' and 'the emancipation of Muslim communities that are capable of understanding the doctrine of tawhid [the unity of God] and the expression of its deep meanings for individual and social life'.[6] Da`wa is thus the act of preaching both to Muslims who are enjoined to rejoin the path of 'true Islam' and to non-Muslims who are invited to convert. The Arabic-language publications of the organization leave no doubt about the matter. Thus, the image of the muhtadi [convert, i.e. 'rightly guided'] occupies a central place: in its newsletter, Al-risala [the message], the agency has been keeping an annual count of the number of converts, accompanied by qissas muhtadiyya, testimonies which underline the strictly voluntary character of conversion to Islam.[7] As El-Affendi puts it, the reasoning behind these organizations was that Christian missionaries had used education and humanitarian aid to 'subvert' African Muslims, and it was therefore essential to give Africans an alternative which would not allow the missionaries to exploit African poverty and thus to 'impose' Christianity (El-Affendi 1990: 280).

Da`wa Islamiya's head office is in Khartoum, but it has an international dimension. Initially, its support came mainly from foreign countries, and its activities came to develop for the most part outside Sudan – as is reflected in the composition of its directorate in 1982. Alongside Sudanese personalities, there were listed representatives of Gulf States (Saudi-Arabia, Kuwait, Qatar, Bahrain, the Emirates), either from ministries or from Islamic institutions which often placed themselves at the service of the foreign policies of host countries. Thus among the directors of Da`wa Islamiya were the secretary-general of the World Islamic League and his assistant, the former secretary-general of the World Assembly of Muslim Youth (Tawfiq al-Qasir, a professor at the University of Riyadh) and the head of the Kuwaiti agency Beit uz-Zakat.

The agency's funding followed a similar pattern. An element of rivalry arose between Libya and the providers of funds from the Gulf. Since the 'First of September Revolution' of 1969 that brought Muamar Gadaffi to power, Libya had been seeking to extend its influence in Africa. The Libyan *jamahiriya* ('state of the masses') had its own agencies for this purpose, such as Jami`yyat Da`wa Islamiya, based in Tripoli (Otayek 1986). The Sudanese Da`wa Islamiya seemed to Libya an opportunity to extend its influence, and so it was helped by support from Jami`yyat Da`wa Islamiya in Tripoli, towards the building of its headquarters in Khartoum.[8]

This Libyan initiative displeased the Gulf governments. At the time, Iranian influence was marginal on the African continent and provided no challenge to the hegemonic projects of the conservative Gulf states (Chouet 1994). By contrast, the revolutionary aspect of the Libyan programme worried these conservative regimes and most of all Saudi-Arabia. Gadaffi's Libya had established some distance between itself and Western countries, and was aligning itself with the Soviet Union (El-Kikhia 1997). In this context, Saudi-Arabia – anti-communist and making use of Islam in its external relations – was considered a guarantor of Western interests to protect the Red Sea region from Soviet influence, just as the Western powers also relied on the Shah of Iran in the Persian Gulf. In 1976, after the attempted coup in Sudan, an agreement to meet the challenge of Libyan subversion was signed between Sudan, Egypt and Saudi-Arabia (Otayek 1983: 10). The Islamic orientation of the Libyan regime was in danger of entering a competition with the Saudi ambition of monopolizing Islamic legitimacy in the world of Sunni Islam, which included Sudan and other African countries. The Saudi authorities were specially afraid that Libya would use Da`wa Islamiya to increase its influence in Chad, and so sought to outbid it financially.[9]

Very rapidly, the providers of funds from the Gulf came to dominate the financing of the activities of Da`wa Islamiya. The report for 1981-9 enables us to distinguish different types of investor who funded its operating programmes in Sudan:[10]

States: the United Arab Emirates, which financed the building of a mosque at the Ministry of Higher Education, and another in the military camp of the *ma`qil* [fort] at Shendi in the north; the state of Kuwait – for the As-Sabah hospital for children at Juba, and a mosque at Wau.

Ministers of governments in their private capacities: Sheikh Khaled Ban Hamad al-Thani, Minister of the Interior for Qatar – an irrigation project at Omdurman.
Companies: the Ben Laden Foundation – 'six Ben Laden schools' in the North and in Khartoum at a cost of $600,000.
Businessmen and financiers: the Saudi, Sheikh Saleh Kamel – reconstruction of schools for $700,000; Sheikh Tariq Ben Laden, also Saudi – 'Ben Laden wells' in the Ramak area of the High Nile.
Islamic banks: the Islamic Development Bank – a hospital at Luwa, secondary schools for Eritrean refugees in the East of Sudan.
Other Islamic institutions: the World Islamic League – the fitting out of the As-Sabah Hospital at Juba, funded by Kuwait; the Kuwaiti Beit uz-Zakat – the 'Kuwait maternity centre' at Mayo, mosques in the Nuba mountains, and clinics and other services for displaced populations.
Charitable institutions: the International Islamic Charitable Organization (Kuwait) – a mosque in the village of Abu Ju in Jezira; the Africa Muslim Agency – two mosques.

The 1991 report, which also includes Da`wa Islamiya's programmes outside Sudan, confirms the predominance of finance from the Gulf, as well as the variety of different sources. This predominance might lead us to conclude that it was an organization controlled by the Gulf states. This conclusion however would take for granted the assumption that local agencies have no room for manoeuvre in the field.

Da`wa Islamiya in the Sudanese domestic scene: control by the Islamists
The case of Da`wa Islamiya in Sudan shows that such an assumption is wrong. It was indeed a tool of the Gulf states in pursuit of influence in Africa. But gradually it came to be diverted from its initial objective to become one of the instruments of a local political movement which sought to take power: the tendency led by Hassan al-Turabi within the Sudanese Islamist movement.

By contrast with other countries in the Middle East, in Sudan it was within a political environment dominated by religious references that contemporary forms of Islamism developed. 'Popular' forms of Islam have had a marked influence in Sudan. It has been argued that this was one of the factors which explains why the growth of the Muslim Brothers movement from the 1940s to the 1960s was slow (Ibrahim 1992).

A new form of Islamism did develop slowly, partly on account of contacts with the Muslim Brothers of Egypt in 1944-5, when Sudan was still under the Anglo-Egyptian condominium. Periods of multi-party politics were favourable to the growth of the movement (Niblock 1991). The foundation of the Islamic Charter Front (*jebha al-mithaq al-islami*) in 1964 marked the entry on the stage of Hassan al-Turabi. In the 1970s, he began to oppose the traditional orientation of the Sudanese Muslim Brothers, led by Al-Sadiq Abd al-Majid, and this rupture was formalized in 1985 with the formation of the National Islamic Front (*al-jebha al-qawmiya al-islamiya*) led by al-Turabi.

After Nimayri's coup in 1969, the opposition was severely repressed, and certain officials such as Turabi were imprisoned. Others sought refuge abroad, including Sadiq al-Mahdi, leader of the Umma party, who was welcomed in Libya by his personal friend, Muamar Gadaffi (Otayek 1986: 40f.). The militant Islamists who took the path of exile took advantage of this period to build up contacts and overseas networks, for instance in import/export businesses, as potential support for later political activity.

When Nimayri proposed a policy of 'national reconciliation' on 27 May 1977, the Islamists seized the opportunity of this turning-point to play a role on the Sudanese political scene. On their side, after the return of their leader Sadiq al-Mahdi to Khartoum, the Mahdists played the game for a time, while the Khatmiya remained mistrustful.[11] The leader of the Islamic Charter Front, Hassan al-Turabi, was freed and agreed to assume some political responsibilities, then became attorney-general, in charge of justice. This period was also utilized to establish Islamic institutions in Sudanese society. Contacts made during the period of exile were mobilized to stimulate investment in Sudan.

There grew up an Islamic economic sector including banks and investment houses. One of these was the Faysal Islamic Bank, founded in May 1978 in Khartoum, of which a large minority stake was owned by Prince Muhamad Bin Faysal, the Saudi founder of the project and a personal friend of al-Turabi since the beginning of the 70s (Marchal 1995: 20). This bank set up subsidiaries such as the Islamic Insurance Society and the Islamic Investment Society (Ahmed 1997, Medani 1997). The climate was favourable for these institutions to flourish, for the Nimayri regime announced the application of *shari`a* in September 1983. Then on 9 December of the same year a committee set up by the President announced that no bank was authorized to operate a system of loan interest. The Muslim Brothers' control over economic institutions provoked the hostility of the Khatmiya, whose rich traders reacted to the success of the Faysal Islamic Bank by setting up in 1982 the Sudanese Islamic Bank in order to keep their monopoly over retail commerce (Ibrahim 1992: 45-9).

When Da`wa Islamiya was launched, various Sudanese political elements drawing their legitimacy from Islam sought to benefit from the organization's activities. Much was at stake. It was in fact a composite entity comprising a variety of institutions that were financially and administratively autonomous. Thus it was active in the investment sector with the Don Fodio Benevolent Foundation for Commerce and Contracting (*mu'assasa don fodio al-khairya lil-tijara w l-muqawalat*), which operated in the import-export field and made investments in real estate, timber and textiles. Regarded as a 'welfare company', it was exempt from tax. The Don Fodio Foundation invested in Kenya, Nigeria and other foreign countries, as well as in Sudan, and it contributed 20 per cent to Da`wa Islamiya's budget.[12]

Da`wa Islamiya also invested in the African Council for Private Education, with schools aimed at the children of rich Sudanese and foreign diplomats in Khartoum; in a centre for research and training in *da`wa*; in media production studios;[13] and also in charitable works. To begin with, one branch was active in this field, the African Society for the Care of Mothers and Children (which later became independent). In 1981, the Islamic African Relief Agency (IARA – *al-wekalat al-islamiya al-ifriqiya lil-ighatha*) was founded.

It soon developed its activities at the international level, initially in many African countries but also in other continents, for instance in Peshawar during the Afghan war, under the name of ISRA. In a Da`wa Islamiya leaflet published in Arabic in 1985, IARA was described as 'the first relief organization of this kind on the African continent, amid an impressive number of foreign and evangelical agencies'. This agency 'had established in a short time a solid base of Islamic work in this new field for *da`wa* methods, by means of competence, precision and security in the provision of relief services'.[14] From the beginning, then, relief programmes were explicitly conceived as being subsidiary to preaching.

At the beginning, too, influential members of the Islamist movement were providing a bridge, more or less officially, between the planning of *da`wa* and the political project. Thus Mohamed Abd Allah Jar al-Nabi, believed to be a principal funder of the Sudanese Islamist movement, was a member of the African Council for Private Education. When, in 1986, he opened an office of his company in Sudan, it diversified from commerce into construction, and its first project was of a charitable nature. With \$10 million of Kuwaiti financing, his company built the Kuwaiti Village of Compassion (*qariat hanan al-kuwaitiya*): this project, designed for a thousand children, mainly from Eritrea, was in fact a project of Da`wa Islamiya's.[15]

On a political chess-board where the principal parties adopt Islam as a key rallying-point, we must not generalize and assume that all the Sudanese representatives in the hierarchy of Da`wa Islamiya were part of the Islamist tendency led by al-Turabi. Other tendencies were represented, such as some businessmen of the Khatmiya and the Ansar al-Sunna al-Muhammadiya ('supporters of the Prophet Muhammad's Tradition', an orthodox group not known for its direct political activism). Moreover, the apparent clarity of political confrontations could be disturbed by the play of interpersonal relations within the elite. The marriage in Khartoum of Hassan al-Turabi, leader of the National Islamic Front (NIF), to Wisal al-Mahdi, sister of Sadiq al-Mahdi, head of the Umma, was a prominent case of a kinship bond which happened to unite two rival political leaders in a way that would not have been predictable otherwise.

Nevertheless, it is true that Islamist officials close to the al-Turabi tendency were specially numerous in the managing board of Da`wa Islamiya. One was Ahmed Mahjub Haj Nur, one of the three judges presiding at the appeal court in Khartoum who decided in 1985 on the death penalty for apostasy of Mahmud Muhammad Taha, the leading intellectual and leader of the Republican Brothers. Taha, who had founded the Republican Party in 1945 calling for the independence of Sudan, had developed a spiritual, non-political reading of Islam, which remains today an inspiration for many young educated Sudanese.[16]

Signs of growing control over Da`wa Islamiya by the Islamists multiplied during the 80s, and provoked some reactions. Da`wa Islamiya became an issue in the domestic political conflict: when Nimayri turned against the Islamists in 1984, conscious as he was of the influence that they had acquired over the workings of power and authority, some employees of Da`wa Islamiya were arrested. When interviewed in 1996, the executive director of the organization recognized that Nimayri's action had had a political aim: 'At the beginning of the 80s, there was no multi-party system. ... When the Nimayri regime tried to outlaw the organization, it was a political act. But it hurt a few people who were sent to prison, not the activities of the organization as a whole'.[17] The regime collapsed in 1985 before the organization could be outlawed.

Nimayri's successor was Swar al-Dahab, who led the Transitional Military Council between 1985 and 1986 towards a new period of multi-party politics. Jazuli Dafallah, president of the Doctors' Union, then became first minister in an interim government (Holt and Daly 1988: 217-225). Once their missions were carried out, both men moved from the sphere of politics to that of charity. Swar al-Dahab was appointed president of Da`wa Islamiya, and Jazuli Dafallah honorary president of the Islamic African Relief Agency. A simple calendrical coincidence? Dafallah's appointment is unsurprising, in that he was known for his closeness to the Muslim Brothers, which became public when he openly supported the Islamic laws adopted in 1983.

As for Swar al-Dahab, his career is more surprising. Coming from the Khatmiya, it appears that when he was president of the Transitional Military Council, the Islamists proposed a deal to him. If he would not abrogate the Islamic laws of 1983, they would give him the post of president of Da`wa Islamiya, which was prestigious but also of material significance. Certain sources suggest that the honorarium was some $30,000 per month, in addition to the use of an official car. A different version has been given however by Nimayri himself, in an interview published in *Al-Wasat*.[18] Returning from his exile in Egypt to take part in presidential elections in Sudan in the autumn of 2000, the former president of Sudan is settling scores. He openly criticizes Swar al-Dahab, whom he had named Minister of Defence just before his departure for the United States for medical consultations, which the minister made use of to effect a coup. Nimayri calls Swar al-Dahab a coward (*jaban*) and claims that he had also appointed him as 'the head of the Islamic relief agency'. Whichever version of the facts is true, both are evidence of the strategic and coveted status of the directorship of Da`wa Islamiya – a position which also allowed al-Dahab to take the number two position in the Cairo-based World Islamic Council for Da`wa and Relief (see p.75), founded in 1988 and headed by the Sheikh Al-Azhar. Da`wa Islamiya was more and more at the heart of the political battle, even if it is hard to determine how much real control of the organization was exercised by the Islamists.

When the leader of the Umma party, Sadiq al-Mahdi, became prime minister in 1986, the Islamists of the NIF, led by al-Turabi, strengthened by their relative electoral success, claimed a share of power and set their conditions.[19] A new power struggle set in, between Da`wa Islamiya and the government, dominated by the Umma party. Sadiq al-Mahdi had welcomed the foundation of the agency: during the Nimayri period, he had taken part in meetings of its managing board, and considered it a means to attract external Arab finance to counterbalance the influence of Western NGOs in dealing with Sudan's humanitarian problems. Some years later, Da`wa Islamiya was treated by Sadiq al-Mahdi as an instrument in the service of the competing Islamist party, the NIF. 'We took a negative attitude', said the head of the Umma party in an interview in Khartoum in May 1996, 'when we noticed that they were not sincere in their humanitarian activities, using the resources for the purposes of the political confrontation'.[20] The attorney-general outlawed the organization in 1986, but its jurists were successful in having the decision annulled for want of legal proof. Was it the Umma party's aim in doing this to destabilize the NIF? In 1996, at a meeting at his house in Omdurman, Sadiq al-Mahdi acknowledged this readily and said he regretted having failed to do so. Did the Umma party have its sights set on Da`wa Islamiya? That is what the secretary-general of the organization asserted: he suspected the Umma party of having seen in the agency 'a type of popular activity that could be useful to it' for domestic political ends, and that the other political side, the NIF, should not benefit from. According to Dr Al-Amin, the Umma party had been trying 'to get its hands' on every organization in Sudan.[21]

International to begin with, Da`wa Islamiya came more and more to be thought of as an instrument of the NIF's on the domestic political scene in Sudan – which obviously upset the other political formations. Ironically, the agency's leaders replied to criticisms – both from the Nimayri and the Sadiq al-Mahdi regimes – precisely by emphasizing that the international character of the organization was proof that it could not be the tool of any domestic political agenda. In an interview published by *Sudanow* in 1985, Mubarak Qasmallah, its director, stated that

> the agency is not part of the Muslim Brothers at all. It is an international agency belonging to all Muslims, wherever they are and whatever their political orientation. Thus, what Nimayri did surprised me deeply, because it was he who, in 1980, exerted himself to convince the conference members that its headquarters should be in Sudan. ... All the funding comes from outside Sudan.[22]

In reality, the external funding did not mean that the agency's policies derived from a truly international dimension: the process of 'NIFization' of the agency which began in the 1980s was reinforced after the June 1989 coup which brought Omar al-Bashir to power.

The initial project of *da`wa* was far from disappearing; but the power struggle between those who defined Da`wa Islamiya's policies was moving on. External investment in the service of *da`wa* in Africa was channelled by a local political force. Displaced from power by the 30 June 1989 coup, Sadiq al-Mahdi was free in his criticism of the 'politicization' of the agency – which he had not been able to capture for his own party. Here is what he told me in 1996:

> They succeeded in grasping the resources of rich Muslims from Saudi-Arabia and Kuwait ... who considered it a duty to work for the islamization of Sudan's non-Muslims. The NIF appealed to them as follows: 'If you put your resources in our hands, we will be able to convert the non-Muslims of Sudan, and indeed of Africa'. That was the pretext ... for grasping resources which they proceeded to use for another purpose. By politicizing these agencies, they involved them in the political confrontation, at the risk of weakening them and putting their future in doubt.[23]

Thus Da`wa Islamiya gradually became a partisan organization, made use of both in Sudan and in its transnational networks. In the Sudan of the 1980s, it was one means among others to establish the influence of the NIF. And in common with some other organizations, it was clearly seen at the time as an organization in the service of NIF, a true lever of power behind the scenes. Rumour says that it was in the studios of Da`wa Islamiya in the Ryad quarter of Khartoum that the president recorded his first televised address announcing the successful coup.

After June 1989: the nation first, or Islamism first?

After the coup by General Omar al-Bashir on 30 June 1989 which overturned Sadiq al-Mahdi, the new regime's Islamist orientation became clear in the ensuing months (Marchal 1992, Sidahmed 1997). Even if al-Bashir did not flaunt any sympathy for the Islamists, it turned out to be the men of the NIF in the shadows who held the true reins of the new power. Though he occupied no official position until his election as parliamentary Speaker in 1996, Hassan al-Turabi was considered the 'grey eminence' of the new regime. In April 1991, he founded the Arab and Islamic People's Conference, with himself as secretary-general, which was intended to be a platform for Islamist and Arab nationalist movements. For this Islamist ideologue, every effort had to be made to further the 'civilizing' project of islamization. The social welfare sector was critical. In an interview given in 1997, al-Turabi welcomed the resources that had been mobilized to support this policy: 'Gradually, in Sudan, we are making progress along the road of total islamization. As the state does not make available enough resources for this responsibility to be taken up, zakat and waqf, which are collective assets according to Muslim ideas, allow us to support a system of social welfare' (al-Turabi 1997: 166). These financial levies, justified by the Islamic tradition of good works, would be used to top up state taxation and thus make possible a programme of extensive control of society, and hence of retaining political power.[24] The zakat levy would also assist the war effort, a war openly characterized as jihad in order to gain support for it, in which the combatants were *mujahidin* and the casualties martyrs, a war to be fought both by a regular army and by popular defence forces (Baillard and Haenni 1997: 88, Sidahmed 2002).

In this context, the denunciation of international humanitarian aid as the hand of the foreigner served to justify the maintenance of policies for controlling the work and/or resources of NGOs or international agencies. This denunciation was made in the name of the defence of Islam and/or the nation. At the time of the famine which threatened Sudan again in 1991, al-Turabi castigated those whom he accused of wanting to use international aid to interfere with Sudan's international affairs:

> Some people want to use the drop in agricultural production, due to the drought, to tie our hands. It is preferable that several thousands of people should die rather than allow the international crusade to come to our help. ... We will never declare a famine as long as we are an Islamic nation. ... We will never allow international aid organizations to do what they want in our country and to oppose the plans of the Islamic Revolution in the South.[25]

In language less inflamed but similar in content, the president of Islamic African Relief Agency (IARA/ISRA), interviewed in Khartoum in 1996, denounced the international NGOs which he had suspected since the 1980s of contributing to a policy which he wittily described as a 'Sudanese Yalta' – aiming to divide Sudan into zones of influence like the Allies in 1944. According to the deliberately provocative analysis of Abdallah Suleyman al-`Awad, CARE's sphere of influence was the Kordofan region, Oxfam's was the west, ADRA's (Adventist Relief Agency) the north, and World Vision's the south.[26]

It would be a mistake to see in these opinions a hostility to the very principle of humanitarianism, especially when the speaker is head of a relief agency. But they indicate the viewpoint of those who condemned any use of humanitarian aid that did more of a bad turn than a good turn to their own interests. Legitimate arguments, in defence of culture and sovereignty put at risk by humanitarian aid, were deployed in the service of local strategies to control the activities of international agencies. In other words, the vaunted objective was to encourage the activities of Sudanese agencies; but in practice, it was often those agencies, Sudanese or international, near to the Islamist tendency that were the ones to profit from this policy.

After the model of the Missionary Societies Act of 1962 which aimed to control missionary activities, measures to control international NGOs had already been taken under the government of Sadiq al-Mahdi (1986-9). This process intensified after the coming to power of Omar al-Bashir in 1989. When questioned about these measures, Ghazi Salah Eddine Atabani, an influential official in the NIF and then president of the National Congress, defended them by invoking two principles consistent with themes that were being developed on the international scene: reaffirming the sovereignty of the state, and showing preference for local organizations.[27]

It was thus in the name of respect for national sovereignty that the Sudanese government laid down conditions for the implementation of Operation Lifeline Sudan (OLS). Set up in April 1989, this was an arrangement supervised by the United Nations for coordinating relief to populations affected by the war that had been fought since 1983 between the government in northern Sudan and rebel movements in the South. The arrangement provided for activities in the northern sector being supervised by the authorities in Khartoum, while coordination of cross-frontier activities in the southern sector would be the responsibility of Unicef's office in Kenya (Karim 1996).

In the same way, it was officially to encourage local organizations that the Humanitarian Affairs Commission (HAC – a merger in 1996 of the Relief and Rehabilitation Commission and the Commission for Voluntary Agencies) was entrusted with a precise task of controlling the voluntary organizations operating in Sudan. Thus, the Country Agreement signed in 1993 made the continued operation of international agencies – work permits, import of goods, access to displaced persons' camps – conditional on their forming partnerships by 'twinning' with Sudanese organizations.

If this policy of twinning soon proved unrealistic (Karim 1996: 50 and 97-8), the growth of local organizations, encouraged by the government, showed tangible results. New organizations were founded such as the Foundation for Peace and Development, while existing agencies, particularly Da`wa Islamiya and Islamic African Relief Agency, experienced a new lease of life.

Whether coincidentally or not, the suspicion expressed with regard to the international agencies, especially since 1989, corresponded to an increase in the number of international Islamic relief agencies working in northern Sudan.[28] These included the British-based agencies Islamic Relief and Muslim Aid, the International Islamic Relief Organization (IIRO) and Lejnet al-Bir al-Dawliya (Committee for International Charity) from Saudi-Arabia, the Africa Muslim Agency from Kuwait, as well as the Muwaffaq al-Kheiriya with its headquarters in Jersey – all of which opened offices in Khartoum and developed programmes in various regions after the beginning of the 1990s. As the executive manager of Muwaffaq al-Kheiriya admitted in an interview in 1996, the launch of an office in Khartoum had been facilitated by the authorities: Muwaffaq al-Kheiriya were granted facilities such as a building plot for an office, exemption from customs and taxes, and free transportation of relief to the South.[29] Thus the Islamist critique of international practices of humanitarian aid was of benefit to other practices of humanitarian aid – local or international, but Islamist.

Criticisms of Islamist use of humanitarian aid

In Khartoum, there were many criticisms of the Islamist control over aid, voiced sometimes by the staff of international NGOs and often by Christian Sudanese organizations, which vigorously denounced the close collaboration between the government authorities and Islamic organizations. In an interview conducted in 1996 in Khartoum, Toby Maduot, president of the Sudan Democratic Forum and the Society Dinka Rek, painted a picture of the Islamic NGOs as surrogates for the governmental policy of the North, serving the interests of the 'war against non-Muslims in the South' and working to convert them. For him, the policy of reception for displaced persons in the camps set up in the outskirts of Khartoum was part of this strategy: the Islamic agencies put the displaced persons 'at the mercy of the NIF', and 'food is used as a weapon to convert as many people as possible to Islam'.[30] An even harsher analysis was given to me by the secretary-general of the Sudan Council of Churches (SCC), a federal institution set up in 1967 with some thirteeen member churches.[31] According to Rev. Enoch Tombe, the NGOs were in the service of the NIF which sought to prolong the war in order to be able to islamize the South. He said that 'Christian communities are bound to lose members in the Islamic hands which are protected by the government'. According to him, the policy was part of a broader aim, the islamization of Africa, deriving from a duty to 'to fill the vacuum' motivated by the strong assumption that 'Africans have no religion and are pagans'.[32]

External observers have also emphasized the practice of islamization and its political aims. Some have taken sides and become spokesmen for the sufferings of the Christians, as in the case of Jacques Monnot's book, whose very title, *The drama of South Sudan: Chronicle of a forced islamization*, is expressive (Monnot 1994). For Abdou Maliqalim Simone, the policy of 1991-2 consisted of dislodging the displaced populations from their temporary residence in Khartoum to put them in camps in the outskirts of the capital, 'providing special food relief and employment to those converting to Islam' (Simone 1994: 68), and this was due to the regime's fear of seeing an Africanization of Khartoum develop. As for Donald Petterson, United States ambassador to Khartoum between 1992 and 1994, he was able to observe on various occasions the alignment of certain NGOs with government policy. Petterson was allowed to fly to the 'transition zone' between North and South. On 27 September 1993 he went to Malakal (500 miles south of Khartoum) where there were 95,000 displaced persons with nothing but their clothes, some very sick. He noted that there were no international NGOs present and that 'the area in the vicinity of the town had been divided into five parts, each of which was the responsibility of one of the five Sudanese NGOs working there'. He reports that a local official whispered to him that 'the Islamic NGOs (four of the five NGOs at Malakal) were using relief supplies as a tool to Islamize people in the camps' (Petterson 1999: 31).

On the question of islamization, it is not always easy to distinguish between the forced and the voluntary conversions. Thorough field research with the recipients of aid would be needed to better understand their relations with the various different aid providers, after the model of Barbara Harrell-Bond's pioneering study which showed how aid is sometimes imposed on beneficiaries (Harrell-Bond 1986). The extreme sensitivity of the issue could lead to special difficulties for any researcher who was outside the aid system.

I experienced this myself in 1996 when I asked to visit the Jabal Awliya camp, one of the main camps for displaced persons (along with another, Dar as-Salam) on the outskirts of Khartoum. It was Abdallah Suleyman al-`Awad (of whom more below) who arranged this. After a delay required to get leave to make the journey, I left on Saturday 11 May 1996 to visit the camp in a 4 by 4 car belonging to the Islamic African Relief Agency and driven by one of their staff. We were accompanied by a young state employee, responsible for the coordination of Khartoum refugees, who was to play his part well in representing the authorities. When I prepared to take some photographs on arrival at the camp, he intervened and stopped me taking them, saying he had orders to do so, though I had an authority to take photographs and a press card obtained from the Ministry of Culture. Families were surviving in temporary tents during very hot weather, totally dependent on humanitarian organizations, some Sudanese (Da`wa Islamiya, IARA, Sudanese Red Crescent, SUDRA, Sudan Council of Churches) but three of them Islamic international agencies (Muwaffaq, IIRO and Africa Muslim Agency), as well as MSF Holland which was mainly concerned with sanitation. Everything seemed to be done to prevent me from meeting any staff of Christian agencies, of whom it was said that they did not work on Saturdays. I visited the clinics and feeding centres run by IARA and Da`wa Islamiya, and talked with their staff.

The IARA administrator in the camp explained to me that his organization did not set out to practice da`wa. But when we discussed a particular given project, it became clear that things were not quite so clear-cut. For instance, in order to confront the scourge of AIDS which was spreading in the camp, IARA had put in place a programme of prevention by means of the distribution of condoms supplied by the World Health Organization. But there was a problem with lack of stocks. The distribution of condoms was not the only means of prevention. The administrator emphasized the importance of getting across a message about sound morals, whether through the help of religious leaders, or more directly in the case of those 'without religion' – by which was meant the 'animists'. Thus material aid was accompanied by an educational dimension. This was also to be found in IARA's programmes to dissuade displaced persons from practising female excision, a practice specially common among those who came from Kordofan and Darfur.[33] But what did the beneficiaries think? I had no idea: when I asked to speak with some of the inmates in the camp, I was told that we were short of time, and we got back up in the car and returned to Khartoum. Even if I had been allowed to sound out the opinions of the displaced persons in the camp, they would probably have hesitated to speak in the presence of their aid suppliers.

The question of the political and religious use of aid must be considered in its context. Often, Islamic NGOs are denounced by other organizations that do not wish to be marginalized. Among others, the Sudan Council of Churches (SCC) complained about the contrast between the privileges given by the state to Islamic organizations and the obstacles put in the way of organizations linked to the SCC such as SUDRA and SUDANAID.[34] But this denunciation derived from the strategy of an organization that was suffering from not being allowed to implement its own missionary programme freely. The constitution of the Sudan Council of Churches provided in fact for the organization 'to assist the members of the Churches in the extension of God's Kingdom by spreading the Good News of Salvation'.[35]

Sometimes, the aid providers found themselves at the heart of international political matters. Thus, after the attempt on the Egyptian president Hosni Mubarak's life in Addis Ababa in June 1995, the spotlight turned to the Khartoum regime, which was under suspicion of serving as a rear base for international 'terrorism' with an Islamist orientation. Furthermore, some aid suppliers were suspected of giving cover to these activities. For instance, the newsletter *Africa Confidential* sought to demonstrate a 'Khartoum connection', noting in its issue for 7 July 1995 that one of the people arrested by the Ethiopian authorities was a Sudanese working for the organization Muwaffaq al-Kheiriya, described as a 'NIF agency'.[36] This resulted in a lawsuit against *Africa Confidential*. Interviewed in Khartoum in 1996, the executive manager of the organization, Sirag Al-Din Abdul Bari, denied the allegations and emphasized its international and humanitarian character.[37] But this episode cost the Khartoum regime a United Nations resolution.

After the attacks on US embassies in Tanzania and Kenya in August 1998, Sudan was again singled out: the United States launched a missile on a medicine factory on the outskirts of Khartoum. However, with time there has been progress towards normalization. To prove its engagement in the 'war against terrorism' after the 11 September 2001 attacks on New York and Washington, the Sudanese government submitted a detailed report in December 2001 to the Counter-Terrorism Committee set up under Resolution 1373 (2001) of the UN Security Council. Annexed to the report is a letter from the President of Sudan, Omar al-Bashir, addressed on the day of the attacks to his American counterpart, George W. Bush, to remind him that 'we strongly condemn all acts of terrorism, reaffirming our willingness to cooperate with you, and the international community, to combat all acts of terrorism'. The Sudanese authorities set out in this 47 page document the measures taken by them to combat 'terrorism', their close cooperation with the American government services, and the results of an enquiry conducted by the Sudanese Central Bank, rebutting the allegation that Usama bin Laden was a founder and shareholder of Al-Shamal Islamic Bank, a leading Islamic financial institution in Sudan.[38] Thus with time, Sudan's signs of conduct seem to have paid off. Hassan al-Turabi's marginalization seems to have been enough to give the appearance of a less Islamist regime, even though some major figures in the movement remain in key posts. The image of Sudan has changed, and criticism has become less virulent.

Humanitarian politics and pragmatism win out over ideological differences

In order to help us escape the ready-made binary opposition of 'Western/Christian' and 'Islamic', three points may be made in conclusion. First, competition has been intense between the groups and movements presenting themselves as legitimate representatives of a correct conception of Islam. This considerable diversity has been reflected in competition between Islamic aid organizations. The rivalry between the partisans of Sadiq al-Mahdi's Umma party and the Hassan al-Turabi tendency has continued to intensify. When the officials of the Umma party lost hope of influence over Da`wa Islamiya or the IARA after the June 1989 coup, they founded another charitable organization. In an interview carried out in March 1997 for the well-informed study published by African Rights, Nasr al-Din al-Hadi al-Mahdi, of

the Umma party, spoke of the recent foundation of the Sudanese Community
Islamic Relief Organization, based in Saudi-Arabia. The Umma party thus hoped to
redirect the donations of Sudanese expatriates, including zakat contributions, by
offering them an alternative to the Islamic organizations working in the zones
controlled by the Sudanese NIF (African Rights 1997: 195-6).

A second point is that, as well as confrontation, some processes of cooperation,
even of hybridization, may be observed. A striking case is the strategies implemented
by the Islamic [African] Relief Agency (IARA-ISRA), based in Khartoum. For
IARA-ISRA, the search for support from NGOs and international organizations
began in the 1980s. The career of Abdallah Suleyman al-`Awad, the founder, later
chairman of the agency, is an example of hybridization. A medical doctor by training
and a militant Islamist, he was for many years employed in Alexandria at the East
Mediterranean Regional Office of the World Health Organization. As he explained
himself in an interview conducted in 1996, this position enabled him to assimilate
the culture of an international organization and appreciate all the advantages that
would accrue to his new organization from participation in the various consortia of
international NGOs. At the same time, giving some humanitarian legitimacy to his
organization enabled it to avoid the accusations that were directed against Da`wa
Islamiya, of which IARA was initially a branch – that it was making use of
humanitarian aid for political purposes.

Declaring that he preferred 'field dialogue' to 'intellectual dialogue between Islam
and Christianity', Abdallah Suleyman al-`Awad tried from early on to convince
Christian or Western agencies to work with him, reminding them that as Christians
they wanted to help the poor, just as Muslims wanted to help the poor.[39] Seeking to
implement the idea of twinning with international NGOs, the IARA worked in
partnership on specific projects with agencies such as World Vision, the Lutheran
Federation, Oxfam, ADRA and MSF Holland. It proved more difficult, according to
al-`Awad, to work with the French MSF. Sometimes, IARA obtained public funding.
For instance, in 1998 the Islamic American Relief Agency (also using the
abbreviation IARA), a sister agency of the Sudanese one, was awarded two grants
from the US Agency for International Development (USAID), totalling $4.2 million,
for projects in Mali. (In December 1999, the US State Department decided to
suspend this grant in the context of investigation into the armed attacks in 1993 on
the World Trade Center and in 1998 against the American embassies in Nairobi and
Dar as-Salaam. The director of IARA-USA stated in his defence that his agency,
registered since 1984 in Columbia, Missouri, had nothing to do with Sudan and had
never been accused of activities linked to 'terrorism'. He announced his intention to
appeal against the decision.)[40]

Furthermore, having been granted consultative status with the UN Economic and
Social Council (UNECOSOC), IARA worked with UN agencies such as the High
Commissioner for Refugees or Unicef. Finally, al-`Awad played a key role in
enabling his agency to become an active member of international NGO forums. He
helped found the Forum of African Voluntary and Development Organizations
(FAVDO) in Dakar and was vice-president for a time. Proud of having enabled a
'Third World organization' to be admitted to the International Council of Voluntary
Agencies (ICVA) in Geneva, he became a member of ICVA's executive council in
1986 and vice-chairman in 1990.

A third point: what may be called the transition to humanitarianism of an Islamist organization can lead it, perhaps unexpectedly, to adopt a pragmatic and critical position with regard to the Islamist project. Thus, ISRA-UK (the UK branch of IARA-ISRA) distanced itself from the Khartoum regime because the regime's policies made fund-raising for the humanitarian agency difficult. Interviewed in Birmingham in 1996, Abdul Samad Summers, manager of the organization's British branch, told the following story to illustrate the prejudice felt against his agency on account of all that was being said in the media about the predicament of the Christians in Sudan. Summers, while accompanying an official of the Methodist Church on a visit to Bosnia to evaluate a joint project in Tuzla, had to reply to the questions of devout Christians who were concerned by information coming from Sudan: about the massacres of Christian priests, about Christian believers crucified, and about children captured in the South of Sudan, taken to the North and forcibly converted. Following this exchange, Abdul Samad Summers took the opportunity of a stay in Khartoum to raise the matter with a Sudanese army general. He said that he had enquired of the general, what was all this about people being crucified? He explained that he had to work with different groups worldwide: if the Churches were subjected to discrimination in Sudan, it raised a serious problem for fund-raising.

In conclusion, though many differences may be identified between different forms of humanitarian aid, the element of pragmatism seems to be common to them all. Whatever the principles justifying a project, it can only be realized if it gets support. Like their Christian or Western equivalents, Islamic relief agencies must bow to the rules of communication and marketing.

THE BALKAN CASE

Transnational Islamic networks in Bosnia-Herzegovina

An 'Islamic reading'

'At the dawn of the twenty-first century, the new world order has inflicted in the Balkans a scourge on Islam and the Bosnian Muslims, equivalent to that produced by the preceding world order in Palestine' – thus, in June 1993, the journal *Sarajevo*, published in Arabic by an Islamic organization active in Bosnia. During the Bosnian conflict (April 1992 – December 1995), the analogies advanced between Bosnia and a 'new Palestine', with its mass of refugees without land, were frequent and aimed at stirring up manifestations of 'Islamic solidarity' with Bosnian Muslims.

The Serb nationalists skilfully played on the presence of 'Islamic NGOs' and *mujahidin* to sustain their propaganda on the 'Islamic threat', and certain Western capitals were concerned to see the Balkans beginning to bring up the rear in an unrestrained Islamic militantism (Ranstorp and Xhudo 1994). Had Bosnia become a new 'bastion of Islamic fundamentalism'?

When the Bosnian conflict broke out, certain elements formulated an 'Islamic reading', which described the war as an aggression against Islam and the Islamic community. These elements often had a strategy to use the situation to foster an Islamic renewal in the Balkans after the fall of communism. But this interpretation of the conflict did not convince the whole of Muslim world, nor did it convince all the Bosnian Muslims.

In the Muslim world as a whole, different elements turned commitment in Bosnia into an aspect of 'Islamic legitimacy', which actually exposed situations of conflict. Bosnia became all the more important a stake in these rivalries because the Balkans, barely emerging from Communism, were pushing back the imaginary frontiers of the *umma*. The organizations in the field sought both to reislamize Muslim populations and also to position themselves in the internal configurations of local Islam. In fact, their interventions were largely aimed at not abandoning the Balkan region to a competitive state or Islamist movement – a competition that was to be used locally and to fuel local political rivalries.[1]

* by Jérôme Bellion-Jourdan

After Afghanistan, Bosnia as a new cause for Islamic mobilization

We have already outlined in Chapter 4 how, during the resistance to the Soviet invasion of Aghanistan in 1979, a number of states made use of Islamist movements to promote their own interests.

With the Gulf War against Iraq in 1990-91, the American and Saudi strategy of using transnational Islamist networks arrived at a turning-point. The United States were decried for their imperialism, and Saudi-Arabia was denounced for having – by means of a *fatwa* delivered by the principal Saudi religious authority, Sheikh bin Baz – given legitimation to the presence on the territory of the two holy places, Mecca and Medina, of 'infidel' American troops.

From now on, Usama bin Laden, formerly an unofficial representative of Saudi policies in Afghanistan, made many statements denouncing the United States and the Saudi regime. This cost him his Saudi nationality in April 1994. But thanks to his charisma as a *mujahid* and his financial means, bin Laden remained a reference point for the combatants, at a time when the Afghan jihad was losing direction. For the volunteers who came to fight the Soviet enemy were faced by disillusion after disillusion: after the retreat of the Soviet troops in 1989, then the fall of Muhammad Najibullah's communist regime in April 1992, the Afghan conflict was changed into a civil war between different Muslim factions, on the basis of ethnic and religious (Sunni-Shi`a) divisions.

The conflict in Bosnia, which flared up in April 1992, coincided with the fall of Najibullah in Kabul and the drift of the Afghan conflict into civil war. Certain Muslims saw in the Bosnian conflict an 'Islamic cause' to replace the Afghan jihad. But to what extent in practice did this conflict become a catalyst for a new mobilization at the level of the *umma*, capable of bringing combatants and charitable organizations to a new commitment in the field, as the Afghan conflict had done?

Before April 1992, the fall of communism made a certain revival of Islam possible in the Balkans. But Muslim leaders were already drawing attention to the threat that Serb nationalism meant for the Muslims of the region. Thus in August 1991 Jakub Selimoski, *reis-ul-ulema* of the Islamic Community (*Islamska Zajednica*) in Yugoslavia, addressed a memorandum to 'all Islamic organizations and institutions in the world' to appeal for their support as 'atheist communist ideologies are replaced by exclusively nationalistic ideologies which have assumed, especially in the eastern parts of the country, open anti-Islamic tendency'. In case of a war against Muslims in the Balkans, 'protection of faith, life, honour and property becomes a religious obligation, and the responsibility for our destiny falls on the entire Muslim Ummet'.[2]

When the conflict flared up in Bosnia, the pan-Islamist current within the Democratic Action Party (Stranka Demokratske Akcije or SDA), the main Muslim party, played the card of Islamic mobilization, in the face of the opposition of those parties known as 'citizen', i.e. non-communitarian (Bougarel 1996). Thus, on 18 and 19 September, the mosque in Zagreb, whose senior imam Mustafa Ceric was one of the founders of the SDA, organized an 'international conference on the protection of human rights in Bosnia-Herzegovina', with representatives from thirty Muslim countries. Attending this conference were some great figures of Islamic militantism: Yusuf al-Qaradawi (a renowned intellectual close to the Muslim Brothers), Muhammad al-Ghazali (a teacher at the University of Al-Azhar), Khurshid Ahmed (president of the Islamic Foundation in Britain, close to the Pakistani *jama`at al-*

islami), and Yusuf Islam (president of Muslim Aid). The conference resolutions presented the conflict as a war of aggression whose aim was to eliminate the Bosnian Muslims. For the first time at the local level, the struggle for the liberation of Bosnia was presented as a jihad that all the Muslims of the *umma* must support.[3]

These local appeals to the unity of the *umma* did not go without responses. The fall of Communism facilitated the setting up of Islamic organizations whose aim was to control, by means of competing strategies, the revival of Islam in the Balkans. Albania was without doubt a key target (Clayer 2001: 150-5) but the deterioration of the political situation in Bosnia suddenly led to this area's becoming a priority. For instance, the International Islamic Relief Organization (IIRO), based in Jeddah, funded in 1991 the foundation of an Islamic Council for Eastern Europe, with Jakub Selimoski as president; and the Director of Islamic Relief, based in Britain, visited Albania and Bosnia, where he gave his support to the founding of a charitable organization Merhamet ('charity'), close to the SDA.[4]

The start of the Bosnian conflict accelerated this implantation. Various elements in the Muslim world produced an 'Islamic reading' of the conflict, both to provoke demonstrations of solidarity and to satisfy their own ambitions (Mitri 1993, Farag 1996). The Islamic humanitarian organizations took part in this process, and the statements of political leaders and *ulama* also contributed to it. A video distributed in 1993 by the British organization Islamic Relief, entitled 'Yugoslavia: the Crime of our Time' illustrates clearly this interpretation of the conflict.

According to this video, the Bosnian conflict was only part of a vast plan of elimination, aimed also at Sandjak, Kosovo and Macedonia. The executioners are 'infidels'. As the commentary hammers home, the communists of yesterday have been replaced by the Serbs today: 'the infidels had tried to exterminate the Muslims in Yugoslavia but now, the masters of communism have handed over power to their compatriots … and the victims were not changed, the means of torture remain the same'. The Serb projects of ethnic cleansing and the destruction of mosques evidently contribute to sustaining this argument. However, the aspects of reality which do not fit into the model of Serbs as executioners and Muslims as victims are obfuscated: the responsibility of the SDA in the triggering of the conflict, military alliances between Croats and Muslims, the presence of Serbs and Croats in the Bosnian army, and so forth.

In this Islamic reading of the conflict, the resistance of Bosnian Muslims, their jihad, was glorified. The figure of Alija Izetbegovic was, of course, honoured. He was known for having been the author in 1970 of an 'Islamic declaration', the manifesto launched under the authoritarian rule of Tito, calling for the 'islamization of those who call themselves Muslims', with the ultimate aim of establishing an 'Islamic power' on the basis of an 'Islamic society' (Izetbegovic 1990 cited in Bougarel 1994: 293). A key activist of the pan-Islamist movement since the 1940s, he, along with others, used the period after the fall of Communism to play an active political role. He became president of the SDA and then of Bosnia, and it was in him that the Islamic organizations rested their hopes of a Muslim resistance to the Serbs, in order thereafter to pursue their projects of Islamic revival in the region.

The promoters of an Islamic understanding of the conflict gave a religious connotation to the categories of friends versus enemies, Muslims versus enemies of Islam. The Bosnian Muslim was a friend because he was a Muslim, the Serb an enemy because hostile to Islam. 'When one part of the body of the *umma* suffers, it is all the parts together which must react' – this *hadith* was taken up as a leitmotiv in the campaign on behalf of Bosnia. From this point of view, even when there was no formal alliance or diplomatic agreement with Bosnian Muslims, whoever did not bring support was not a 'true' Muslim. This type of argument would have found less of an echo if it had not been for the widespread use of the issue of 'Islamic legitimacy' by certain political elements in order to discredit their adversaries. Thus, disseminating an Islamic reading of the conflict made it possible to impose as a publicly accepted norm the commitment of every Muslim to support the Bosnian Muslims; failure to take this responsibility would be to risk seeing one's own 'Islamic legitimacy' being challenged. This did not prevent various elements in the Muslim world from maintaining relationships with the Serbs, such as commercial relationships between Egyptian and Yugoslav companies, but when relationships of this kind were discovered they were condemned by the Islamist movements.

The campaign for Bosnia and competition within it
The proclaimed objective of coming to the help of Bosnian Muslims, and the types of action envisaged – humanitarian aid versus military commitment – concealed competition among the different elements. Three types of configuration emerged, allowing us to identify different interventions and uses of transnational networks during the Bosnian conflict. First, the use of these networks in the course of competition between states, as in the case of Saudi-Arabia versus Sudan or Iran; second, conflict between a government and its Islamist opposition, using the Bosnian cause as a way to delegitimize its power, as in the case of Egypt; and third, competition between Islamic organizations set up in the West which used their commitment in favour of Bosnia to increase their influence over Muslim minorities, as in the case of Britain.

Officially, and in keeping with their membership of the international community, the states in the Muslim world respected the resolutions of the United Nations (resolution 713 of the UN Security Council imposed an embargo on all arms intended for states that had been part of the former Yugoslavia, see Nagan 1994), and did not intervene directly in the Bosnian conflict. The statements of principle and resolutions adopted at the summit meetings of the Organization of the Islamic Conference (OIC) were not followed through (an example being the ultimatum of 15 January 1993 fixed by the OIC for lifting of the arms embargo). But in practice this façade of state non-intervention concealed 'non-governmental' activities under the remote control of certain states in competition with one another. This was the case with Saudi-Arabia, which, after the 1990-91 Gulf War, feared that Iran and Sudan would exploit the anti-Saudi hostility of certain Islamist groups.

In the Bosnian conflict, Sudanese activity was channelled principally through Da`wa Islamiya and Islamic Relief Agency, which were present in the field since 1992. These two organizations were reputed to be close to the National Islamic Front, which had held the reins of power *de facto* since 1989 (see Chapter 6). Moreover, the Sudanese regime allowed Usama bin Laden to settle in Khartoum in 1994, building up his economic activities there and setting up training camps for combatants, some of whom joined the Bosnian front. For the Saudi regime, the presence of bin Laden in Sudan signified an external threat (the threat of his mobilizing Islamists hostile to Saudi-Arabia) but also the potential to stoke up an increasing domestic opposition; for indeed, since 1993 an Islamist opposition began to denounce openly the corruption and pro-Western orientation of the Saudi regime. On the other hand, the Saudi authorities had to take into account Iranian strategies in the Balkans. At that time, the Saudis feared that Iran would try to control Sunni Islamist movements, using Sudan as an intermediary. The visit of the Iranian President, Hashemi Rafsandjani, to Khartoum in December 1991 was seen as a sign of rapprochement between Sudan and Iran. In 1992, Iran sent some *pasdaran* (Guardians of the Revolution) to stiffen the leadership of the Bosnian combatants. Thus at the time of the Bosnian conflict, both the Sudanese and the Iranian strategies were resulting in a requestioning of the Saudi regime's Islamic legitimacy, and hence its security.

Faced with this, the regime made use of a tried and tested strategy, raising the stakes. The International Islamic Relief Organization (IIRO), an agency created by the World Islamic League, embarked, under the local name of IGASA (the local pronunciation of *al-ighatha*), on sizeable humanitarian programmes aimed at the Bosnian Muslims who had taken refuge in Croatia and Slovenia. In September 1992, a second structure was set up, directed (as in the Afghan conflict) by Prince Salman ben Abd al-Aziz: the Saudi High Committee for Aid to Bosnia-Herzegovina. These so-called NGOs were in fact para-statal structures corresponding to the Saudi strategy in Bosnia, which was to control the territory so that Bosnian refugees and foreign combatants would not become clients of groups or states hostile to the regime.

The campaign for Bosnia, as well as being an object for competition between states, also provoked conflicts on the domestic political stages of various Muslim countries. The case of Egypt shows how an opposition movement could use this campaign to promote its own 'Islamic legitimacy' and thereby to denounce the illegitimacy of the powers-that-be. The Muslim Brothers – as the main opposition movement, albeit unauthorized and at one remove from the political scene – used their influence in the professional associations to launch initiatives in support of Bosnia. Thus, from the start of the conflict the humanitarian branch of the influential Medical Doctors' Union, the Human Relief Agency, worked in refugee camps in Croatia. At a number of meetings, religious leaders and personalities close to the Muslim Brothers, such as Muhammad al-Ghazali of the University of al-Azhar, put pressure on the Egyptian authorities so that the Bosnian conflict might be supported as a jihad equivalent to the Afghan one. In response, the government refused to make any military commitment – for reasons of foreign policy (the UN's embargo on arms, and fear that the SDA might create an Islamic state in Bosnia) combined with internal factors (the experience of 'Afghan Arabs' who had returned to Egypt to swell the ranks of the armed Islamist groups).

Thus the campaign for Bosnia was also a stake in domestic politics: the Muslim Brothers denounced as illegitimate the power of a government that disregarded the 'Islamic duty of solidarity'. Confronted by the Muslim Brothers' unsettling initiatives, the Egyptian authorities eventually reacted. Starting in 1993, and more openly in 1995, the government penalized the Human Relief Agency, which was suspected of being a front for illegal activities benefiting the armed Islamist groups Gama`at Islamiya and Al-Jihad (Shaqiq 1995). Several of the organization's key members were arrested, and its funds were frozen and transferred to the Egyptian Red Crescent Society, whose president was Suzanne Mubarak, the wife of President Hosni Mubarak. This kind of domestic confrontation had a parallel in Turkey with the case of the German-based agency Internationale Humanitäre Hilfe, which was made use of in the political strategy of Turkey's principal Islamist party, Refah Partisi or Party of Prosperity (Bilici 1997).

And third, the Bosnian conflict gave rise to a process of competitive campaigning among minority Muslim populations. This was particularly true of Britain, but the process could be observed in France or the USA as well. No more than on the occasion of the 1990-91 Gulf War or the Rushdie affair was there any unanimous reaction of a supposed 'Muslim community'. As in the case of those two events, the initiatives taken in support of Bosnia were indicative of competition between organizations that wished on the one hand to increase their influence with Muslim populations, and on the other to be recognized as leading interlocutors by the public authorities. In Britain, two opposite types of institution may be distinguished. The first type defended the idea of humanitarian aid to the Muslims of Bosnia, and it was attacked by the second type, which called for military commitment.

As for the first type, the Bosnian conflict gave rise to a substantial development in Islamic charities. Numerous 'Muslim charities' were founded – such as Helping Hands, Children's Relief Fund and so forth – but the most active were those that had already developed a transnational network. Apart from Muslim Aid, it was Islamic Relief that experienced the greatest expansion. Founded in 1984 by Hany El Banna, then an Egyptian medical student at the University of Birmingham, this organization saw a quadrupling of its donations to fund its programmes to help Bosnian Muslims. If these organizations had their own Islamic reading of the conflict – the oppression of Bosnian Muslims just because of their adherence to Islam – they confined themselves to humanitarian programmes and refused any sort of military commitment. Regulated by the UK Charities Acts, which forbid charitable organizations to get involved with any political activity, these agencies played the card of respectability in order to gain the recognition of the British authorities.

By contrast, other Islamic organizations opted for a radically different strategy, calling for military commitment. Apart from organizations such as Hizb al-Tahrir (Party of the Liberation),[5] which reportedly took part in the recruitment of volunteers for the war in Bosnia, the most striking is that of an embryonic organization founded in January 1992, the Muslim Parliament of Great Britain. The leader of this organization, Kalim Siddiqui, adopted a strategy already tried out at the time of the Rushdie affair when he was director of the Muslim Institute, a pro-Iranian organization based in London: the strategy of radicalizing the debate within the British Muslim community and provoking the British authorities (Kepel 1994). In October 1992, the Muslim Parliament organized a demonstration in Trafalgar Square, bringing together some hundreds of individuals who chanted slogans glorifying jihad in Bosnia. In November 1993, Siddiqui presided over a 'world conference' on Bosnia, during which Islamic personalities condemned the 'Muslim charities' as agents of the West and of the Saudis, that contented themselves with delivering humanitarian aid to the Bosnians rather than giving them the means to defend themselves with. In the same way, the Muslim Parliament launched in June

1993 a 'Fund to arm Bosnia' which was rapidly outlawed by the British authorities.[6] In short, the provocations of the Muslim Parliament gave the organization a certain visibility but proved to be too radical to exert a real influence over British Muslims. In fact, on this point at least, the picture with minority Islam was the same as with the Muslim governments: there was no mass campaign to come to the help of the Bosnian Muslims. Campaigning resulted from various elements seeking to increase their capital of 'Islamic legitimacy' on the local and the international level. What is presented as an expression of 'Islamic solidarity' is by no means a homogeneous phenomenon, flowing from the immutable essence of Islam.

Bosnia as the new site of jihad

'Freedom fighters', '*mujahidin*', 'terrorists': such are the terms that were used to designate the cluster of foreign combatants coming from different regions of the *umma* to fight in Bosnia. They came in groups at once heterogeneous in character and secret, with seemingly only one factor in common: participation in a jihad. Though there were some overlaps, four types of foreign combatant may be identified: the 'Afghan Arabs', the militants from armed Islamist groups, the pro-Iranian combatants, and the new volunteers.

First, the 'Afghan Arabs' included Arab combatants who had taken part in the Afghan war, of different origins (Egyptian, Saudi, Yemeni, Algerian and so forth) and with different ideological commitments, and they seemed to have little in common except this strong engagement with the Afghan jihad. The Afghan war had indeed created networks of mutual acquaintance, more or less formalized, marked by points of reference such as bin Laden or the late Abdallah Azzam. Convinced that their duty was to defend Muslims of the *umma* wherever they were threatened, certain of these combatants were ready to fight on 'lands of jihad' such as Kashmir, the Philippines or Bosnia.

The second type included combatants from the armed groups of the Muslim world that sent men to fight in Bosnia. These groups defended a particular cause in a given country: Groupe Islamique Armé (GIA) in Algeria, Gama`at Islamiya and Al-Jihad in Egypt, Movement of the Partisans[7] in Pakistan, and so forth. Some of these combatants had taken part in the campaign in Afghanistan or had lived there in military training camps. Pro-Iranian combatants formed a third category on their own. The most numerous to intervene in Bosnia were the *pasdaran*. But starting in 1992, combatants also arrived in Bosnia from Hizbullah, the pro-Iranian Shi`a group (see Chapter 5).

Fourth and last, the Bosnian conflict was an opportunity for some young people to embark on combat for the first time. Given the tight control exercised by some states such as Saudi-Arabia, Egypt and Algeria, the volunteers coming from the Muslim world were much fewer than on the occasion of the Afghan war. By contrast, young Muslim volunteers from the Western countries were more in evidence. Belonging to the fringe of young men attracted by the reislamization movements, they responded to the appeal of organizations such as the Muslim Parliament in Britain, or committed themselves independently. Some of them had earlier taken part in military training courses organized in the outskirts of Peshawar in Pakistan.[8] And finally, among the new combatants were Muslims from the Balkans, especially ethnic Albanians from Kosovo and Albania.

Participation of the mujahidin in the Bosnian conflict

Different channels, more or less formalized, facilitated the advance of combatants during the first months of the conflict. In 1992, the Office of Services (*maktab al-khidamat*), founded by Abdallah Azzam in Pakistan, opened a branch in Zagreb, Croatia, from where the combatants moved on to different positions in central Bosnia. Certain Islamic NGOs such as the Third World Relief Agency (TWRA) or the Muwaffaq Foundation seem to have also arranged for combatants to reach the front.[9] If the training of certain combatants was undertaken in military training camps on the Afghan-Pakistani border or in Sudan, other camps were opened too in Bosnia.

In the first phase of the conflict, the participation of foreign combatants was hardly controlled. The appeal to jihad launched in Zagreb in September 1992 was met with reticence by the heads of the Islamska Zajednica – literally 'Islamic Community', the institution supervising the Muslim community – and by the high command of the Bosnian army, who refused to adopt a religious reading of the conflict. The foreign combatants took advantage of the weak degree of control exercised by a Bosnian army still in the process of being recruited, and were able to group themselves into autonomous 'Muslim units' or to create their own units. These were marked by a strong stress on religious practices and by a definition of the conflict as a jihad. In Travnik in central Bosnia, Abu Abdul Aziz, a Saudi veteran of different jihads (Afghanistan, Kashmir, Philippines) took charge of the 'Muslim forces' (*Muslimanske snage*), a unit including Bosnian Muslims and combatants from the Muslim world, but also from Europe and the United States. He claimed to be 'the principal commander of all the *mujahidin* of Bosnia' and announced that he would not obey the orders of the Bosnian army.[10] But in November 1992 the 'Muslim forces' merged with the 7th Battalion of Zenica to form the 7th Muslim Brigade, the first and principal 'Muslim unit' integrated into the ranks of the Bosnian army.

The presence of foreign combatants alongside the Bosnians provoked some clashes. The foreigners, trained in the idea of a universal jihad to 'defend Islam', saw in Bosnia only one jihad among others such as those in Kashmir or the Philippines. But behind this proclaimed universality of jihad there were concealed in reality some very particular conceptions of Islam and of conflict in its name. In Bosnia, as earlier in Afghanistan, some of the foreign combatants transformed the conflict: they fought one jihad against the enemies of Islam, and another in parallel against local conceptions of Islam. A good example is the above-mentioned 7th Muslim Brigade, composed of both Bosnians and foreigners. In the brigade, the Bosnian commander was at the same time a sheikh in the Sufi brotherhood *nakshibendi*, and the combatants practised some Sufi rites such as the *zikr*, an untiring repetition of formulas and divine names. But the foreign combatants sought to impose their own conception of Islam: the Salafi conception which Abu Abdul Aziz, among others, adhered to.[11] This condemns Sufism together with all forms of popular religion. These religious divergences provoked violent altercations, and led in 1993 to the murder of a Bosnian combatant by a foreigner. Finally, schism in the brigade proved inevitable: in August 1993, a specific battalion, called El-Mudzjahid, was founded for the foreign combatants, who were later joined by other Bosnian Muslims that were attracted by Salafi Islam.

Insofar as their numbers remained limited to a maximum of 4,000 to 6,000, the military capacity of the foreign combatants must not be exaggerated. But their weak manpower was balanced by the great mobility of their units and the effectiveness of their forms of operation. Their role must in fact not be judged only by their military capacity; certain groups of combatants seem also to have been used for tactical purposes by the Croat and Serb forces. Thus in 1992-93, when the Serbs wanted to break up the Croat-Muslim alliance, it would seem that they let *mujahidin* pass through their territory so as to make the Croats feel the dangers of the 'Islamic threat'.

It would appear that certain Islamic NGOs took part in providing arms as well as humanitarian aid to the Bosnian army and the groups of *mujahidin*. In July 1993, the Croat police searched the offices of several organizations in Zagreb and claimed that they had seized arms there. The Egypt-based Human Relief Agency and two Saudi organizations, IIRO and Al-Haramain,[12] were accused of making common cause with the *mujahidin*. We should recall that up till the spring of 1993, the strategic alliance between the Council of Croat Defence (HVO) and the Bosnian army allowed the HVO to deduct its own share of convoys financed by the Muslim world and passing through Croatian territory. The campaign conducted during summer 1993 by the Croatian authorities against the Islamic NGOs was aimed, then, at cutting off the Muslim forces' supply lines. But in a conflict where, locally, the parties were face-to-face and sometimes lent one another, or bought from one another, arms and munitions, this campaign could not reach all the supply lines for arms: certain organizations actually bartered humanitarian aid from the Muslim world for Serb arms. In regions where certain Serb units had difficulties in obtaining food and medicines, the Egypt-based Human Relief Agency would seem to have engaged in such transactions of exchange.[13]

Starting from the end of 1993, a second phase began with the Bosnian army's attempting to regain control over the activity of foreign combatants and 'Muslim units'. In June 1993, the new minister of the interior, Bakir Alispahic, took repressive steps against certain foreign units that were out of control. Similarly, at the end of that year the reorganization of the Bosnian army included the reintegration of certain units that until then had been autonomous, such as the 'Handzar division' and 'Green legion' in central Bosnia.[14] The unit called El-Mudzjahid kept its position in the 3rd Corps of the Bosnian army, but a new commandant, an Algerian called Abu al-Mali, took charge of it.

Integrated into the Bosnian army, the units consisting of foreign combatants now became the objects of official recognition. If the 'citizen' parties still refused to consider the Bosnian conflict as a jihad, some political, military and religious leaders adopted this interpretation. At the heart of the Bosnian army, new promotions allowed officers close to the SDA and favourable to an Islamic reading of the conflict to be nominated. The Islamska Zajednica, directed since April 1993 by Mustafa Ceric, appointed imams in certain units. On two occasions, Izetbegovic expressed in public his gratitude to the foreign combatants. In December 1993, he visited the El-Mudzjahid unit, and in January 1995 he was present at Zenica for a march past of the 7th Muslim Brigade, accompanied by a visitor whose presence was noticed, Ayatollah Ahmad Jannati, president of the Iranian committee for the support of Bosnia.

From war to the post-war period: 'combatants' or 'terrorists'?

Within the religious and military circles that considered the Bosnian conflict to be a jihad, there was no consensus as to its nature or its aims. Was it merely a combat *against* the Serb aggressor or was it also a struggle *for* the setting up of an Islamic state in Bosnia? The position of the foreign combatants was often clearer: participation in the conflict was not merely defensive but also aimed at the reislamization of local populations. In the same way, the participation of the *mujahidin* did not follow the calendar of international negotiations. Indeed, for some of them a peace accord would only be legitimate if it allowed for the setting up of an Islamic state.

From this point of view, the Washington accords setting up the Croat-Muslim Federation in March 1994 were seen as a betrayal of the aim of jihad. Questioned in August 1994, the Saudi commandant Abu Abdul Aziz described it as the worst scenario imaginable.[15] Even more clearly, the Dayton accords were denounced as a Western diktat aimed at depriving the Muslims not only in Bosnia but in the whole world of a victory allowing them to set up an Islamic state in the Balkans. After leaving Sarajevo and on his way to Zagreb, a Yemeni combatant stated in December 1995 that the *mujahidin* and the Bosnian army were on the point of completely liberating Bosnia. Some combatants had the idea of taking up the struggle against the Croats, even of declaring jihad against Izetbegovic.[16]

In October 1995, a civilian was killed and 29 others wounded in a car-bomb attack in the Croatian town of Rijeka. Was the conflict being pursued by means of 'terrorist' activities? In reality, this attack reflected a change in the pattern of violence, on account of factors external to the local context. The new conflict reflected the opposition between Gama`at Islamiya and the Egyptian government. On 12 September 1995, an Egyptian, Talal Fuad Qassem, was arrested in Croatia; a former spokesman for Gama`at Islamiya, imprisoned in 1981, he reached Afghanistan in 1988 having served his sentence, but then, risking the death penalty in Egypt, he was granted political asylum in Denmark. During the Bosnian conflict, he took part in the military training of groups of *mujahidin* and had many contacts with members of the Gama`at Islamiya present in Croatia, Macedonia, Bulgaria and Turkey. In arresting him, the Croat authorities took the side of the Egyptian authorities and triggered a spiral of repression and revenge, for the attack in Rijeka was claimed by the Gama`at Islamiya in Cairo, and then defended by Anouar Chaaban, formerly the Egyptian director of the Islamic cultural centre in Milan and commandant of a group of *mujahidin* in central Bosnia. In reprisal, Chaaban and five other *mujahidin* were killed on 14 December 1995 in Zepce by the Croat HVO – deaths for which the Gama`at Islamiya in Cairo appealed for revenge. This chain of events shows the pattern of local Bosnian jihad overlapping with that of another local jihad focused on Egypt; the first blamed the Croats as obstacles to the setting up of an Islamic state, while the second blamed them as accomplices of the Egyptian authorities.[17]

The Dayton accords were all the more decried by the foreign combatants because they meant not only a halt in their struggle for an Islamic state, but also signed, in a way, their expulsion orders from Bosnian territory. It was again owing to the United States that the honourable figure of the 'combatant' was transformed into the blameworthy figure of the 'terrorist'. Having let the foreign combatants commit themselves in Bosnia to a form of jihad replacing that in Afghanistan, the United

States now denounced the 'terrorist' risk that they represented – mainly not for the local populations, but for American troops. About 20,000 American soldiers were to take part in the Implementation Force (IFOR), the international peacekeeping force commanded by NATO which took over from the United Nations' protection force (Forpronu). Moreover, Article III of the military section of the Dayton accords obliged the various parties to demobilize foreign combatants, and the American negotiator Richard Holbrooke, visiting Sarajevo in December 1995, insisted to the Bosnian authorities that the group of *mujahidin* should have left Bosnian soil by 20 January 1996.

As before in Afghanistan, the American rhetoric on 'terrorism' made every foreign combatant a potential terrorist, setting a dilemma for the Bosnian authorities: expelling the former combatants and risking their hostility, or not expelling them and having to face American retaliatory measures. They tried to combine a discreet and symbolic recognition of the role of the *mujahidin* with organizing their departure. Before the signature of the accords on 14 December 1995, Izetbegovic went to the training centre of the El-Mudzjahid unit in Zenica, and decorated several combatants with the Golden Lily, the highest Bosnian military award. The Islamska Zajednica, whose leadership met at Zenica on 23 December, received a delegation of combatants and published a communiqué expressing its 'gratitude to the *mujahidin* of the Muslim world for the sacrifice and good deeds that they have accomplished in Bosnia'.[18]

From December 1995, the foreign combatants left Bosnian soil in small groups, passing through Zagreb. But before leaving, some of them committed acts of looting at the expense of civilian populations, for instance in Podbrezje, a suburb of Zenica with a large Croatian population.[19] Thereafter, their paths separated and little is known about them. Some risked returning to countries of origin – Saudi-Arabia, Egypt, Algeria – which repressed them as 'terrorists'; others, frustrated by demobilization, joined networks ready to lead them towards other jihads. But despite American pressures, some foreign combatants did stay in Bosnia, or return there.

If the majority of foreign combatants left Bosnian soil before February 1996, the pressure exerted on the Bosnian authorities by the United States did not prevent some dozens of former *mujahidin* from settling there. Those who had contacts with Islamic NGOs managed to stay as employees of these organizations, notably in their offices in Zenica or Travnik. But these redeployments were always temporary, for after the war most of the Islamic NGOs reduced their activities, even closing down their offices. Other careers began to define themselves: some became clients of certain networks of the SDA, some formed Islamic micro-societies, some drifted into crime.

Islamic NGOs between *ighatha* and *da'wa*

The military involvement of the mujahidin has been only one face of the external support given to the Bosnian Muslims. Another important role was played by the Islamic relief organizations that started to operate soon after the conflict broke out. Were these organizations used as a cover for military and violent activities? The question was repeatedly raised during the war – whether by the media in search of a scoop, by governments wishing to discredit such organizations' activities, or by other NGOs in an attempt to disclose that these competitors were not genuinely humanitarian – and it has continued to resonate up to now, especially since 11 September 2001.

There is no doubt that some organizations were closely linked with groups that had a military agenda or with *mujahidin*. Allegations that some organizations smuggled arms have been substantiated by hard data. But it would be too narrow an approach to study these organizations only for their possible links with the military. Many Muslim relief organizations during this war did undertake relief programmes in an attempt to address its humanitarian cost, but also to respond to the perceived risk of a dilution of Islamic identity in the Balkans.

A majority of the Muslim NGOs intervening during the Bosnian conflict were members of a federal association, the World Islamic Council for Da`wa and Relief (*al-majlis al-`alami li-l da`wa wa-l-ighatha* – see p.75). In this Council, which was divided into several branches (*da`wa*, finance, media and so forth), the IIRO presided in Jeddah over a General Committee for Relief (*lajnat al-ighatha al-`ama*) which coordinated the charitable organizations.[20] From the strength of this position, the Saudi agency had a leading role since the start of the conflict, and took part in the first international conference on aid to refugees from Bosnia, which assembled delegates from 25 countries in Vienna in April 1992. The General Committee for Relief started a Council for Coordination of Humanitarian Organizations, initially in Zagreb but afterwards relocated to Sarajevo when the state of the war allowed humanitarian organizations to work inside Bosnia. In 1995, eleven organizations took part in this Council – the only coordinating group for Islamic humanitarian agencies active in Bosnia.

A common identification with Sunni Islam united these diverse organizations. Moreover, it is at this pole that we find those that promoted a Salafi or Wahhabi conception of Islam. Most of these organizations had developed considerably during the Afghan war, in the course of which the Saudis, Wahhabi themselves, relied on movements of Salafi inspiration to counter the influence of Iran. These organizations clearly displayed the priority they give to relief programmes (*ighatha*); but their humanitarian activities in Bosnia were often combined with missionary activities (*da`wa*) aimed at the Bosnian Muslims.

Here we may note a difference from the humanitarian operations directed from Iran: the Iranian humanitarian programmes in Bosnia were not accompanied by any Shi`a proselytization, with the exception of one Shi`a organization based in Britain, Dar al-Tabligh ('House for the propagation of Islam'), which succeeded in converting some Bosnian Muslims to Shi`ism. Iranian humanitarianism was itself heterogeneous. Bosnians received support from organizations such as the Foundation for the Oppressed (*Bonyad-e mostaz'afin*) and the quasi-governmental Iranian Red Crescent (Bagherzade 2001). Moreover, a special agency was founded from Iran specially to intervene in Bosnia, the Iranian Islamic Centre for Help to the People of Bosnia-Herzegovina, and this would seem to have discreetly taken part in arming the Bosnian army.[21] However, our analysis is focused on Sunni organizations.

Numerous other organizations intervened in Bosnia. As well as those we have already noted, Muslim organizations based in the United States developed large-scale programmes, such as Mercy International (founded in 1986, with a growing presence on the international scene) and ICNA Relief (a branch of the Islamic Circle of North America, which is close to the Pakistani Jama`at i-Islami). Indeed, most Islamic organizations gave aid to the Bosnian Muslims and had had some degree of presence in the field. The Turkish Refah intervened through Internationale Humanitäre Hilfe (IHH), based in Germany. The humanitarian branch of the Movement of Islamic Youth of Malaysia (*Angkatan Belia Islam Malaysia* – ABIM) opened a Malaysian Relief Centre in Sarajevo. The Ahmadiyya movement – based in London, with a historical background in Pakistan and considered a heterodox sect by the majority of Islamist movements – created a humanitarian structure for Bosnia, Humanity First.

The priority of keeping Muslim populations where they were

For the majority of the Islamic NGOs, the Islamic reading of the Bosnian conflict was inseparable from that of the humanitarian crisis that followed it. Thus, the management of this crisis by the Western and international humanitarian agencies was often denounced as the pursuit of war by other means, in a conflict where the displacement of population had become a tool serving the ultimate aim of territory control. Humanitarian organizations were confronted with an 'unsolvable dilemma' (Destexhe 1993: 177). Evacuating civilian populations to protect them could in fact contribute to the policy of ethnic cleansing. Alternatively, refusing to evacuate them would have meant taking the risk of exposing them to even more serious exactions. The Office of the UN High Commissioner for Refugees (UNHCR), perceived as favouring the exodus of Muslim populations, was held to be supporting the ethnic cleansing by the Serbs; and the Western NGOs which came to 'change the identity of Muslim populations' were accused of taking over from the Serbs in their wish to blot out all trace of 'Islamic identity'. Behind these accusations the main priority of the Islamic NGOs was clear: the maintenance – or renewal – of an Islamic identity in Bosnia. These organizations feared that the exodus of Muslim populations might jeopardize the very presence of Islam in Bosnia, and that they might settle in countries that would not guarantee them the maintenance (or renewal) of their Islamic identity. To face this problem, the Islamic NGOs concentrated on two priorities that promoted a form of alternative, Islamic humanitarianism: taking care of refugees, and keeping Muslim populations inside Bosnia.

The first years of the Bosnian conflict were marked by a major flow of Muslim populations fleeing in the direction of Croatia, before being directed on to other countries. The main objective of the Islamic NGOs was therefore to make it easier for Muslim refugees to stay in the region, in the interests of their eventual repatriation. Among the Islamic agencies, it was the Saudi agencies (IIRO/IGASA and the Saudi High Committee) that took charge of the largest number of refugee camps in Croatia and Slovenia, generally with the agreement of the local authorities and UNHCR. Their main activities were distribution of food, medical care, psychological support (especially for women who had been raped) and teaching. In April 1993, the Islamic NGOs who belonged to the coordinating Council took responsibility for more than 50,000 refugees in Croatia and 80,000 in Slovenia.[22] Some agencies such as Muslim Aid rapidly put in place programmes for the return of the refugees to Bosnia. But in the face of a massive inflow of refugees and the difficulties of repatriation, a second objective emerged: to organize the departure of Muslim refugees, and especially students, to Muslim countries such as Jordan and Palestine, even if on the whole these had received few refugees by comparison with some European countries. From the viewpoint of the heads of Islamic NGOs, if

Muslim refugees were to leave for countries where Muslims were in a minority, their 'Islamic identity' would be threatened. Also – and this became a third objective – the Islamic agencies tried, with the help of their branches in various countries, to arrange for the reception of these populations in Europe. The IIRO opened reception centres in Austria and Hungary. In London, Muslim Aid and Islamic Relief supported the creation of an Islamic Centre for Bosnia, to facilitate the settling in of refugees.[23]

In parallel with this policy of taking care of refugees, the Islamic NGOs developed programmes to avoid the departure of Bosnian Muslims, which also allowed them incidentally to turn the beneficiary populations into clients. Thus these NGOs took part actively in the reception of people who were displaced within the Bosnian territory, especially in the camps around Zenica, which accommodated more than 40,000 such people, and around Tuzla, where several thousand displaced persons arrived after the fall of the enclave of Srebrenica in July 1995. Among the projects given priority by these organizations, we may note the support for local activity by means of economic micro-projects: for Islamic Relief, a salmon farm at Zenica; for Muslim Aid, a programme to cultivate mushrooms.[24] To confront the consequences of the war, programmes in the health field were more and more numerous. The Egyptian relief committee took charge of the provision of basic supplies for the Bosnalek medical factory in Sarajevo; the Saudi High Committee and IGASA/IIRO supplied materials for the hospitals in Sarajevo and opened their own clinics – not far from those of the Iranian Red Crescent. Finally, the importance attached by most of these organizations to the sponsorship of orphans was coupled with their desire to keep Muslim populations in place: in 1994, IGASA/IIRO alone offered more than 6,500 orphans an annual sum of $640, as well as taking responsibility for their health and education.[25]

After the war, the activities of the Islamic NGOs were much reduced, and from 1996 onwards some of them even closed their offices. Different reasons may explain this development: on the one hand, the Islamic NGOs stood aside for the extensive programmes organized by Western NGOs (see Vukadinovic 1996); on the other hand, some of them, being linked to groups of foreign combatants, were invited to close down. Despite this general tendency, other organizations remained active, especially the Saudi organizations. Priority was now given to reconstruction: from the start of May 1997, the World Islamic Council for Da`wa and Relief was entrusted with the supervision of an International Society for the Reconstruction of Bosnia, whose headquarters was sited in the United Arab Emirates.[26]

From the communitization of humanitarian aid to reislamization
The universality of Western humanitarian aid was often criticized by the Islamic NGOs. It was essentially on the issue of identity that the more virulent criticisms were articulated. It was alleged that Western NGOs, under the cover of universality, were seeking to export highly particular conceptions and practices that violated the usages and rights of local Muslim populations. As in Sudan and elsewhere in Africa, fear of competition from missionaries was evidently strong: it often led to all Western agencies, including secular ones, being assimilated to missionary organizations. Thus, an Islamic Relief video stated in 1993 that '[Bosnian] children are met by Christian agencies or evangelists who can convert them to Christianity

and later send them to Bosnia-Herzegovina as priests or missionaries'.[27] When it was mentioned in reply that there was a difference between confessional and secular organizations such as the Red Cross or MSF, the latter were accused of exporting Western cultural models – whether emancipation of women, or culinary practices – which were claimed to be incompatible with the local culture.

In Bosnia, the leaders of the Islamic NGOs, both local and transnational, joined to denounce the danger that international humanitarian aid would intervene to compromise 'Muslim identity'. Thus in July 1992, Edah Becirbegovic, president of the charity 'Merhamet' (close to the SDA), denounced as an attack on Bosnian Muslim practices the sending by UNHCR of food-aid parcels containing pork.[28] Non-consumption of pork was thus turned into a collective norm, whereas in fact many Bosnian Muslims were in the habit of eating it.

This dispute about pork highlighted the shift from a humanitarian discourse that aimed to guarantee rights, into a communitarian discourse that sought to impose duties. The shift consisted of passing a norm at an individual level (a guarantee of individual rights) to the collective level (the duties of the Muslim community). Thanks to such a shift, the Islamic NGOs and their religious authorities highlighted what concerned them: not eating pork was not only a right guaranteed to a Muslim individual, but a duty applying to all Muslims. Thus, claiming the right of individual Muslims not to eat pork was in reality a device to assert that the communal norm ought to be the religious prohibition on pork consumption, as imposed by local religious elements. After he became Reis-ul-Ulema, Mustafa Ceric also denounced in October 1994 the delivery of pork by the United Nations as 'a constraint imposed on the Bosnian Muslim nation, which offends its way of life and eating'. The communitarian dimension and the project of reislamization were clear when he added: 'we must reject all European filth: alcohol, drugs and prostitution'.[29] The denunciation by 'Merhamet' or the Islamska Zajednica of a Western humanitarian aid that would violate the 'rights of Muslims' was actually part of a global process of reislamization that sought to impose the 'duties of Muslims' on the Bosnian Muslims.

Islamic NGOs and reislamization projects
Thus the skilful use of the idea of specific rights for Muslim populations could be used to justify the programmes of Islamic NGOs, which did not necessarily distinguish the humanitarian from the religious dimension, and even used *ighatha* (material relief) to undertake *da`wa* (spiritual relief). Three types of reislamization could be observed in most of these organizations: the celebration of religious festivals; a militant form of *da`wa*; and Islamic educational programmes. This is considered reislamization in that it emphasizes Islamic rituals, teachings and values addressed to a population of nominal Muslims characterized by having lived for decades under a secular regime.

If the Islamic NGOs had programmes similar to those of their Western equivalents – health, food distribution, economic micro-projects – they also developed other projects aimed at Muslims on important dates in the Islamic calendar. At the time of Ramadan, they organized *iftar* meals in refugee camps or Bosnian towns and villages: for instance, during Ramadan in 1994, IGASA and other Islamic organizations arranged for the distribution of one *somun* (traditional round loaf used for *iftar*) per family.[30] At the end of Ramadan, for the *ramazanski bajram*, the Islamic NGOs offered presents or new clothes to the children. On the occasion of the *kurban bajram*, the same organizations distributed pieces of sacrificed meat, or alternatively – in the modern version of the sacrifice chosen by Islamic Relief and Human Appeal International – tins of meat ritually sacrificed in Australia. These celebrations were meant to create a feeling of community between Bosnian Muslims and the entire *umma*.

Another means of reislamization was by means of *da`wa* carried out by the staff of these organizations. But a summary sociological analysis, based on my stay in Bosnia in 1998, suggests that not all of them were of a militant vocation. Three types of staff could be identified. First, permanent staff and volunteers recruited for their combination of ideological commitment and professional competence. These could include a former *mujahid* who became an employee, a militant from an Islamist movement, and a doctor who gave up some of his time to the organization. Second, local employees of foreign origin, often Arabs, recruited for their linguistic competence in Serbo-Croat as much as for their ideological commitment; many of these had formerly studied at the universities of Sarajevo and Belgrade. Third, Bosnians recruited on the basis of professional competence rather than ideological conviction. Hence, working in an Islamic NGO could be no more than a straightforward professional opportunity.

But a number of these employees, especially those who came from foreign countries, were militants who had their own idea of Islam and practiced *da`wa* to bring back their Bosnian 'brothers' into the 'right path'. Like many others, an employee of the Kuwait-based Organization for the Renewal of Islamic Tradition was of the opinion that Muslims here had turned their back on their faith and would be punished by war until they returned to the right path.[31] If *da`wa* was limited sometimes to an invitation without being linked to Islamic obligations, it could also be accompanied by a coercive element. Distribution of aid to women depended on their wearing the Islamic veil; to men, on their visiting the mosque, giving up alcohol or wearing beards. The heads of some organizations, such as Islamic Relief, denied the existence of such practices, which damaged their image. Actually, the reality in the field depended on the type of people on the spot who were distributing food. Some employees admitted that their convictions led them to refuse to deliver a parcel of humanitarian aid to a woman in a mini-skirt or to a man who was drunk.

Finally, the activity of *da`wa* was closely linked to various forms of educational project. The building of mosques and the proliferation of Quranic schools, often linked to centres for aid distribution, provided many opportunities for the distribution of different types of Islamic literature. This continued after the war: during my visit to Sarajevo in December 2001, I noticed at least two huge mosques built since my previous visit in 1998. One, the King Fahd Bin Abdul Aziz Al Saud Mosque, financed by Saudi-Arabia, had become the base of the Saudi High Committee; the other, the Mosque of Independence (Djamija Istiqlal) was funded by Indonesia. The contrast was striking between these brand-new religious monuments and nearby housing, damaged by mortar shells and bullets during the war and still not repaired since 1995.

During the war, in the same way as the content of *da`wa* varied according to who was practising it, the content of the literature was also varied. Some organizations, such as Islamic Relief, limited themselves to distributing copies of the Quran (100,000 copies in Bosnia and Albania), and small leaflets reproducing *suras* of the Quran or summarizing the main principles of Islam. Others, such as IGASA/IIRO, also distributed video cassettes by Ahmed Deedat, a South African Islamist militant much appreciated for his debates with Christian evangelists and for his virulent attacks on Salman Rushdie's *Satanic Verses*. Finally, certain organizations stepped up the distribution of radical literature which, in many cases, had already been circulating in Bosnia: particularly the writing of the Egyptian radical, Sayyid Qutb, the Muslim Brother who was hanged in prison in 1966 (see above, p.37), or of the Pakistani Abu Ala Mawdudi, the founder of Jama`at I-Islami.

Given the large number of agencies that intervened in Bosnia, disseminating different conceptions of Islam, these reislamization projects often became controversial. Thus, proselytization by militants of the Ahmadiyya movement aimed at Bosnian refugees was denounced on several occasions by British Islamic agencies:[32] the Islamic Centre for Bosnia-Herzegovina in London obtained the support of the Islamic Foundation (close to the Jama`at i-Islami movement) to publish books putting Bosnian Muslims on guard against the Ahmadiyya movement. For their part, the Ahmadiyya considers that the charity they set up, Humanity First, provided aid without any conditions. I was told that the Calife of the movement in London received Bosnian women refugees as they were, without *hijab* and wearing mini-skirts. Ahmadis blamed organizations such as Muslim Aid and Islamic Relief for imposing conditions.[33]

Relations between transnational and local organizations

The emphasis so far has been on external providers of aid. But as regards their interactions with local organizations, what were the effects of the solidarity of the *umma* on internal Islam institutions in Bosnia? I will show how the SDA did its best to control this external influence in favour of an 'official' project of reislamization by the Muslim community. But the independent activities of some transnational networks, linked with the strategies of some local 'outsiders', resulted in the expression of a degree of hostility towards the SDA and its wish to maintain control over Bosnian Islam. Faced by this potential conflict, what were the reactions of the Bosnian authorities?

The parallel networks of the SDA and 'official' reislamization

The foundation of the Third World Relief Agency (TWRA) preceded the Bosnian conflict, and even the fall of Communism; for it was founded in 1987 by two Sudanese, Fatih al-Hassanain and his brother Sukarno al-Hassanain, who were close to the National Islamic Front in Sudan, their aim being to support the Islamic revival in Eastern Europe and the Soviet Union.[34] Fatih Al-Hassanain's contacts with Balkan Muslim leaders dated back as far as the 1960s and 1970s, when he had studied medicine in Sarajevo and made friends with Izetbegovic and other leaders of the Bosnian pan-Islamist tendency. The establishment of TWRA in Vienna enabled Fatih al-Hassanain to play a central role in the Balkans: in 1991, he became Secretary-General of the Islamic Council for Eastern Europe financed by the IIRO and chaired by Jakub Selimoski, then Reis-ul-Ulama of Yugoslavia.

The singularity of TWRA became clear after the Bosnian conflict broke out. Apart from Fatih al-Hassanain, several representatives of the Bosnian pan-Islamist movement were numbered among its leaders.[35] In October 1992, al-Hassanain was appointed representative of Bosnia in the First Austrian Bank in Vienna. By the end of 1992, the agency had offices in Sarajevo, Zagreb, Moscow, Budapest and Istanbul.

Unlike other Islamic NGOs, TWRA knew no allegiance to any state or Islamist movement in the Muslim world, and so could benefit from financing from various elements in competition. Its main funder was Saudi-Arabia, but some revenue also came from Iran, Sudan, Pakistan, Brunei and Malaysia. Usama bin Laden would seem to have also supplied it with funds. More than $350 million passed through the agency's accounts between 1992 and 1995, of which $231 million was in 1993 alone.[36] So the representatives of the pan-Islamist movement within the SDA made use of TWRA to fund certain activities of this party: in 1992, it subsidized the publication of the first numbers of *Ljiljan* ('the lily'), a journal close to the SDA edited by Dz. Latic.

Above all, TWRA allowed the same pan-Islamist current to get round certain legal restrictions. At the local level, the Bosnian republican institutions were bypassed in favour of the SDA's parallel network (Bougarel 2001: 91-6); at the international level, the UN's resolutions on the arms embargo were flouted. For the main function of the agency during the Bosnian conflict was certainly to supply the Bosnian army with arms. This activity of TWRA was discovered in September 1993, when the Slovene authorities intercepted at Maribor airport a consignment of humanitarian aid from Sudan, which actually contained arms. Within TWRA, Fatih Al-Hassanain and Hassan Cengic were the architects of these transactions.

This role of TWRA had a broader context. During the Bosnian conflict, the SDA organized a vast parallel system which aimed to monopolize material resources that came from the *umma*, to the disadvantage of the official institutions and ministries (for defence, refugees and so forth) of the Bosnian Republic. To do this, the SDA turned not only to TWRA, but also to other satellite organizations that channelled funds coming from abroad. This was true of the charitable organization Merhamet, chaired first by Edhem Sahovic and then by Edah Becirbegovic, both members of the pan-Islamist tendency of 'young Muslims' in the 1940s (Bougarel 1994); and of the Foundation for the Families of Martyrs (*shahid*) and war invalids, also Fatma, an organization set up to care for orphans. Finally, with the appointment of Mustafa Ceric to the post of Reis-ul-Ulema in April 1993, the SDA took control of the Islamska Zajednica, a major interlocutor with foreign donors.

The control of these various organizations allowed the SDA to extend its influence over Bosnian Muslims. Certainly, within the party, 'pan-Islamism' was an implicit and changing line of behaviour rather than a clearly defined political project. But the desire to reislamize the Muslim community was shared by the whole pan-Islamist tendency, whether this goal was a finality in itself – to guarantee the Islamic morality of the society – or merely a preliminary to the setting up of an Islamic state. From this point of view, the SDA and the institutions linked to it presented themselves as the sole legitimate representatives of the Bosnian Muslims.

Concretely, the effort by organizations linked with the SDA to monopolize the financial support of the Muslim world had a measure of success. The TWRA succeeded in channelling considerable sums that were mainly used to supply 'Muslim units' of the Bosnian army with arms. The Islamska Zajednica took advantage of the increase in its material resources to advance its interests: it extended its network of *medrasa*s over the Bosnian territories, and succeeded in introducing into the curricula of public schools religious teaching which was optional – but strongly recommended, the allocation of humanitarian aid being often dependent on the carrying out of this teaching. As for the activities of Merhamet, they developed with the help of the financial support of various Islamic NGOs, but also some Western NGOs attracted by a Muslim charitable organization that preached cooperation with those of other Bosnian communities: the Catholics' Caritas, the Orthodox Church's Dobrotvor, the Jewish La Benevolencia.[37] In fact, the tendency of aid organizations to give priority to their own community members increased. After the breakdown in the Croat-Muslim alliance in 1993, Merhamet concentrated on territories under Muslim control, and Caritas on territories under Croat control (Duffield 1994).

However, the Islamska Zajednica and Merhamet were quickly outstripped by the independent strategies of certain Islamic NGOs. Merhamet sought control over aid coming from the Muslim world and coordination of the work of all the Islamic NGOs. But it had to give up this goal, in the face of organizations that did not agree to submit the dissemination of their Islamic publications to the prior approval of the Islamska Zajednica, or insisted on only delivering aid to Muslims, or simply refused any control by other parties over their work.[38] Similarly, the Islamska Zajednica wished to oversee the development of religious institutions, but had to come to terms with the setting up of many independent projects by Islamic NGOs that were not under its control – such as the construction of mosques or Islamic centres, the setting up of Quranic schools, and visits by imams from abroad.

Transnational elements, local outsiders and 'wild' reislamization
The autonomy of action of certain Islamic transnational organizations posed an obstacle to the SDA and its satellite organizations in their wish to control the reislamization of Bosnian Muslims. But it turned out to be a resource for some religious leaders whose careers had taken them outside the SDA's circles, and who even contested the control that this party had over Islam in Bosnia. Thus the use of the resources of the *umma* sustained a conflict which went back to the 1980s, between the main leaders of the Association of Ulemas (Salih Colakovic in Mostar and Halil Mehtic in Zenica), who were close to the Salafi wing of Islam, and representatives of the pan-Islamist tendency, who were partisans of a form of political Islam. The pan-Islamists finally took control of an Islamska Zajednica reduced to Bosnia-Herzegovina in April 1993, with the nomination of Mustafa Ceric as the new Reis-ul-Ulema (Bellion-Jourdan 2001b).

The grip of the pan-Islamist tendency on the principal religious institutions pushed its opponents back to a peripheral position. In reaction, these poles of peripheral opposition, particularly Mostar and Zenica, came to rely on certain transnational networks to increase their autonomy. Thus the resources of the *umma* were used to escape control by the centre, indeed to develop an oppositional type of activity.

During the Bosnian conflict, the region of Mostar, jammed between Serb and Croat territory, was not a priority zone for the various transnational Islamic networks. However, Colakovic knew how to play the transnational card and cultivated many foreign contacts. From the beginning of the conflict, he left Bosnia and relied on the logistics provided by Islamic Relief. In May 1992, he undertook an international tour with the director of Islamic Relief, Hany El-Banna, and gave many talks in Europe, the United States and the Arab world. Continuing to be introduced abroad as chairman of the Islamic religious institutions in Bosnia,[39] Colakovic appointed himself the spokesman for the sufferings of the Bosnian Muslims. For Islamic Relief's fund-raising strategy, these talks were much more effective than a leaflet. For his part, Colakovic acquired international fame and obtained funding, especially from the Gulf, which he made use of to position himself on the Bosnian religious scene. Returning to Bosnia in 1995, he became director of the medrasa in Mostar, and founded a large Islamic Centre in that town. This functioned outside the structures of the Islamska Zajednica, being linked to the Bosnian Congress, an organization of Bosnian Muslims who had settled in the United States and were hostile to the SDA, accusing Izetbegovic of misuse of funds intended for the Bosnian state.[40]

The region of Zenica and Travnik, in central Bosnia, was the principal centre of activity for Islamic NGOs and *mujahidin*: humanitarians and Islamic combatants conducted a *da`wa* there, accompanied by a measure of violence. It was in this region particularly that the official reislamization undertaken by the Reis-ul-Ulema Ceric was paralleled by independent reislamization projects, which benefited from local protection. In Zenica, Halid Mehtic was appointed mufti in 1994. Chairman of the Association of Ulemas and close to Salih Colakovic, he took advantage of his position as mufti to protect the *mujahidin* and Islamic NGOs that opposed the 'official' Bosnian Islam. The aim was to question the legitimacy of the pan-Islamist tendency by attacking its pretensions to a monopoly of Islamic legitimacy.

Among the organizations that benefited from the protection of Mehtic, the most important was the Kuwaiti-based Organization for the Renewal of Islamic Tradition. The headquarters of this agency, directed by a Palestinian, was set up in Zenica in 1993. In 1994, it was supporting more than 700 orphans, giving them 50 deutschmark per month; it was also distributing aid that depended on beneficiaries following religious instruction, and on women wearing the veil and men wearing beards. Moreover it had links with groups of *mujahidin* and distributed radical leaflets with which their author, Imad al-Misri, instructed combatants in the camp at Podbrezje.[41]

One of al-Misri's leaflets distributed by this Kuwaiti agency was entitled 'Conceptions which we must correct', and it called for the application of *shari`a* in Bosnia, denounced infidels, and condemned socialism and democracy as enemies of God.[42] This agency became specially embarrassing for the Islamska Zajednica when it disseminated conceptions of Islam which were contrary to the Hanafi practices of Bosnian Islam. Al-Misri's leaflet did indeed forbid Bosnian Muslims to 'tell the beads' after prayer and to celebrate the Prophet's birthday, and also discouraged men from shaving their beards and women from taking part in the *mevlud* or ceremonies in honour of the Prophet.[43] Clearly the Kuwaiti agency was seeking to tear Bosnian Muslims, and particularly the younger generations, from the Hanafi *madhhab* or school. As an indication of its desire to implant foreign religious practices in Bosnia, the Organization for the Renewal of Islamic Tradition created in July 1994 a Balkan Islamic Centre, intended to take over from the organization in Zenica.

Fear of 'afghanization' and of an Islamic opposition

The more the variety of Islamic transnational networks and the largely independent nature of their activities made themselves felt, the more the Bosnian political and religious leaders expressed openly their fear of an 'afghanization' of Bosnia, by which they meant the degeneration of the Afghan conflict which was precipitated by the intervention of external elements. Mustafa Ceric, invited to the Second Arab and Islamic Popular Conference in Khartoum in December 1993, denounced, in an interview that he gave to an Egyptian daily,[44] the tensions that divided the different Islamist movements, and made explicit reference to the Afghan situation: 'You know that the Pharaoh of the Twentieth Century is [the Secretary-General of the United Nations] Boutros-Ghali. It is he who, unfortunately, decides the fate of Muslims, and we must speak of this in all frankness, for Islamic organizations and forces do not succeed in agreeing among one another, even over the smallest things. We used to complain about the Communist Soviet Union ... but Islamic movements make war among one another. We see the image of Afghanistan and that has an influence on the entire Islamic *umma*.'

This anxiety on the part of the Bosnian authorities may be explained in part by the coincidence in time of the drift in the Afghan conflict and the secession of Fikret Abdic in the region of Bihac, which provoked confrontations among Bosnian Muslims beginning in September 1993. But this secession ultimately failed.

In fact, this fear of an 'afghanization' of Bosnian society relates to the fears of the SDA and the Islamska Zajednica of seeing an opposition develop to their own conception of Islam. Certainly, the vast majority of Bosnian Muslims remained impermeable to the Islamic NGOs' and the *mujahidin*'s reislamization projects. To a great extent, ostentatious Islamic practices – such as wearing of the veil or the beard, frequenting mosques, and so forth – became less noticeable with the departure of the foreign combatants and, above all, with the reduction in the activities of the Islamic NGOs following the Dayton accords. Already during the war, some Bosnians adopted a pragmatic attitude – assenting, but without conviction, to conditions imposed by the provider in order to get relief or employment. A secularised Muslim woman interviewed during the study conducted by Ivana Macek in Sarajevo said:

> Once I wanted to apply as a secretary in a Kuwait humanitarian organization. My husband told me not to, because I'd have to cover myself. What can I do? I told him, I'll cover myself when I enter the building. I'll put on a long skirt. If I don't put a scarf my children shall be hungry. When I leave the building, I'll get out of these clothes. That is what the majority does. (quoted in Macek 2000: 194)

But it would be incorrect to conclude that the actions of transnational Islamic networks had no durable effects on Bosnian society. Their radical language did find a certain echo, especially with the populations who were most affected by the war.

After the war, neither the question of refugees and displaced persons, nor that of former combatants, was resolved. Refugees and displaced persons were confronted with the inefficacy of policies for their return, which were slowed down, even prevented, by various parties who were in the way. The former combatants faced serious material difficulties, and felt they did not receive sufficient recognition of their role in the war. These social frustrations were, for some of them, balanced by the conviction of having discovered the 'true Islam' by frequenting the militants of the Islamic NGOs and the *mujahidin*. The expression of their frustration could then take the form of opposing those who, from the SDA or the Islamska Zajednica, claimed a monopoly of Islamic legitimacy.

Among the refugees living in western Europe, some, especially in London or Vienna, expressed their hostility to the version of Islam defended by SDA and by the Islamska Zajednica. But it was in Bosnia that, after the war, emerged the most organized form of opposition, with the creation of the Organization of Active Islamic Youth (*Organizacija Aktivne Islamske Omladine* – OAIO). Then led in Zenica by Adnan Pezo, a young war invalid, it recruited most of its members from Bosnian veterans of the El-Mudzjahid unit. Several thousands of young Bosnians had fought in this unit beside the *mujahidin*; among them, many felt unrecognised and had suffered from the discreet dissolution of El-Mudzjahid as part of the application of the Dayton accords. The group benefited from the charisma of Imad al-Misri, who gave numerous lectures on its behalf.[45] The OAIO built up a presence in towns under Muslim control. Relatively discreet in the immediate post-war period, it became more visible at the end of 1997. During the month of Ramadan (December 1997 – January 1998) it distributed tracts calling on Muslims not to involve Christians in Muslim festivals, and not to wish them a happy Catholic or Orthodox Christmas. These steps represented also an indirect challenge to the Islamic legitimacy of the SDA and the Islamska Zajednica. The militants of OAIO went so far as to call Alija Izetbegovic a *munafiq* or hypocrite, which is a very strong term in the vocabulary of Islamic controversy.

The reaction of the Bosnian authorities, from perplexity to repression
The SDA and the Islamska Zajednica claimed to be the sole custodians of Islamic legitimacy in Bosnia. But the activity of certain 'brothers' of the *umma* allowed the young Bosnian Muslims to make use of the Islamic register to challenge that legitimacy. On the one hand, this challenge advanced a claim to Islamic truth outside the Hanafi *madhhab*, and so questioned the Islamska Zajednica's reislamization projects. On the other hand, it was sustained by a criticism of the 'hypocrisy' of SDA staff who made use of Islam to achieve power without achieving any 'Islamic project' in Bosnia. Faced by this challenge, the heads of the SDA and the Islamska Zajednica seemed caught unawares, as was shown by their tendency to react in the short term through denunciation and repression.

Already, during the war, the appeals of Mustafa Ceric for the solidarity of the *umma* in the jihad in Bosnia had given way to denunciation of the perverse results of that same solidarity of the *umma*. In September 1994, criticizing sharply the polygamy practised by the 'brothers' who had come to Bosnia, he recalled that *shari`a* marriages were invalid unless preceded by a civil marriage: 'Our Muslim brothers come from everywhere in the world, marry our women and our girls, then divorce them. I am afraid of such anarchy. The problem of polygamy must be gradually resolved'.[46] In 1994 too, the Islamska Zajednica denounced the Islamic NGOs who were trying to convert Bosnian Muslims to conceptions of Islam different from those of the Hanafi *madhhab*, and obliged them to obtain a prior authority from the Islamska Zajednica before being allowed further their activities. As previously in Afghanistan, the term Wahhabi became a generic term used to denounce all efforts to import into Bosnia foreign Islamic concepts and practices. They certainly had in mind organizations that followed the Wahhabi conception of Islam that obtains in the Saudi kingdom; but the term Wahhabi was also used to denounce other organizations – particularly certain ones close to the Muslim Brothers – that, following the Salafi movement, reject all distinctions between *maddhab* within Sunni Islam. Thus in April 1995, the Kuwait-based Organization for the Renewal of Islamic Tradition had to stop making its distribution of food aid dependent on the abandonment of the Hanafi *madhhab*, on pain of being outlawed by the Bosnian government.[47]

During the post-war period, the violent activities – 'terrorism' or banditry – of certain *mujahidin* remained for a time unpunished. But from 1997 onwards, they served as a pretext for a vast campaign of repression against groups that might sustain the Islamic opposition. In January 1997, the murder of an Egyptian convert to Shi`ism by a Sunni Tunisian, in front of the Balkan Islamic Centre in Zenica, was used to justify a series of raids by the Bosnian police. The following month, a tribunal in Zenica obliged the Kuwaiti organization and the Balkan Islamic Centre to close their doors.[48] On 18 July 2001, Imad al-Misri was arrested on an Egyptian warrant. The Organization of Active Youth launched a campaign for his release.[49]

A number of round-ups were organized in milieux linked to the former *mujahidin*. The first, in November 1997, centred on the village of Guca Gora: about forty foreigners and Bosnian Muslims were arrested and accused of having committed several attacks and murders since the end of the war. At the same time, the heads of the Islamska Zajednica showed their desire to penalize those who were hostile to them. Another round-up took place in September 1998, shortly after the attacks on the American Embassies in Nairobi and Dar-es-Salaam. Centred on the town of Bugojno in central Bosnia, it was aimed principally at young Bosnian Muslims who were veterans of the El-Mudzjahid unit and active in the OAIO.

In the aftermath of 11 September 2001, the control of Islamist militants or alleged Islamist militants has intensified. Several individuals have been arrested, and some of them extradited to their countries of origin or to Guantánamo Bay to be detained by the US authorities on suspected links with 'terrorist' activities.[50] The activities of some NGOs – including the Saudi High Committee for Aid to Bosnia-Herzegovina, the TWRA and the Islamic Relief Agency – have been further investigated (International Crisis Group 2001: 15). After a request by the USA indicating suspicion that Islamic charities were channelling funds for 'terrorism', the police authorities of Bosnia's Muslim-Croat federation announced in November 2002 the banning of the Saudi-based al-Haramain Foundation and the US-based Global Relief Foundation, as well as of Bosanska Idealna Futura (BIF), which took over in 2000 the activities in Bosnia of the US-based Benevolence International Foundation.[51]

Conclusion

At first sight, the presence of Islamic transnational networks seems to confirm the idea of an 'Islamic civilization' expressing its solidarity towards the Muslims in the Balkans, who were placed in the front line of a conflict between 'civilizations' as forecast by Samuel Huntington (1996). However, analysis of the motivations of the different elements involved brings out the highly varied and conflictual character of the campaigns in support of Bosnia, and their articulation in a diversity of local contexts.

In reality, the Bosnian conflict took place during a period of transition, when allegiances and lines of force were being renegotiated in the Muslim world. As from 1990, the end of the cold war hastened the drift in the Afghan conflict, but opened up new horizons at the same time – in the Balkans, the Caucasus, central Asia. Above all, the 1990-91 Gulf War seriously undermined the credit that Saudi-Arabia enjoyed among the principal Islamist movements. In this context, the Bosnian conflict appears to have been like a movement of ideological convergence, turning up to reinforce the idea so dear to Islamist movements of an antagonism between an oppressed Islam and an oppressive West, which thus takes over from the Soviet executioner.

A few years later, when clashes in 1998 between the Serbian police and the Army for the Liberation of Kosovo (UCK) led to a major crisis in Kosovo, one could have expected a similar reaction and ideological convergence from the *umma*. It was indeed possible to read the situation as one of Muslim (Albanian Kosovar) victimhood at the hands of non-Muslim (Serb) aggressors. However, only a weak level of mobilization, even from Islamist parties, could be detected – even from Pakistan, where I was at the time. Generally speaking, the external military support seems to have been limited, and if some Islamic NGOs did develop humanitarian programmes, the scale of involvement was minor compared to the programmes to support Bosnian Muslims.

Why such a difference? First, by contrast with Bosnia, Western intervention was prompt, with a campaign of NATO air strikes from 2 March to 3 June 1999 that led to agreement on the withdrawal of Serb forces from Kosovo. In a sense, Muslim victims of Serb aggression were being rescued by the West, which hardly fitted in with an 'Islamic reading'. Second, there was no Kosovan equivalent to the pan-Islamist movement that had developed within the SDA in Bosnia. Third, the international context had evolved. The USA, which had tolerated the involvement of *mujahidin* and Iran during the Bosnian conflict, warned the Army for the Liberation of Kosovo against developing such links with the outside world; and for its part, Iran was now actively working on normalization of its relations with Western countries (Bougarel and Clayer 2001: 53). Finally, those who had become involved at the time of the Bosnian conflict grew frustrated: many employees of Islamic NGOs and militants were disappointed to realize that Balkan Muslim thinking and behaviour were at odds with Salafi or other orthodox understandings of Islam, and so were less impelled to come in support of their 'brothers'.[52]

As we have seen, not only did the projects to reislamize the Bosnian people not have the success that was counted on, but the variety of styles of reislamization attempted by the external agencies resulted in a diversification of available Islamic identities – which was the opposite of the original aim of the Bosnian pan-Islamist tendency.

The internal challenges to the political system put in place by the SDA could clearly be sustained by external influences, disappointed by the transformation of the 'Islamic cause' into a *pax Americana*. Those who had seen in Izetbegovic a Muslim leader capable of establishing an Islamic state in the Balkans were no longer able to recognize the politician who from now on obeyed the directives of an international system dominated by the United States.

'Did Alija Izetbegovic betray us, or did we betray ourselves?' asked an Egyptian political scientist, in the title of an article published in October 1997.[53] This article, commenting on a project to establish diplomatic relations between Bosnia and Israel which would prove the allegiance of the Muslim leader to the United States, does not content itself with criticizing Izetbegovic: the author reconsiders the campaigns of the Muslim Brothers, humanitarian agencies and Islamic combatants that supported the 'Bosnian Muslims'. 'We did not ask enough questions about the nature of the struggle, its horizons and limits, and about the important role of the international system which was able to trifle with us and with them, at the heart of the Bosnian conflagration'. The Muslim Brothers had in fact been allowed to make Bosnia an 'Islamic cause' replacing that of Afghanistan – in order that these networks would not come and sustain the Islamist movement Hamas in Palestine. In fact, it was during the Bosnian conflict, in September 1993, that the Israeli-Palestinian Oslo accords were signed – to be denounced by the Islamist movements. 'During this period', adds the author, 'we forgot Palestine and its *intifada* and we went to fight in Bosnia. And Arafat, Rabin and Hussain [then King of Jordan] confiscated from us the *intifada*, Jerusalem and the mosque of Omar.' Paradoxically, Bosnia's salience as a 'new Palestine' in the Islamic cause resulted in the situation in Israel/Palestine being overshadowed.

CONCLUSION*

In your research: you're proving that there is no relief aid and everything is politics. ...When your research is published, the result will be to explain that Muslim relief agencies are little known in the West because the humanitarian dimension is lacking. In fact, Muslims want to promote their confessional interests. On the other hand, Christians are non-confessional, working purely for the sake of humanity and Christian values.

This sarcastic challenge came to one of us from a former Pakistan commissioner for Afghan refugees.[1] We accept the proposition that all humanitarian aid has a political dimension, as explained in the Introduction. Is it not possible and valid, though, for people seen as coming from Christian cultures to try to stand back from them and be as even-handed as possible? In this book, for instance, we have shown how the intended non-confessionality of the Red Cross movement was compromised almost from its beginnings by the unfortunate choice of its primary emblem; and how, more recently, relief aid to the non-Muslim areas of southern Sudan by Euro-American agencies has been interpreted in the Muslim north as a prolongation of the colonial missionary endeavour. Another recent development has been for Western agencies to be suspected, in Sudan and elsewhere, of smuggling in the modern secularism that is opposed as godlessness or *kufr* by strict Muslims.

Since the beginnings of our respective research projects in the mid-1990s, we have taken little account of Samuel P. Huntington's 'clash of civilizations' thesis (Huntington 1997). Edward Said and numerous other scholars have pointed out its errors of gross over-simplification (Said 2000a: 139-43, 2000b: 569-90, Bayart 1996). As far as Islam is concerned, it would seem that Huntington has taken one of the most controversial elements in classical Islamic thinking, the partition of the world into *dar al-Islam* ('realm of Islam') and *dar al-harb* (literally 'realm of war', i.e. non-believers), and inverted it, opposing the West to the Rest in an equally aggressive dichotomy. However, Huntington has undeniably tapped into the *Zeitgeist*, and the media waves, with such success that he has even been credited with predictive acumen. Though almost all world statesmen have distanced themselves from the 'clash' thesis, it crops up continually in both public and expert debate and is lent plausibility by the mutual reinforcement of the stereotypes of an ultra-consumerist 'West' and a fundamentalist 'Islam' (Halliday 1995: 110).

---

* by Jonathan Benthall and Jérôme Bellion-Jourdan

One of the few sociological attempts to test the Huntington model against comparative empirical data concludes that an objective, as opposed to stereotypic, cleavage between Western and Muslim societies may exist, but it is one unnoticed by Huntington (the issue of gender equality and sexual liberalization, where the Muslim world remains on the whole conservative). The authors of that research do support Huntington's broad claim that 'religious legacies leave a distinct and lasting imprint on contemporary values' (Norris and Inglehart 2002). This is indeed an assumption that has underpinned our own research into organized charity, though we stress that such heritages are always selectively rebuilt to fulfil contemporary objectives. It is noteworthy that one of the first books on international NGOs, published in 1951 by a UN official, L.C. White, drew attention to their growing importance, but gave attention to Christian organizations only – with a single exception, the World Jewish Committee – and used Christian imagery such as seeking the 'kingdom of God' to describe the incipient movement (White 1951: 166-97). The association between the Christian religion and humanitarian aid was nevertheless later weakened by such events as the foundation of Médecins Sans Frontières (MSF) by Bernard Kouchner and others after the Biafran war of 1967-70, for the principal roots of the 'French doctors' were in medicine and journalism (Benthall 1993: 124-39).

On another level, Huntington does not make the mistake of assuming organized charity to be an exclusive feature of the West. He draws attention to the use of Islamic charitable efforts, especially in war-torn areas, to promote political goals – but he regards 'kin-country rallying' as an inter-civilizational norm. Organized charity for him would presumably come under the heading of the 'commonalities of civilization', manifestations of 'thin' minimalist morality – a concept he borrows from Michael Walzer (Huntington 2002: 318). However, it seems to us that since Huntington permits himself to foreground the 'religious legacy' of each civilization in the fields of international relations and political analysis – at the expense of other global divisions such as those of class, social race and technology – he should, in order to be consistent, have included and allowed for the unifying features of these legacies as well as the sources of friction.

We hope the early chapters of this book will have shown conclusively that the commonalities between Judaeo-Christian and Islamic charitable traditions are, in Walzer's terms, 'thick', that is strongly embedded in institutions. Some minor specificities in the Islamic tradition have been pointed out: the special concern for orphans, the links with a specific religious calendar (Ramadan, *qurbani* and *umra*), the compatibility of family and public interests in waqf settlements. However, these are overshadowed by the common Judaeic roots in tithing and in offerings to God as the true owner of all wealth.

The abuse of charitable activities to fulfil personal, political or military aims can also be considered a practice shared in various traditions. We mentioned in our Introduction that it has become received wisdom to expose the political aspects of humanitarianism. This is overdue but should be applied consistently, and not arbitrarily by Westerners to discredit the activities of Muslim charities or vice versa. We cannot therefore fairly characterize the raising of funds for arms rather than alms as a monopoly of Muslims. At various times, certain Christian clergy have been involved with facilitating the supply of arms in order to benefit causes they were passionately committed to. During the years before the founding of the Irish Free

State in 1921, for instance, a large number of Catholic priests and monks were in trouble with the British police and military authorities (Coldrey 1988: 259-68). And during the Nigerian civil war of 1967-70, numbers of Christian clergy became deeply committed to the cause of the Biafran enclave. 'Arms kept Biafra going and it was well-known that, in the early days, the Churches had condoned the despatch of mixed cargoes [i.e. including both aid supplies and arms] to Uli [airport]' (de St Jorre 1975: 241).

Nor can we consider the intermittent abuse of the privileges of charitable organizations as an Islamic trait. The tight regulation of charities in the United Kingdom today would not have arisen unless it were needed to prevent serious financial and other abuses. Recently, Zionist extremists in the United States, and Hindu extremists in Britain, have both been accused of making use of charitable organizations to raise funds for inappropriate ends.[2]

The major Western aid organizations have never existed in a political vacuum. Both Save the Children Fund and Oxfam owe their origins to campaigns to stir opinion in Britain against economic blockades, whose victims were, respectively, Eastern Europeans at the end of the First World War and Greeks during the Second (Freeman 1965, Black 1992). The Red Cross Movement is independent in principle, but in practice has always had close relations with governments. Xavier Emmanuelli, a leading light in Médecins Sans Frontières, once published a stinging polemic arguing that humanitarian action was essentially private and should never be co-opted by governments (Emmanuelli 1991), then a few years afterwards was appointed minister for humanitarian action in the French Government.

The borrowing of the humanitarian figleaf by governments either to excuse themselves for taking no action against war crimes, or to make their own wars more palatable, has become highly sophisticated. A French journalist pointed out caustically in 1991 that the secretariat for humanitarian action 'can be seen as the after-sales service for the gun manufacturers who occupy the neighbouring ministries'.[3] During the short war against the Taliban, Britain's minister for international development and humanitarian aid, Clare Short, was appointed a member of the inner War Cabinet. In the summer of 2002, President George W. Bush's administration was inviting aid agencies to tender for an aid fund in anticipation of the need for reconstruction in Iraq after the planned war to depose, in the name of human rights, Saddam Hussain. Back in the 1990s, the US government experimented with using aid explicitly to stimulate political change in Sudan and North Korea. The new Bush administration has somewhat retreated from this policy, but US overseas aid is still closely linked to wider foreign policy goals. According to one observer, President Bush's encouragement of 'faith-based' initiatives 'risks polarising the NGO community, and pitting Judaeo-Christian values against those of other religions, notably Islam' (Stoddard 2002: 4).

It is true that substantive differences between the Christian and Muslim traditions show up in the practice of voluntary associations today. Perhaps the most salient is a reluctance to give the same degree of assistance to non-co-religionists as to co-religionists and prospective converts. However, we need to remind ourselves that secular universalism is the result of a long history of battles between the defenders of religious, that is Christian, control over society and those who argued that the secular nation-state should protect the rights of its citizens, including freedom of religion.

Modern secular NGOs therefore emerged as an outcome of this process of secularization, which has been only partially accomplished and is always reversible.

Christian missionary activity and humanitarian aid have been progressively de-linked from each other ever since the foundation of the Red Cross movement, but there still remain some major aid organizations such as the World Vision International and some American Protestant missions which combine the two. We have underlined the tensions in the field of Islamic charities, oscillating between adaptation to internationally recognized secular principles of humanitarian aid and attempting to reinject religious values.[4] Both Islamic and evangelical Christian charities experience a tension between religious universalism and secular universalism.

We must conclude by sounding a sceptical note about the validity of unqualified claims to universalism in the humanitarian field – whether they are grounded in secular principle or in religious doctrine. Henry Dunant founder of the ICRC, Bernard Kouchner of Médecins Sans Frontières, Hany El Banna of Islamic Relief – all in turn ran up against obstacles to universalism. The ICRC saw itself perceived as a Crusader organization by the Ottoman soldiers; MSF was confronted by Afghan men who would not allow male French doctors to look after Afghan women; Islamic Relief has had to deal with Albanian Muslims who had no wish to go to the mosque rather than the discotheque (Bellion-Jourdan 2002a: 392-6).

On the one hand, some Islamic charities seek an accommodation with the international humanitarian norm which dictates that, in principle, aid should be given to all in need without discrimination. On the other hand, Western critical thought, much indebted to cultural anthropology, has developed the idea of 'respect for difference' and hence of 'cultural rights'. A number of Islamic NGOs appear to be drawing on this idea in order to develop a doctrine of what might be called 'cultural proximity' or a communitarian approach to aid. It is claimed that women Muslim refugees, for instance, have special cultural needs that can be catered for only by Muslim agencies (Chapter 4, p.84; Bellion-Jourdan 2002a: 378-91, 416-18). A British analyst of Islamic and Western aid in conflict areas has defended this position, arguing that if the providers and beneficiaries of aid share the same belief-system, this can benefit the recovery process (Strand 1998). The extent of competition between Muslim agencies in recent war zones – as we have documented in the cases of Afghanistan, Bosnia and Sudan – and the cultural and ideological gaps between them and their beneficiaries, are surely enough to cast doubt on this argument, though the need for aid providers to show cultural sensitivity is not in dispute.

We have tried in this study to challenge naivety about all forms of organized charity and aid – Islamic, Western and other – but also not to lose sight of the authenticity of the charitable impulse: Rousseau's *pitié de soi*, compassion for a fellow species-member. This takes an Islamic form in emphatic calls for generosity, compassion and care for others, so that even smiling at a neighbour or helping a blind person may be forms of charity (Boisard 1985: 128) – which brings us back to the bodily act of charity with which our analysis started. But at the individual and *a fortiori* at the organizational level, there is the constant risk of imposing a conception of the good in the presumed interests of distressed and vulnerable people.

Humanitarians seek aid without politics, a universal ideal. But for the foreseeable future, the worldwide reality is the politics of aid.

ABBREVIATIONS

ACBAR	Afghan Coordination Body for Afghan Relief (Pakistan)
ADRA	Adventist Relief Agency
AMAL	Afwaj al-Muqawameh al-Lubnaniyeh (Lebanese Resistance Battalions)
BBC	British Broadcasting Corporation
CIA	Central Intelligence Agency (USA)
CNN	Cable News Network
DFID	Department for International Development (UK)
FAVDO	Forum of African Voluntary Development Organizations
FIS	Front Islamique du Salut (Algeria)
FLN	Front de Libération Nationale (Algeria)
GIA	Groupe Islamique Armé (Algeria)
GONGO	Government Organized NGO
GUVS	General Union of Voluntary Societies (Jordan)
HAC	Humanitarian Affairs Commission (Sudan)
IAIB	International Association of Islamic Banks
ICRC	International Committee of the Red Cross
ICVA	International Council of Voluntary Agencies
IDB	Islamic Development Bank
IFRCS	International Federation of Red Cross and Red Crescent Societies
IGASA	local name used by IIRO in Bosnia (=*al-ighatha*)
IHH	Internationale Humanitäre Hilfe (Germany)
IHL	International Humanitarian Law
IIRO	International Islamic Relief Organization
INTRAC	International NGO Training and Research Centre, Oxford
IR(W)	Islamic Relief (Worldwide)
ISRA	Islamic Relief Agency
JNRCS	Jordan National Red Crescent Society
MDA	Magen David Adom (Red Shield of David – Israel)
MDI	Munazamat ad-Da`wa al-Islamiya (Sudan)
MENA	Middle East and North Africa
MSF	Médecins Sans Frontières
MSP	Mouvement de la Société pour la Paix (Algeria)
NATO	North Atlantic Treaty Organization
NGO	Non-Governmental Organization

NIF	National Islamic Front (Sudan)
NWFP	North-Western Frontier Province (Pakistan)
OIAO	Organizacija Aktivne Islamske Omladine (Organization of Active Islamic Youth – Bosnia)
OIC	Organization of the Islamic Conference
OLS	Operation Lifeline Sudan
PRCS	Palestine Red Crescent Society
SCC	Sudan Council of Churches
SDA	Stranka Demokratske Akcije (Democratic Action Party – Bosnia)
SPLM/A	Sudanese People's Liberation Movement/Army
TWRA	Third World Relief Agency
UN	United Nations
(UN)ECOSOC	(United Nations) Economic and Social Council
(UN)HCR	(United Nations) High Commissioner for Refugees
Unicef	United Nations Children's Fund
UNRWA	United Nations Relief and Works Agency (Middle East)
USAID	United States Agency for International Development
WFP	World Food Programme
WHO	World Health Organization

GLOSSARY OF ISLAMIC AND ARABIC TERMS

AWQAF Plural of *waqf*.

BA`ATHISM An ideology with elements of both Arab nationalism and state socialism, generally secular yet acknowledging the cultural centrality of Islam to Arabs; founded by a Syrian Christian, Michael Aflaq, and others after the Second World War; later the Ba`ath Party came to power in Iraq and Syria. Ba`ath is a Quranic word meaning resurrection or rebirth.

BONYAD Foundation (Iran).

CALIPHATE The Islamic state or nation established after the death of the Prophet. Caliph = literally 'deputy'.

CRESCENT (*hilal*) Crescent moon emblem associated with pilgrimage and with Ramadan – the Islamic calendar being lunar – and since the 18th century increasingly used in the flags, etc., of Muslim states. See Red Crescent.

DA`WA Missionary activity, literally call or invitation.

DHIMMI Non-Muslim with protected status in an Islamic state, on payment of a poll tax.

FATWA Formal legal opinion or ruling delivered by a mufti.

FITRAH See *zakat al fitr*.

HADITH Traditional 'saying' or action of the Prophet, or his tacit approval of sayings made or actions taken in his presence. Authoritative collections were compiled around the ninth century CE.

HAJJ The annual pilgrimage to Mecca at a stipulated time of year; every Muslim is required to undertake this once in his or her life if possible (see *rukn*, `*umra*).

HALAL Lawful, especially of food.

HAMAS The common name for two distinct Islamist movements founded in both Palestine and Algeria. The word means 'enthusiasm' and is also (in Palestine) an acronym in Arabic (*harakat al-muqawama al-islamiya*, Islamic Resistance Movement).

HARAM Anything forbidden in shari`a law, e.g. gambling.

AL-HARAMAIN The two Holy Places (Mecca and Medina).

HASHEMITES The present ruling dynasty of Jordan, now headed by King Abdullah – descendants of the Prophet.

HAWALA Financial deed of exchange.

HIJAB Head covering for women.

HIJRA Muhammad's emigration from Mecca to Medina in 622 CE, from which base the Muslim calendar is calculated.

HIZBULLAH 'Party of God', Lebanese Shi`a resistance movement.

HUBS *Waqf* in North Africa.

`ID AL-KABIR The major feast, or `id el-adha – the feast of the sacrifice, performed at the end of the annual Hajj. Sheep or other animals are slaughtered, and some of the meat distributed to the poor.

IFTAR Ramadan evening breakfast.

IGHATHA Relief aid.

IJTIHAD The process of creatively interpreting the existing body of law in order to adapt to the current situation.

IKHWAN AL-MUSLIMIN See Muslim Brothers.

IMAM Prayer leader, leader of a religious community. To be distinguished from the special use of this term in Shi`ism, connoting one of the spiritual descendants of Ali, the Prophet's son-in-law.

ISLAM Submission to the will of God as revealed to the Prophet Muhammad, or spiritual commitment; the religion based on this.

ISLAMISM (Arabic *Islamiya*) a neologism coined by the Islamic revivalists themselves. Islamism, as opposed to Islam, denotes a political ideology that holds that all areas of life should be regulated by reference to Islam or at least one interpretation of it. The terms 'integrism' or 'fundamentalism' are also used by observers.

JIHAD Exertion of one's power 'in the path of God'. Also, the defence of Islam; the war against unbelievers as ordained by the *Shari`a*. A term whose connotations are particularly dependent on context.

JIZYAH Tax levied on *dhimmi*s (q.v.)

KAABA The large cubic stone in the centre of the Grand Mosque in Mecca.

KAFIR One guilty of *kufr*, denial of God.

KEMALISM The policy of dissociating Islam from state power, instituted in Turkey by General Mustafa Kemal (Atatürk); in 1928 Turkey was declared a secular state.

KHUTBA Friday sermon.

KUFR Denial of God.

MADHHAB One of the legal schools or traditions of Sunni Islam (Maliki, Hanafi, Maliki, Shafi`i).

MAGHREB North-West Africa.

MUFTI See *fatwa*.

MUJAHID A fighter in *jihad* (q.v.).

MUJTAHID An authority who makes decisions in Islamic law.

MULLAH Islamic scholar or doctor of the Shari`a law; a term used especially in Turkey and Iran, but not in the Arab world.

MUSLIM One who has submitted to God; one who follows the religion revealed to and established by the Prophet Muhammad.

MUSLIM BROTHERS (*al-ikhwan al-muslimin*) A society founded in Egypt by Hassan al-Banna in 1928, which became very influential in the 1940s and has spread to other countries. Its policy is in general to 'islamize' virtually all aspects of public and private life.

NISAB The minimum amount of assets on which *zakat* is payable.

NIYYAH Intention.

OTTOMAN (TURKISH) EMPIRE This dates from around the 14th century and was at its zenith during the 16th-17th centuries, since when it gradually declined and was broken up, to be finally dissolved after the First World War. The Sultan in Constantinople (now Istanbul) used to be both head of the Empire and spiritual leader (caliph) of the majority of Muslims.

PASDARAN Guardians of the Revolution (Iran).

PROPHET (*nabi*) One of a line of divinely inspired religious leaders including Adam, Noah, Abraham, Moses and Jesus, but particularly the last of this line (according to Muslims), Muhammad, the 'Seal of the Prophets'. 'The Prophet' is the usual way in which a Muslim refers respectfully to Muhammad.

QURAN (or KORAN) The body of revelations received by Muhammad.

QURBANI Festive sacrifice, especially on the `Id al-kabir (q.v.)

RAMADAN The ninth month of the Muslim calendar, a holy month during which eating, drinking and sexual intercourse are forbidden from dawn to dusk. A time when believers are enjoined to sympathize with the poor and give charitable alms, but also a festival during which family and friends are visited in the evenings and special food is then eaten.

RED CRESCENT (*al-hilal al-ahmar*). One of the two emblems recognized by the Red Cross and Red Crescent Movement, and used by most, but not all, national societies in the Islamic world. See Crescent.

REIS Leader.

RIBA Usury or bank interest.

RUKN (pl. ARKAN – 'pillar') The 'pillars of Islam', the five religious duties prescribed for every Muslim: *shahada* (the profession of faith); *salat* (regular prayers every day); *zakat* (q.v.); *saum* (fasting and abstinence during ramadan, q.v.); *hajj* (q.v.).

SABIL ALLAH The 'path of God', i.e. all acts pleasing to God.

SADAQA Voluntary payment of charitable alms, as opposed to *zakat* which is in principle a religious obligation.

SALAFI This word, from the Arabic word for ancestor, characterizes those in favour of following the precedent of the Prophet and his companions. In the 19th century, Salafism referred to the reformist movement of scholars who sought to reinterpret the original sources in the light of modern needs. Today, it is largely used to refer to movements that seek to impose, sometimes if necessary by force, a return to the way of life of the Prophet and his companions.

SHARI`A Islamic law, which theoretically should govern all aspects of a Muslim's life.

SHEIKH A venerable old man; also a learned man, a hereditary ruler, a tribal elder, a senator, etc.

SHI`A (hence SHI`ITES, SHI`ISM) The 'party' of those Muslims who recognize Ali, the Prophet's son-in-law, as his rightful successor. The official branch of Islam in Iran; Shi`ites form an important minority in some other Arab countries and in Pakistan and Turkey, and a majority in Bahrain and Iraq.

SHIRK 'Associating' other entities with God, i.e. polytheism.

SUFISM The principal mystical school of Islam, named from the wool (*suf*) which its original members wore. Sufi brotherhoods have played a major missionary role for Islam, especially in Africa and Southeast Asia, partly because of their openness to linkages with other religions and customs.

SUNNA The sum of the sayings and doings (hadith) of the Prophet, which are complementary to the law as established in the Qu'ran.

SUNNI The branch of Islam which upholds customs based on the Sunna (q.v.), as opposed to the Shi`a branch and some others.

SURAH One of the 114 chapters of the Qu'ran.

TAQWA Piety.

`ULAMA (sing. `alim) 'Learned men', guardians of law and tradition, generally trained in one of the traditional religious universities.

UMMA Community of believers, especially the community deemed to include all Muslims. Also, a nation.

`UMRA A lesser pilgrimage to Mecca, which can be made at any time of year (see hajj).

`USHR An Islamic tax on agricultural production, comparable to the Christian institution of the tithe (from the Arabic word for 'tenth').

WAHHABISM Reformist school in Islam deriving from the ultra-conservative 18th century religious reformer Muhammad ibn Abd al-Wahhab, who was opposed to Arab customs such as visiting saints and tombs as deviating from belief in the absolute unity of God. This school lays down strict rules on personal behaviour and dress, and is the official version of Islam in Saudi-Arabia. The Saudi king is the leading sheikh, chief imam, head of the Saudi clan, and head of state, though still subject to Shari`a.

WAQF (pl. AWQAF) Religious endowment. Ministry of Awqaf = Ministry of Religious Affairs.

ZAKAT (or ZAKA) One of the pillars (*rukn*, q.v.) of Islam; the religious obligation to make an annual payment for charitable purposes based on a proportion of one's assets.

ZAKAT AL FITR A special *zakat* (q.v.) payment supposed to be made just before the `id al-fitr or breaking of the Ramadan fast.

ZAWIYA Sufi establishment (North Africa).

NOTES

INTRODUCTION

1. *The Times*, 10 May 1996.
2. These have included the Benevolence International Foundation, Worth, Illinois; the Global Relief Foundation, Bridgeview, Illinois; and the Holy Land Foundation for Relief and Development, Richardson, Texas (*The Non-Profit Times*, 1 January 2002). In nearly all cases, the charges appear to have been denied: for instance by the Al-Haramain Foundation, based in Saudi-Arabia (*Al-Sharq Al-Awsat*, London, 3 May 2002); and by the Muwaffaq Charitable Foundation, also based in Saudi-Arabia but now no longer operating, which forced a statement of apology from the London newsletter *Africa Confidential* in 2001, after it linked the group with an assassination attempt in Africa (*Dawn* Internet edition, 11 October 2001). U.S. Treasury officials raided the offices of the International Islamic Relief Organization (IIRO) in Virginia in March 2002 (*Washington Times*, 'U.S. demands data on Islamic charities', 22 March 2002). In September 2001, the UK's Charity Commission investigated an allegation in *The Times* that the IIRO in England had been under CIA scrutiny, but found that the English charity had been inactive since 1997, and before then its activities appeared to have been minimal (Charity Commission website, 'Investigations', 16 April 2002). In January 2002, the Charity Commission froze assets of the Saudi-funded International Development Foundation (*The Times*, 16 January 2002) but they were released in April 2002 owing to lack of compromising evidence (*Daily Telegraph*, 3 March 2003).
In August 2002, some US relatives of victims of the 11 September attacks launched a lawsuit against the IIRO and the World Assembly of Muslim Youth and other organizations, claiming three trillion dollars in punitive damages. Officials of the two charities rejected the accusations totally (*Jordan Times*, 18 August 2002). In December 2002, Saudi officials announced the setting up of a 'high commission' to oversee Saudi charities and new guidelines to clamp down on abuses, in the wake of allegations that charitable donations from the wife of the Saudi ambassador to Washington might have been diverted to reach the 11 September 2001 hijackers (Reuters, 3 December 2002).
3. In this book we tend to use the word 'Muslim' to refer to people who at a given point in time call themselves or are regarded as Muslims, and 'Islamic' to refer to policies or actions which seek to put Islamic teaching into practice.
4. For general coverage of radical Islam, see Kepel 2002a, Ruthven 2002. A book in French covering some of the same ground as ours was published in Paris just as our first draft had been submitted to the publisher (Ghandour 2002). Abdel-Rahman Ghandour writes from extensive field experience with aid agencies in Muslim societies. Though his book contains a number of factual errors and indulges in some sweeping statements about radical Islam as an international movement, it offers some stimulating ideas and its general conclusions are not dissimilar to ours.

5. Both authors have published articles on the topic since 1996 (see authors' acknowledgments). The material has been substantially revised and brought up to date for this volume.

6. This analysis was stimulated by Jean Leca's summing-up speech at the end of a conference on NGOs and humanitarianism organized by the University of La Rochelle in April 2001.

CHAPTER 1: FINANCIAL WORSHIP

1. The other four pillars are, in order, the *shahada*, or 'there is no god but God, and Muhammad is his Prophet'; *salat*, observance of the five daily ritual prayers; *sawm*, fasting in the month of Ramadan; and *hajj*, performance of the pilgrimage to Mecca once in a lifetime by those able to do it.

2. The summary given here draws both on publications and on conversations with experts.

3. For comment on this category, see Décobert 1991: 222-5.

4. For an example of this discussion, see Hamidullah 1959, ii: 617-28.

5. Omar Bakri Muhammad appears to be following the Maliki school of law, which argues for the importance of the State in administering *zakat*, whereas the British-based charities he is criticizing follow the Hanafi or Shafi`i interpretation (Weiss 2002: 29).

6. *Jordan Times*, 11 February 1995.

7. *Jordan Times*, 21 August 2002.

8. As Leach (1983: 52-53) and others have noted, the sacrifice of firstborn children was widespread in the geographical context of the Old Testament. Leach follows Frazer in emphasizing the apotropaic or evil-preventing role of this form of sacrifice, and it is true that a pattern of preference for the second son as the sacred heir (Abel, Isaac, Jacob) runs through the biblical narrative. However, vegetable sacrifice was also a marked feature of the Near Eastern historical background, as in Egypt (MacCulloch 1913, van der Toorn 1995: 2053), though there is comparatively little evidence from the Levant as opposed to North Africa, where the custom survived into modern times (for Algeria, see Doutté 1908: 491, 493).

On firstlings in Hebraic religion, W. Robertson Smith argued that these had less in common with firstfruits than with the first three years' produce of a new orchard which was not to be eaten as it was 'as if uncircumcised to you' (*Leviticus* 19. 23; Smith 1927: 24-241, 462-465, see also notes by his editor Stanley A. Cook 583-584). The semiotic connections between circumcision, blood-sacrifice and the cutting of fruit are beyond the scope of this discussion. The Quran mentions in scathing terms the pre-Islamic custom of burying young girls (*wa'd al-banat*, Q. 16. 58-59, 81. 8-9), which was interpreted by Robertson Smith (1885: 279-285) as a form of human sacrifice, though not by all the Arabic sources. More generally, the biblical background to Quranic teaching about tithing for the poor was recognized by some classical commentators such as the great Persian scholar of the early twelfth century, Zamakshari. (I am grateful to Professor Sarah Stroumsa for the preceding two points in this note.) On Muslim birth rituals, see Aubaile-Sallenave 1999.

9. This is said to refer to the breakdown of the irrigation of the Yemen or the Marib dam.

10. Traditional biblical scholarship was however uncertain as to the separation between tithes and firstfruits (Strahan 1913). For a study of the biblical theology of material possessions, in the tradition of Christian commentary with a strong didactic element, see Blomberg 1999.

11. This corresponds to 'St James's reservation' in New Testament theology, based on *James* 4. 15.

12. An as yet unpublished thesis appears to apply Mary Douglas's ideas in a comparable way (Katz 1999).

CHAPTER 2: WAQF AND ISLAMIC FINANCE

1. In Geertz's retrospective of his career as an anthropologist, he notes that during the period between 1963 and 1986, there were huge changes in Sefrou, including disintegration of the

bazaar economy and an explosion of residential land prices by 1,000 per cent between 1960 and 1970 (Geertz 1995: 11-17).

2. The IDB cooperates with a number of OIC-associated agencies: the Statistical, Economic and Social Research and Training Centre (Ankara), the Islamic Chamber of Commerce, Industry and Commodity Exchange (Karachi), the Islamic Centre for Development of Trade (Casablanca), the Islamic Foundation for Science, Technology and Development (Jeddah) and the Islamic Centre for Technical Vocational Training and Research (Dhaka) (Meenai 1989). Iran has now joined the membership.

3. For further details see *Encyclopedia of Islamic Banking*, London: Institute of Islamic Banking and Insurance, 1995, 389-93.

4. Al-Cheikh Youssef al-Qaradawi. *Shakhsiyya al-`am al-Islamiya*. Cairo: Maktaba Wahba, 2001. The profile adds that Qaradawi is married to a lady descended from the Hussainian Hashemites, and has four daughters and three sons. See also Kepel 2002b: 69-79.

5. Source: Interview with a former Islamic bank executive, Paris, February 1998, JB-J.

6. Meenai personally considers that 'the Bank's assistance should solely focus on the economic uplift of the Muslim communities instead of any religious activities' (Meenai 1989: 152).

7. *Sudanow*, September 1991, p.17. In the mid-1980s the Sudanese pounds converted at about 2.50 to the US$.

8. Interview with IIRO official published in *Al-Nur*, 20 September 1992.

9. See entries on Al-Baraka and IDB in *Encyclopedia of Islamic Banking*.

10. *Al-Hayat*, 10 January 2003.

11. For Islamic theorists, money and capital are not synonymous, money being only potential capital requiring an entrepreneur to transform it into productive use. There are parallels with Marx's theory of capital and Schumpeter's theory of entrepreneurship (Ahmed 1990). It has recently been argued that one of the sources for Islamic finance is the 'critical accounting' theory originated by Trevor Gambling, who had been in turn influenced by the anthropologist Mary Douglas (Maurer 2002).

12. Islamic equity (ordinary share) funds are now said to total some $3.3 billion worldwide, a decline from the peak of $5 billion in 2000 which had grown from only $800 million in 1996. Among the more than 100 equity funds are some run by large Western banks such as Citibank (USA), and UBS and Pictet (Switzerland). Many of these funds were hard hit in 2001 by the fall in high technology stocks, which they had specially favoured. There are Dow Jones and *Financial Times* Islamic Market Indexes. (Source: Failaka International Inc., www.failaka.com)

CHAPTER 3: RED CRESCENT POLITICS

1. The Kazakhstan 'Red Crescent and Red Cross Society' is thus a technically irregular entity within the Movement. Like Israel (see later in this chapter), Kazakhstan has filed reservations about the present rules relating to the emblems. Eritrea also uses both emblems. These societies, like the Palestinian Red Crescent, are classed as 'pending recognition and admission'.

2. ICRC press release, 18 October 2001. 'Agreement on the Organization of the International Activities of the Components of the International Red Cross and Red Crescent Movement', 26 November 1997, *International Review of the Red Cross*, March 1998, 322, 159-76. *Strategy for the International Red Cross and Red Crescent Movement*, November 2001.

3. The heart is in fact a symbol in Christianity – of spiritual love and ardour – but a subsidiary one.

4. In 1999, a Working Group on the Emblem was set up by the Movement to find a lasting solution to the problem. It agreed to propose a new protocol to be added to the Geneva Conventions, proving for 'an additional emblem devoid of any political, cultural or religious connotations' to meet the requirements of those National Societies that had difficulty in using the existing emblems. It was intended that a diplomatic conference in Geneva should

complete the process in October 2000. However, this has been postponed because of serious events in the Middle East. The emblem proposed is a red diamond shape, provisionally called the 'red crystal', which according to the results of commissioned research bears no negative connotations in any known culture and has the same name in many languages. This additional emblem would be available both for 'indicative' use (as the everyday logo of a National Society) and for the 'protective' use that applies when a National Society, and the medical services of its country's armed forces, are involved in conflict. The ICRC is strongly committed to resolving the problem as soon as possible, and in an interview with the author in July 2002 a senior director stated that all parties were now agreed in the principle of the change but not as to the timing. See Bugnion 2000; statement by Christina Magnuson, co-chair of the Joint Working Group on the Emblem, 31 December 2001, *International Review of the Red Cross*, no. 844, 1156-8.

5. Dunant also published *L'Esclavage chez les Musulmans et aux Etats-Unis* (Geneva, Flick, 1863); on the cover is a translation of St Paul's words 'There is neither Jew or Greek' in large Arabic characters. Dunant was an intelligent traveller in North Africa and learnt the Arabic alphabet; a devout Protestant Christian, he was impressed by Arab hospitality and piety. Jacques Pons' study shows the origins of the ICRC to have been more embedded in the colonial ethos of the day than had previously been recognized (Lonca 1968, Pons 1979, Descombes 1988). During the last part of his life, when Dunant became recognized as a public figure after years of being forgotten, he became prominent in the international peace movement and criticized Europe for its treatment of the Far East. For analysis of Muslim influences on International Humanitarian Law, see Zemmali 1997, Cockayne 2002: 597-608.

6. *Bulletin international des Sociétés de Secours aux Militaires Blessés*, no. 28, October 1876, 173-6. Translated from the French. The obsolete term 'Mohammedan' has been followed in translation.

7. For a fuller account of the origins of the Turkish Red Crescent, see Boissier 1985: 303-12. Boissier records that during the Russo-Turkish War of 1877, the Russian military authorities did their best to instruct troops in the proper treatment of the wounded, whereas the Turks did not. The president of the International Committee of the Red Cross protested in a personal capacity against the conduct of the Turkish army. See also Anderson 1968: 118-19.

8. *Bulletin international*, no. 29, January 1877, p.1-3.

9. *The Work of the British Red Cross Society in Three Continents, 1912-14*, London 1915 (British Red Cross archive).

10. 'Charity has no geographical limits. The needy Greeks, Armenians and Jews of Turkey receive help from their co-religionists and from the charitable societies of Europe and America. The Russian refugees in our town are the object of international care and sympathy. The Red Crescent asks the Muslims of the world to adopt the Mosque and Baïram days [first day of feast following Ramadan, and the 'Major Feast', *'id al-kabir*] and hopes that Muslim sympathy will manifest itself on a large scale. Muslim journals appearing different languages are requested to reproduce the above text.' *Bulletin du Croissant Rouge Ottoman*, no. 8, April 1922. (Translated from the French.)

11. 'Le croissant-rouge mauritanien: une organisation humanitaire à l'image d'un pays', *Etudes du Développement* no. 2, Institut Henry-Dunant, Geneva, 1986. (Translated from the French.)

12. ICRC archives, Geneva.

13. The question of the emblems arose in the course of the ICRC's activities during the Palestine-Israel conflict between 1945 and 1952. It then played a strategic role when it was under attack for having failed to help the victims of the Nazi concentration camps during the Second World War , and was under threat of dissolution by the International Red Cross Movement (Junod 1996).

14. The Red Crescent national societies include Afghanistan, Algeria, Bahrain, Bangladesh, Djibouti, Egypt, Iran, Iraq, Jordan, Kirghistan, Kuwait, Libya, Malaysia, Mauritania, Morocco, Pakistan, Palestine Qatar, Saudi-Arabia, Somalia, Sudan, Syria, Tunisia, Turkey, Turkmenistan, United Arab Emirates, Uzbekistan and Yemen. All have the crescent facing

like a C except for Pakistan, Tunisia and Turkey, which are reversed. A third possible orientation, like a C tilted 22 degrees anti-clockwise, is also permitted under the Geneva Convention but is not in use (Bugnion 1977: 69).

15. The original Christian symbols were the fish and the *chi-rho* monogram (X-P – the first two letters of Christ's name in Greek).

16. ArabicNews.com, 29 June 2001.

17. OIC press release, 22 November 2000, and interviews with officials of the Movement.

18. Convention adopted in Niamey, Niger, in 1982.

19. OIC press release, 21 April 2001.

20. For general discussions of tensions between Islam and Western conceptions of human rights, see Mayer 1999, and (for a particularly sceptical account) Halliday 1996. For a criticism of Mayer's position as 'axiomatic' and 'orientalist', see Strawson 1996. Zemmali's comparative study of a specific theme in Islamic law and IHL is exemplary (Zemmali 1997).

21. From a speech at an academic conference in Khartoum, *Monde Arabe Maghreb Machrek*, 148, April-June 1995 (translated from French translation).

22. The president, Younis Al-Khatib, wrote, a few days before his own detention by the Israeli army on 2 April 2002, that the PRCS welcomed an investigation of the allegations that its ambulances had been misused. 'I am concerned that this event may have been a deliberate attempt to tarnish the image of our ambulances'. Source: *al-Ittihad*, newsletter of International Federation of Red Cross and Red Crescent Societies, Regional Delegation for the Middle East and North Africa, issue 2, April 2002, 1-2.

23. 'Meeting between the Palestine Red Crescent Society and the Magen David Adom of Israel under ICRC auspices on the Protection of Medical Services and Cooperation', 21 December 2000.

24. In October 2001, Dr Bernadine Healy was forced to resign as salaried President of the American Red Cross, after part of a $540 million disaster fund raised from the public for the victims of 11 September was applied to routine funding of their activities. Healy had repeatedly criticized the ICRC and the Federation for not formally recognizing the Magen David Adom, and sought to cut off funding from the American Red Cross. However, her two year period of office was successful in making American Red Cross programmes more effective (Hansch 2002).

25. In 1992, the president of the French Red Cross, Georgina Dufoix (also a close political supporter of President Mitterrand), was forced to resign after a hard-line Palestinian leader, Georges Habash, was admitted to Paris for medical treatment under Red Cross auspices.

26. Quoted in Bellion-Jourdan 2002a p.192 n. The Iranian Red Crescent may have sent arms to the Shi`a Afghan opposition in 1997, under cover of a humanitarian convoy (Ghandour 2002: 184).

27. Decisions 30 (1995) and 45 (1997) of the General Assembly of the International Federation.

28. Of the Standing Commission's nine members, four represent the ICRC and the Federation, and of the remaining five current members, both Mohammed Al-Hadid and Dr Al Swailem represent Red Crescent National Societies – an indication of the prominence of these Societies in the internal politics of the Movement.

29. See n.4. According to one report, some Muslim countries do not want to see the double cross/crescent emblem disappear, as it seems to them a guarantee of neutrality (Ghandour 2002: 317).

CHAPTER 4: HELPING THE 'BROTHERS'

1. The extensive literature on transnational groupings includes Badie 1995, Keck and Sikkink 1998, Rosenau 1990, Pagnucco 1997.

2. Among the few studies that attempt to relate Islamic tradition to contemporary activity is an article on the Organization of the Islamic Conference by Sohail H. Hashmi, which concludes

that current commitments to humanitarian intervention are not at the level which Islamic tradition would legitimate (Hashmi 1993).

3. On the concept of *jihad* in historical perspective, see Kelsay and Johnson (eds.) 1991.

4. For accounts of Arab engagement in the war in Afghanistan see for instance Hyman 1994, Rubin 1997.

5. Interview in Arabic, *Al-Jihad*, no. 5, 21 April 1985, 20-2.

6. Brochure published by the Committee.

7. Interview with the Director, 25 June 1998.

8. See Chapter 5 for discussion of the powerful foundations have developed in Iran, also Ghandour 2002: 272-7.

9. *Nida'ul Islam*, no. 14, July-September 1996, www.islam.org.au

10. Ahmed Zaidan, '*Tanzim al-qa`ida wa ta'rikhuhu … fi Dau' mahakamat new york*' [Al-Qa`ida's structure and its history … in the light of the trial in New York], *Al-Hayat*, 16 February 2001.

11. Interview with Commissioner for Afghan Refugees, Peshawar, 26 May 1999.

12. *Al-ta'sis wa l-injazat* (foundations and realizations) 1985-1995, Islamic Coordination Council, Pakistan, July 1996 (in Arabic).

13. Abdel Rahman Mohamed Said, *Mudhakkira hawla mustaqbal al-ta`lim fi afghanistan* (Memorandum on the future of teaching in Afghanistan), ISRA Peshawar.

14. Abdallah Azzam, *`ibar w basa'ir li-l-jihad fi l-`asr al-hadir* (Lessons and insights for the jihad in the contemporary period), Peshawar: Edition al-Jihad, 1986-87.

15. 'Coordination system of the International Islamic Council for Da`wa and Relief', Cairo, 1993 (in Arabic and English).

16. Interviews with the director of ACBAR, Peshawar, 19 May 1999; regional director of ISRA, Peshawar, 20 May 1999. On the different arrangements for coordinating humanitarian action in Afghanistan, see Bennett 1995.

17. 'Mujahid Osama Bin Ladin Talks Exclusively to "Nida'ul Islam" About the New Powder Keg in the Middle East', www.islam.org.au/articles/15/LADIN.HTM

18. *Frontier Post*, 8 April 1993.

19. Aamer Ahmed Khan, 'The forsaken warriors', *The Herald*, August 1993, 57-63.

20. 'Riyadh says 125 Saudi detainees held in the Guantánamo center', AFP, 26 August 2002.

21. ISRA (Islamic Relief Agency, also evoking *al-isra'*, the Prophet Muhammad's Night Journey) was the name taken by IARA for its international network, with a few exceptions such as IARA-USA. The UK-based Islamic Relief Worldwide (IRW) is a different entity from ISRA and keen to distance itself from its Sudanese counterpart, but there may have been a link in the past. According to my ISRA informants, initially Hany El Banna, an Egyptian medical student at Birmingham University, now head of IRW, was asked on a visit to Sudan to open a branch in the UK. For reasons reportedly related to disagreement between the Egyptian Muslim Brotherhood and the political trend led by Hassan al-Turabi, Hany al-Banna started his own organization instead, in Birmingham. ISRA then opened its own branch in Britain. Birmingham now hosts both the headquarters of IRW and an office of ISRA-UK (affiliated to the Khartoum headquarters of IARA-ISRA).

22. *Yugoslavia: The Crime of Our Time*, Islamic Relief video, 1993; *Relief News: Newsletter of Islamic Relief Worldwide*, Spring 1994, no. 5; *The Independent*, 8 December 1992.

23. 'A conversation with Fadi Itani, UK manager of Islamic Relief', *Inspiration Magazine* (Islamic Relief magazine), 1998, 8-9.

24. Interview, 8 May 1998.

25. Interview with Yusuf Islam by Mohamed Mahjoub Haron, *Sudanow*, August 1986, 31-2; interview with Suhaib Hassan, *Q-News*, 16 February – 1 March 1996, p.7.

26. *Daily Telegraph*, 2 March 1996.

27. *Q-News*, 9 October 1992, 2-9 July 1993, 25 June 1993.

28. *Al-Nur*, Cairo, 22 September 1992.

29. Brochure, Islamic Relief Agency.

30. Interview with official, Malaysian Relief Centre, Sarajevo, January 1998.

31. International Conference on Uprooted Muslim Women. Sharjah Declaration: Recommendations. Sharjah, 12-15 November 1994.

32. 'Inside Europe', CNN, 31 August 2002.

33. The code was initially signed by Caritas Internationalis, Catholic Relief Service, International Federation of Red Cross and Red Crescent Societies, International Save the Children Alliance, Lutheran World Federation, Oxfam, World Council of Churches, ICRC.

CHAPTER 5: NGOs IN THE CONTEMPORARY MUSLIM WORLD

1. A report on the effectiveness of international NGOs was commissioned in 2002 by Vietnam's Ministry of Foreign Affairs, and concluded that international NGOs contributed some $80 million per year towards poverty alleviation and other development goals, and were valued at all levels across the country. Civil society within Vietnam is however still closely regulated. (Information supplied by Lin Menuhin.)

2. An account of the accident may be found in *The Times*, 20 February 2002 ('Cooker fire kills 370 on Egyptian train'), and in other newspapers. Fund-raising for all charities is tightly regulated in Egypt, as are the activities of international Islamic NGOs. This country, despite being the most populous in the Arab world, has refrained from founding international Islamic NGOs – a principal reason being Saudi-Arabia's determination not to be outshone by Egypt as a core state of the Arab-Islamic world (Ghandour 2002: 192, 288-90).

3. Islamic Relief, annual report, 1999, and personal interviews with Islamic Relief officials. According to a former Islamic Relief employee, the funding for this innovative project in Mali originates from Malian residents in France, where there is a branch of Islamic Relief.

4. Translated from the Arabic with the help of Jamal Nusseibeh. Hugh Roberts, Andrea Liverani and Mark Sinclair provided helpful information for the section in this Chapter on Algeria.

5. I am grateful to the French research centre CERMOC in Amman for access to research on the Jordanian voluntary sector by Abla Amawi and Brigitte Curmi.

6. Anne Sofie Roald's study contains rich and irreplaceable material on the Islamist movements in Jordan and Malaysia, to which she had privileged access as the wife of an Islamist. She gives special attention to the relations between the women's movement and the Islamist movement in Jordan.

7. In other countries, the issue is sometimes sidestepped with a reference to the urgent humanitarian needs of Muslims. It becomes a live issue with 'non-Abrahamic' indigenous minorities such as some of the Nilotic peoples of southern Sudan ('animists'). In such contexts, it would seem that even the more tolerant interpretations of Islam cannot easily overcome the traditional, almost visceral dread of paganism and polytheism (*shirk*) which is deeply rooted in the Quran. This may be a principal reason why charitable and humanitarian institutions in Sudan have been so ruthlessly manipulated by the Islamist government in Khartoum in the context of civil war (see Chapter 6).

8. Cf. also François Burgat on the Middle East and North Africa more generally: 'If, for some decades, the mosques have had such a success, it is certainly because people speak of God there, but also because the vocabulary used to do so derives from the only domain which has resisted the cultural pressure of the North. In this case, the apparent return of the religious should be seen less as the resurgence of the sacred in a secular universe, than as the rehabilitation of the referents, especially political ones, of the local culture, which are invited to rediscover – at the conclusion of the colonial parenthesis – their lost ambition to universality.' (Burgat 1995: 108, translated from the French).

9. I have sometimes used one of these boxes as a visual aid for lectures on Islamic charities, and challenged the audience to give evidence of any model of a Christian church being fitted with a slot as a collecting box. The hypothesis is that money is not generally regarded by

Muslims as contaminating to spirituality, as it is in the Christian tradition (though not the Jewish). An American informant has told me, however, that in parts of the USA models of churches are indeed used as collecting boxes.

10. The failure of Islamist movements in the region to try to restrain the growth of virulent anti-Jewish propaganda is one of their most serious obstacles to gaining international sympathy. Hamas's charter positively endorses anti-Jewish conspiracy theories (Mishal and Sala 2000: 45, 175-99). Such propaganda, defended by the radical Palestinian resistance as a retaliation for the ethnic exclusivism of the Israeli state, fuels a vicious circle of counter-propaganda.

11. For an analysis of the Quranic origins of the imagery of fructifying seedcorn, commonly used as a graphic device by Islamic charities, see Ghandour 2002: 47, 133.

12. In Jordan, too, the Ministry of Awqaf sees no necessity to publish accounts of its administration of *zakat*, merely indicating that the donations are subject to change and that their donors 'have complete trust in the fund' (*Jordan Times*, 21 August 2002).

13. For comparative evidence from Accra, Ghana, which has a population of some 1.5 million, about eleven per cent of whom are Muslims, see Sulemena Mumuni's survey of Islamic NGOs in the city, which have grown sharply in number since 1972 (Mumuni 1992). She concludes that whereas these organizations have tried to uplift the socio-religious status of Muslims in Ghana – especially through sponsoring mosques and scholarships – they are not specially active in disaster relief and have done very little in campaigns against AIDS, environmental pollution and the like.

CHAPTER 6: WESTERN VERSUS ISLAMIC AID?

1. 'Fifteen years in the field of *da`wa* and public service' [translated from the Arabic].

2. *Al-Hayat*, 21 February 2001. The agreement on memorandum resulted from negotiations in Geneva between a delegation of the National Popular Conference (of al-Turabi) and the SPLA (of John Gorang).

3. Interview, 28 April 1996.

4. Two fraternities, sub-divided into a number of branches, became specially important in the nineteenth century: the Qadiriya, founded in Iraq in the twelfth century by Abd al-Qadir al-Jilani, and the Tijaniya, founded in Morocco and Algeria in the nineteenth century by Abu al-Abbas Ahmad al-Tijani. The African branches of these fraternities were to a great extent inspired by their equivalents in the Arab world.

5. Interview, Khartoum, 5 May 1996.

6. Aims of the organization as set out in a booklet published to mark its 15th anniversary, *Khamsa `ashara `aman di majal ad-da`wa w l-khidmat w l-ighatha*, Khartoum, 1995, p.6.

7. No. 59, p.6 and 9.

8. The Libyan agency provided funding towards the total cost of $822,708, with the participation (in the vague expression of the annual report) of 'the Kuwaiti people' (Da`wa Islamiya, *Kottayeb al-mashru`at* (1981-1989), p.6).

9. Interview with former employee of an Islamic financial institution, Paris, 26 February 1998.

10. Da`wa Islamiya, *Kottayeb al-mashru`at* (1981-1989).

11. The Mahdists withdrew from power in September 1983, so marking their dissatisfaction with the setting up of 'Islamic laws'.

12. Interview with Abdessalam Suleyman, executive director of Da`wa Islamiya, Khartoum, 12 May 1996.

13. The studios of the World Foundation for the Production of Information produced propaganda documentaries for Sudanese television after the coup of 1989. Source: Dr Karuri, its director, 9 May 1996.

14. Da`wa Islamiya, *Dalil*, Khartoum, 1985.

15. Da`wa Islamiya leaflet, 1982.

16. Taha's principal work, *The Second Message of Islam* (1967), distinguished between two levels of Quranic revelation. The verses revealed to the Prophet to reform the pagan Arab society, and to found the Muslim community through the setting up of a system of laws (*shari`a*) had only a limited bearing in the historical context of early Islam. For Taha, *shari`a* was 'only a transitory stage, never conceived for the modern world'. By contrast, the true message of Islam lay in the verses that set out moral principles of good conduct, valid for every age and addressed to the whole of humanity. Taha was condemned and executed in 1985, for his 'apostasy' in propagating this liberal reading of Islam (Howard 1998).

17. Source: interview with Dr Abdessalam Suleyman, executive director, Khartoum, 12 May 1996.

18. *Al-Wasat*, 29 January 2001.

19. On the transition and the 'democratic' period between 1985 and 1989, see Salih 1990; Woodward 1990: Chapter 6.

20. Interview with Sadiq al-Mahdi, former prime minister (1986-9) and current leader of the Umma party, Khartoum, 15 May 1996.

21. Interview with Dr Al-Amin Mohamed `Uthman, secretary-general, Da`wa Islamiya, 22 April 1996.

22. *Sudanow*, September 1985, p.28. Similarly, after the prohibition order in 1986 the agency responded with a press release describing the decision of the attorney general as 'purely political and without foundation despite its appearance of legality' (*Sudanow*, May 1986, p.5)

23. See n.20.

24. In the Ministry of Finance and Economy's report for the year 1994-95, zakat funds were integrated together with other state revenue. *Al-`ard al-iqtisadi* 1994-95, Khartoum, October 1995, p.104f.

25. Hassan al-Turabi's words reported in the Kuwaiti publication *Sawt al-Kuwait*, 25 March 1991 (translated from the Arabic).

26. Source: interview with Dr Abdallah Suleyman al-`Awad, Khartoum, 5 May 1996.

27. Source: interviews, Khartoum, 21 April and 6 May 1996.

28. The president of the Humanitarian Affairs Commission (HAC) denied that the number of Islamic agencies had increased in Sudan since 1989. This could not be checked, as the list of NGOs provided by the HAC did not include the dates when they began operating. Source: interview with Fath Abu al-Qadi, president of HAC, Khartoum, 9 May 1996.

29. Interview with Sirag al-Din Abdul Bari, Executive Manager, Sudanese office of Muwaffaq al-Kheiriya, 4 mai 1996.

30. Interview with Toby Maduot, 3 mai 1996.

31. The SCC was founded in 1967 through the unification of two institutions that antedated Independence, the Northern Sudan Christian Council (NSCC) and the Sudan Evangelical Council for the South (SECS).

32. Source: interview with Rev. Enoch Tombe Stephen, secretary-general, Sudan Council of Churches, Khartoum, 3 May 1996.

33. Interview, 11 May 1996.

34. See n.30.

35. Sudan Council of Churches, *Constitution*, Khartoum, 1995.

36. Sudan/Egypt. Calling the Shots after Addis Ababa. *Africa Confidential*, 36: 14, 7 July 1995.

37. Interview, 4 mai 1996.

38. The report recalls that Usama bin Laden, who had arrived in Khartoum in 1994 after leaving Afghanistan, had been expelled from Sudan in 1996. According to this document, Al-Shamal Islamic Bank obtained agreement in April 1983, after a request from the government of northern Sudan, with the Saudi company Al-Shamal For Investment and Development Co., and with the Saudi business-man Saleh Abdallah al-Kamil. In April 1984, the bank issued shares for subscription, and the main founders were (in addition to the three named above) the Faysal Islamic Bank of Sudan and the Saudi, Omer Abdallah Kamil. Final authorization for the launching of the bank was granted in April 1990. According to the

documents, Usama bin Laden was neither a founder nor a shareholder. However, a letter from Mohamed S. Mohamed, the bank's general manager, admits that Usama bin Laden was indirectly an account holder in the bank, through the medium of two companies (Al Hijra Construction and Development, registered in Sudan in March 1992, and Wadi El Agig, a Saudi company). *Report of the Government of the Sudan submitted pursuant to paragraph 6 of Security Council resolution 1373 (2001)*, December 2001, S/2001/1317.

39. Interviews with Abdallah Suleyman al-`Awad, then chairman of IARA-ISRA, Khartoum, 1 and 5 May 1996.

40. Judith Miller, 'Terrorists Rely on a Few Islamic Charities, U.S. Suspects', *International Herald Tribune*, 21 February 2000, p.5.

CHAPTER 7: THE BALKAN CASE

1. Though this Chapter is primarily based on my own research based on visits to Bosnia, Britain and Egypt in 1998, I am specially grateful to Xavier Bougarel, French expert on Bosnia, for having allowed me to consult his thesis before publication (Bougarel 2000), and to Esad Hecimovic, a dedicated Bosnian journalist, who shared his analysis with me when I met him in January 1998 in Zenica and in December 2001 in Sarajevo.

2. Jakub Selimoski, 'Memorandum about the Muslim Community in Yugoslavia, its Position and Views on the Solution of the Present Political Crisis', *Glasnik Rijaseta IZ-e u SFRJ*, LIV:5, July-August 1991, 615-19.

3. Conference resolution published in *Ljiljan*, 28 September 1992, p.9.

4. Interview with director of Islamic Relief Worldwide, Birmingham, May 1998.

5. Hizb al-Tahrir is a radical Islamist organization founded by Cheikh Taqiuddine al-Nabahani in 1953 in Jordan. It campaigns for the re-establishment of the unity of the Muslim world around the Caliphate, which was abolished in 1924.

6. Video of conference organized on 13-14 November 1993 in London, Bosnia and the Global Islamic Movement, Muslim Parliament. *Q-News*, 9 October 1992 and 25 June 1993.

7. Harakat ul-Ansar was founded in 1993 in Pakistan, with the initial objective of campaigning for the annexation of Kashmir to Pakistan.

8. *Le Monde*, Paris, 11 July 1996.

9. Bosnian Congress (www.xs4all.nl/~frankt/Bosnian_congress) for TWRA; *L'Express*, 3 July 1995, for *Muwaffaq*.

10. *Globus*, Zagreb, 16 October 1992.

11. Before leaving for the jihad in Bosnia, Abu Abdul Aziz met Nasir al-Din al-Albani, director of the Jordanian Salafi movement Ahl al-Hadith ('people of the Hadith') and obtained his agreement. MSA News (Muslim Students of America), www.msanews.mynet.net

12. Al-Haramain, based in Riyadh, has a substantial office in the USA (Al-Haramain Education Centre). This organization issued *fatwa*s in the name of Sheikh bin Baz, the Saudi religious leader, and disseminated Wahhabi conceptions of Islam.

13. *Al-Wafd*, Cairo, 4 July 1997; *Al-Ahram*, Cairo, 11 July 1994.

14. The 'Handzar division', named after an SS division founded in Bosnia in 1943, consisted of combatants from Sandjak and Kosovo, officered by veterans from Afghanistan (Robert Fax, 'Albanians and Afghans fight for the heirs to Bosnia's SS past', *Daily Telegraph*, 29 December 1993). The 'Green legion' consisted of Bosnian combatants and *mujahidin*. It was dissolved in February 1994, some of its members were given prison sentences, and others were dispersed in various units of the Bosnian army.

15. Interview with Abu Abdul Aziz, reproduced on MSA News web-site, see above.

16. *Akhbar al-yom*, Cairo, 30 December 1995.

17. *Ljiljan*, Sarajevo, 14 September 1995; *Al-Ahram*, 13 September 1995; *Ljiljan*, 15 September and 20 December 1995; AFP report, Cairo, 18 December 1995.

18. *Akhbar al-yom*, 30 December 1995; *Preporod*, xxvii: 1, 1 January 1996, p.3.

19. AFP report, 5 January 1996.

20. *Guide to the International Islamic Council for Da`wa and Relief, Cairo*, 1994.

21. *Ljiljan*, 9 June 1993.

22. *Al-Ahram*, 26 April 1993.

23. Interview with official of BiH Islamic Centre, London, May 1998.

24. Islamic Relief brochure, November 1996; Muslim Aid *Annual Review*, 1995.

25. IIRO *Newsletter*, 8 May 1994.

26. *Al-Muslimun*, Cairo, 2 May 1997.

27. Islamic Relief video, *The Crime of Our Time*, see above.

28. *Preporod*, xxiii.12, 15 July 1992, p.4

29. *The Guardian*, London, 15 October 1994.

30. *Ljiljan*, 16 February 1994.

31.*The Times*, London, 22 October 1994.

32. *Q-News*, 5 March 1993.

33. Meeting at headquarters of Ahmadiyya, London, 4 April 1998.

34. On the TWRA, see *Washington Post*, 22 September 1996.

35. These included Hasan Cengic and Dzjemaludin Latic – who were accused jointly with Izetbegovic at the time of the law-suit in 1983 against the Bosnian pan-Islamist movement (see Bougarel 1994), Husein Zivalj (another co-accused, who became Bosnian Ambassador to Austria in 1994), and two of Izetbegovic's close advisers, Irfan Ljevakovic and Faris Nanic.

36. *Washington Post*, 22 September 1996.

37. In December 2001, I met some Bosnian youths and asked them about the experience they had of a communitized humanitarian aid during the war. One, born of a mixed marriage at the second generation (with both Muslim and Serb grandparents), told me of the difficulties of getting humanitarian aid from the Muslim or Christian organizations as he did not belong to the Muslim, Catholic or Orthodox communities. Furthermore, he was not shy to claim that he was, and still is, an atheist. He did therefore get relief from the local Jewish organization. A different view of the reality is given by the apologetic book on charitable work published by Merhamet (Bavcic 1997).

38. Interview with official of Merhamet, Sarajevo, January 1998.

39. *Al-Sha`b*, Cairo, 29 October 1993.

40. 'The White Paper on Alija Izetbegovic', Bosnian Congress web-site www.xs4all.nl/ ~frankti/Bosnian_congress.

41. *Ljiljan*, 5 March 1997 and 3 May 1995.

42. *The Times*, 22 October 1994.

43. *Ljiljan*, 26 April 1995.

44. *Al-Sha`b*, 28 December 1993.

45. Esad Hecimovic, 2001. Bosnia: a safe haven for terrorists? *Transitions Online*, 25 September.

46. *The Guardian*, 15 October 1994.

47. *Ljiljan*, 26 April 1995.

48. *Ljiljan*, 3 March 1997.

49. See n.44.

50. 'Six terror suspects detained in Bosnia handed over to the US.' AFP, 18 January 2002.

51. 'Bosnia bans Islamic charities after US request', Reuters, 29 November 2002.

52. Recently, according to one report, Albania has been offered Christian and liberal Turkish alternatives and so resisted the attempted incursions of Saudi charities. But rural Kosovo, one of the most abjectly poor regions in Europe and neglected by the West since the conflict, has been targeted with some success by the Saudi Joint Committee for the Relief of Kosovo and Chechnya (Blumi 2002).

53. *Jaridat al-dustur*, Cairo, 29 October 1997.

CONCLUSION

1. Former Commissioner for Afghan Refugees, Peshawar, 19 May 1999, interview with Jérôme Bellion-Jourdan.
2. For a raid on 4 January 2001 by FBI and New York City police on a community centre in Brooklyn run by followers of the Jewish 'terrorist' groups Kach and Kahane Chai: Matthew A. Levitt, 'Charitable and Humanitarian Organizations in the Network of International Terrorist Financing', testimony to US Subcommittee on International Trade and Finance, Committee on Banking, Housing, and Urban Affairs, 1 August 2002. On Sewa International (UK)'s alleged (but denied) support of communal indoctrination by Hindu extremist groups in India: Channel Four News, 12 December 2002.
3. Edouard Mir, *Libération*, 20 December 1991.
4. Since the Islamic revolution in Iran, International Humanitarian Law has been challenged by Muslim states on such legal issues as forced pregnancies and the gender balance of judicial personnel (Cockayne 2002: 616-25).

* * *

POSTSCRIPT

As this book was going to press, a major study of early Sufism in south Asia was published by Riazul Islam, a senior Pakistani historian (Islam 2002). This includes material on *futūh*, a Persian term indicating the unsolicited charity on which many Sufis came to depend and its bulk distribution in a supposedly equitable manner every Friday. It was the main basis of the economy of their *khanqah*s or communal halls. Riazul Islam argues that Indian Sufism in practice did not live up to its extremely high moral ideals, and in particular failed to establish institutional poor relief apart from free kitchens (*langar*s). Sufism's other-worldly orientation came to be assaulted since the nineteenth century by Muslim revivalists who sought to revive the this-worldly orientation of their religion (Robinson 2003).

BIBLIOGRAPHY

Abu-Sahlieh, Sami A. Aldeeb. 1994. *Les Musulmans face aux droits de l'homme*. Bochum: Verlag Dr Dieter Winkler.

El-Affendi, Abdelwahab. 1990. 'Discovering the South': Sudanese dilemmas for Islam in Africa. *African Affairs* July, 89: 356, 371-389.

African Rights. 1997. *Food and Power in Sudan: A Critique of Humanitarianism*. London: African Rights.

Ahmed, A.S. 1990. Economie islamique, principes et réalités. *Revue tiers monde* 31 (122), April-June: 405-35.

Ahmed, Einas. 1997. Banques islamiques et sociétés islamiques d'investissement. *Politique Africaine* June, 66: 39-48.

`Ali, `Abdullah Yusuf. 1989. *The Meaning of the Holy Qur'an*. Beltsville, MD: Amana Publications.

Anderson, Dorothy. 1968. *The Balkan Volunteers*. London: Hutchinson.

An-Naim, Abdullahi A. 1996. A new Islamic politics: faith and human rights in the Middle East. *Foreign Affairs* May/June: 122-6.

Antoun, Richard T. 1989. *Muslim Preacher in the Modern World: A Jordanian Case Study in Comparative Perspective*. Princeton: Princeton University Press.

----2000. Civil society, tribal process, and change in Jordan: an anthropological view. *International Journal of Middle East Studies* 32: 441-63

----2001. A reply to Jonathan Benthall. *International Journal of Middle East Studies*. 33: 670-2.

Arda, S. Adam. 1994. The establishment, development and features of the Turkish Banking Sector (*Vakifbank*). In F. Bilici, ed., *Le waqf dans le monde musulman contemporain*. Istanbul: Institut Français d'Etudes Anatoliennes, 71-84.

Arjomand, Said Amir. 1998. Philanthropy, the law, and public policy in the Islamic world before the modern era. In Warren F. Ilchman et al., ed., *Philanthropy in the World's Traditions*. Bloomington: Indiana University Press: 109-132.

Arkoun, Mohammed. 1977. *Essais sur la pensée islamique*. Paris: Maisonneuve and Larose.

Arous, Zoubir. 2000. *Al harakat ul-majmu`iat ul-islamiyah bil-jaza`ir: al-awsulu, alwaqi`u wal-afaq* (The Islamic associative movement in Algeria: roots, reality and perspectives). Cairo: Medbouli.

Aubaile-Sallenave, Françoise. 1999. Les rituels de naissance dans le monde musulman. In Pierre Bonte et al., eds., *Sacrifices en islam: Espaces et temps d'un rituel*. Paris: CNRS Editions, 125-160.

Ayeb, H. 1995. Les inondations de novembre 1994 en Egypte. *CEDEJ Egypte Monde Arabe* 22: 159-178.

Babadji, R. 1991. The associative phenomenon in Algeria. In M. Camau, ed., *Changements Politiques au Maghreb*. Paris: CNRS.

Badie, Bertrand. 1992. *L'Etat importé: l'occidentalisation de l'ordre politique*. Paris: Fayard.

----1995. *La fin des territoires. Essai sur le désordre international et sur l'utilité sociale du respect.* Paris: Fayard.

Bagherzade, Alireza. 2001. L'ingérence iranienne en Bosnie-Herzégovine. In Xavier Bougarel and Nathalie Clayer, eds., *Le nouvel islam balkanique: les musulmans, acteurs du post-communisme, 1990-2000.* Paris: Maisonneuve and Larose: 397-428.

Baillard, Isabelle and Patrick Haenni. 1997. Libéralité prétorienne et Etat minimum au Soudan. L'effort civique entre la poudre et les travaux publics. *Egypte/Monde Arabe,* 32:4 trimestre: 71-96.

Baitemann, Helga. 1990. NGOs and the Afghan war: the politicization of humanitarian aid. *Third World Quarterly.* January, 12:1: 62-85

Banerjee, Mukulika. 2000. *The Pathan Unarmed: Opposition and Memory in the North West Frontier.* Oxford: James Currey.

Barnes, J.R. 1987. *An Introduction to Religious Foundations in the Ottoman Empire.* Leiden: Brill.

Barr, James. 1961. *The Semantics of Biblical Language.* Oxford: OUP.

Bavcic, Uzeir (ed.) 1997. *Humaniticki Aspecti Djelovanja Dobrotvornih Drustava U Ratnim Uvjetima* (Humanistic aspects of charitable societies' work under war conditions). Sarajevo: Merhamet.

Bayart, Jean-François. 1996. *L'illusion identitaire.* Paris: Fayard.

Bayat, Asef. 2002. Activism and social development in the Middle East. *International Journal of Middle East Studies,* 34: 1-28.

Bekkar, Rabia. 1997. Taking up space in Tlemcen: the Islamist occupation of urban Algeria (interview). In J. Beinin and J. Stork, eds., *Political Islam,* London: I.B. Tauris: 283-91.

Bellion-Jourdan, Jérôme. 1997. L'humanitaire et l'islamisme soudanais. Les organisations Da'wa Islamiya et Islamic African Relief Agency. *Politique Africaine* June, 66: 61-73.

----2001a. Les organisations de secours islamique et l'action humanitaire. *Esprit,* August-September, 173-185

----2001b. Les réseaux transnationaux islamiques en Bosnie-Hercégovine. In X. Bougarel and N. Clayer, eds., *Le nouvel islam balkanique. Les musulmans acteurs du post-communisme. 1990-2000.* Paris: Maisonneuve et Larose: 429-472.

----2002a. *Prédication, secours, combat: l'action humanitaire des ONG islamiques entre da`wa et jihad.* Unpublished doctoral thesis, Institut d'Etudes Politiques de Paris.

----2002b. Le médecin, le militant et le combatant: figures contemporaines de l'engagement dans la 'solidarité islamique'. *Genèses,* 48, September: 52-76.

Ben Ashoor, Yadh. 1980. Islam and international humanitarian law. *International Review of the Red Cross.* March-April.

ben Néfissa, Sarah. 1995. Associations égyptiennes: une libéralisation sous contrôle. *Monde arabe* 150: Oct-Dec: 40-47.

Bennett, Jon (ed.) 1995. *Meeting Needs: NGOs in Coordination and Practice.* London: Earthscan.

Bensaid, Said. 1987. Al-Watan and al-Umma in contemporary Arab use. In G. Salame, ed., *The Foundations of the Arab State.* London: Croom Helm: 149-74.

Benthall, Jonathan. 1993. *Disasters, Relief and the Media.* London: I.B. Tauris.

----1999. Two takes on the Abraham story [review article on Brisebarre 1998 and Delaney 1998]. *Anthropology Today,* 15: 1. February: 1-2.

----2000. Civil society's need for de-deconstruction. *Anthropology Today* 16:2, April 2000, 1-3.

----2001. A comment on Richard T. Antoun, 'Civil society, tribal process, and change in Jordan: an anthropological view'. *International Journal of Middle East Studies* 33: 668-70.

Berg, Herbert. 1997. The implications of, and opposition to, the methods and theories of John Wansbrough. *Method and Theory in the Study of Religion.* 9:1, 3-22.

Berkey, Jonathan. 1992. *The Transmission of Knowledge in Medieval Cairo.* Princeton: Princeton University Press.

Bilici, F. 1994. Introduction to F. Bilici ed. *Le waqf dans le monde musulman contemporain.* Istanbul: Institut Français d'Etudes Anatoliennes: 9-18.

----1997. Le parti islamiste turc (Refah Partisi) et sa dimension transnationale. *Les Annales de l'Autre Islam*, 4, 35-60.

Bitter, Jean-Nicolas. 1994. *Un outil de travail pour les organisations humanitaires face au radicalisme islamiste: typologie et images réciproques*. Lausanne: Institut Romand de Pastoral.

----2003. *Les dieux embusqués: une approche pragmatique de la dimension religieuse des conflits*. Geneva: Droz.

Black, Maggie. 1992. *A Cause for Our Times: Oxfam, the First 50 Years*. Oxford: OUP.

Blomberg, Craig L. 1999. *Neither Poverty nor Riches: A Biblical Theory of Possessions*. Downers Grove, IL: InterVarsity Press.

Blumi, Isa. 2002. Indoctrinating Albanians: dynamics of Islamic aid. *ISIM Newsletter*, 11: 9.

Boisard, Marcel A. 1985. *L'Humanisme de l'Islam*. Paris: Albin Michel (3rd ed.)

Boissier, Pierre. 1985. *History of the ICRC from Solferino to Tsushima*. Geneva: Henry Dunant Institute.

Bonte, Pierre. 1999. Sacrifices en islam: textes et contextes. In P. Bonte et al., eds., *Sacrifices en islam: Espaces et temps d'un rituel*. Paris: CNRS Editions: 21-61.

Bougarel, Xavier. 1994. Un courant panislamiste en Bosnie-Herzégovine. In Gilles Kepel, ed., *Exils et royaumes: les appartenances au monde arabo-musulman aujourd'hui*. Paris: Presses de la FNSP: 275-99.

----1996. *Bosnie: anatomie d'un conflit*. Paris: La Découverte.

----2000. *Islam et politique en Bosnie-Herzégovine: le parti de l'action démocratique*. Doctoral thesis in political science, Paris, IEP, unpublished.

----2001. L'islam bosniaque, entre identité culturelle et idéologie politique. In X. Bougarel and N. Clayer, eds., *Le nouvel islam balkanique. Les musulmans acteurs du post-communisme. 1990-2000*. Paris: Maisonneuve et Larose:79-132.

Bowie, Katherine A. 1998. The alchemy of charity: of class and Buddhism in northern Thailand. *American Anthropologist*, 100:2, 469-81.

Bradbury, Mark. 1995. *Aid Under Fire: Redefining Relief and Development Assistance in Unstable Situations*. London: HMSO.

Brenner, Louis (ed.) 1993. *Muslim Identity and Social Change in Sub-Saharan Africa*. London: Hurst.

----2000. *Controlling Knowledge: Religion, Power and Schooling in a West African Muslim Society*. London: Hurst.

Brisebarre, Anne-Marie. 1993. The sacrifice of `Id al-Kabir: Islam in the French suburbs. *Anthropology Today*, 9:1, Feb.: 9-12.

----et al. 1998. *La fête du mouton: Un sacrifice musulman dans l'espace urbain*. Paris: CNRS Editions.

Bugnion, François. 1977. *The Emblem of the Red Cross: A Brief History*. Geneva: ICRC.

----1989. The red cross and red crescent emblems *International Review of the Red Cross*. 272, September-October: 408-419.

----2000. Towards a comprehensive solution to the question of the emblem *International Review of the Red Cross*, no. 838, June 2000, 427-78, reprinted by ICRC as offprint, August 2000.

Burgat, François. 1995. *L'Islamisme en face*. Paris: Editions de la Découverte.

Burton, John. 1977. *The Collection of the Qur'an*. Cambridge: CUP.

----1994. *An Introduction to the Hadiths*. Edinburgh: University of Edinburgh Press.

Cahen, C. 1961. Réflexions sur le waqf ancien. *Studia Islamica* 14: 37-56.

Carapico, Sheila. 1998. *Civil society in the Yemen*. Cambridge: CUP.

Carré, Olivier. 1984. *Mystique et politique: lecture révolutionnaire du Coran par Sayyid Qutb, Frère musulman radical*. Paris: Editions du Cerf.

----1992. Religion et développement dans les pays musulmans: éléments d' <économie islamique>. *Social Compass*. 39:1.

Caulkins, Douglas. 1996. Voluntary Associations. In D. Levinson and M. Ember, eds., *Encyclopedia of Cultural Anthropology*. New York: Henry Holt: 1351-56.

Chamberlain, Michael. 1994. *Knowledge and Social Practice in Medieval Damascus, 1190-1350*. Cambridge: CUP.

Chouet, Alain. 1994. L'islam confisqué: stratégies dynamiques pour un ordre statique. In Riccardo Bocco and Mohamed-Reza Djalili, eds., *Moyen-Orient: migrations, democratisation, mediations*. Paris: PUF: 371-401.

Cizakra, Murat. 1995. Venture Capital. In *Encyclopedia of Islamic Banking*, London: Institute of Islamic Banking and Insurance: 145-8.

Clayer, Nathalie. 2001. Albanie: le enjeux de la réislamisation. In X. Bougarel and N. Clayer, eds., *Le nouvel islam balkanique: les musulmans acteurs du post-communisme, 1990-2000*. Paris: Maisonneuve et Larose: 133-76.

Clayton, Andrew (ed.). 1996. *NGOs, Civil Society and the State: Building Democracies in Traditional Societies*. Oxford: INTRAC.

Cockayne, James. 2002. Islam and international humanitarian law: from a clash to a conversation between civilizations. *Review of the International Committee of the Red Cross*, September, 84, 597-625.

Coldrey, Barry M. 1988. *Faith and Fatherland: The Christian Brothers and the Development of Irish Nationalism 1838-1921*. London: Gill and Macmillan.

Constantin, François. 1993. Leadership, Muslim identities and East African politics. In Louis Brenner, ed., *Muslim Identity and Social Change in Sub-Saharan Africa*. London: Hurst and Co., 48-53.

Cragg, Kenneth. 1956. *The Call of the Minaret*. New York: OUP.

Dagorn, René. 1981. *La Geste d'Ismaël d'après l'onomastique et la tradition arabes*. Geneva: Librairie Droz.

Danawi, Dima. 2002. *Hizbullah's Pulse: Into the Dilemma of Al-Shahid and Jihad Al-Bina Foundations*. Privately published.

Daraz, Issam. 1993. *Al-gha'idun min afghanistan: ma lahum w ma 'alahim* (The returning veterans from Afghanistan: for and against) Cairo: Al-Dar al-Masriya li-l-Nashr w l-Islam.

de St Jorre, John. 1975. *The Nigerian Civil War*. London: Hodder and Stoughton.

Décobert, Christian. 1984. L'aumône et l'écrit. *Annuaire de l'Afrique du Nord*, XXIII, 109-27.

----1991. *Le Mendiant et le Combattant*. Paris: Seuil.

Deguilhem, Randi. 1995. Approche méthodologique d'un fonds de waqf. In R. Deguilhem, ed., *Le waqf dans l'espace islamique: outil de pouvoir socio-politique*. Damas: Institut français d'études arabes de Damas, 45-70.

Delaney, Carol. 1998. *Abraham on Trial*. Princeton: Princeton U.P.

Delorenzi, Simone. 1999. *Contending with the Impasse in Humanitarian Action: ICRC Policy since the End of the Cold War*. Geneva: ICRC.

Descombes, Marc. 1988. *Dunant*. Geneva/Lucerne: Ed. René Coeckelberghs.

Destexhe, Alain. 1993. *L'humanitaire impossible*. Paris: Armand Colin.

Donner, Fred M. 1998. *Narratives of Islamic Origins: The Beginnings of Islamic Historical Writing*. Princeton, NJ: Darwin Press.

Doughty, Charles M. 1936 [1888]. *Travels in Arabia Deserta*. London: Cape.

Douglas, Mary. 1993. *In the Wilderness: The Doctrine of Defilement in the Book of Numbers*. Sheffield: JSOT Press.

Doutté, Edmond. 1908. *Magie et religion dans l'Afrique du Nord*. Algiers: Typographie Adolphe Jourdan.

Duffield, Mark. 1996. The symphony of the damned: racial discourse, complex political emergencies and humanitarian aid. *Disasters*, September, 20:3, 173-93.

Dumper, Michael. 1994. *Islam and Israel: Muslim Religious Endowments and the Jewish State*. Washington, D.C.: Institute of Palestine Studies.

Dwyer, Kevin. 1997. Beyond a boundary: 'universal human rights' and the Middle East. *Anthropology Today* 13:6, December, 13-17.

Edhi, Abdul Sattar. 1996. *Edhi, an Autobiography: A Mirror to the Blind*. As narrated to Tehmina Durrani. Islamabad: National Bureau of Publications.

Eickelman, Dale F. 1992. Mass higher education and the religious imagination in contemporary Arab societies. *American Ethnologist*. Nov. 643-55.

Emmanuelli, Xavier. 1991. *Les Prédateurs de l'Action Humanitaire*. Paris: Albin Michel.

Ereksoussi, M.K. 1962. The Koran and the humanitarian conventions. *International Review of the Red Cross*. May.

Eshel, David. 2002. Hamas resists pressure as Israel targets Arafat. *Jane's Intelligence Review*. January, 14.1, 12-15.

Esposito, John L. 1992. *The Islamic Threat: Myth or Reality?* New York: CUP.

Ettinghausen, R. 1971. Hilal (ii) – In Islamic Art. *Encyclopaedia of Islam*, vol. III, 2nd edn., Leiden: E.J. Brill, 381-5.

Farag, Iman. 1996. Ces musulmans de l'ailleurs: la Bosnie vue d'Egypte. *Monde arabe Maghreb-Mashrek*, January-March, 151, 41-50.

Feierman, Steven. 1998. Reciprocity and assistance in precolonial Africa. In W.F. Ilchman et al., eds., *Philanthropy in the World's Traditions*. Bloomington: Indiana University Press, 3-24.

Firth, Raymond. 1996. *Religion: A Humanist Interpretation*. London: Routledge.

Fischer, Michael M.J. and Mehdi Abedi. 1990. *Debating Muslims: Cultural Dialogues in Postmodernity and Tradition*. Madison: University of Wisconsin Press.

Fraser, Cary. 1997. In defense of Allah's Realm: religion and statecraft in Saudi foreign policy strategy. In S.H. Rudolph and J. Piscatori, eds., *Transnational Religion and Fading States*. Boulder: Westview Press, 212-42.

Freeman, Kathleen. 1965. *If Any Man Build: The History of the Save the Children Fund*. London: Hodder and Stoughton.

Freij, Hanna Y. and Leonard C. Robinson. 1996. Liberalization, the Islamists, and the stability of the Arab State: Jordan as a case study. *The Muslim World*. 86:1, 1-32.

Galloux, Michel. 1997. *Finance islamique et pouvoir politique. Le cas de l'Egypte moderne*. Paris: PUF.

Garnsey, Peter. 1988. *Famine and Food Supply in the Graeco-Roman World*. Cambridge: CUP.

Geertz, Clifford. 1979. Suq: the bazaar economy in Sefrou. In C. Geertz et al., eds., *Meaning and Order in Moroccan Society*, Cambridge: CUP, 123-313.

----1995. *After the Fact*. Cambridge, MA.: Harvard University Press.

Geremek, Bronislaw. 1994. *Poverty: A History*. Oxford: Blackwell.

Gerges, Fawaz A. 2002. Introduction to D. Danawi, *Hizbullah's Pulse: Into the Dilemma of Al-Shahid and Jihad Al-Bina Foundations*. Privately published.

Ghandour, Abdel-Rahman. 2002. *Jihad humanitaire: Enquête sur les ONG islamiques*. Paris: Flammarion.

Al-Ghannouchi, Rachid. 2000. Secularism in the Arab Maghreb. In Azzam Tamimi and John L. Esposito, eds., 2000. *Islam and Secularism in the Middle East*. London: Hurst, 97-123.

Gilsenan, Michael. 1982. *Recognizing Islam*. London: Croom Helm.

Girod, Christophe. 1994. *Tempête sur le Désert. Le Comité International de la Croix-Rouge et la Guerre du Golfe 1990-1991*. Brussels: Bruylant.

Glassé, Cyril. 1991 (2nd ed.). *The Concise Encyclopaedia of Islam*. London: Stacey.

Grandin, Nicole. 1993. *Al-markaz al-islami al-ifriqi b'il khartum*. La République du Soudan et la propagation de l'Islam en Afrique noire. In R. Otayek (ed.) *Le radicalisme islamique au Sud du Sahara. Da`wa, arabisation et critique de l'Occident*. Paris: Karthala, 97-120.

Haddad, Yvonne. 1995. Islamist depictions of Christianity in the twentieth century: the pluralism debate and the depiction of the Other. *Islamic and Christian-Muslim Relations*, 7.1, 75-93.

Halbertal, Moshe and Avishai Margalit. 1992. *Idolatry*. Cambridge, MA.: Harvard University Press.

Halliday, Fred. 1996. *Islam and the Myth of Confrontation: Religion and Politics in the Middle East*. London: I.B. Tauris.

Hamer, John H. 2002. *America, Philanthropy, and the Moral Order*. Lewiston: Edwin Mellen Press.

Hamidullah, Muhammad. 1945. *Muslim Conduct of State*. Lahore: Sh. Muhammad Ashraf.

---- 1959. *Le Prophète de l'Islam*. Paris: J. Vrin.

Hanafi, Hassan. 1996. Methods of thematic interpretation of the Qur'an. In S. Wild, ed., *The Qur'an as Text*, Leiden: Brill.

Hann, Chris and Elizabeth Dunn (eds.) 1994. *Civil Society: Challenging Western Models*. London: Routledge.

Hansch, Steve. 2002. *Humanitarian Policy Watch*. Winter, 20-1.

Harrell-Bond, Barbara E. 1986. *Imposing Aid. Emergency Assistance to Refugees*. Oxford: OUP

Harrison, Simon. 1992. Ritual as intellectual property. *Man (n.s.)*, 27:2, June, 225-244.

Hashmi, Sohail H. 1993. Is there an Islamic ethic of humanitarian intervention? *Ethics and International Affairs* 1993, vol. 7, 55-73.

Hassan, Yusuf Fadl and Richard Gray (eds.) 2002. *Religion and Conflict in Sudan*. Nairobi: Paulines Publications Africa.

Hathaway, Jane. 1998. Review of Deguilhem *op.cit.*, *International Journal of Middle Eastern Studies*, 3o/1, Feb 1998 121-123.

Hawting, G.R. 1999. *The Idea of Idolatry and the Emergence of Islam: from Polemic to History*. Cambridge: CUP.

Hayward, C.T.R. 1980. Appendix: The Aqedah [Binding of Isaac]. In M.F.C. Bourdillon and M. Fortes, eds., *Sacrifice*, ed., London: Academic Press.

Hazan, Pierre. 2002. *Humanitarian Policy Watch*. Winter, 24-5.

Henninger, Joseph. 1981. Pre-Islamic Bedouin religion. In Merlin L. Swartz, trans. and ed., *Studies on Islam*, New York: OUP.

Holt, P.M. and M.W. Daly. 1988. *A History of the Sudan from the Coming of Islam to the Present Day*. London, New York: Longman

Hosny, M.M. 1995. The role of religious board. In *Encyclopaedia of Islamic Banking*, London: Institute of Islamic Banking and Insurance, 95-103.

Hours, Bernard. 1993. *Islam et développement au Bangladesh*. Paris: L'Harmattan.

Howard, Stephen W. 1998. Mahmud Mohammed Taha: a remarkable teacher in Sudan. *Northeast African Studies*, 10:1, 83-93.

Hubley, Martin. 1997. 'Arab Afghans and Islamist Movements. A Unifying Factor?' Unpublished paper presented at BRISMES, Oxford, July.

Huntington, Samuel. 1996. *The Clash of Civilizations and the Remaking of World Order*. New York: Simon and Schuster.

Husaini, Musa Ishak. 1956. *The Moslem Brethren: The Greatest of Modern Islamic Movements*. Beirut: Khayyat.

Hyman, Anthony. 1994. Arab involvement in the Afghan war. *Beyrut Review*, summer, no.7, 73-89.

Ibn Warraq 2000. *The Quest for the Historical Muhammad*. New York: Prometheus Books.

Ibrahim, Riad. 1992. Factors contributing to the political ascendancy of the Muslim Brethren in Sudan. *Arab Studies Quarterly*, Summer-Autumn, 12: 3-4, 33-53.

Ibrahim, Saad Eddim. 1988. Egypt's Islamic activism in the 1980s. *Third World Quarterly*. April. 10.2: 632-57.

ICRC 1993. *Extraits des chroniques arabo-islamiques*. Geneva: ICRC.

Ilchman, Warren F., Stanley N. Katz and Edward L. Queen II (eds.) 1998. *Philanthropy in the World's Traditions*. Bloomington: Indiana University Press.

International Crisis Group. 2001. *Bin Laden and the Balkans: the Politics of Anti-Terrorism*. Brussels: ICG Balkans Report no. 119, 37p.

INTRAC. 1998. *Direct Funding from a Southern Perspective: Strengthening Civil Society?* Oxford: INTRAC NGO Management and Policy series no. 8.

Islam, Riazul. 2002. *Sufism in India: Impact on Fourteenth Century Muslim Society*. Oxford: OUP.

Israeli, Raphael. 1993a. *Muslim Fundamentalism in Israel*. London: Brassey's.

----1993b. *Fundamentalist Islam and Israel: Essays in Interpretation*. Lanham, MD: University Press of America.

Izetbegovic, Alija. 1990. *Islamska deklaracija* (Islamic declaration). Sarajevo: Bosna.

Izutsu, Toshihiko. 1959. *The Structure of the Ethical Terms in the Koran.* Tokyo: Keio Institute of Philological Studies.

----1965. *The Concept of Belief in Theology: A Semantic Analysis of Iman and Islam.* Tokyo: Keio Institute of Cultural and Linguistic Studies.

Jaber, Hala. 1997. *Hezbollah: Born with a Vengeance.* London: Fourth Estate.

Jadaane, Fahmi. 1992. Umma musulmane et société islamique. *Pouvoirs*, 1992, no. 62, 31-43.

Jaussen, A. 1948. *Coutumes des Arabes au pays de Moab.* Paris: Maisonneuve.

Jorand, Anne-Liliane. 2002. 'The Challenge of Integration: Hizballah within the Lebanese political system' MSc. dissertation, Middle East Politics, SOAS, London.

Junod, Dominique-D. 1996. *The Imperiled Red Cross and the Palestine-Eretz-Yisrael Conflict 1945-1952.* London and New York: Kegan Paul International.

Kane, Oussama. 1997. Muslim missionaries and African states. In Susanne H. Rudolph and James Piscatori, eds., *Transnational Religion and Fading States.* Boulder: Westview Press, 47-62.

Karim, Ataul (et al.) 1996. OLS: Operation Lifeline Sudan: A review. [Unpublished].

Katz, Marion Holmes. 1999. 'Purified Companions: The Development of the Islamic Law of Ritual Purity' Abstract of prizewinning dissertation (Humanities), 1998 Malcolm H. Kerr Dissertation Award. *Middle East Studies Association Bulletin*, 33.1, Summer, 46.

Keck, Margaret E. and Kathryn Sikkink. 1998. *Activists beyond borders: Advocacy networks in international politics.* Ithaca: Cornell University Press.

Kelsay, John and James Turner Johnson (eds.). 1991. *Just War and Jihad: Historical and Theoretical Perspectives on War and Peace and Western and Islamic Traditions.* New York and London: Greenwood Press.

Kepel, Gilles. 1987. *Les Banlieues de l'Islam: Naissance d'une religion en France.* Paris: Seuil.

----1994. *A l'Ouest d'Allah.* Paris: Seuil.

----2002a. *Jihad: The Trail of Political Islam.* London: I.B. Tauris.

----2002b. *Chronique d'une guerre d'Orient.* Paris: Gallimard.

Khatib, Abdullah. 1994. *The Experience of NGOs in Jordan: A Brief Description.* Amman: GUVS.

Al-Khayyat, Abdul-Aziz. 1993. *Az-zakat wa tatbiqat-ha w-istithmarat-ha* [Zakat and its applications and profitable uses]. Amman: Ministry of Awqaf and Islamic Affairs.

El-Kikhia, Mansour O. 1997. *Libya's Qaddafi. The Politics of Contradiction.* Gainesville: University Press of Florida.

Kister, M.J. 1990. *Studies in Jahiliyya and Early Islam.* London: Variorum.

Kochan, Lionel. 1997. *Beyond the Graven Image: A Jewish View.* London: Macmillan.

Kouchner, Bernard. 1991. *Le malheur des autres.* Paris: Odile Jacob.

Kozlowski, Gregory L. 1985. *Muslim Endowments and Society in British India.* Cambridge: CUP.

----2000. Religious authority, reform, and philanthropy in the contemporary Muslim world. In Warren F. Ilchman et al., ed., *Philanthropy in the World's Traditions*, ed. Bloomington: Indiana University Press, 279-308.

Kuran, Timur. 1989, 1990. Economic justice in contemporary Islamic thought. *International Journal of Middle East Studies* 21: 171-91, 22: 376-7.

----2001. A response to Bill Maurer. *Anthropology Today* 17.3: 28-9.

Labat, Severine 1995. *Les islamistes algériens: entre les urnes et le maquis.* Paris: Seuil.

Lammens, Henri. 1914. *Le berceau de l'Islam: l'Arabie occidentale à la veille de l'Hégire.* Rome: Papal Biblical Institute.

Lapidus, Ira M. 1988. *A History of Islamic Societies.* Cambridge: CUP.

Layard, A.H. 1853. *Discoveries in the Ruins of of Nineveh and Babylon.* London: John Murray.

Layish, A. 1994. The Muslim waqf in Jerusalem after 1967: beneficiaries and management. In F. Bilici, ed. *Le waqf dans le monde musulman contemporain.* Istanbul: Institut Français d'Etudes Anatoliennes, 145-68.

Leach, Edmund. 1983. *Structuralist Interpretations of Biblical Myth.* Cambridge: CUP.

Leca, Jean. 1997. Opposition in the Middle East and North Africa. *Government and Opposition* 32:4, autumn, 557-77.

Legrain, J.-F. 1991. *La voix du soulèvement palestinien.* Cairo: CEDJ.

----1996. *Les Palestiniens, l'adversité et Allah.* Le Monde, 13 March.

Leo Africanus 1526. *Description of Africa.* Part 3, 'Kingdom of Fez'.

Lindenmeyr, Adèle. 1998. From repression to revival: philanthropy in twentieth-century Russia. In W. Ilchman et al., ed., 1998. *Philanthropy in the World's Traditions.* Bloomington: Indiana University Press. 309-331.

Lohmann, Roger A. 1994. Buddhist commons and the question of a third sector in Asia. *Voluntas.* 6:2, 140-158.

Lonca, Anour. 1968. Henry Dunant apprend l'Arabe. *Musées de Genève* no. 81, Jan.

McChesney, R. 1991. *Waqf in Central Asia: Four Hundred Years in the History of a Muslim Shrine,* 1480-1889. Princeton: Princeton University Press.

MacCulloch J.A. 1913. Firstfruits. In *Encyclopaedia of Religion and Ethics* (ed. J. Hastings), Edinburgh: Clark.

Macek, Ivana. 2000. *War Within: Everyday Life in Sarajevo under Siege.* Uppsala: Uppsala University.

Madigan, D.A. 1995. Reflections on some current directions in Qur'anic studies. *Muslim World,* 85: 345-362.

Madison, Bernice. 1960. The organization of welfare services. In C.E. Black, ed., *The Transformation of Russian Society: Aspects of Social Change since 1861.* Cambridge, MA.: Harvard University Press.

Makki Mohamed Ahmed, Hassan. 1989. *The Christian Design: a Study of the Missionary Factor in Sudan's Cultural and Political Integration: 1843-1986.* Leicester: Islamic Foundation.

Maloney, Suzanne. 2000. Agents or obstacles? Parastatal foundations and challenges for Iranian development. In P. Alizadeh, ed., *The Economy of Iran: Dilemmas of an Islamic State.* London: I.B. Tauris: 145-76

Mannan, M.A. 1986. *Islamic Economics: Theory and Practice.* London: Hodder and Stoughton.

Marchal, Roland. 1992. Le Soudan entre islamisme et dictature militaire *Maghreb-Machrek.* July-September, n°137, 56-79

----1995. Eléments d'une sociologie du Front National Islamique Soudanais. *Les Etudes du CERI,* September, no. 5.

Marett, R.R. 1935. *Head, heart and hand in human evolution.* London: Hutchinson.

Marx, Alfred. 1994. *L'offrande végétale dans l'Ancien Testament.* Leiden: Brill.

Marx, Emanuel. 1967. *Bedouin of the Negev.* Manchester: University of Manchester Press.

Massad, Joseph A. 2001. *Colonial Effects: The Making of National Identity in Jordan.* New York: Columbia University Press.

Maurer, Bill. 2001. Engineering an Islamic future: speculations on Islamic financial alternatives. *Anthropology Today* 17:1, 8-11.

----2002. Anthropological and accounting knowledge in Islamic banking and finance: rethinking critical accounts. *Journal of the Royal Anthropological Institute* 8.4: 645-68.

Mauss, Marcel. 1990 [1925]. *The Gift.* English trans. London: Routledge.

Mawdsley, Emma et al. 2002. *Knowledge, Power and Development Agendas: NGOs North and South.* Oxford: INTRAC.

Maybury-Lewis, David. 1992. *Millennium: Tribal Wisdom and the Modern World.* New York: Viking.

Mayer, Ann E. 1999. *Islam and Human Rights: Tradition and Politics* (3rd edition). Boulder, CO.: Westview Press.

Medani, Khalid. 1997. Funding fundamentalism: the political economy of an Islamist State. In Joel Benin and Joe Stork, eds., *Political Islam.* Berkeley: University of California Press, 166-77.

Meenai, S.A. 1989. *The Islamic Development Bank: A Case-Study of Islamic Cooperation.* London, New York: Kegan Paul.

Milliot, L. 1918. *Démembrements du Habous.* Paris: Ernest Leroux.

Milton-Edwards, Beverley. 1996. *Islamic Politics in Palestine.* London: Tauris Academic Studies.

----2002. Researching the radical: The quest for a new perspective. In H. Donnan, ed., *Interpreting Islam,* London: Sage, 32-50.

Mishal, Shaul and Avraham Sela. 2000. *The Palestinian Hamas*. New York: Columbia University Press.

Mitchell, Richard P. 1969. *The Society of the Muslim Brothers*. London: CUP.

Mitri, Tarek. 1993. La Bosnie-Herzegovine et la solidarité du monde arabe et islamique. *Monde arabe Maghreb-Mashrek*, January-March, 139, 123-36.

Moe, Henry Allen. 1961. Notes on the origin of philanthropy in Christendom. *Transactions of the American Philosophical Society*, 105:2, 141-4.

Monnot, Jacques. 1994. *Le drame du Sud-Soudan. Chronique d'une islamisation forcée*. Paris: L'Harmattan.

Moorehead, Caroline. 1998. *Dunant's Dream: War, Switzerland and the History of the Red Cross*. London: HarperCollins.

Mumuni, Sulemena. 2002. A survey of Islamic Non-Governmental Organisations in Accra. In H. Weiss (ed.), *Social Welfare in Muslim Societies in Africa*, Uppsala: Nordiska Afrikainstitutet, 138-61.

Musil, Alois. 1928. *The Manners and Customs of the Rwala Bedouins*. New York: American Geographical Society.

Nagan, Winston P. 1994. Rethinking Bosnia and Herzegovina right to self-Defence: a comment. *International Committee of Jurists; The Review*, 52, 34-46.

Naqui, Ali Muhammad. 1991. *A Manual of Islamic Beliefs and Practice*, ed. J. Cooper. Qom, Iran: Ansariyan Publications.

Niblock, Tim. 1991. Islamic movements and Sudan's political coherence. In Hervé Bleuchot et al., eds., *Sudan: History, Identity, Ideology*. London: Ithaca Press, 253-68.

Norris, Pippa and Ron Inglehart. 2002. Islam and the West: testing the 'Clash of Civilizations' thesis. *Comparative Sociology* 1:2.

Norton, A.R. (ed.) 1995. *Civil Society in the Middle East*. Leiden: Brill.

Novossyolov, Dimitri. 1993. The islamization of welfare in Pakistan. In Dale F. Eickelman, ed., *Russia's Muslim Frontiers*. Bloomington: Indiana University Press.

Oakley, Peter (ed.) 2001. *Evaluating Empowerment: Reviewing the Concept and Practice*. Oxford: INTRAC.

Ostrower, Francie. 1995. *Why the Wealthy Give: the Culture of Elite Philanthropy*. Princeton: Princeton University Press.

Otayek, René. 1986. *La politique africaine de la Libye (1969-1985)*. Paris: Karthala.

Pagnucco, Ron (ed.) 1997. *Transnational Social Movements and Global Politics beyond the State*. New York: Syracuse University Press.

Parry, Jonathan. 1986. The Gift, the Indian gift and the 'Indian gift'. *Man (n.s.)*, 21.3, 453-73.

Payton, Robert L. 1989. Philanthropic values. In R. Magat, ed., *Philanthropic Giving: Studies in Varieties and Goals*. New York: CUP, 29-45.

Petterson, Donald. 1999. *Inside Sudan: Political Islam, Conflict and Catastrophe*. Boulder: Westview Press.

Piscatori, James. 1991 (ed.) *Islamic Fundamentalism and the Gulf Crisis*. Chicago: American Academy of Arts and Sciences.

Pons, Jacques. 1979. *Henry Dunant l'Algérien*. Geneva: Grounauer.

Prochaska, Frank. 1995. *Royal Bounty: The Making of a Welfare Monarchy*. New Haven: Yale University Press.

Pugh, Michael, 2002. Like it or not, humanitarians *are* political. *Humanitarian Affairs Review*, Winter 2002, 5-7.

Al-Qaradawi, Y. 1994 (21st edition). *Fiqh az-zakat. Dirasa muqarana li'ahkamiha w falsafatiha fi Dau' al-qur'an w al-sunna*. (The law of zakat: comparative study of its modes and philosophy in the light of the Quran and Sunna). Cairo: Librairie Wahiba. 2 vols.

Qasim, Ahmad. 1994. The waqf in Tunisia in the 18th and 19th centuries [in Arabic with abstract]. In F. Bilici, ed. *Le waqf dans le monde musulman contemporain*. Istanbul: Institut Français d'Etudes Anatoliennes, 7-55.

Qutb, Sayyid. 1978. *fi Zilal al-Qur'an* (In the Shade of the Quran). Beirut, Cairo: Dar-al-Shuruq.

Ranstorp, Magnus and Gus Xhudo. 1994. A threat to Europe? Middle East ties with the Balkans and their impact upon terrorist activity throughout the region. *Terrorism and Political Violence*, Summer, 6.2: 196-223.

Rashid, Ahmed. 2000. *Taliban: Islam, Oil and the New Great Game in Asia*. London: I.B. Tauris.

Rieff, David. 1999. Le Kosovo a-t-il sonné le glas des organisations indépendantes? *Humanitarian Affairs Review*, Autumn 1999, 28-31.

Ringgren, Helmer. 1962. The pure religion. *Oriens*. XV: 93-96.

Roald, Anne Sofie. 1994. *Tarbiya: Education and Politics in Islamic Movements in Jordan and Malaysia*. Lund: Lund University.

Robinson, Francis. 2003. Between two worlds (review of Islam 2002). *Times Literary Supplement*, 24 January, 9.

Rodriguez-Mañas, Francisco. 2000. Charity and deceit: the practice of iT`am al-T`am [meals and temporary accommodation] in Moroccan Sufism. *Studia Islamica*, 59-90.

Rogerson, J.W. 1980. Sacrifice in the Old Testament: problems of method and approach. In M.F.C. Bourdillon and M. Fortes, eds., *Sacrifice*. London: Academic Press.

Rosenau, James A. 1990. *Turbulence in World Politics*. Princeton: Princeton University Press.

Rouadjia, Ahmed. 1990. *Les frères et la mosquée: Enquête sur le mouvement islamiste en Algérie*. Paris: Karthala.

Roule, Trifin J. 2002. Post-911 financial freeze dries up Hamas funding. *Jane's Intelligence Review*. May, 14.5, 17-19.

Roy, Delwin. 1991. Islamic banking *Middle Eastern Studies*. 27:3, July, 427-56.

Roy, Olivier. 1998. *The Failure of Political Islam*. Cambridge, MA.: Harvard University Press (first published in French in 1992, Paris: Seuil).

----2001. 'Civil society in the new Central Asia', seminar, Institute of Ismaili Studies, London, 16 February.

Rubin, Barnett B. 1995. *The Search for Peace in Afghanistan: From Buffer State to Failed State*. New Haven and London: Yale University Press.

----1996. *The Fragmentation of Afghanistan: State Formation and Collapse in the International System*. Lahore: Vanguard Books.

----1997. Arab Islamists in Afghanistan. In John L. Esposito, ed., *Political Islam: Revolution, Radicalism or Reform?* Boulder: Lynne Reiner.

Ruel, Malcolm. 1982. Christians as believers. In J. Davis, ed., *Religious Organization and Religious Experience*, London: Academic Press.

Rugh, Andrea B. Reshaping personal relations in Egypt. In M. Marty and R. S. Appleby, eds. *Fundamentalism observed*. Chicago: American Academy of Arts and Sciences.

Ruthven, Malise. 2002. *A Fury for God: The Islamist Attack on America*. London: Granta Books

Saad-Ghorayeb, Amal. 2002. *Hizbu'llah: Politics and Religion*. London: Pluto Press.

Sabra, Adam. 2000. *Poverty and Charity in Medieval Islam: Mamluk Egypt, 1250-1517*. Cambridge: CUP.

Sadiq, C.M. 1995. Islamic Insurance (Takaful): Concept and Practice. In *Encyclopedia of Islamic Banking*, London: Institute of Islamic Banking and Insurance, 197-208.

Sahlins, Marshall. 1958. *Social Stratification in Polynesia*. Seattle: University of Washington Press.

Said, Edward. 2000a. *The End of the Peace Process*. London: Granta Books.

----2000b. *Reflections on Exile*. London: Granta Books.

Salame, Ghassan. 1987. Islamic and politics in Saudi-Arabia. *Arab Studies Quarterly*, 9:3, Summer, 306-26.

----(ed.) 1994. *Démocraties sans democrates: politiques d'ouvertures dans le monde arabe et islamique*. Paris: Fayard.

Salih, Kamal Osman. 1990. The Sudan, 1985-89: the fading democracy. *Journal of Modern African Studies*, 28, 199-224.

Salih, M.A. Mohamed. 2003. Islamic NGOs in Africa: the promise and peril of Islamic voluntarism. In A. de Waal, ed., *Islamism and its Enemies in the Horn of Africa*. London: C. Hurst.

Schacht, Joseph. 1964. *An Introduction to Islamic Law*. Oxford: Clarendon Press.

Schervisch, Paul G. 1993. The sound of one hand clapping: the case for and against anonymous giving. *Voluntas* 5:1. 1-26.

Schimmel, Annemarie. 1992. *Islam: an Introduction*. Albany: State University of New York Press.

Schultze, Reinhard. 1990. *Islamische Internationalismus im 20 Jahrhundert. Untersuchung zur Geschichte der islamische Weltliga*. Leiden: Brill.

Shaqiq, Munir (ed.) 1995. *Al-umma fi 'am: taqrir hawali al-siassiya wal-iqtisadiya al-islamiya* (The umma in a year: report on Islamic politics and economics). Cairo: 1995.

Sharma, Sanjay. 2001. *Famine, Philanthropy and the Colonial State: North India in the Early Nineteenth Century*. New Delhi: Oxford University Press.

Sidahmed, Abdel Salam. 1997. *Politics and Islam in Contemporary Sudan*. Richmond: Curzon.

----2002. The unholy war: Jihad and the conflict in Sudan. In Hassan, Y.F. and R. Gray, eds., *Religion and Conflict in Sudan*. Nairobi: Paulines Publications Africa, 83-96.

Silber, I.F. 2002. Echoes of sacrifice? repertoires of giving in the great religions. In A.I. Baumgarten, ed., *Sacrifice in Religious Experience*, Leiden: Brill, 291-312.

Simone, Abdou Maliqalim. 1994. *In Whose Image? Political Islam and Urban Practices in Sudan*. Chicago: University of Chicago Press.

Sirageldin, Ismail. 1996. *Islam, Society and Economic Policy*. Economic Research Forum for the Arab Countries, Iran and Turkey, Working Paper 9529.

Smith, W. Robertson. 1885. *Kinship and Marriage in Early Arabia*. Cambridge: University Press.

----1927 (3rd edition). *Lectures on the Religion of the Semites*. London: A.and C. Black).

Sommaruga, Cornelio. 1992. Unity and plurality of the emblems. *International Review of the Red Cross*. 289, July-August, 333-8.

Speight, R. Marston. 1988. The function of hadith. In A. Rippin, *Approaches to the History of the Interpretation of the Qur'an*, Oxford: Clarendon Press.

Stoddard, Abby. 2002. Trends in US humanitarian policy. *Humanitarian Policy Group Briefing*, 3, April. London: Overseas Development Institute.

Strahan, J. 1913. Firstfruits: Hebrew. In *Encyclopaedia of Religion and Ethics* (ed. J. Hastings), Edinburgh: Clark, VI: 41-45.

Strand, Arne. 1998. *Bridging the Gap Between Islamic and Western NGOs Working in Conflict Areas*. MA dissertation in Post-War Recovery Studies, University of York.

Strawson, John. 1996. Encountering Islamic law. *Pakistan Law Review* (on-line) www.geocities.com/paklawreview/strawson1.html.

Sullivan, Denis J. 1992. *Private Voluntary Organizations in Egypt: Islamic Development, Private Initiative and State Control*. Gainesville: University Press of Florida.

Tamimi, Azzam and John L. Esposito (eds.). 2000. *Islam and Secularism in the Middle East*. London: Hurst.

Thesiger, Wilfred. 1964. *The Marsh Arabs*. London: Longman.

Tourabi, Hassan. 1997. *Islam: avenir du monde* (interviews with Alain Chevalérias). Paris: J.C. Lattès.

Townsend, Janet. 2002. A question of trust? *Ontrac, Newsletter of INTRAC, Oxford*, 22, September, 7.

van der Toorn, Karel. 1995. Theology, Priests, and Worship in Canaan and Ancient Israel. In Jack M. Sasson, Jack M., ed., *Civilizations of the Ancient Near East*, New York: Scribner's, 2043-58.

van Leeuwen, Richard. 1995. The Maronite waqf of Dayr Sayyidat Bkirki in Mount Lebanon during the 18th century. In R. Deguilhem, ed., *Le waqf dans l'espace islamique: outil de pouvoir socio-politique*. Damas: Institut français d'études arabes de Damas, 259-75.

Vatikiotis, P.J. 1987. *Islam and the State*. London: Croom Helm.

Verges, Meriem. 1997. Genesis of a mobilization: the young activists of Algeria's Islamic Salvation Front. In J. Beinin and J. Stork, eds., *Political Islam*, London: I.B. Tauris, 292-305.

Vesely, Rudolf. 1995. Procès de la production et rôle du waqf dans les relations ville-campagne. In R. Deguilhem, ed., *Le waqf dans l'espace islamique: outil de pouvoir socio-politique.* Damas: Institut français d'études arabes de Damas, 230-41.

Vukadinovic, Nebodsa. 1996. La reconstruction de la Bosnie-Herzégovine. Aide internationale et acteurs locaux. *Les Etudes du CERI,* 21, December.

de Waal, Alex. 1997. *Famine Crimes: Politics and the Disaster Relief Industry in Africa.* London: James Currey.

----2002. Anthropology and the aid encounter. In J. MacClancy, ed., *Exotic No More: Anthropology on the Front Lines.* Chicago: University of Chicago Press, 251-69.

Waines, David. 1995. *An Introduction to Islam.* Cambridge: CUP.

Waldman, Peter. 1992. Clergy capitalism: mullahs keep control of Iranian economy with an iron hand. *Wall Street Journal,* 5 May.

Wansbrough, John. 1977. *Qur'anic Studies: Sources and Methods of Scriptural Interpretation.* Oxford: OUP.

----1978. *The Sectarian Milieu: Content and Composition of Islamic Salvation History.* Oxford: OUP.

Watt, W. Montgomery. 1953. *Muhammad at Mecca.* Oxford: Clarendon Press.

Weber, Max. 1952 [1918]. *Ancient Judaism.* English trans. Glencoe, IL.: Free Press.

Weiss, Holger. 2002. *Zakat* and the question of social welfare. In H. Weiss, ed., *Social Welfare in Muslim Societies in Africa* (Uppsala: Nordiska Akrikaininstitutet), 7-38.

Weiss, Thomas G. 1994. UN responses in the former Yugoslavia: moral and operational choices. *Ethics and International Affairs,* 21, Dec., 1-22.

Werbner, Pnina. 1985. The organization of giving and ethnic elites: voluntary associations amongst Manchester Pakistanis. *Ethnic and Racial Studies.* 8: 3, July.

----1988. Sealing the Koran: symbolic orientations among Pakistani migrants. *Cultural Dynamics,* I.1, 77-95.

Westermarck, Edward. 1908. *The Origin and Development of the Moral Ideas.* London: Macmillan.

----1926. *Ritual and Belief in Morocco.* London: Macmillan.

White, Lyman Cromwell. 1951. *International Non-Governmental Organizations: Their Purposes, Methods and Accomplishments.* New Brunswick: Rutgers University Press.

Wild, Stefan (ed.). 1996. *The Qur'an as Text.* Leiden: Brill.

Wilkinson, J.C. 1987. The *Imamate Tradition of Oman.* Cambridge: CUP.

Williams, Raymond. 1961. The Long Revolution. London: Chatto and Windus.

Woodward, Peter. 1990. *Sudan, 1898-1989: The Unstable State.* London: Lester Crook Academic Publishing.

Yediyildiz, B. 1985. *Institution du vaqf au XVIIIe en Turquie.* Ankara: Imprimerie de la Société d'Histoire Turque.

Yousaf, Mohammad. 1991. *Silent Soldier: the Man behind the Afghan Jihad.* Lahore: Jang Publishers.

---and Mark Adkin. 1993. *The Bear Trap: Afghanistan's Untold Story.* Lahore: Jang Publishers.

Zemmali, Ameur. 1997. *Combattants et prisonniers de guerre en droit islamique et en droit international humanitaire.* Paris: A. Pedone.

INDEX

Frequently occurring words such as 'Islam', 'Arab', 'NGO' and 'charity' have not been indexed.

Abd-Allah, 'U. H. 10-11
Abd al-Majid, Al-Sadiq 116
Abdic, Fikret 148
Abdul Bari, Sirag Al-Din 125
Abedi, M. 8
Abu Bakr 56
Abu-Goura, A. 60-4
Abu-Sahlieh, S. 10
Abu Zayd, N. 28
accountability 107-8
Adkin, M. 72
Adventist Relief Agency 121
El-Affendi, A. 114
'Afghan Arabs' 132, 134
Afghanistan 33, 46, 52, 68, 69-84, 129, 138
Africa 20-1, 92, 111-27
Africa Confidential 125, 163
Africa Muslim Agency 122, 124
African Council for Private Education 118
African Islamic Centre (Khartoum) 113
African Rights 43, 125-6
African Society for the Care of Mothers and Children 117
Aga Khan 49; Foundation 89, 92
Ahl al-Hadith 172
Ahmadiyya 140, 144
Ahmed, A.S. 165
Ahmed, Khurshid 129
Albania 79, 156, 173
alcohol 142-3
Algeria 6, 34, 41, 58, 74, 92-8, 110, 134
`Ali, A. Y. x, 23
Ali, fourth Caliph 33

Alispahic, B. 136
Almohad dynasty 35
AMAL (Lebanon) 108-9
Al-Amal City, Gaza 65
Amawi, A. 169
America *see* United States; American Red Cross 58, 61-2, 67-8, 167
Al-Amin, M. U. 119-20
Amman 13, 54, 59, 61-2, 65, 103-4
'animists' 169
Ankara 68
An-Naim, A.A. 88
Ansar al-Sunna al-Muhammadiya 118
anthropology, cultural 5, 8, 26-8, 90, 156
anti-Judaism 4, 110, 170
Antoun, R. 13, 92
Aoun, General M. 110
Appia, L. 47, 52
Al-Aqsa Fund 43
Arab and Islamic People's Conference 121
Arab Red Crescent and Red Cross Societies, Conference of 53
Arafat family 66
Arjomand, S.A. 31
Arkoun, M. 15
Arous, M. 95, 97
Asad, T. 90
Association des Oulémas 95
Atabani, G. S. E. 122
Atatürk 36 *and see* Kemalism
Aubaile-Sallenave, F. 164
Austria 141
al-`Awad, A. S. 121, 124, 126, 171, 172
Ayeb, H. 87

Al-Azaideh, A. Q. 64
Al-Azhar University 26, 40, 73, 132
Aziz, Abu Abdul 135, 137
Azzam, Abdallah 73-4, 134-5, 168

Bab El-Oued (Algiers) 93
Babadji, R. 96
Babylonian law 32
Badie, B. 89, 167
Bagherzade, A. 139
Baillard, I. 121
Baitemann, H. 74
Bakri Muhammad, Omar 84, 164
Balkans 128-52
Banerjee, M. 57
Bangladesh 36, 43, 51
El-Banna, Hany 133, 147, 156, 168
al-Banna, Hassan 40, 105
Al-Baraka 39, 42-3
Barnes, J. R. 30, 32-3
Barr, J. 24
base communities (South America) 89
al-Bashir, Omar 111-25
Basma bint Talal, Princess 100-1
Bavcic, U. 173
Bayart, J.-F. 153
Bayat, A. 87, 89, 108
beard 69, 102, 143, 147, 148
Becirbegovic, E. 142
Bedouin 14, 17, 19-21, 61
Bekkar, R. 96
Belcourt (Algiers) 92-3
Bellion-Jourdan, J. 3, 146, 156, 167, 174
ben Ashoor, Y. 56
ben Badis, Abdelhamid 95
Bencheikh, S. 104
Benevolence International 150, 163
Benevolencia, La 146
Ben Laden Foundation 73, 116; group of
    companies 73 *and see* bin Laden
Ben Laden, Tariq 116
Benlakhdar, A. 97
ben Néfissa, S. 87
Benthall, J. 2-3, 24, 45, 58, 87, 90, 92, 107,
    154
Berg, H. 8, 27
Berkey, J. 34
Biafran war 154-5
Bible 8, 22-8, 164
Bilici, F. 30-1, 35, 37, 133
bin Baz, Abdul Aziz Abdullah 36, 83,
    129, 172
Bin Faysal, Prince Muhamad 117

bin Laden, Usama 72-3, 76-7, 125, 129,
    131, 134, 145, 168, 171, 172 *and see* Ben
    Laden
Birmingham 78-9
Bitter, J.-N. 52, 57-8, 75
Black, M. 155
Black September (Jordan) 54, 100
Blumi, I. 173
Boisard, M. 18, 57, 70, 156
Boissier, P. 166
Bonte, P. 23
Book, People of the 57, 101
bonyad 36, 72, 107, 139
Bosanska Ideala Futura 150
Bosnia-Herzegovina 6, 65, 75-9, 79, 81-2,
    128-52
Boucebci, Fondation Mahfoud 96-7
Bougarel, X. 129-30, 145, 151, 172
Bouras, Mohamed 95
Bouslimani, M. 97
Bouteflika, Abdelaziz 95
Boutros-Ghali, B. 148
Bowen, J. 8
Bowie, K.A. 91
Bradbury, M. 55
Brenner, L. 92, 113
Brisebarre, A.-M. 14, 23
Britain 5, 12, 36, 49, 51, 67, 78-80, 88, 95,
    101, 107, 111-2, 122, 127, 129-31, 133-
    4, 139, 144, 155-6, 163-4, 168; British
    Muslims 10, 11, 78-83, 106, 134; British
    Red Crescent Society 49-50; British Red
    Cross 49, 58, 166
Bugnion, F. 47, 51-2, 167
Bulgaria 49
Burgat, F. 169
Burton, J. 7, 27, 169
Bush, George W. 106, 125, 155

Cahen, C. 32
Cairo 33-4, 75, 88 *and see* Al-Azhar
Caius Gracchus 16
Carapico, S. 91
CARE 121
Caritas 87, 146, 169
Carré, O. 8, 16, 18, 37-40, 70
Catholic Church 96, 112, 155; Catholic
    Relief Services 169 *and see* Caritas
Caulkins, D. 90
Cengic, H. 145
Central Intelligence Agency (CIA) 67, 163
Ceric, Mustafa 129, 136, 142, 145-9
CERMOC Amman 169

Chaaban, A. 137
Chad 115
Chamberlain, M. 34
Charities Acts 4, 133
Charity Commission 84, 163
Charles, Prince 84
Chemseddine Bouroubi 93-4
Christian Aid 87, 91
Christianity 4, 19, 36, 87, 164; and Islam 5, 7-8, 14-17, 21-8, 32, 47-68, 70, 83, 89, 91-2, 108, 111-27, 144, 149, 153-6; *and see* missionaries, Christian
Circassian Charitable Association 99
circumcision 164
Citibank 165
civil society 89-91
civilizations, 'clash' of 150, 153-4
Cizakra, M. 43
Clayer, N. 130
Clayton, A. 90
Cockayne, J. 57, 166, 174
Colakovic, S. 146-7
Coldrey, B.M. 155
Committee for the Islamic Call 73
Communism 101, 128-30 *and see* Soviet Union
communitization of aid 141-2, 156
Constantin, F. 113
Cook, S.A. 164
Council for the Coordination of Humanitarian Organizations (Bosnia) 139
Cragg, K. 14-15
Croatia, Croats 136-7, 146
Crusades 47, 53, 112, 156
Curmi, B. 169

Dafallah, J. 118-19
Dagorn, R. 23
al-Dahab, S. 119
Daly, M.W. 119
Damascus 34
Danawi, D.109
Dar al-Mal al-Islami 38-9, 41
Dar al-Tabligh 137
Daraz, I. 69
*da`wa* 40-1, 70-5, 138-9, 142-3; Da`wa Islamiyya 6, 111-27, 131, 170
Dayton accords 137-8, 148
Décobert, C. 10, 21-6, 31, 164
Deedat, Ahmed 144
Deguilhem, R. 33
Delaney, C. 23-4

Delorenzi, S. 58
Democratic Action Party, Bosnia 129 *and see* SDA
Department for International Development (UK) 78
Descombes, M. 166
Destexhe, A. 140
Don Fodio Benevolent Foundation 117
Donner, F. 26-7
Doughty, C. 20
Douglas, M. 8, 24-7, 165
Doutté, E. 164
Dow Jones Islamic Market Index 165
Duffield, M. 146
Dufoix, G. 167
Dumper, M. 36
Dunant, H. 47, 65, 166
Dunn, L. 90
Dwyer, K. 87

Edhi Foundation 2, 18-19, 80
Egypt, medieval 19, 34; modern 2, 28, 30, 38-9, 51, 72-7, 82, 88, 98, 102, 105, 113, 116, 132-4, 169
Eickelman, D. 8
emblems, red cross and red crescent 45-55, 165-6
Emirates, United Arab 58, 84, 115, 141
Emmanuelli, X. 155
Encyclopedia of Islamic Banking 165
Enlightenment, the 86, 105
Ereksoussi, M K. 56
Eritrea 118, 165
Eshel, D. 106
Esposito, J.L. 87, 109
Ethiopia 47
Ettinghausen, R. 53

Fahd, King 72
faith and works 26
faith-based initiatives 155
Farag, I. 130
Fatma 145
Faysal Investment Bank 117, 171
Faysal, King 39
FBI 174
Feierman, S. 21, 30
Financial Times Islamic Market Index 165
firstfruits 4, 5, 21-28, 164
Firth, Sir R. 86-7
Fischer, M. 8
Forum of African Voluntary and Development Organizations 126

Foundation for the Families of Martyrs 145

Foundation for the Oppressed and the Self-Sacrificers (Iran) 107, 139

France 133, 155, 169; French Red Cross 67

Fraser, C. 71

Frazer, Sir J. 164

Freeman, K. 155

Freij, H.Y. 99

Freud 24

Front de Libération Nationale (FLN) 95-7

Front Islamique du Salut (FIS) 96

Galloux, M. 38-9

Gama'at Islamiyya 132, 134, 137

Gambling, T. 165

Garaudy, R. 89

Garden, Parable of the 21-28

Garnsey, P. 17

Gaza 65-6

Geertz, C. 35, 164-5

Gellner, E. 91

gender 26, 99, 100, 154, 174

General Union of Voluntary Societies (Jordan) 99-100

Geneva Conventions 45-50, 55-6, 66, 165, 167

Geremek, B. 87

Gerges, F. A. 110

Germany 140

Ghana 170

Ghandour, A.-R. 4, 52, 58, 73, 83, 89, 97, 102, 163, 167-70

Al-Ghannouchi, R. 34

Al-Ghazali, M. 40, 129, 132

Glassé, C. 25, 53

Global Relief Foundation 150, 163

Gordon Memorial Southern Sudan Mission 112

Grameen Bank 43

Gray, R.112

green 5, 21, 28, 64-5, 101, 136, 172; Green Crescent 64-5

Groupe Islamiste Armé (GIA) 97, 134

Guantánamo Bay 77, 150

Gulf states 1, 18, 62, 68, 113, 115-16 *and see* individual states

Gulf War 52, 58, 61-2, 76, 99-100, 129, 130, 133, 151

Habash, G. 167

Haddad, Y. 57

Al-Hadid, M. 60-5, 167

*hadith*s 7-9, 12, 14, 21, 26, 32, 57, 69, 131

Haenni, P. 121

Haigh, W.E. 49-50

hajj 20, 67, 164

Halbertal, M., 25

Halliday, F. 29, 153, 167

Hamas (Algerian) 97

Hamas (Palestinian) 2, 29, 55, 67, 77, 81, 105-6, 152, 167, 170

Hamer, J.H. 87

Hamidullah, M. 17, 56, 164

Hanafi, H. 27

Hanafi school of law 32, 147, 149-50, 164

Hanbali school of law 71

Handzar division (Bosnia) 172

Hann, C. 90, 92

Harakat ul-Ansar 172

al-Haramain Foundation 36, 136, 150, 163, 172

Harrell-Bond, B. 123

Harrison, S. 107

Hashemite Fund for Social Development 14, 100

Hassan of Jordan, Prince 18, 59

Al-Hassan, M. 79-80

Hassan, Y.F. 112

al-Hassanain, Fatih and Sukamo 144-5

Hathaway, J. 31

hawala 39-40

Hawting, G.R. 25

Hazan, P. 47, 68

Healy, B. 167

Hecimovic, E. 172-3

Henninger, J. 25

hijab 102, 143-4, 147

Hinduism 5, 88, 155, 174

Hizb al-Tahrir 133, 172

Hizbullah 6, 55, 88, 105, 108-10, 134

Holbrooke, R. 138

Holt, P.M. 119

Holy Land Foundation for Relief and Development 163

Hosny, M.M. 40

hostage-taking 58

Howard, S. W. 171

Hubley, M. 73

hubs 30-35

al-Hudaybi, Hassan 40

Humanitarian Affairs Commission 122, 171

Humanity First 140, 144

Human Relief Agency 73, 75, 77, 132,
  136
Huntington, S.P. 150, 153-4
Husaini, M.I. 102
Hussain of Jordan, King 60-1, 100-1
Hyderabad, Nizam of 49
Hyman, A. 168
Hymes, D. 90

Ibn Taymiyya 40
Ibn Warraq 28
Ibrahim, R. 116-17
Ibrahim, S.E. 88
ICNA Relief 139
`id al-kabir (Great Feast) 14, 23, 78
IFOR (NATO Implementation Force)
  138
IGASA 132, 140-4
ighatha 69-74, 78, 82, 138-9, 142
Ilchman, W.F. 91
Independent, The 78
India 31, 35, 49, 51, 88, 174
Indonesia 91, 143
Inglehart, R. 154
International African University 114
International Association of Islamic
  Banks (IAIB) 39-40
International Committee of the Red
  Cross (ICRC) 3, 45-58, 61-7, 106, 156,
  165-169
International Crisis Group 150
International Development Foundation
  163
International Federation of Red Cross
  and Red Crescent Societies (IFRC) 45-
  68, 167, 169
International Humanitarian Law 56-7, 83,
  166, 174 and see Geneva Conventions,
  International Committee of the Red
  Cross
International Islamic Charitable
  Organization (Kuwait) 41, 116
International Islamic Relief Organization
  (IIRO) 3, 11, 14, 43, 69, 72-3, 75, 84,
  107, 122, 124; in Bosnia 130, 132, 136,
  139-41; in Jordan 103-4; and UK 163;
  and USA 163
International Society for the
  Reconstruction of Bosnia 141
Internationale Humanitäre Hilfe 133
INTRAC 91
Iqra Foundation 42-3

Iran 71-2, 87-8, 107-10, 115, 131-4, 151,
  165, 174; Iranian Islamic Centre for
  Help to the People of Bosnia-
  Herzegovina 139; Iranian Red Crescent
  50-2, 62, 141, 167
Iraq 20, 46, 58, 61-2, 64, 66, 99, 108, 110,
  129, 155, 170, 191
Irchad Islah (Algeria) 97
Islam, Riazul 174
Islam, Yusuf 80, 130, 168
Islamic African Relief Agency (Sudan) 69,
  71, 74, 114-17, 121-6
Islamic American Relief Agency 126
Islamic Centre for Bosnia 141, 144
Islamic Charter Front 116-17
Islamic Circle of North America 139
Islamic Community (Bosnia) see Islamska
  Zajednica
Islamic Council for Eastern Europe 130,
  144
Islamic Crescent 53-6, 64
Islamic Development Bank 39, 116, 165
Islamic Faysal Bank 42
Islamic finance 37-44
Islamic Foundation 112
Islamic Relief Agency, Sudan (ISRA) 73-
  75, 78, 83, 113, 117, 121, 126-7, 131,
  150, 168
Islamic Relief (Worldwide) 3, 10-12, 36,
  69, 78-82, 92, 103, 107, 122, 130, 133,
  141-4, 147, 156, 168, 169, 172
Islamska Zajednica (Islamic Community,
  Bosnia) 129, 136,138, 142, 145-50
ISRA see Islamic Relief Agency
Israel 2, 13, 36, 38, 52, 55, 63-6, 87, 101,
  106, 109-10, 152, 165, 166
Israeli, R. 88, 102
Itani, F. 79, 168
Izetbegovic, A. 130, 136-8, 144, 147, 149,
  151-2, 173
Izutsu, T. 24-26
Izz al-Din al-Qassam 106

Jaber, H. 109-110
jahiliyya 25
Jama`at i-Islami 71-3, 112, 139, 144
Jannati, Ayatollah 136
Japan 49, 51, 59, 91
Jaussen, A. 22
Jerusalem 30, 36, 53-4, 57, 65, 106, 152
Jesus see Christianity
Jews 17, 21-27, 57, 82, 106, 146, 154, 166
  and see Israel, anti-Judaism

jihad 5, 10-11, 70-4, 76-8, 80-4, 97, 121,
    129-39
Al-Jihad 77
Jihad al Bina (Hizbullah) 109
Johnson, J.T. 168
Jorand, A.-L. 108-9
Jordan 3, 5-6, 9, 11, 13-14, 18, 46, 54, 98-
    107, 169-70; Jordan National Red
    Crescent Society (JNRCS) 59-68
Judaeo-Christian tradition 1, 86, 154 and
    see Bible, Jews, Christians
Junod, D.-D. 166

Kaaba 23, 32
Kach 174
Kahane Chai 174
al-Kamil, Saleh Abdallah 171
Al-Kareh, G. D. 100
Karim, A. 122
Kassam, A. 20
Kazakhstan 165
Keck, M.E. 167
Kelsay, J. 168
Kemal Atatürk 8, 19, 36
Kenya 92
Kepel, G. 41, 88-9, 96, 102, 109, 133, 163,
    165
Khan, A.A. 168
Kharijites 26
Al-Khatib, Y. 66, 167
Khartoum 111-27, 131-2, 148, 167-9
Khatib, A. 100
Khatmiya 111, 117-18
Al-Khayyat, A.-A. 10-13, 16-17
Khomeini, Ayatollah 107
khoms 108
El-Kikhia, M.O. 115
Kister, M.J. 25
Koç Foundation 36
Kochan, L. 25
Kosovo 3, 4, 66, 151, 173
Kouchner, B. 75, 154, 156
Kozlowski, G. 31, 35-6
Kuran, T. 15, 44
Kuwait 9, 38, 41, 61, 64, 72-6, 99, 115-16,
    120, 122, 143, 147-8, 150, 170; Kuwaiti
    Village of Compassion 118

Labat, S. 95
Lalla Malika, Princess 53
Lammens, H. 17, 20-1
La Rochelle, University of 164
Law of Associations (1901), French 2

Layard, A.H. 20
Layish, A. 34, 36
Leach, Sir E. 164
League of Red Cross Societies 45, 63 and
    see International Federation
Lebanon 6, 33, 40, 51, 53, 55, 88, 108-10
Leca, J. 77, 164
Legrain, J.-F. 106
Lejnet al-Bir al-Dawliya 122
Leo Africanus 35
Levitt, M.A. 174
liberation theology 89
Libya 54, 108, 115-16, 170
Lindenmeyr, A. 85
Lohmann, R.A. 91
Lonca, A. 166
London Technical Group 90
lotteries 87, 99
Lutheran Federation 126, 169

MacCulloch, J.A. 164
Macek, I. 148
Madaba 60
Madigan, D.A. 27
madrasa 34, 80, 92, 102, 146-7
Maduot, T. 123, 171
Magen David Adom (MDA) 52, 66, 167
Magnuson, C. 166
al-Mahdi, Nasr al-Din al-Hadi 125
al-Mahdi, Sadiq 116-22, 171
Mahdist movement 111, 170
Mahjub Haj Nur, Ahmed 118
Mahmud II, Sultan 33
Maimonides 17
Makki, H. 112
Maktab al-Khidamat see Office for
    Services to the Mujahidin
Malakal 123
Malaysia 9, 51; Malaysian Relief Centre
    140
Mali 92
Maliki school of law 164
Maloney, S. 36, 107
Mamluks 19, 33-4
Mannan, M.A. 12
Mansour, H. 64
al-Mansur Qalawun, Sultan 33
Marchal, R. 117, 120
Marett, R. 87
Margalit, A. 25
Marinid dynasty 34-5
Marx, A. 22
Marx, E. 20

Marxism 14, 31, 85-6, 89, 165
Masood, Ahmed Shah 74
Massad, J. 101
Maurer, B. 37, 39, 165
Mauritanian Red Crescent 50
Mauss, M. 16-17
Al-Mawardi 15-16
Mawdsley, E. 90, 108
Mawdudi, Abu Ala 144
Maybury-Lewis, D. 20
Mayer, A.E. 87, 167
Mecca 9-10, 14-15, 18, 20-21, 23, 26-27,
    30, 32, 38, 76, 102, 129, 164
Medani, K. 117
Medina 10, 21, 27, 41, 76, 80, 102, 112,
    129
Médecins Sans Frontières (MSF) 55, 63-4,
    75, 142, 154, 156; MSF France 126;
    MSF Holland 124, 126
Meenai, S.A. 42-3, 165
Mehtic, H. 147
Merhamet 130, 142, 145, 173
Mesiane, A. 98
Methodist Churches 83, 127
Milliot, L. 35
Milton-Edwards, B. 29, 102
al-Mirghani, Muhamad Osman 111
Mishal, S. 106
al-Misri, Imad 147-50
missionaries, Christian 6, 11, 41, 74-5,
    105, 111-12, 113-15, 122, 124, 139, 141-
    2, 156
Missionary Societies Act (Sudan) 122
Mission to Lepers 105
Mitchell, T. 7, 16
Mitri, T. 130
Moe, H.A. 87
monarchy 76, 101
Monnot, J. 123
Montenegro 49
Moorehead, C. 45
Morocco 8, 9, 31, 34-5; Moroccan Red
    Crescent 51, 53-4
Mostar 146-7
Mouvement de la Société pour la Paix
    (MSP) 94, 97
Movement of Islamic Youth, Malaysia
    140
Movement of the Partisans 134
Mubarak, Hosni 125, 133
mudabara 39

Muhammad, The Prophet 7-8, 12, 21, 23,
    25, 26-7, 32-3, 41, 56, 64-5, 102, 108,
    112, 118, 147, 156, 164, 168, 171
Muhammad VI of Morocco, King 53-4
Muhammad al-Faysal al-Saoud, Prince 39
Mumuni, S. 170
mujahidin 70-6, 121, 128, 134-9, 143, 148-
    51, 172
Murji'ites 26
Musa Sadr, Imam 108
musharaka 39
Musil, A. 20, 61
Muslim Aid, 10-11, 36, 72-3, 77-82, 107,
    122, 130, 133, 140-1, 144
Muslim Brothers, Society of 2, 7, 40, 71-
    2, 75, 87-9, 97-8, 105, 116-17, 119-20,
    132, 149-50, 168; in Jordan 18, 101-2
Muslim Council of Britain 78
Muslim Institute 133
Muslim Parliament (Britain) 82, 133, 172
Muslim Students of America 172
Muwaffaq al-Kheiriya 122, 124-5, 135

Al-Nabi, Mohamed Abd Allah 118
Nablus 13-14, 104
Nagan, W.P. 131
Najibullah, M. 129
Nasser, Gamal Abdul 37, 71, 113
National Islamic Front (NIF) 118-126,
    131, 144
Nazis 55, 86, 166
New Testament see Christianity
Niasse, Ibrahim 113
Niblock, T. 116
Nigeria 51, 117, 155
Nimayri, President 114-20
Noor al Hussein Foundation 100
Norris, P. 154
Norton, A.R. 91
Norway 66
Novossyolov, D. 11

Office for Services to the Mujahidin 73-4,
    78, 135
Oman 9-10, 29-30, 85-6
Omar Khayyam 31
Omar, second Caliph 32
Operation Lifeline Sudan 122
Order of Malta 87
Organization of the Islamic Conference
    (OIC) 39, 54-5, 131, 165
Organization for the Renewal of Islamic
    Tradition 143, 147, 150

orphans 10, 14, 17, 22-3, 36, 60, 87, 93-4, 100, 102-4, 141, 145, 147, 154
Orthodox Church 105, 146
Oslo accords 152
Ostrower, F. 87
Otayek, R. 115-16
Ottoman Empire 30-3, 37, 47-51, 63, 166 *and see* Turkey
Oxfam 18, 78, 87, 121, 126, 155, 169

Pagnucco, R. 167
Pahlavi Foundation 107
Pakistan 2-3, 9, 10, 18-19, 38, 67-84, 108, 129, 134-5, 139-40, 151, 153, 174; Pakistanis in UK 11-12, 89
Palestine and Palestinians 2-3, 13, 29, 36, 43, 54-5, 59, 67, 73, 77, 81, 94, 97-100, 102-6, 134-5, 139-40, 151-3, 166 *and see* Israel; Palestine Red Crescent Society (PRCS) 65-6, 165, 167
pan-Islamism 38, 129-30, 144-51, 173
Parry, J. 19
pasdaran (Iran) 72, 132, 134
Paul, St 166
Payton, R.L. 87
Persia see Iran
Petterson, D. 123
Pezo, Adnan 149
Pictet bank 165
pillars of religion, five 9, 14, 15, 164
Pipes, D. 4
Piscatori, J. 76
political science 3, 5
politicization of aid 4, 74, 93, 97, 107, 120, 156
Pons, J. 166
Popovitch, L. 47-8
pork 142
prisoners of war 56-7
Prochaska, F. 101
professionalization 70, 76, 79-81, 84, 91
psychotherapy 96-7
Pugh, M. 4

Al-Qa`ida 1-2, 73, 106, 168
Qadiriya 170
Qaradawi, Y. 40-3, 71, 129, 165
Qasmallah, M. 120
Qassem, Talal Fuad 137
Qatar 41, 116
Quran, The 3, 5, 7-28, 32, 37, 40, 47, 56-8, 69, 83, 102-3, 108, 144, 156, 164, 169-70

Al-Qur'an Society 80
qurbani 12, 36, 78, 81, 154
Qutb, S. 7, 16, 37, 40, 70, 144

Ramadan 9, 11, 13-14, 53, 81, 93-4, 142-3, 166
Ramadan/Kippur War (1973) 38, 72
Ranstorp, M. 128
rape, victims of 140
Rashid, A. 11, 67, 73
Red Crescent national societies 73, 85, 103, 139, 141 *and see* Red Cross and Red Crescent
Red Cross and Red Crescent Movement, International 3-5, 45-68, 84, 87, 164; Museum 56-7, 63
Red Lion and Sun Society (Persia) 50
Refah Party 133, 140
refugees 11, 18, 46, 51, 59, 62, 65, 73-5, 98-9, 102-4, 107, 128, 132, 139-52, 156
reislamization 134, 137, 141-4, 146-51
relativism, moral 3
Republican Party (Sudan) 118
riba 16, 37-9, 42, 44, 72
Rieff, D. 4
Ringgren, H. 25
ritual giving 22-7
Roald, A.S. 102, 169
Roberts, Hugh 169
Robinson, F. 174
Robinson, L.C. 99
Rodriguez-Mañas, F. 35
Rogerson, J.W. 22, 27
Rosenau, J.A. 167
Rouadjia, A. 96
Roule, T.J. 106
Rousseau, J.-J. 156
Roy, D. 11, 38
Roy, O. 72, 91
Rubin, B.R. 67, 70, 72, 168
Ruel, M. 26
Rugh, A.B. 87
Rushdie, Salman 133, 144
Russia 48-9, 69 *and see* Soviet Union

Saad-Ghorayeb, A. 109
sabil Allah 32, 70
Sabra, A. 19, 32-4
Sabra and Chatila 63
sacrifice 12, 14, 20, 22-7, 78, 81, 109, 143, 164
sadaqa 9, 18, 20, 24-5, 29, 32, 41, 78, 83
Saddam Hussain 58, 76, 155

Sadiq, C.M. 42
Sahel, the 43, 50
Sahlins, M. 90
Said, A.R.M. 168
Said, E. 90, 153
as-Saïd, Sultan Abu-l-Hassan 35
St James's reservation 164
Saladin 57
Salafi movement 71, 73, 75, 135, 139, 146, 150-1, 172
Salah Abdullah Kamel 39
Salame, G. 71, 77
Salih, K.O. 171
Salih, M. 105, 114,
Salman, Prince 72, 132
Salt 60, 62, 103
Samaritan, parable of the Good 4
Sarajevo 128, 137-45, 148, 169, 172
Sarvath, Princess 59, 100
Saudi-Arabia 5, 11-12, 14, 36, 39-40, 43, 67-77, 82-4, 88, 99, 102-4, 106-7, 113-17, 120, 122, 126, 129, 131-45, 150-1, 163; Saudi High Committee for Aid to Bosnia-Herzegovina 132; Saudi High Committee for Somalia and Bosnia 83, 143, 150; Saudi Joint Committee for the Relief of Kosova and Chechnya 173; Saudi Red Crescent 67
Save the Children Fund 78, 87, 90, 155, 169
Schacht, J. 30
Schervisch, P.G. 14
Schimmel, A.-M. 11
schools and schooling 2, 9, 29, 31, 34, 40, 41, 59, 80-1, 87, 92, 102-6, 116-17, 143, 146, 147
schools of law see Hanafi, Hanbali, Maliki, Shafi`i
Schumpeter, J. 165
Scouts Musulmans Algériens 95
SDA (Bosnia) 130, 142, 145, 148-9
Secours Islamique see Islamic Relief
Sefrou 35, 164-5
Sela 105
Seljuk empire 31
Selimoski, J. 129-30, 144, 172
September 11th 2001: 1, 2, 40, 67, 77, 81, 106-7, 125, 139, 150, 163, 167
Serbia, Serbs 47, 78, 82-3, 128-31, 136-7, 140
Shafi`i school of law 164
Shahid Foundation (Hizbullah) 109
Al-Shamal Islamic Bank 125, 171

Shaqiq, M. 77, 132
Sharif, Basma 104
Sharjah 84, 167
Sharma, S. 88
Sherif, N. 77
Shi`ism 72, 88, 96, 105, 107-10, 129, 134, 139, 167
shirk 25, 27, 169
Short, Rt Hon C. 79, 155
Sidahmed, A.S. 120-1
Siddiqui, K. 133
Silber, I. 22
Simone, Abdou Maliqalim 123
Sirageldin, I. 38
Six Day War 3
'smart aid' 67, 106
socialism 16-17, 38, 85, 90, 97, 147
Solferino 128
Somalia 52, 54, 83
Sommaruga, C. 52
Soviet Union 38, 51, 71, 85, 91, 96, 107, 115, 129, 144, 148, 151
Srebrenica 141
Stevens, Cat 80
Stoddard, A. 155
Strahan, J. 164
Strand, A. 156
Strawson, J. 167
Stroumsa, S. 164
Sudan 3, 6, 28, 36, 39, 42-3, 51-2, 54, 64, 66, 69, 73-5, 79, 111-27, 131-2, 135, 141, 144-5, 153, 155, 156, 166-72; Sudanese Community Islamic Relief Organization 126; Sudan Council of Churches 123-4, 171; Sudanese Red Crescent 124
SUDANAID 124
SUDRA 124
Sudanese Islamic Bank 117
Sudanese People's Liberation Army (SPLA) 111
Sufis 19, 34-5, 97, 113, 135, 174
Suleyman, Abdessalam 170-1
Sullivan, D.J. 88-9
Summers, A.S. 127
Switzerland 45-57, 63
Syria 34, 38, 40, 62, 65, 74, 99, 106, 109

Taha, Mahmoud Muhammad 118, 171
Takiyat Khaski Sultan 30
Taliban 3, 11, 77, 106, 155
Tamimi, A. 87
telethon 100

'terrorism' 1, 77, 81, 106, 125-6, 134, 137-8, 150, 172-4
Thailand 51
'thematic interpretation' 27-8
Thesiger, W. 20
Third World Relief Agency (TWRA)135, 144-5, 150, 172
Tijaniya 113, 170
tithes 18, 22-4, 83, 154, 164
Tombe, Rev. Enoch 123, 171
van der Toorn, K. 164
Touiza, Fondation 97
Townsend, J. 108
transnationalism 2, 38, 70-1, 89, 120, 128-152, 167
Travnik 135, 138, 147
Tunisia 31, 34, 53, 167
al-Turabi, H. 64, 111-25, 168, 170, 171
Turkey 8, 19, 35-6, 53, 108, 133, 137, 140, 166-7, 173 *and see* Ottoman Empire
Turkmenistan 51
Tuzla 141

umma 5, 38, 42, 69-70, 78, 106, 113, 128-31, 134, 143-51
Umma party (Sudan) 116, 119-20, 125-6
`umra 14, 154
UNECOSOC 126
UNHCR 6, 64, 75, 84, 126, 140, 142
Unicef 96, 122, 126
Union Bank of Switzerland 165
United Kingdom *see* Britain
United Nations Security Council 125
United States 2, 5, 36, 55, 63, 72-3, 82, 67, 99-100, 123, 125, 129, 133, 135, 137-9, 147, 151-6, 170; attacks on embassies in Nairobi and Dar as-Salaam 126, 150
universal values 1, 3-5, 45, 47, 52, 55, 57-8, 66, 78, 82-4, 86-7, 101, 141-2, 155-6, 169
UNRWA 98
USAID 126
`Uthman, Al-Amin M. 171
Uzbekistan 51

Vaqif Bank 37
Verges, M. 96
Vie, La 81
Vietnam 86, 169
Vukanovic, N. 141

de Waal, A. 4, 43, 58, 90
Wadi Musa 14, 65

Wahhabism 40, 71, 113, 139, 149-50, 172
Waines, D. 27
Waldman, P. 107
Walzer, Michael 154
Wansbrough, J. 25, 27
waqf 5, 7, 29-37, 41, 44, 106, 121, 154, 164
Weiss, H. 9, 11
Weiss, T.G. 82
Werbner, P. 11-12, 89
West Bank see Palestine
Westermarck, E. 22, 31, 88, 90
White, L.C. 154
Williams, R. 8
Wilkinson, J.C. 10
women's dress 8, 104 *and see hijab*
women's movement 101, 142, 169
women's rights 4, 83-4, 87, 91-2
Woodward, P. 171
World Assembly of Muslim Youth 115, 163
World Bank 43
World Council of Churches 105, 169
World Food Programme (WFP) 75
World Foundation for the Production of Information 170
World Health Organization (WHO) 75, 124, 126
World Islamic Council for Da`wa and Relief 75, 119, 139, 141
World Islamic League 39, 41, 71-4, 113, 115-16, 132
World Jewish Committee 154
World Trade Center (1993 attack) 126 *and see* September 11th 2001
World Vision 87, 105, 121, 126, 156

Xhudo, G. 128

Yediyildiz, B. 31-3
Yemen 66, 91, 134, 137, 164
Young Women's Muslim Association 100
Yousaf, M. 72

Zagreb 129, 135-9
Zaidan, Ahmed 168
zakat 3, 7-29, 37-8, 40-4, 72, 78, 81, 83, 92, 102, 104, 106, 121, 126, 164, 171
Zamakshari 164
zawiya 34-5, 87
Zemmali, A. 56, 166-7
Zenica 135-6, 138, 141, 146-50
Zionism 11, 29, 36, 106, 110, 155